HISTORICAL DICTIONARIES OF EUROPE
Jon Woronoff, Series Editor

26. *Russia*, by Boris Raymond and Paul Duffy. 1998.
27. *Gypsies (Romanies)*, by Donald Kenrick. 1998. *Out of print.*
28. *Belarus*, by Jan Zaprudnik. 1998.
29. *Federal Republic of Yugoslavia*, by Zeljan Suster. 1999.
30. *France*, by Gino Raymond. 1998. *Out of print. See no. 64.*
31. *Slovakia*, by Stanislav J. Kirschbaum. 1998. *Out of print. See no. 47.*
32. *Netherlands*, by Arend H. Huussen Jr. 1998. *Out of print. See no. 55.*
33. *Denmark*, by Alastair H. Thomas and Stewart P. Oakley. 1998. *Out of print. See no. 63.*
34. *Modern Italy*, by Mark F. Gilbert and K. Robert Nilsson. 1998. *Out of print. See no. 58.*
35. *Belgium*, by Robert Stallaerts. 1999.
36. *Austria*, by Paula Sutter Fichtner. 1999. *Out of print. See No. 70.*
37. *Republic of Moldova*, by Andrei Brezianu. 2000. *Out of print. See no. 52.*
38. *Turkey, 2nd edition*, by Metin Heper. 2002. *Out of print. See no. 67.*
39. *Republic of Croatia, 2nd edition*, by Robert Stallaerts. 2003. *Out of print. See no. 74*
40. *Portugal, 2nd edition*, by Douglas L. Wheeler. 2002. *Out of print. See no. 73.*
41. *Poland, 2nd edition*, by George Sanford. 2003.
42. *Albania, New edition*, by Robert Elsie. 2004. *Out of print. See no. 75.*
43. *Estonia*, by Toivo Miljan. 2004.
44. *Kosova*, by Robert Elsie. 2004.
45. *Ukraine*, by Zenon E. Kohut, Bohdan Y. Nebesio, and Myroslav Yurkevich. 2005.
46. *Bulgaria, 2nd edition*, by Raymond Detrez. 2006.
47. *Slovakia, 2nd edition*, by Stanislav J. Kirschbaum. 2006.
48. *Sweden, 2nd edition*, by Irene Scobbie. 2006.
49. *Finland, 2nd edition*, by George Maude. 2007.
50. *Georgia*, by Alexander Mikaberidze. 2007.
51. *Belgium, 2nd edition*, by Robert Stallaerts. 2007.
52. *Moldova, 2nd edition*, by Andrei Brezianu and Vlad Spânu. 2007.
53. *Switzerland*, by Leo Schelbert. 2007.

54. *Contemporary Germany*, by Derek Lewis with Ulrike Zitzlsperger. 2007.
55. *Netherlands, 2nd edition*, by Joop W. Koopmans and Arend H. Huussen Jr. 2007.
56. *Slovenia, 2nd edition*, by Leopoldina Plut-Pregelj and Carole Rogel. 2007.
57. *Bosnia and Herzegovina, 2nd edition*, by Ante Čuvalo. 2007.
58. *Modern Italy, 2nd edition*, by Mark F. Gilbert and K. Robert Nilsson. 2007.
59. *Belarus, 2nd edition*, by Vitali Silitski and Jan Zaprudnik. 2007.
60. *Latvia, 2nd edition*, by Andrejs Plakans. 2008.
61. *Contemporary United Kingdom*, by Kenneth J. Panton and Keith A. Cowlard. 2008.
62. *Norway*, by Jan Sjåvik. 2008.
63. *Denmark, 2nd edition*, by Alastair H. Thomas. 2009.
64. *France, 2nd edition*, by Gino Raymond. 2008.
65. *Spain, 2nd edition*, by Angel Smith. 2008.
66. *Iceland, 2nd edition*, by Guđmunder Hálfdanarson. 2009.
67. *Turkey, 3rd edition*, by Metin Heper and Nur Bilge Criss. 2009.
68. *Republic of Macedonia*, by Dimitar Bechev. 2009.
69. *Cyprus*, by Farid Mirbagheri. 2010.
70. *Austria, 2nd edition*, by Paula Sutter Fichtner. 2009.
71. *Modern Greece*, by Dimitris Keridis. 2009.
72. *Czech State, 2nd edition*, by Rick Fawn and Jiří Hochman, 2010.
73. *Portugal, 3rd edition*, by Douglas L. Wheeler and Walter C. Opello Jr., 2010.
74. *Croatia, 3rd edition*, by Robert Stallaerts, 2010.
75. *Albania, 2nd edition*, by Robert Elsie, 2010.
76. *Malta, 2nd edition*, by Uwe Jens Rudolf and Warren G. Berg, 2010.

Historical Dictionary of Malta

Second Edition

Uwe Jens Rudolf
Warren G. Berg

Historical Dictionaries of Europe, No. 76

The Scarecrow Press, Inc.
Lanham • Toronto • Plymouth, UK
2010

Published by Scarecrow Press, Inc.
A wholly owned subsidiary of The Rowman & Littlefield Publishing Group, Inc.
4501 Forbes Boulevard, Suite 200, Lanham, Maryland 20706
http://www.scarecrowpress.com

Estover Road, Plymouth PL6 7PY, United Kingdom

British Library Cataloguing in Publication Information Available

Library of Congress Cataloging-in-Publication Data

Rudolf, Uwe Jens, 1944-
  Historical dictionary of Malta / Uwe Jens Rudolf, Warren G. Berg. — 2nd ed.
      p. cm. — (Historical dictionaries of Europe ; no. 76)
  Rev. ed. of: Historical dictionary of Malta / Warren G. Berg. 1995.
  Includes bibliographical references.
  ISBN 978-0-8108-5317-1 (cloth : alk. paper) — ISBN 978-0-8108-7390-2 (ebook)
  1. Malta—History—Dictionaries. I. Berg, Warren G., 1924- II. Berg, Warren G., 1924- Historical dictionary of Malta. III. Title.
  DG989.8.R83 2010
  945.8'5003—dc22

                                                                                2009041586

⊗™ The paper used in this publication meets the minimum requirements of American National Standard for Information Sciences—Permanence of Paper for Printed Library Materials, ANSI/NISO Z39.48-1992.

Printed in the United States of America

To

Ruth,
Stephanie,
Michael,
Benjamin,
Marianna,

My mentor Warren Berg and his wife, Jan,

and

The people of Malta

Contents

Acknowledgments

Among the many places on earth that I have had the fortune of visiting for extended periods, Malta occupies a very special place in my heart. The warmth of the people matches the warmth of the sunshine there. Whoever spends some time on these historic and culturally rich islands, will never completely leave them.

Dr. Warren Berg, professor emeritus at Luther College and the original author of this volume, has been a long-time colleague and mentor. It was he who earned a Fulbright visiting professorship at the University of Malta and, in partnership with Bryan Gera, Chairman of Farsons Ltd., Malta, and with support of the Chamber of Commerce of Malta, established a scholarship to enable more than 60 Maltese students to spend from one semester to four years at Luther College. The strong connections Dr. Berg and the Maltese alumni built between Malta and Luther College still bear fruit today. Every spring semester, 12 to 14 students from Luther College and a sister institution, Concordia College in Moorhead, MN, spend a semester studying in Malta and the Mediterranean region. Thank you, Warren!

I am also deeply grateful for the assistance of another colleague, Elizabeth Kaschins, professor emerita at Luther College and librarian extraordinaire, who spent so many hours carefully reviewing the bibliography.

Warmest thanks are also due to Maltese friends Fr. Peter Serracino Inglott, Mark Miceli Farrugia, Maria Mercieca, Fr. Joseph Ellul and the Maltese alumni of Luther College, especially: Victor Galea, Vanessa Frazier, Edward and Gordon Grima Baldacchino, Andrew and Julian Mamo, Ranier Fsadni, Andrew, Michael and Mark Mangion, Santiago Navarro and Ignatio Montalto, whose collective pride in and enthusiasm for their homeland made me curious enough to visit Malta for the first time and whose warm receptions have made me return so many times.

Of direct invaluable assistance in research for this book were the following professors and staff at the University of Malta: Dr. Henry Frendo (Dep't of History), Dr. Raymond Mangion, (Dep't of Public Law), Dr. Peter Xuereb (Chairman, European Documentation and Research Center) Mr. Anthony Mangion, Director of Library Services. For their cheerful service searching out so much material for me over so many weeks and months in the Melitensia section of the library, very special thank yous to Mr Edward Camilleri, Stefan Bezzini, Sylvia Callus, and Kristine Saliba. My sincerest gratitude to all of the above. Finally, any flaws in the text are all my own.

The Maltese Islands

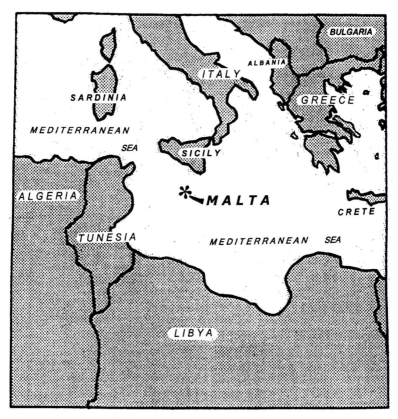

Mediterranean Sea with Malta in the Center

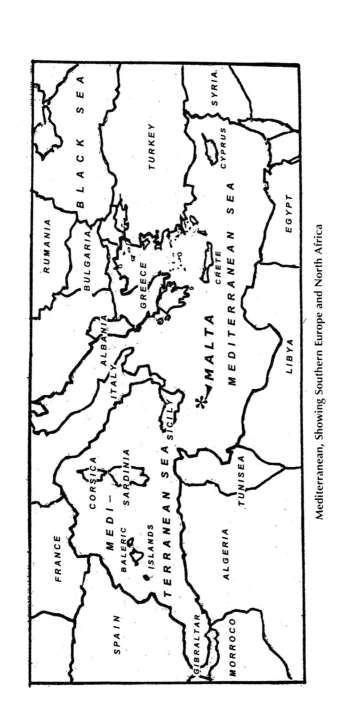

Mediterranean, Showing Southern Europe and North Africa

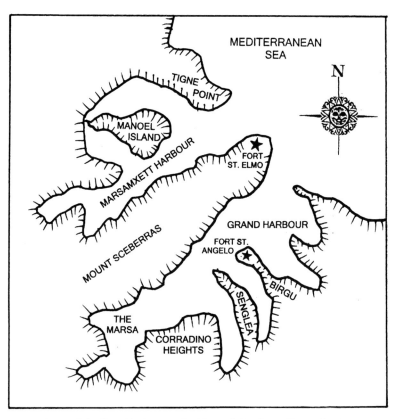

Area of the Two Harbors at the Time of the Great Siege of 1565

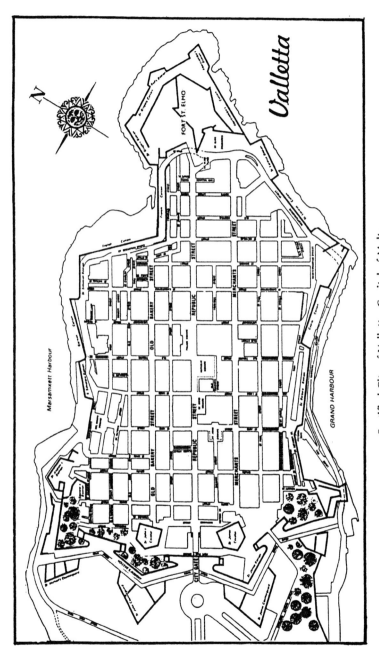

Fortified City of Valletta, Capital of Malta

Editor's Foreword

If ever there was a country strategically located, it is Malta. Over the centuries, this was more of a curse than a blessing, involving it in repeated attacks and periodic invasions as it passed from the hands of one foreign power to another. It was bitterly fought over by European rulers and the Turks, and the balance between Christianity and Islam was often determined here. During World War II, it suffered like no other place. Now that it has finally become independent and the Mediterranean enjoys relative peace and prosperity, Malta's location is more of a blessing, providing commercial advantages and attracting hordes of tourists (but also illegal immigrants). Long a bastion of the West, it has become a member of the European Union and is working more closely with its partners while maintaining beneficial, if sometimes difficult, contacts with North Africa.

Yet, for all its strategic significance and closer relations, Malta is not very well known abroad, and that is a pity. While small in size if somewhat larger in population, consisting only of two major islands, it remains strategically important within the Mediterranean context. It boasts an extraordinary history, one that appears not only in books but also in the visible remnants of older periods, which abound. It clings to an exceptional culture, a mixture of the elements of many other cultures that have been absorbed and assimilated, and the landscape is visually stunning. Many of these facets are described and amplified in this historical dictionary of Malta, which first traces its long and often exciting history in the chronology and then puts the island nation into its proper context in the introduction. The dictionary section has numerous entries on significant persons, places, events, and institutions as well as essential facets of Malta's politics, economy, society, and culture. More can then be learned by consulting some of the titles in the bibliography.

The first edition of this volume was written by Warren Berg, a professor of economics at Luther College, whose initial visit was in 1966 when he taught at the then Royal University of Malta. For several decades, he was the leading American scholar on Malta, and the connection was maintained by some of his colleagues. One of these is Uwe Jens Rudolf, a professor of accounting and management, who has visited Malta a half dozen times already, including a longer stay with Luther's Semester in Malta program in 2003 and a sabbatical in 2005–6 to research the effects of EU membership on the wine industry. In addition, he has served as the director of Luther's international studies program and led numerous study abroad seminars. This experience has motivated him to both update and substantially expand this volume for a second edition, one that will continue to inform and enlighten the growing circle of friends of Malta, within and without.

Jon Woronoff
Series Editor

Reader's Note

1. All entries are alphabetized by the individual words rather than by whole phrases. In the case of names of human beings, the alphabetization is by family name.
2. Maltese words are used in their common form. Where there is a conflict between the British spellings and the American spellings, the latter are used except in the case of place names, political parties, and titles of positions.
3. Where known, exact dates are listed. Others may be qualified with the word "about." For broader time frames, the word "circa" is used.
4. Several forms of cross-referencing have been used with the intention of making the dictionary as easy to use as possible. Citations that are located elsewhere are in **bold type**. Where there are several possible citations—for example, Order of St. John, Knights of St. John, Knights of Malta—all are listed and cross-referenced. Entries that are related but not included in the text are listed under *See also.*

Acronyms and Abbreviations

AD	Alternattiva Demokratika
AFM	Armed Forces of Malta
AM	Anglo-Maltese Party
BA	Bachelor of Arts
BSc	Bachelor of Science
CBE	Commander of the Order of the British Empire
CHOGM	Commonwealth Heads of Government Meeting
CMG	Companion of the Order of St. Michael and St. George
CP	Constitutional Party
DBA	Doctor of Business Administration; sometimes Diploma in Business Administration
DSO	Companion of the Distinguished Service Order
EC	European Community
ECB	European Central Bank
EEA	European Economic Area
EEC	European Economic Community
EMWA	Equality for Men and Women Act
EMU	European Monetary Union
ERM	Exchange Rate Mechanism (of the European Union)
EU	European Union
EVRF	Emergency Voluntary Reserve Force
FAO	Food and Agricultural Organization
FMOM	Friends of the Sovereign Military Order of Malta
Fra'	Frater (Latin: "brother," title for "monk" used by the Knights of Malta)
FWA	Fondazzjoni Wirt Artna
GC	George Cross
GCB	Knight Grand Cross of the Order of the Bath

GCH	Knight Grand Cross of the Royal Guelphic Order
GCMG	Knight Grand Cross of the Order of St. Michael and St. George
GDP	Gross Domestic Product
GWU	General Worker's Union
HMS	Her (or His) Majesty's Ship
HSBC	Hong Kong and Shanghai Banking Corporation
JUD	Doctor of Canon and Civil Law
KBE	Knight Commander of the Order of the British Empire
KCB	Knight Commander of the Order of Bath
Kt	Knight
LLD	Doctor of Laws (Legal Letters)
Lm	Maltese Lira
MBA	Master of Business Administration
MC	Military Cross
MCA	Malta Communications Authority
MCAST	Malta College of Arts, Sciences and Technology
MD	Doctor of Medicine
MEP	Member of the European Parliament
MEPA	Malta Environment and Planning Authority
MEUSAC	Malta European Union Action and Steering Committee
Mgr.	Monsignor, ecclesiastic honorific title
MIC	Malta European Union Information Center
MIMCOL	Malta Investment Management Company Limited
Mjur	Master of Law
MLP	Malta Labour Party (Partit Tal-Haddiema)
MP	Member of Parliament
MTA	Malta Tourism Authority
M.U.S.E.U.M.	Society of Magister Utinam Sequatur Evangelium Universus Mundus
MVO	Member of the Royal Victorian Order
MWP	Malta Workers' Party
NATO	North Atlantic Treaty Organization
NBM	National Bank of Malta
NCPE	National Commission for the Promotion of Equality
NECC	National Euro Changeover Committee
NGO	Nongovernmental organization

OBE	Officer of the Order of the British Empire
OECD	Organization for Economic Cooperation and Development
OSCE	Organization for Security and Cooperation in Europe
PAR	Partito Anti-Reformista
PCP	Progressive Constitutional Party
PDN	Partito Democratico Nazionalista
PfP	Partnership for Peace
PhD	Doctor of Philosophy
PM	Prime Minister
PN	Nationalist Party (Partit Nazzjonalista)
PP	Partito Popolare
PU	Partito Unionista
QC	Queen's Counsel
RAF	Royal Air Force
RMA	Royal Malta Artillery
RUM	Royal University of Malta
SDA	Society of Christian Doctrine
SMEs	Small and Medium (Sized) Enterprises
SMOM	Sovrano Militare Ordine di Malta—The Knights of Malta
SS	Steam Ship
SThD	Doctor in Sacred Theology
UEFA	Union of European Football Associations
UHM	Union Haddiema Maghqudin
UM	University of Malta
UN	United Nations
UNESCO	United Nations Educational, Scientific and Cultural Organization
UNHCR	Office of the United Nations High Commission for Refugees
UPM	Unione Politica Maltese
VAT	Value Added Tax
VC	Victoria Cross
VSM	Victim Support Malta
WHO	World Health Organization
€	Euro

Chronology

BCE

ca. 5200–4500	Ghar Dalam Phase. First human settlers.
ca. 4500–4400	Grey Skorba Phase.
ca. 4400–4100	Red Skorba Phase.
ca. 4100–2500	Megalithic Temples constructed.
ca. 2500–800	Bronze Age.
ca. 800–480	Phoenician Colonization.
ca. 700–600	Greek Presence.
ca. 480–218	Carthaginian Rule.
264–146	Punic Wars (Rome against Carthage).
264–241	First Punic War.
221–202	Second Punic War.
149–146	Third Punic War.

Roman Rule

218 Romans seize control of Malta when Consul Sempronius Longus sails to Malta to accept the surrender of the Carthaginians.

CE

60 Shipwreck of St. Paul the Apostle.

117 The islands become a *municipium* under Emperor Hadrian.

395 Roman rule ends.

395–535 Visigoth or Ostrogoth presence on Malta?

Byzantine Rule

535–870 Byzantine Rule.

454 Maltese islands occupied by the Vandals?

464 Maltese islands occupied by the Goths?

533 Islands restored to Byzantine Rule?

Arab Rule

870 **28–29 August to 1090:** Arab rule.

1048 First Byzantine attempt to regain islands.

Norman Rule

1091–1194 Norman conquest.

1091 Malta annexed to Sicily.

1122 Arab uprising.

1127 King Roger reconquers the Maltese islands.

1144 Second Byzantine attempt to regain the islands.

1154 John made bishop of Palermo and Malta.

1154–1205 Genoese influence.

Swabian Rule

1194–1266 Swabian rule.

1224 Final expulsion of the Arabs from Sicily and Malta.

Angevin Rule

1266–1283 Angevin rule.

1282 Sicilian Vespers.

Aragonese and Castilian Rule

1283–1412 Aragonese rule.

1283 **12 July:** The "Battle of Malta." The Aragonese led by Roger de Lauria enter Grand Harbour and destroy the Angevin fleet.

1350 Establishment of Maltese nobility.

1350–1357 First incorporation into Royal Domain.

1393–1397 Time of the Tyrants.

1397 Second incorporation into Royal Domain. Universita established in Gozo. Petitions to Sicily.

1420 Malta becomes feudal possession of Don Antonio Cardona.

1421 **7 March:** Malta and Gozo are transferred to Don Gonsalvo de Monroy.

1423 Muslim forces attack the Maltese islands, devastate the countryside, and take many inhabitants as slaves.

1425 Gozitans revolt against Don Gonsalvo de Monroy.

1428 **20 June:** Last incorporation into Royal Domain.

1429 **September:** Tunisian Saracens attempt capture of the islands, taking about one-third of the Maltese population captive.

Rule of the Knights

1530 **23 March:** Charles V, King of Sicily and Malta, grants Malta to the Knights of St. John. **26 October:** The Order sails into Grand Harbour to take possession of Malta.

1551 **July:** Dragut's raid on Gozo, capturing and enslaving most of the population.

1561 Inquisition officially established.

1565 Great Siege.

1566 **28 March:** Founding of Valletta.

1568 **21 August:** Death of Jean Parisot de la Valette and burial in Valletta.

1571 **7 October:** Battle of Lepanto.

1573 Foundation stone laid for St. John's Co-Cathedral.

1578 Consecration of St. John's Co-Cathedral.

1592 Opening of Jesuits College (Collegium Melitense) in Valletta.

1615 **21 April:** Wignacourt Aqueduct completed.

1676 **19 December:** School of Anatomy and Surgery founded at the Sacred Infirmary.

1732 **9 January:** Manoel Theatre dedicated.

1768 Jesuits expelled and property transferred to the Knights by papal order.

1769 **22 November:** Conversion of Jesuits College to a university.

1775 **9 February:** Uprising of the Priests.

1784 Creation of a legal code, *Diritto Municipale*, under Grand Master Rohan.

1792 **19 September:** Decree is issued by the revolutionary government of France, seizing all possessions of the Knights of St. John located in France.

French Occupation

1798   The Inquisition is abolished. **12 June:** French invasion, Napoleon lands in Malta. **18 June:** Grand Master Ferdinand von Hompesch, the 71st grand master and only German ever elected grand master of the Knights of St. John, withdraws from Malta with many of the Knights, relocating the Order in Russia. **1-2 August:** Napoleon's navy suffers defeat at the Battle of Aboukir Bay. **2 September:** Maltese revolt against the French.

1799   **17 January:** Dun Mikiel Xerri is executed by the French. The British take the islands under their protection in the name of the King of Two Sicilies.

British Rule

1800   **4 September:** British occupation begins; French troops depart. **11 September:** Congress is dissolved.

1802   **27 March:** Treaty of Amiens. **15 June:** Declaration of Rights is issued by the Consiglio Popolare.

1807   **18 September:** Mgr. Ferdinando Mattei is appointed first Maltese-born bishop of Malta.

1809   **23 June:** Anglo-Maltese bank is established.

1812   **1 May:** Banco di Malta established. **18 July:** Russia agrees to let the British take over control of Malta.

1813   **16 July:** The Bathurst Constitution (Malta's first constitution). **5 October:** Sir Thomas Maitland is installed as first governor of Malta.

1814   **30 May:** The Treaty of Paris is signed. Malta is declared free of the plague. **15 July:** The police force is established.

1815   The Congress of Vienna affirms the Treaty of Paris.

1819   The Universita is dissolved.

1828   **10 April:** Vatican Church-State Proclamation abolishes right of sanctuary in criminal matters and lay ecclesiastical jurisdiction.

1831 **20 June:** The See of Malta is made independent of the See of Palermo.

1833 **May:** Construction begins on the Mosta Dome.

1835 **1 May:** The First Council of Government is granted under British rule. Four of the seven are official members, and three are appointed, two of them Maltese.

1839 **14 March:** Abolition of press censorship. **20 March:** Laying of the cornerstone for St. Paul's Anglican Cathedral by Queen Adelaide, the first member of British royalty to visit Malta.

1846 **February:** Carnival riots.

1849 **11 May:** Letters patent grant a new constitution, setting up Council of Government with eighteen members, eight Maltese elected members.

1866 **9 October:** The Royal Opera House is dedicated.

1869 **16 November:** Opening of the Suez Canal.

1870 Referendum on ecclesiastics serving on Council of Government.

1881 Creation of Executive Council under British Rule.

1882 Anglo-Egyptian Bank founded in Malta.

1883 Malta Railway begins operation.

1885 First postage stamps issued.

1886 Surgeon Major David Bruce discovers microbe causing Malta fever.

1887 Council of Government with "dual control" under British rule.

1888 Simmons-Rampolla Agreement between Great Britain and the papacy concerning the Church in Malta.

1896 **1 December:** Electricity officially inaugurated in Malta.

1902 **29 December:** Accidental discovery of the Hypogeum under the site of housing development in Paola.

1903 **16–21 April:** King Edward VII visits Malta. **3 June:** Knutsford Constitution withdrawn. **August 1903–April 1904:** Five elections held with elected members always resigning immediately after election. Chamberlain Constitution comes into force. Return to the 1849 form of Council of Government under British rule.

1905 **23 February:** Tram service begins.

1906 **15 October:** Steam ferry service across Grand Harbour is inaugurated. **30 October:** New dry docks, the largest in the world, are completed and put into operation (causing a recession since it was the end of work for many). **25 June:** Dr. Themistocles Zammit discovers source of Malta fever. **17 December:** The Barracca Lifts built by Macartney McElroy start operating. First bus service starts operations.

1907 **22 December:** St. Aloysius' College opens its doors.

1908 **9 November:** Malta Boy Scouts Association established. **22 December:** First motion pictures shown in Malta.

1909 **15 January:** First submarine to enter Grand Harbour is the German U-3.

1912 Dun Karm writes his first poem in Maltese. **22 April:** The Royal Commission's report on dire economic state of Malta is issued. It recommends that Maltese language be used in lower courts in lieu of Italian.

1914–1918 World War I. Malta becomes known as the nurse of the Mediterranean. After receiving 1,640 wounded from the campaign on the Gallipoli Peninsula, facilities are expanded to 25,000 beds.

1915 **12 February:** First flight in Malta, a seaplane from HMS *Ark Royal*. **20 July:** Tarxien Temples discovered by Dr. Themistocles Zammit.

1917 **8 May:** Dr. Enrico Mizzi is arrested and charged with sedition because of pro-Italian speeches. Mizzi was elected in October, but Francesco Azzopardi, former council member, sued to annul election because of Mizzi's conviction, and the court awarded Azzopardi the seat.

1919   **25 February:** National Assembly convened by Dr. Filippo Sciberras. **7 June:** Sette Giugno riots. **20 November:** Granting of a new constitution for Malta announced.

1920   **15 October 15:** Labour Party (Camera del Lavoro) established.

1921   **30 April:** Self-government is granted under British rule: letters patent are read and proclaimed by Lord Plummer, installing a new constitution effective 16 May. **1 November:** First Parliament opens, inaugurated by Edward, Prince of Wales. Joseph Howard named prime minister.

1923   **2 February:** "Innu Malti" played for the first time in public at the Manoel Theater. **14 October:** Dr. Francesco Buhagiar becomes prime minister upon resignation of Joseph Howard.

1924   Compulsory Attendance Act requiring school attendance passed. **24 September:** Sir Ugo P. Mifsud becomes Prime Minister. **19 November:** National Museum of Archeology opened under direction of Dr. Themistocles Zammit.

1927   **28 February:** Governor Sir Walter Norris Congreve dies and is buried at sea on 4 March. **7–10 August:** General elections, Sir Gerald Strickland becomes prime minister.

1930   Constitution suspended because of Church actions under British rule.

1931   Malta Railway ceases to operate.

1932   Constitution restored under British rule. Sir Ugo Mifsud becomes prime minister.

1933   **2 November:** Constitution withdrawn. Malta reverts to the Crown colony status it held in 1813.

1934   **1 January:** Malti and English become dual official languages.

1935   Rediffusion Radio begins.

1936   Constitution revised to provide for nomination of members to Executive Council.

1939 Constitution revised to provide for a Council of Government with some elected representatives under British rule. **1 September:** Germany invades Poland.

1939–1945 World War II.

1940 10 June: Italy declares war on Great Britain. **11 June:** Italy launches first air raids on Malta, beginning the Great Siege of World War II.

1941 10 January: HMS *Illustrious* bombed and severely damaged, repaired and attacked again, departs Malta several weeks later. **26 July:** Italian E-boat attack on Grand Harbour.

1942 13 February: Enrico Mizzi and other detainees deported to Uganda. **15 April:** Award of the George Cross to the people of Malta. **14–15 August:** Operation Pedestal convoy arrives in Grand Harbour.

1943 20 June: George VI arrives in Grand Harbour for a visit. **7 July:** Lord John Gort announces that Malta is to receive self-government as soon as possible after war. **9–10 July:** Invasion of Sicily launched from Malta. **8–10 September:** Italian fleet surrenders in Malta. **5 October:** General Workers' Union organized. **17 November:** Winston Churchill visits Malta. **8 December:** President Franklin D. Roosevelt arrives in Malta to present citation.

1944 28 August: Last air raid on Malta.

1945 2 February: Churchill and Roosevelt meet in Malta prior to the Yalta Conference with Stalin. **25 October:** British government announces that a commissioner is to visit Malta to discuss new constitution.

1946 20 January: National Assembly begins to meet, resulting in 1947 Constitution under British rule.

1947 17 June: International telephone service is inaugurated. **5 September:** MacMichael Constitution restores self-government under British rule and grants suffrage to all men and women over the age of 21. **25–27 October:** General elections are held, the first in which women are permitted to vote. Dr. Paul Boffa becomes prime minister.

1949 Treaty creating North Atlantic Treaty Organization signed.

1950 **2–4 September:** General elections. **26 September:** Dr. Enrico Mizzi becomes prime minister.

20 December: Dr. Giorgio Borg Olivier becomes prime minister upon sudden death of Enrico Mizzi.

1951 **16 February:** Parliament is dissolved.

1952 **6 February:** King George VI dies. **23 April:** Sir George Borg retires as chief justice. Dr. L. A. Camilleri replaces him.

1952: Conditions of Employment Regulation Act provides legal framework for labor relations.

1953 **11 May:** Coronation incident in which Parliament votes against local celebration of the coronation of Queen Elizabeth II. **2 June:** Coronation of Queen Elizabeth II. **17 June:** Borg Olivier requests dominion status of Great Britain. **15 October:** Governor dissolves the Legislative Assembly.

1955 **12 January:** Paul Boffa resigns as leader of the Malta Workers Party. **8 March:** Dom Mintoff becomes prime minister upon resignation of Borg Olivier. Roundtable conference held.

1956 **14 February:** Referendum on Integration with Great Britain is boycotted by the Nationalists and the Catholic Church. Incident at Rediffusion.

1958 Caravaggio incident. **24 April:** Dom Mintoff resigns as prime minister. Borg Olivier declines forming alternative government. Colonial governor takes direct administration under British rule.

1959 **19 February:** The 1947 MacMichael Constitution is revoked. **15 April:** Interim Constitution provides for an Executive Council under British rule.

1961 Blood Commission provides for a new constitution, allowing for a measure of self-government and recognizing a quasi-state of Malta. **17 March:** Archbishop Michael Gonzi issues interdict against Malta Labour Party leader Dom Mintoff and all the members of the party's executive committee. **29 September:** Broadcasting Authority of Malta is established.

1962 **17–19 February:** General elections, Borg Olivier chosen premier under Blood Constitution. **20 August:** Borg Olivier requests independence for Malta within the Commonwealth.

1964 **2–4 May:** Referendum on Independence Constitution. **21 July:** Stolper report issued. Malta signs Anglo-Maltese Mutual Defense Agreement with Great Britain as part of independence negotiations.

Malta Statehood

1964 **21 September:** Malta granted independence, becoming a sovereign nation within the British Commonwealth. "Innu Malti" is recognized as the national anthem. **1 December:** Malta becomes 114th member of the United Nations.

1965 **25 January:** Malta joins Council of Europe. Din l'art Helwa is founded.

1966 **August:** Great Britain declares intention to run down its military presence in Malta by 1968.

1967 **23 January:** Malta ratifies the European Convention on Human Rights. **4 September:** Malta applies for a special relationship with the European Economic Community (EEC).

1968 **17 April:** Central Bank is established. **24 July:** Malta joins the International Monetary Fund (IMF). **21 October** Discussions between Malta and the EEC begin.

1970 **5 December:** Malta enters into an association agreement with the EEC.

1971 **17 June:** Dom Mintoff elected prime minister. **3 July:** Sir Anthony Mamo is sworn in as the first Maltese national to serve as governor-general.

1972 **26 March:** A military base agreement is signed by Malta, Great Britain, and other North Atlantic Treaty Organization nations. The King's Own Malta Regiment is disbanded. **16 May:** The change to a decimal monetary system is instituted. The government bars the U.S. Naval Forces from using Malta as a liberty port.

1973   **21 March:** Air Malta is established by act of Parliament. **31 March:** NATO dismantles military bases in Malta.

1974   **1 April:** Air Malta's inaugural flight departs. **17 April:** Government writes off 12.5 million liri debt owed by Malta Drydocks. **13 December:** Malta officially becomes a republic, remaining in the Commonwealth. Sir Anthony Mamo is elected first president.

1975   **15 July:** Civil marriage bill is published by Parliament.

1976   **27 December:** Dr. Anton Buttigieg becomes second president.

1979   **31 March:** Declaration of Malta's neutrality. Military base agreement is terminated. Loss of 30 million British pounds revenue as British forces leave. First Freedom Day celebrated. **15 October:** The headquarters of the *Malta Times* are set on fire by political activists. **13 December:** A new national stadium is inaugurated at Ta' Qali.

1980   **23 August:** A territorial dispute with Libya comes to a head when the Libyan navy threatens an Italian oil drilling operation leased by the Malta government. The United Nations mediates the dispute. **29 October:** Former Prime Minister Borg Olivier dies.

1981   **4 March:** Malta publishes its declaration concerning neutrality, barring foreign troops on Malta's soil. Malta's dockyards are no longer allowed to repair U.S. or Soviet ships. **9 November:** Parliament is dissolved. **22 November:** A clash between supporters of the Malta Labour Party and the Nationalists turns ugly as stones are thrown, cars are set on fire, and more than a dozen people are injured. **12 December:** Almost 95 percent of the eligible voters turn out on election day. Although the Nationalists gain the majority of the votes, the Malta Labour Party gets 34 seats versus the Nationalists' 31 due to Malta's system of proportional representation. **18 December:** Dom Mintoff is sworn in as prime minister.

1982   **16 February:** Agatha Barbara is elected third president, the first woman to hold the office. **13 March:** Colonel Muammar Gaddafi stops in Malta on his way back from Vienna. As a result, relations between Malta and Libya are restored.

1983   **20 February:** Two Libyan army officers hijack a Libyan Arab Airlines plane with 160 passengers on board and redirect it to Malta.

23 February: Dom Mintoff negotiates release of the passengers. The hijackers are arrested and returned to Libya one month later. **29 March:** A political boycott of Nationalists is ended when twenty-five NP members are sworn in. **27 April:** Paul Xuereb resigns his seat in Parliament to allow Karmenu Mifsud Bonnici to take his place. **2 May:** Mifsud Bonnici is sworn in as senior deputy prime minister and minister of labor. **5 May:** President Buttigieg dies. **27 June:** Church Property Act empowering the State to seize Church property is passed. It was an attempt by the Labour government to dismantle Church schools, making education free for all. Nationalist party MPs walk out in protest. **10 August:** Malta joins the World Bank.

1984   21 September: A protest against the Government's closure of several Church schools is put down by force, using tear gas for the first time in Malta, and sets off a season of discontent and political violence. A bomb explosion, the first of twenty such incidents during the remainder of 1984, damages the government computer center in Dingli. **22 December:** Dom Mintoff resigns. Carmelo Mifsud Bonnici becomes prime minister. **29 December:** The Caravaggio painting, *St. Jerome*, is stolen from St. John's Co-Cathedral.

1985   13 December: One of the deadliest hijackings ends in Malta where an EgyptAir flight from Athens is forced to land.

1986   15 April: Malta tips off Libya about approaching U.S. planes about to attack.

1987   23 March: Fire destroys the roof of the Mediterranean Center. **12 May:** Dr. Eddie Fenech Adami becomes prime minister, returning the Nationalist Party to power.

1988   Freeport Corporation is organized. **15 April:** United Nations Institute on Aging is established in Valletta. **August:** Malta Council for Science and Technology is set up. **8 October:** Institute for International Maritime Law is established at the University of Malta. **21 December:** Pan Am flight 103 explodes over Lockerbie, Scotland, killing all 259 people on board. A Libyan Airline employee stationed in Malta and working for the Libyan secret service is later convicted of placing a suitcase containing the bomb on a flight originating in Malta.

1989   4 April: Dr. Vincent Tabone is elected president by the House of Representatives. First gathering of Knights of St. John since their departure in 1798 is held in Malta. **2–3 December:** U.S.-Soviet summit between Mikhail Gorbachev and George H. W. Bush takes place on a ship anchored at Malta.

1990   25 May: Pope John Paul II pays the first ever papal visit to Malta. **16 July:** The government formally applies for full membership in the European Community. Guido de Marco is elected president of 45th UN General Assembly. **1 November:** Malta Stock Exchange is established.

1992   8 February: The new Malta International Airport terminal is inaugurated. **22 February:** The Nationalist Party wins the national election. **26 March:** Dr. Alfred Sant is elected leader of the Malta Labour Party.

29 May: Queen Elizabeth II and Prince Philip in Malta for the inauguration of the Siege Bell Memorial. Fiftieth Anniversary of Operation Pedestal celebrated. **24 July:** Maritime Museum is opened in Vittoriosa.

1993   Malta signs international convention banning the use of chemical weapons. **6 January:** First university degree courses offered in Gozo. **25 February:** After serving only seven years, convicted hijacker Ali Rezaq is released to the shock and dismay of the U.S. government. **25–29 May:** The Fifth Games of the Small States of Europe are held in Malta. **26 September:** First Malta International Airshow held. **20 November:** First elections for local councils held.

1994   2 February: Broadcasting Authority approves license for Malta Labour Party to operate Super 1, a new television station. **4 April:** Dr. Ugo Mifsud Bonnici elected fifth president. **May 28:** President Mifsud Bonnici officiates at opening of the National Archives. **25 June:** European Union (EU) leaders meeting in Corfu confirm that Cyprus and Malta will be included in next EU enlargement. **23 September:** Malta Financial Services Centre begins operations as an autonomous body responsible for local and offshore financial activity. **25 October:** General Workers' Union calls general strike, paralyzing Malta, to protest value added tax scheduled to take effect on 1 January. **14 December:**

Maltese students now able to study at European universities under the ERASMUS Programme.

1995 1 January: Value added tax (VAT) is introduced. **13 January:** Ministry of Social Policy establishes a department to ensure equality for women in all sectors. **3 February:** Libyan tanker *Um El Faroud* explodes in the dry docks, killing nine workers. **26 April:** Malta joins NATO Partnership for Peace, which the Malta Labour Party (MLP) opposition contends is a violation of Malta's neutrality as written into the Constitution. **27 July:** Brucellosis (Malta fever) epidemic peaks at 129 cases. **31 July:** Parliament appoints Joe Sammut as first ombudsman of Malta. **1 September:** Malta Drydocks Council refuses to bid on ship repair work for U.S. ships, citing the neutrality clause of the Malta Constitution. **21 October:** Postal service privatized as Posta Ltd. takes over mail delivery. **29 October:** Assassination in Malta of Libyan citizen and jihad leader Fathi Shqaqi raises tension between Libya and Malta. Israeli agents are suspected to be responsible. **27–28 November:** Malta is accepted as a partner in the Euro-Mediterranean Partnership launched at the Barcelona Conference.

1996 26 October: MLP candidate Dr. Alfred Sant is elected the fifth prime minister since independence, gaining 50.7 percent to the NP's 47.85 percent of votes cast. **23 November:** Foreign Minister George Vella formally withdraws Malta's bid to join the European Union.

1997 1 January: A Malta-based launch collides with a larger ship off the coast of Sicily, and 280 people drown. **9 June:** Two Turkish hijackers commandeer an Air Malta flight on its way to Istanbul but surrender in Cologne. **13 July:** Appledore report regarding restructuring of the dockyards issued. **27 July:** Posta Ltd. goes into liquidation. The postal service is taken over by the postmaster general until a new company can be set up.

1998 8 June: Mintoff's vote against the government's stance on the Cottonera project creates a crisis. **5 September:** Over 95 percent of voters turn out for elections that return the Nationalist Prime Minister Edward Fenech Adami to power. **10 September:** Malta reactivates application to join EU.

1999 **2 May:** Professor Guido de Marco appointed president. **22 November:** Minister of finance presents a white paper on government plans to privatize government services and enterprises. **12 December:** Malta-flagged oil tanker *Erika* breaks in two south of Brest, causing a major environmental disaster **31 December:** St. James Cavalier Centre for Creativity opened.

2000 **23 January:** Passage of first equal opportunities law to protect handicapped. **4 February:** Malta Film Commission is launched with Winston Azzopardi appointed as film commissioner. **10 February:** New laws on dual citizenship come into effect. **15 February:** Formal accession negotiations between Malta and the EU are opened. **12 March:** Local council elections in 23 towns and villages give the PN 49.3 percent and MLP 48.8 percent of the votes. **25 May:** Seven of the eight chapters in negotiation for EU membership are provisionally closed. EU launches the Socrates program for Malta. **14 June:** Formal decision taken by EU Enlargement Commission to close the first seven chapters with Malta. **19 June:** Organisation for Economic Co-operation and Development (OECD) removes Malta from its list of tax havens. **23 June:** Explosion at Marsa power station leads to a total shutdown of the country's two sources of electrical power at Marsa and Delimara. **4 July:** Wardens are established and operating in 54 localities throughout Malta and Gozo. **14 July:** Joseph Sammut is reappointed ombudsman for a second and final term of five years. **20 July:** Hal Saflieni Hypogeum is inaugurated after a nine-year restoration and conservation project partly funded by UNESCO. **11 August:** Foundation to establish the Malta College of Arts, Sciences and Technology is signed into law. **22 September:** St. James Center for the Arts is opened after a Lm4 million renovation of the St. James Cavalier. **1 October:** Malta signs an association agreement with the EU, allowing Maltese to fully participate in educational programs for youth. **21 October:** A new movement called *Iva Malta fl-Ewropa* (Yes! To Malta in Europe) is established to promote Malta's EU membership. **14 December:** Malta signs the United Nations convention against international organized crime and protocols on trafficking of people (especially women and children) and illegal immigrants.

2001 **10 March:** Turnout of 71 percent of eligible voters for local council elections. Malta Labour Party gains majority with 49.3 percent versus 48.1 percent for the Nationalists and 2.6 percent for the independents. **14 March:** On a state visit to Bulgaria, President De Marco survives a car accident that kills one man. **14 April:** Neolithic Temples at World Heritage Site Hagar Qim are damaged by vandals, causing a national outcry and a protest march. **8–9 May:** Pope Jean Paul II visits Malta. **27 June:** Malta negotiates the right to restrict European Union workers from access to Maltese jobs for seven years upon joining EU, whereas Maltese workers will be able to work in EU immediately upon Malta's accession. **16 December:** A power transmission cable between Malta and Gozo is commissioned.

2002   16 January: Dr. Noel Arrigo sworn in as new chief justice. **31 March:** Small retail shops are permitted to open for business on Sundays. **23 April:** Italian oil company ENI begins drilling for oil in Maltese waters. **25 April:** Malta signs agreement to sell 40 percent of Malta International Airport. **9 May:** First International Fireworks Festival in Malta organized by Malta Tourism Authority. **4 August:** Chief Justice Noel Arrigo and Judge Patrick Vella are arraigned on bribery charges. **25 August:** Judge Vincent De Gaetano sworn in as new chief justice of Malta. **22 September:** Former Prime Ministers Mintoff and Mifsud Bonnici launch Front Maltin Inqumu (Front Maltese Awake), a group opposing Malta's joining the European Union. **21 October:** Industrial and Employment Relations Act is passed, consolidating and updating labor laws to eliminate discrimination and to introduce gender mainstreaming and family friendly policies. **13 December:** Formal negotiations for Malta's joining the EU are concluded in Copenhagen, Denmark.

2003   1 January: Deadline for Malta to have all necessary laws in place for joining the European Union. **February:** Equality for Men and Women Act is passed by Parliament. **8 March:** Referendum vote held with 91 percent of eligible voters turning out, of which 53.6 percent approve Malta's joining the EU. **12 April:** Turnout of 96 percent of eligible voters in national elections returns Nationalists to power with a 51.7 percent majority and 35 seats versus 47.6 percent and 30 seats for the MLP. Alternattiva Demokratika receives only 0.7 percent of the votes, thus gaining no seats. **16 April:** Prime Minister Eddie Fenech Adami and Foreign Affairs Minister Joe Borg sign Malta's accession to the EU in Athens. **2–7 June:** The 10th Games of the Small States of Europe are held in Malta. **19 June:** The draft of a Constitution for Europe is published by the EU. **14 July 20:** House of Representatives ratifies the EU accession treaty. **15 July:** Thirteen years to the day that Malta applied for membership, President Guido de Marco signs the European Union Act, clearing the way for Malta to join the EU. **9 August:** The new Cottonera Marina is inaugurated. **17 August:** The new Marine Mammals Protection Regulations (2003) are issued. **29 October:** Malta signs the Council of Europe's Convention on Nationality, designed to make it easier to acquire a new nationality or recover a former one. **27 September:** New regulations titled the Flora, Fauna and Natural Habitats Protection Regulations of 2003 are published, bringing Malta's regulations in line with those of the EU. **29 September:** Malta becomes a member of the International Commission for the Conservation of Atlantic Tunas (ICCAT). **13 October:** Malta joins the European Economic Area. **5 November:** Drydocks and Malta Shipbuilding are restructured as Malta Shipyards, eliminating 900 workers. **10 November:** The Ta' Kandja pumping station in Siggiewi is sabotaged and the water contaminated with petroleum.

2004   23 January: Dr. Janet Mifsud appointed first "equality promotion" commissioner. **7 February:** Prime Minister Eddie Fenech Adami resigns from party leadership. **3 March:** Dr. Lawrence Gonzi wins race for Nationalist Party leadership and becomes prime minister "in waiting." **20 March:** Dr. Tonio Borg elected deputy leader of Nationalist Party and deputy prime minister. **22 March:** Eddie Fenech Adami resigns as prime minister and from Parliament. **23 March:** Lawrence Gonzi sworn in as prime minister. Three women announced as cabinet members. **29 March:** Eddie Fenech Adami elected president of Malta. **29 April:** The celebration for Malta's joining the EU begins.

Member of the European Union

1 May: Malta becomes a member of the EU. **12 June:** Turnout of 82 percent of Maltese and Gozitan voters go to polls to elect EU parliamentarians. **21 June:** Local council elections held: Labour—68 (50.2 percent), Nationalist—68 (46.4 percent), AD—1 (1.5 percent), and Independents—3. **3 July:** John Dalli, minister of foreign affairs, resigns and is replaced by Dr. Michael Frendo, parliamentary secretary.

17 July: The introduction of the environment tax causes an uproar from unions and social partners. **26 July:** The eco tax is postponed. **3 November:** Negotiations between the government and the General Workers' Union to restructure the dockyards are concluded, whereby Malta Shipbuilding and Malta Dockyards are restructured as Malta Shipyards, greatly reducing the workforce. **22 October:** Malta's first EU commissioner, Dr. Joe Borg, begins term as commissioner for fisheries and maritime affairs. **December 12:** Chief Justice Joseph Said Pullicino appointed ombudsman by unanimous parliamentary vote.

2005   13 January: Protest by illegal immigrants at Safi Barracks detention center results in scuffle with armed forces guards, causing injuries to 26 detainees and two guards. Amnesty International calls for investigation into alleged undue use of force. **16 January:** EU grants Malta €4 million (US$5 million) for restoration work on eight cultural and tourist sites, including the Hagar Qim temples and the city of Mdina. **26 February:** Domus Romana reopened to the public after refurbishing. **23 March:** Malta-Gozo helicopter service resumed. **5 April:** Smoking is no longer allowed in any entertainment establishment without a smoking room. **8 April:** EU determines that Malta qualifies for Objective 1 funding category after all. **2 May:** The Maltese lira enters the EU's Exchange Rate Mechanism (ERM II). **14 June:** The government launches the National Euro Changeover Committee (NECC) to formulate and implement a specific plan dealing with all aspects pertaining to the final adoption of the euro. **7 July:** The Maltese Parliament unanimously ratified the EU Constitution. **22 July:** BirdLife Malta and BirdLife International submit a formal complaint to the European Commission about Malta's failure to adequately transpose and enforce the Birds Directive into national law. **23 August:** The Emission Alert SMS 4 Clean Air campaign is launched by the Malta Transport Authority. **24 September:** Malta applies for full membership in the Organisation for Economic Co-operation and Development (OECD). **28 September:** The Malta Aviation Foundation's Battle of Malta Memorial Hangar at Ta' Qali is inaugurated. **1 October:** U.S. government buys land to build a US$50 million embassy compound at Ta' Qali. **2 October:** Five youths from Qrendi are killed in the nation's worst traffic accident. **3 October:** Prime Minister Gonzi meets with President Bush in the White House. **14 October:** Restoration works at the Ggantija temples, which suffered a collapsed wall from heavy rains in September 2003, are completed with Lm36,000 from the EU Solidarity Funds. **21 October:** Atlantica S.p.A. di Navigazione signs an agreement to buy the government's 69 percent shares in Sea Malta. **26 October:** Prime Minister Gonzi announced that the electricity surcharge has been raised from 17 percent to 55 percent to offset rising oil prices. Petrol prices are now to be reviewed monthly instead of every quarter. **3 November:** Announcement of National Reform Programme, with an investment of €227,569,863 to strengthen the country's competitiveness, economic growth, environmental protection, and job creation in line with the EU's Lisbon Agenda. **25–27 November:** Malta hosts the Commonwealth Heads of Government Meeting (CHOGM) for which Queen Elizabeth II and Prime Ministers Tony Blair (UK) and John Howard (Australia) visit Malta. **7 December:** The Italian shipping company, Grimaldi, decides against buying government's Sea Malta shares. As a result, the Maltese company is liquidated five days later. **18 December:** Malta obtains a net EU budget package of €455 million (US$575 million) over a seven-year period.

2006 16 January: Victor A. Galea is elected president of the Malta Chamber of Commerce and Enterprise. **2 February:** Ian Micallef, president of the Chamber of Local Authorities, is named vice president of the EU's Committee of the Regions. **4 February:** New regulation makes it illegal for anyone under 16 years of age to consume alcohol. The European Parliament is finally able to interpret its plenary sessions into Maltese after four interpreters of Maltese are added to the staff. **6 February:** EU Commissioner for the Environment Stavros Dimas officially admits that an exemption from a specific article of the Birds Directive was discussed during Malta's accession negotiations, weakening the EU's stance against Malta's continuation of spring hunting. **10 February:** The Malta Environment and Planning Authority (MEPA) obtains €200,000 from the EU Transitional Facility to assist in implementing the EU environmental *acquis* with a "polluter pays" principle. **14 February:** Reacting to the global bird flu threat, the government suspends hunting at sea and rounds up all wild ducks. **22 February:** Illegal immigrants tear down fences at three detention centers. The detainees do not seem interested in escaping but rather drawing attention to their living situation. **11 March:** The opposition wins local elections with 53.9 percent of the votes. Prime Minister Lawrence Gonzi states that low turnout played a significant part in the Nationalist Party's poor showing. **14 March:** The government nominates former Attorney General Anthony Borg Barthet as its member on the European Court of Justice (ECJ) for a further six-year term. **27 March:** The Dubai company TECOM and the Malta government sign an agreement regarding the company's plans to build a Lm110 million IT center called SmartCity at Fort Ricasoli in which the government is to have a 9 percent interest. **30 March:** The Government adopts the European Union's Birds Directive. **31 March:** Family and Social Solidarity Minister Dolores Cristina establishes the Commission on Domestic Violence. **15 May:** The Cabinet approves the government plan to sell for €220 million (US$300 million) its 60 percent stake in Maltacom to TECOM Investments of Dubai, the company behind the SmartCity project. TECOM also agrees to invest about Lm30 million in new state-of-the-art technology for Maltacom in the first three years. **26 May:** The Forni Sea Passenger Terminal, part of the Valletta Waterfront project, is officially opened by President Edward Fenech Adami. Malta is now able to handle home-porting passenger operations (cruises starting and ending in Malta). **26 June:** Close to 400 illegal immigrants escape from the detention center before being rounded up and returned to the center several hours later. **25 July:** The House of Representatives votes 33–28 in favor of the controversial extension of the building development zones. **6 August:** The Sigma report on Malta is released. A joint effort by the OECD and the EU to evaluate the 10 new EU member states' "regulatory management capacities" praises the Civil Service and the Malta Environment and Planning Authority for their efficiency and regulatory capacities but urges more administrative simplification. **11 August:** The European Union officially launches its first joint border patrol mission to slow the influx of illegal immigrants from Africa to European shores. **6 September:** Malta's first women judges, Magistrate Abigail Lofaro and lawyer Anna Felice, are sworn in by President Fenech Adami. **7 September:** The leading budget airline, Ryanair, announces its first routes to Malta, making over four million seats available. **12 September:** Prime Minister Lawrence Gonzi announces that the Euro-Mediterranean Parliamentary Assembly is to be based in Malta. Italy and Libya agree to collaborate in dealing with illegal immigration and human trafficking by launching joint patrols in Libyan waters. **15 October:** Thousands fill the streets of

Valletta for its first Notte Bianca. **31 October:** Archeological investigations unearth traces of a Bronze Age settlement and Roman remains at the historic Santa Margerita Cemetery in Rabat. **12 November:** Beginning in 2008, Malta will receive a minimum of €300,000 (US$400,000) annually from the European Return Fund to be used for the repatriation of illegal immigrants to their country of origin.

2007 **24 January:** Mgr. Paul Cremona is installed as the archbishop of Malta. **27 February:** At a press conference, Prime Minister Gonzi announces that in January 2007, the government formally submitted Malta's application to join the eurozone and to adopt the euro. **10 March:** Turnout of 68 percent of eligible voters for local council elections at 16 localities in Malta and six in Gozo. The MLP won 53 percent, the NP 44 percent, AD and independents 3 percent of the votes cast. **24 April:** The final agreement on SmartCity Malta, projected to be the biggest foreign investment ever in Malta, is signed. **11 May:** STMicroelectronics, a major manufacturer, threatens to pull out of Malta if it does not receive substantial financial support from the government. **3 June:** Over 5,000 Maltese faithful witness the canonization of George Preca, who is canonized as the first saint of Malta by Pope Benedict XVI. **9 June:** A new conservative party, Azzjoni Nazzjonali, is launched by former PN member Josie Muscat. **15 June:** Electric car public transport system is introduced in Valletta. **24 June:** An all night session of the European Council leads to a compromise on the controversial EU Constitution Treaty. Now referred to as the Reform Treaty, it ensures a sixth parliamentary MP for Malta, putting it on equal footing with Luxembourg. **29 June:** Prime Minister Gonzi inaugurates the controversial Lm220 million hospital, Mater Dei. **10 July:** The EU finance ministers unanimously vote to approve Malta's entry into the eurozone with the conversion rate of €1 = Lm0.4293.

2008 **1 January:** The euro replaces the Maltese lira as the official currency of Malta. **11–12 February:** Malta hosts the EU–League of Arab States Foreign Affairs Ministerial Meeting of 27 EU and 22 Arab states' foreign ministers. **19 February:** Internet provider GO signs an agreement with Emirates Company to lay a second underwater Internet cable from Italy that will expand capacity nine-fold. **20 February:** New harbor terminal at Mgarr, Gozo is inaugurated. **8 March:** National elections return Gonzi as prime minister. **12 March:** Following the close election victory by the Nationalist Party, President Fenech Adami appoints 14 new cabinet members. **30 March:** All border controls are lifted in Malta for travel within the Schengen area as the Schengen Agreement comes into full force. **11 April:** US and Malta sign a visa waiver agreement to permit Maltese to enter the United States without a visa. **25 April:** European Court of Justice bans spring hunting in Malta for 2008. **6 June:** Dr. Joseph Muscat is elected the new leader of the Malta Labour Party, succeeding Dr. Alfred Sant. **3 August:** The EU approves the release of the first batch of funds under the 2007–13 financial program, signaling the biggest ever investment in Malta, which should contribute toward a dramatic upgrading of the island's infrastructure. **8 August:** Malta signs double taxation avoidance treaty with the United States. **30 December:** A record 1.3 million tourists visited Malta in 2008, a 4 percent increase over 2007.

2009 28 January: The government launches a €10 million grant program to subsidize private investment in alternative energy solutions. **February:** Opponents, fearing damage to the historic structure, succeed in convincing the government to abandon controversial plans for an underground expansion to St. John's Co-Cathedral Museum. **4 April:** George Abela is unanimously elected the eighth president of Malta. **18 April:** Italy and Malta become involved in a dispute over which country should accept 140 illegal immigrants rescued near Lampedusa by a Turkish freighter. **23 April:** The General Workers' Union and the Malta Dockers' Union meet to settle a dispute over which union should represent the workers at the Malta Freeport. **30 April:** Malta hosts international firework festival. **17 May:** *Agora*, the first major film entirely produced in Malta, premieres at the Cannes film festival. **6 June:** The lowest percentage of eligible voters since 1955 turns out to vote for the Maltese members of the European Parliament and some of the local councils. **10 September:** The European Court of Justice declares that Malta must follow EU Birds Directive banning spring hunting.

Introduction

Whether the Mediterranean Sea is the "cradle of civilization," as is so often stated, may be open to debate; that Malta is at its center is not. Situated in the middle of the Mediterranean Sea, this tiny island group consisting of very rocky terrain with soil of limited quality has an amazingly rich history. The scope of Malta's story is compelling and vast, especially when contrasted with its tiny size. Home to the oldest free-standing, man-made structures known to the world—older even than the pyramids and Stonehenge—Malta, at one time or another, has been invaded and occupied by most of the civilizations bordering the surrounding sea.

From about 800 BCE until 1979, the Maltese have been ruled by outsiders: Phoenicians, Carthaginians, Romans, Arabs, Byzantines, and various other European powers—Spanish, Italian, French, and British forces have taken turns controlling the archipelago. Their primary goal was always either to protect or attack shipping.

Malta's chief resource, its strategic location guarding major trade routes through "the narrows" between it and Sicily, together with its natural deep-water harbors, has made it a highly desirable piece of real estate throughout history. The Grand Harbour is one of the finest in the world. More recently, since joining the European Union on 1 May 2004, Malta serves as a cultural as well as geographic bridge between Europe and the Arabic-speaking countries of North Africa.

LAND AND PEOPLE

The Maltese archipelago is located approximately 100 kilometers (60 miles) south of Sicily, 288 kilometers (180 miles) east of Tunisia, and

355 kilometers (220 miles) north of Libya. It is almost equidistant between Gibraltar on the west and Alexandria on the east.

The nation consists of three inhabited islands, Malta, Gozo, and Comino, and several tiny, uninhabited ones, encompassing 316 square kilometers (122 square miles) in total area. Malta is the largest at 246 square kilometers, Gozo at 67, and Comino covering barely 2.59 square kilometers (or 95, 26, and 1 square miles, respectively). The longest distance on the island of Malta from the northwest to the southeast is approximately 27 kilometers, and the widest is 14.5 kilometers (17 and 9 miles). For Gozo, the corresponding distances are 14.5 kilometers and 7 kilometers (9 and 4.5 miles).

Situated at 36 degrees latitude north, the archipelago has a typical Mediterranean marine climate featuring hot, dry summers and mild, wet winters. June, July, and August are the hottest months with temperatures often in excess of 35 degrees Celsius. Winters are mild with low temperatures around 10 degrees during January and February.

Although the island of Malta contains rural areas devoted to agriculture, Gozo is known as the "green island" because of its greater agricultural development. Both islands are quite hilly, but there are no rivers and just a few streams. Numerous harbors and bays surround the island of Malta; Gozo, however, has relatively few.

According to the most recent census taken in 2005, Malta's population is estimated to be 405,000. About 92.5 percent live on Malta and the remainder on Gozo. The population of the tiny island of Comino is limited to the staff of a single resort hotel serving the needs of visiting vacationers. Leaving aside the anomalies of Monaco and the Vatican, only Singapore has a population density greater than that of Malta, which has 1,260 inhabitants per square kilometer. Malta's population, largely concentrated in the area around the Grand and Marsamxett Harbours, was growing by over 9 percent in the decade from 1985 to 1995. This growth slowed in the following decade to about 6 percent, and by 2015, the population is projected to begin a gradual decline.

In the various guidebooks, Maltese are described as being very friendly, patriotic, stubborn, bright, hardworking, and resilient. A report by a royal commission from 1911 stated that the Maltese "type is South European . . . but fairer in colour, in the towns at any rate . . . a strong, hardy race . . . temperate, thrifty and industrious . . . though lacking self confidence."[1] This is understandable for a people who, until recently, had no control over their own destiny. Threatened with death or capture and enslavement by hostile forces, Malta's native peoples had to endure a hardscrabble existence. This might explain some contradictory character traits: the Maltese have lived through the centuries with a certain "us versus them," insider versus outsider, ruled versus rulers dichotomy. Even today, the nation is sharply divided into two camps: on the one hand, those resisting, consciously or not, the influences of globalization and on the other, those with international perspectives and ambitions, open to the outside world, willing to embrace foreign investment and influence.

Though fairly equally split along two party lines on many other issues, the Maltese share a common fervor to express their political views; it is not at all unusual to have 80 or 90 percent voter turnout in national elections. They are also staunchly united about their religion. Ninety-five percent profess to be Roman Catholics, and much of Maltese social life centers on the Church.

Other than its passionate, hardworking people, the limestone on which the islands sit, a sunny climate, and deep, natural harbors, Malta has no resources. This has meant that limited harvests have to be supplemented by trade with outsiders, the greater part of Malta's exports consisting of services. Whether as a way station for Phoenician traders or ship repairs and refueling for the British navy, for centuries the Maltese have relied on trade in services as a significant contributor to the country's gross national product.

Advances in modern technology, such as long-range and nuclear weapon systems, have greatly diminished the military value of its strategic location, while Malta's population and dependence on trade with other countries has grown. Almost 100 percent of its energy needs are met by imported oil. To date, attempts at finding oil reserves on land or in the territorial waters surrounding Malta have been unsuccessful.

Whether because of their closer proximity to Italy or strong loyalty to the pope in Rome, certainly since the arrival of the Knights, the Maltese people have considered themselves to be European. This makes it all the more remarkable that the linguistic legacy of the Arab invaders survived so many centuries of Italian and European influence so that even today, the devoutly Roman Catholic population appeals to God as "Allah." Only recently have the Maltese begun to leverage their country's ability to serve as Europe's "bridge" to Arab cultures and economies of North Africa.

The Maltese language (Malti) was long thought to have been derived from the language spoken by the Phoenicians and Carthaginians, who colonized the islands from 800 to 218 BCE. However, more recent studies have proposed that Maltese has its roots in the dialects of Arabic spoken in Northern Africa, especially Tunisia. In any case, it is a curious mixture of Semitic words and structures, including Romance and English words, a unique legacy of Malta's various invaders/occupiers. The Maltese language has existed in written form for only about 200 years, using the Roman alphabet along with a few diacritical marks. Until the middle of the last century, it was considered a "kitchen language," mainly used by the less educated. The educated class, government, and the law courts spoke Italian and later English. The "language question," whether Italian or English should be favored, was long-standing controversy dividing many Maltese. It was not until the mid-1930s, when a standard Maltese orthography evolved, that the Maltese language became a factor in building a national identity. Today, Maltese and English are the two official languages. Maltese has also gained international standing as one of the official languages of the European Union (EU).

PREHISTORIC INHABITANTS

The Maltese archipelago was once inhabited by many animals no longer found there today, including dwarf hippos and elephants, whose remains were found in Ghar Dalam, the "Cave of Darkness." This is evidence that in earlier periods of the ice age, which ended around 12000 BCE, a land bridge connected the African and European continents. It is probable that humans followed the same travel paths, but no evidence of human settlement prior to 5000 BCE has been found. The only human evidence in the cave, two teeth, was found in 1917. These were long thought to have belonged to Neanderthal man but more recently were carbon-dated as coming from Neolithic man (5200–4000 BCE).

The first settlers undoubtedly came from Sicily about 5000 to 4000 BCE, probably settling Gozo first and then Malta. Beginning around 3600 BCE, these early Maltese built temples of huge rock slabs set in circular patterns. The structures became increasingly intricate and ornate and, judging from the various items discovered, were used for the worship of one or more deities. In order to construct such massive edifices, there must have already been a fairly cohesive social organization. Archeologists surmise that after about 800 years, the islands' inhabitants must have become sufficiently successful in agriculture to enable them to develop a societal structure that allowed some individuals to specialize in temple building and worship activities.

About 2500 BCE, the structures became used more as burial places. Archeologists have excavated six of the 23 temple sites discovered on Malta and Gozo. Their style of construction is not found anywhere else in the world. They represent the oldest free-standing, human-made structures known to exist anywhere on earth, predating the great pyramids of Egypt and Stonehenge by a thousand years. Because they have only recently been reexposed to the elements, there is serious concern about atmospheric damage as well as vandalism. The government, with the help of EU funding, has greatly improved the protection and management of these sites and is building a protective covering over some of them.

The Bronze Age dates from about 2500 to 700 BCE. The people of this era were of a different race and culture, distinguished by their copper and bronze tools and weapons. These inhabitants were thought to have been more preoccupied with warfare, moving away from the exposed temple sites to the high ground near Marsaxlokk, a site more easily defended against foreign invaders. A series of urns containing cremated human remains were discovered at the site of the Tarxien temples, the first evidence of cremation on Malta.

PHOENICIANS, GREEKS, AND CARTHAGINIANS

Around 800 or 700 BCE, Phoenicians from the Levant began inhabiting the Maltese islands. Several of their rock-cut tombs and cave dwellings have been uncovered on Malta and Gozo. An inscription on a stone column dedicated to "our Lord Melqart, Lord of Tyre," written in both the Carthaginian Phoenician language and classical Greek, indicates interaction with Greek colonies on nearby Sicily as well. The Phoenicians founded Carthage at present day Tunis and established a great naval and commercial presence in the Mediterranean, including control over Malta until 218 BCE, when the Romans drove them off in the second Punic War.

ROMAN RULE

When the Romans defeated the Carthaginian as rulers of the Mediterranean Sea, Malta came under Roman control and was governed by the propraetor of Sicily. Later, it received a propraetor of its own, directly responsible to the emperor in Rome, giving Malta and Gozo the status of *municipia*, which allowed them to mint their own coins. Some of those coins bear Punic as well as Latin inscriptions, attesting to the fact that a form of Punic language survived among the general population.

Two main cities, one called Melite, located on the site of present-day Mdina, and another on Gozo named Gaulos, existed during the Roman rule. The remains of several dozen villas, some baths and numerous Roman catacombs and other burial sites are scattered about the islands. The most impressive and best preserved of the villas, located just outside of the walls of Mdina, has been restored as a museum.

Although details of Roman rule over Malta are very scarce, it must have been a fairly peaceful and prosperous era. Beyond serving as a way station for shipping and the occasional pirate raids in the region, economic activity on the islands seems to have revolved around agriculture. A letter by the Roman statesman Cicero mentions the quality of Malta's honey and linen. Judging by the number of olive presses found on the sites of Roman villas, there must have been extensive olive oil processing during Roman times.

Around 60 CE, a ship carrying 275 passengers, including St. Paul and St. Luke, was wrecked on the island of Malta during a storm. The biblical account of the event and of the three months that followed are important to Christians everywhere but are of particular concern to the Maltese. Although the first evidence of practicing Christians dates from several centuries later, the Maltese generally consider St. Paul's arrival on Malta as the "time we became Christians." At any rate, there is no doubt that Malta is a Christian nation even today, both written into the Constitution and by practice.

When the Roman Empire fell to invading Vandals, it is presumed that they also laid siege to Malta, but there is no concrete evidence of that nor of any other impact on the islands by the Visigoths and Goths, who later controlled Sicily and, therefore, presumably Malta until well into the sixth century.

BYZANTINE RULE

Byzantine forces drove the Vandals out of Sicily in 533 CE. A letter written in 592 CE by Pope Gregory to Lucillus, the first known bishop of Malta, indicates that Malta was already a secure part of the Eastern Roman Empire. Little other evidence remains from this period, but it was during the Byzantine rule that Christianity became firmly established on the islands. Greek trading activity and other cultural influences were strong until the arrival of the Arabs. They swept across the North African coast causing a northward retreat of the Byzantines, whom they evicted from Sicily and finally Malta in 870 CE.

ARAB RULE

Very little is known about the period when the Arabs occupied Malta. Aghlabid Arabs from North Africa invaded Malta in 869 and 870, laying waste to the country, killing most of its inhabitants, and capturing the remainder as slaves.

Other than the Semitic structure of the Maltese language and a majority of place names plus a few Arab tombstones, there is strikingly little physical evidence left from the two centuries of Arab control in Malta. This may well be because, unlike the large, difficult to move megalithic temples, smaller structures were often dismantled in later centuries and recycled to build new buildings or rubble walls.

THE MIDDLE AGES

In the middle of the 11th century, Normans conquered much of southern Italy and Sicily. After the Great Schism of 1054 split the Latin and Byzantine churches, Pope Nicholas II and the Norman leader Robert Guiscard signed an agreement under which Guiscard, in exchange for being named duke of Puglia and Calabria, promised to restore Christianity to Sicily by conquering the Arab rulers of the region. Robert summoned his younger brother, Roger I, from Normandy to assist in the campaigns and installed him as count of Sicily after the successful capture of Palermo in 1072. Guiscard admired and adapted some aspects of the Arab culture. He treated his Greek and Arabic subjects with tolerance and respect, employing their artists and builders in his court. After several unsuccessful raids, mainly to quell piracy in the region, Guiscard conquered the Arabs occupying Malta in 1091. He followed a similar approach of allowing his Arab subjects to remain under the rule of their emir, so long as they paid tribute to the Sicilian ruler. Although Roger I, and his son Roger II, are credited with building many churches in Malta, they also permitted the Muslims and Jews under their control to worship openly and freely.

After Constance, the daughter of Roger II, married into the Hohenstaufen line of German rulers, the Swabians, under Henry VI, took control of the Kingdom of Sicily and, therefore, Malta. Charles of Anjou, supported by Pope Clement IV, conquered Sicily in 1266. The Angevins were in power until the Sicilians revolted against their French oppressors in 1282, allowing the Aragonese to seize control. Throughout these power shifts, the rulers of Sicily installed feudal lords on Malta, who taxed the inhabitants. This ended temporarily about 1397, when Gozo and Malta became part of the royal domain. Both islands were ruled by a "hakem," or local governor, appointed by the king of Sicily. In the following three decades, Malta was handed back to feudal lords and returned to the royal domain, albeit a much weakened kingdom that left Malta exposed to attacks by Muslim invaders from North Africa.

THE ORDER OF ST. JOHN

After their defeat by the Turks and the expulsion from their stronghold on the Island of Rhodes, the Knights of St. John roamed the Mediterranean for several years. Finally, in 1530, they were offered the Maltese islands for an annual rental fee of one Maltese falcon. The offer was reluctantly accepted, and the Order moved its navy and equipment to the Island of Malta. Work on improving the fortifications was begun immediately, causing an improvement in the local economy. The reaction of the Maltese was positive because of the new jobs and the greater protection the Knights could give against the constant threat of pirates and other marauders. The Maltese nobility, never accepted as equals by the aristocratic Knights, did not have the same positive reactions to their new overlords, and their opinion did not improve over the years.

The Great Siege in 1565 is the second major historical event celebrated by the Maltese (after the shipwreck of St. Paul). The Turks arrived with the largest fleet of ships ever seen in the Mediterranean up to that time, carrying 40,000 of the finest soldiers that Suleiman the Magnificent could muster. Although expecting a quick victory, they also carried equipment for a lengthy siege. Dragut, the overall commander, arrived after the battle had started and brought an additional 1,500 soldiers.

Against these numbers, there were approximately 8,500 defenders, including 592 Knights, 5,830 Maltese militia and irregulars, and 1,230 mercenary soldiers. The remainder were galley slaves released on a pledge of faithful service.

The siege lasted 110 days, from 21 May to 8 September, with battle after battle fought following fierce bombardments by the Turks. Several times the Knights were able to avoid what seemed like sure defeat. Although Dragut was killed in one of the early battles, leadership passed to the equally qualified Mustapha Pasha. Two events led to the end of the siege and the retreat of the Turks. First was a daring raid out of Mdina by the Knights' small cavalry on the Turkish camp at Marsa. They burned and destroyed most of the supplies and equipment and killed everyone, sentries and wounded alike. When he received word of the attack, Mustapha, fearing encirclement, called a retreat from a battle that was close to a Muslim victory. Soon after, a relief army from Sicily landed at the northern end of the island. When that intelligence was given to Mustapha, he ordered an immediate and total withdrawal from Malta. Only 15,000 of the original invading army of approximately 40,000 lived to return to Constantinople.

As the siege was about to begin, Queen Elizabeth I of England wrote that she feared for all of Christian Europe if the Turks prevailed in Malta. Her statement indicates the level of apprehension felt throughout Europe over past Muslim successes and the threat of further advances. After the victory, a joyous relief replaced the apprehension and caused an outpouring of wealth to the Knights. The result was a great improvement in the Order's treasury, which permitted it to embark upon the construction of the fortified city of Valletta and the repair of the siege damages.

In subsequent years, the Order became commonly known as the Knights of Malta. It continued to improve the island's fortifications as well as the architectural enhancement of the newly established city of Valletta, which soon became known throughout Europe for its beauty. The feared return of the Turks never took place, and the Order's fighting capability gradually deteriorated.

FRENCH OCCUPATION

The French Revolution caused the loss of the Order's wealth and landholdings in France. In addition, the loyalty of the Knights of the French Langue became doubtful. Finally, in 1798, Napoleon's forces invaded without opposition and took control of the island of Malta. The invaders were welcomed by the Maltese, who had long since grown tired of the Knights and now viewed them as lazy and arrogant intruders upon their land. The French permitted the Knights to leave with their personal property. The Order finally settled in Rome in 1834 after numerous legal attempts to regain their position in Malta.

Although the French had been welcomed with high expectations by the Maltese, those expectations were soon turned into anger as the new invaders began looting. Property belonging to the Order was seized, including many items to which the Maltese could have made some degree of legitimate claim. What aroused the greatest anger, however, was the looting of the churches, actions that completely turned around the attitudes of the populace. Clergy, farmers, and nobility took up arms to attack the French troops. In their anger, mobs gained control of Mdina and then forced Napoleon's army of occupation to retreat into fortified Valletta where it was subjected to a complete blockade.

Knowing that they were too weak to defend themselves even if they did overcome the French forces, the Maltese sent a delegation to the British naval vessels anchored off the island. The request was for assistance to both dislodge the French and come to the islands as a protecting force. The British, having defeated Napoleon at the Battle of the Nile, accepted, and the French garrison was forced to surrender. As a repeat of earlier history, the newcomers were welcomed almost as saviors.

BRITISH RULE

In 1802, under the Treaty of Amiens, Malta was to have been returned to the Order of St. John. The Maltese protested vehemently both the decision and the fact that they had been given no voice in the discussions. In the end, it did not matter as both sides broke the terms of the treaty. That provided the British with enough time to have second thoughts. Under the Treaty of Paris in 1814, Britain was awarded Malta as a colonial possession. Because they had invited the British to Malta as equals in ousting the French, the Maltese reacted angrily to the treaty, justifiably upset that they were to have new colonial masters. The Treaty of Paris is an example of how differently the two parties perceived their relationship, and it would prove to be an irritant for many years to come as Malta became a major British naval base.

It is fair to say that the arrival of the British began a love/hate relationship under which the dominant feeling fluctuated from time to time. A Maltese saying is that "all foreign nations are bad but the British are least bad." Malta's strategic importance as a base for the British navy grew with the opening of the Suez Canal in 1869. This lifted prosperity in the islands, and the Maltese relationship with their British overlords became almost positive as the British military provided resources and jobs. However, when downturns came, Maltese resentment at being British "servants" resurfaced. With each new constitution, the British felt that they were making serious concessions to the Maltese. But when the Constitution was received with less than total gratitude, it was usually replaced with something even more irritating to the local population.

WORLD WAR I

World War I brought a period of great prosperity to the islands. Because it often served as many as 20,000 sick or wounded Allied military personnel at one time, Malta became known as the "nurse of the Mediterranean." However, the sharp economic downturn after the war led to unrest. On 7 June 1919, a demonstration in Valletta to protest the price of bread turned ugly. In three separate incidents, inexperienced, poorly trained British soldiers fired on crowds, killing two Maltese and one Gozitan. The next day, a fourth was bayoneted and killed. These events have become known as the Sette Giugno riots, and the four dead are revered as political martyrs. It is said that Maltese Nationalism was born during the event of those two days, and 7 June is still celebrated as a national holiday.

The tragedy gained the attention of the British, and one result was the new Constitution of 1921, the first ever to refer to Malta as a nation. It created a dual system of government: a democratically elected legislature to deal with all matters of local concern and an administrative head appointed by the British to deal with colonial matters (essentially, foreign affairs and defense). The top official of the first was the prime minister and of the second, the colonial governor. For a variety of reasons, the Constitution was suspended in 1930, restored in 1932, and suspended again in 1933. Self-government in Malta did not return until 1947.

WORLD WAR II

The third major historical event for Malta was World War II. Surprisingly, the British War Cabinet considered using Malta and Gibraltar as bribes to keep Italy out of the war. As late as 28 May 1940, the matter was put to a vote of the five members of the British War Cabinet but lost—three, no; two, yes. Then, on 10 June 1940, Italy declared war and began the bombing of the islands, primarily Malta. The Italian attacks on Malta pretty much settled the language question that had been debated for so many years. When the bombs began to fall, streets in Valletta were renamed from their Italian names to English and Maltese names.

The German Air Force joined the Italians in November 1941, and the bombing intensified. As a result, Malta gained the dubious distinction of being by far the most heavily bombed place of the entire war. The great majority of bombs were dropped in the area surrounding Grand Harbour, concentrating the destructive effect to an even greater extent.

An invasion by the Italians early in the war would most certainly have been successful as there were minimal defense works in place. Also, a later invasion planned jointly by the Germans and Italians would likely have succeeded had it been carried out. Even the fierce bombings could have been much more effective if the bombers had concentrated on the electric power plant at the Marsa end of Grand Harbour. A loss of power would have drastically reduced Malta's ability to fight. Any one of these actions would have eliminated this festering sore for the Axis powers. That the attackers did not execute them became an important factor in the eventual Allied victory in the war.

Planes and submarines out of Malta were a severe hindrance to the flow of supplies to the Axis forces in North Africa. German General Erwin Rommel was to write later that Malta's conscience had to carry the burden of the deaths of thousands of German and Italian soldiers.

On the other hand, Axis planes and surface vessels were able to almost completely stop the flow of supplies to the islands. Always dependent upon imports, the minimum needs were placed at 26,000 tons (23,587 metric tons) of cargo monthly. Only 26,000 tons arrived in total during the first six months of 1942. Both civilians and military forces were on extremely short rations, and the surrender was deemed to be only days away. Finally, however, the remains of a huge convoy named Operation Pedestal (the Maltese call it "il konvoy Santa Marija") limped into Grand Harbour: four severely damaged cargo ships and a sinking tanker, the SS *Ohio*. There is no doubt that this convoy saved Malta from certain surrender. That it arrived at all was only at a tremendous cost in human lives, ships, and matériel.

In April 1942, King George VI awarded his nation's highest civilian honor, the George Cross, to the people of Malta. A depiction of the medal appears in the upper left corner of the nation's flag.

May and June 1943 were months of beehive activity in Malta as preparations for the invasion of Sicily were made. New airfields were built on Gozo to become the home base for a USAAF Fighter Group. Everywhere supplies and equipment were being stockpiled, and amphibious vessels were made ready. The nerve center was the underground War Headquarters at Lascaris in the bastions of Valletta. D-Day was 10 July 1943, and the invasion fleet of 3,000 ships and major landing craft departed carrying 115,000 British Commonwealth and 66,000 American soldiers. After the invasion, the fervor of war preparations declined, and Malta began its rebuilding. A deserved tribute to the importance of the Battle of Malta was contained in an editorial in the *New York Times*: "if we want to find the spot where the tide began to turn, Malta is as good as any."[2] Considering that the first bombs dropped on Malta came from Italian aircraft, it was only fitting that the surrender of the entire Italian navy take place there. It did just that in early September 1943.

INDEPENDENCE AND NATIONHOOD

Although Malta's wartime experience diminished the anti-British attitudes that had existed earlier, it did nothing to dampen the desire for true self-government and eventual independence. In politics, there evolved a two-party system, the Malta Labour Party (MLP) and the Nationalist Party (NP). Both desired to reduce the power of the Church in political activities; although, the NP was more subtle in its approach.

The war had been a great equalizer. It had a democratizing effect on the Maltese population, which had suffered shoulder to shoulder, rich alongside poor, working class beside professionals. In 1947, women gained the right to vote in national elections, and the MLP, traditionally seen as more pro-British than the NP, gained in popularity. Opinions about the manner in which Malta should free itself from rule by and dependency on Great Britain were divided. The NP supporters wanted Malta to become a dominion like Canada, while the MLP wanted integration into the United Kingdom, including representation in the British parliament.

A rising political star, Dominic (Dom) Mintoff, came on the scene as a forceful speaker and combative debater, very successful at rallying followers. Educated in England as a Rhodes scholar, he was initially strongly pro-British. He pushed hard for Malta to become integrated into the Empire, going so far as to suggest that the new state be called "The United Kingdom of Great Britain, Northern Ireland and Malta." The British government was not interested, and Mintoff soon changed his strategy to work for complete independence. He took over the MLP leadership and was elected prime minister in 1955 but resigned three years later, protesting the firing of several dockworkers. The ensuing riots caused the British government to revoke the Constitution.

In the election of 1962, after Malta had been granted a new constitution, the powerful Archbishop of Malta, Michael Gonzi, issued an interdict stating that anyone voting for Mintoff was committing a mortal sin. Many accused the British government of enlisting the Catholic Church to interfere with the elections in order to help the NP win. Whether this is true or not, the NP won and elected Giorgo Borg Olivier as prime minister. Mintoff still garnered enough votes to be reelected and served as leader of the minority.

Certainly, independence for former colonies was in the air during the 1960s, but even today, there is disagreement about when the country actually gained its independence. Most agree that this took place on 21 September 1964, when Malta was granted independence from Great Britain, becoming a constitutional monarchy, a sovereign nation in the British Commonwealth. Yet, the British retained the right to maintain a military presence for another 10 years. Because the Nationalist Party was in power from 1962 to 1971, which included the time of official independence in 1964, the MLP supporters took the view that independence really came when the British troops finally pulled out in 1979, a withdrawal that was negotiated by Mintoff during his regime.

An independent Malta quickly took its place as a nation among nations. A few months after independence, it became the 114th member of the United Nations and joined the Council of Europe.

ECONOMIC AND SOCIAL DEVELOPMENT

The new nation was faced with the necessity of freeing its economy in a very short time frame from dependence upon funds from its military occupiers. First of all, the naval dockyards would have to be converted from military to commercial use. Infrastructure for tourism was lacking; hotels, restaurants, nightclubs, and swimming pools would have to be constructed where few existed before. Tourism would also require a complete retraining in skills and attitudes for those who would be employed in the industry. Britain, throughout its rule over Malta, was one of the world's great industrial powers. One wonders why Malta could not have been made a greater beneficiary of that expertise. Instead, when independence arrived and the British departed, Malta was left with a minuscule managerial class. That was the greatest void in its attempt to become economically viable.

Furthermore, Malta would need small factories for the development of light industry; potential entrepreneurs would need access to, among other things, a modern banking system, a stable monetary system, an efficient communication network, and reliable power sources. Malta would need to develop desalination plants as water needs increased with economic growth. These were immense challenges that required unusually strong and effective leadership. Reelected as prime minister in 1971, Mintoff led an aggressive restructuring of the economy. The government nationalized many businesses to provide jobs and minimize competition. The Dockyards, Malta Shipping, and Air Malta were all state owned. Mintoff promoted self-sufficiency, banning many imports in order to support local products.

He also made significant changes in Maltese foreign policy. One of the matters of continual disagreement was the amount of the annual rent Malta received from the British. In 1972, an agreement was signed to permit the North Atlantic Treaty Organization (NATO) to maintain its Mediterranean base in Malta. In 1974, the new nation became a republic, shedding its allegiance to the British monarchy but retaining membership in the British Commonwealth. In 1979, under a declaration of full neutrality, all military agreements were terminated, and the remaining British forces stationed in Malta departed. Mintoff made the democratic Western powers uneasy: he forced NATO out of Malta, barred U.S. ships from entering Malta's harbor for repairs or refueling, and forged new relations with Libya and communist countries, such as Cuba, China, and Russia.

The decade of the mid-1970s to mid-1980s became a time of considerable political unrest in Malta. The Parliament was dissolved in 1981. Party headquarters were destroyed as party rivalries between the MLP and the NP boiled over into mob violence, bombings, and several unsolved murders. Although not directly implicated in the violence, alleged false arrests and police brutality were attributed to some of his follower's, and Mintoff's fiery rhetoric did little to calm political tensions.

In the general elections of 1981, 95 percent of the electorate turned out to vote. Although the Nationalists gained the majority of votes, Malta's system of proportional representation enabled the Labourites to gain 34 seats in Parliament to the NP's 31, returning Mintoff as prime minister. The passage of an act in 1983, allowing the government to seize Church property in its attempt to dismantle Church schools, further enflamed passions among the opposition.

Mintoff and the MLP lost the election in 1987 to Edward "Eddie" Fenech Adami and the Nationalists. Fenech Adami was elected prime minister and began a long process of changing course, reversing much of what Mintoff had done. Socialism was in retreat, and the communist states were failing. Malta became the world's center stage when it hosted the US/USSR summit. Malta formally applied to become a member of the European Union (EU).

MEMBERSHIP IN THE EUROPEAN UNION

The single most significant event in Malta since World War II and gaining independence was becoming a member of the European Union on 1 May 2004, a process that took almost 35 years and involved numerous hurdles and setbacks. Recognizing its economic and political vulnerability as a small island nation and fearful of being shut out of Europe in a rapidly globalizing world, Malta, under the leadership of Prime Minister Borg Oliver, had entered into an association agreement with the European Community in 1970.

After the Nationalists replaced the MLP in the elections of 1987, the government, under Prime Minister Fenech Adami, embarked on the ambitious goal of joining the EU by applying for full membership in July 1990 against staunch opposition from the MLP. Membership required, among many other changes in the political and economic structure of the nation, that Malta adopt a value added tax (VAT) system of taxation. The move proved to be very unpopular and resulted in a brief return to power of the MLP in 1996 with the election of Alfred Sant as prime minister. One of his first actions was to suspend the application for EU membership, stalling the process until the NP was returned less than two years later. Formal negotiations for Malta's membership began in 2000.

As promised by the NP during the electoral campaign, a referendum was held in March 2003. Ninety-one percent of the eligible voters actually cast ballots, 53.6 percent of them favoring EU membership. In a somewhat peculiar twist, the opposition leader, Sant, tried to argue that because the referendum lacked approval of the majority of eligible voters, it had failed. A month later, the NP pro-EU stance was further validated when Fenech Adami, riding a wave of EU optimism, was reelected and signed the accession treaty in Athens, Greece, four days later, paving the way for Malta's becoming a member of the EU on 1 May 2004.

It is difficult to exaggerate the immensity of the challenges Malta has had to overcome in order to conform its economic, political, legal, and social structure to the requirements of EU membership. Deficit spending, high inflation, and debt had to be brought under control. The economy had to be shifted away from one that was inefficient and state run with an emphasis on job security to one that was privatized, more competitive, and market-driven. The government had to adopt and adapt 80,000 pages of the *acquis* to Maltese law. Ingrained habits and customs, such as a casual attitude toward the environment, waste of resources, littering, pollution, and bird hunting (not to mention ignoring laws and regulations!), had to be changed. Malta had to eliminate high duties that protected local industry and bring inflation and deficits under control. The government needed to put into place standards regarding the rights of women, children, and handicapped persons and force inefficient industries to rationalize or shut down. The case of the dockyards, a labor union stronghold where an expectation of lifetime employment reigned, was a particularly sensitive issue. Membership in the EU has greatly bolstered the politicians' ability to muster support for these difficult changes.

On the other hand, Malta's prospective rewards are considerable as well: access to EU funding in the amount of 900 million euros in the 2007–13 budget, supporting infrastructure improvements; access for Maltese to much larger markets, jobs, and education in the wider EU; and access to technological assistance and the electrical grid of Europe, to name just a few.

Once EU membership was assured, Fenech Adami stepped down and Lawrence Gonzi was elected prime minister to replace him. Gonzi has continued the NP policies, making the most of EU membership to gain funding and legal support for structural reforms. Malta has succeeded in revising its laws to attract more banks and become a leading center for financial services. The "SmartCity" development and Internet gambling investments are expected to create more jobs, and a push to bring low-cost airline service to Malta has helped to support the vital tourism sector of the economy.

Many serious challenges still face Malta in the coming years as well: how to deal with a flood of immigrants coming from North Africa, how to maintain economic competitiveness in the face of the growing competition posed by cheaper labor from China, India, and elsewhere, and how to combat the threat of climate change that could have especially harsh consequences for small island nations like Malta. The enthusiasm for the EU has also worn off a bit as the global economic downturn begins to take effect and the Maltese electorate support for the party in power is beginning to wane. Fortunately, in reviewing what the Maltese have endured over the millennia, there is reason to believe that they will survive and thrive in the face of these challenges as well.

NOTES

1. Henry Frendo, *Party Politics in a Fortress Colony: The Maltese Experience* (Valletta, Malta: Midsea Books, 1979), 1.

2. George Hogan, *Malta: The Triumphant Years 1940–43* (Malta: Progress Press, 1978), 163.

The Dictionary

– A –

ABELA, DR. GEORGE (1948–). Dr. George Abela was elected **president** of the Republic of Malta on 4 April 2009, the eighth president to serve independent Malta and the first elected by unanimous approval of both **political parties** in **Parliament**. It was also the first time that a ruling party nominated a candidate for president coming from the party in opposition.

The son of a port worker, Abela was born in Qormi on 22 April 1948. He was educated at the Lyceum and studied at the **University of Malta**, where he earned a BA in English and a law degree; he worked in private practice for over 30 years, specializing in civil, commercial, and industrial law. In 1995, he earned a master's degree in law. For 25 years, Abela acted as legal consultant to the General Workers Party and helped various **trade unions** in their negotiations with the Maltese government, especially the restructuring of Air Malta and the port reform negotiations of June 2007, in which Abela represented workers' interests.

Abela has also been a lifelong supporter of sports in Malta, especially football (soccer). He served as the president of his local club, Qormi FC, and as president of the Malta Football Association from 1982 to 1992. Under his leadership, the national football team of Malta was raised to a professional level with full-time paid professional players, and the national stadium was significantly upgraded. He served as Malta's representative to Union of European Football Associations (UEFA) and sat on the Court of Arbitration for Sports headquartered in Lausanne, Switzerland.

In 1992, Abela was elected deputy leader of the **Malta Labour Party (MLP)** in charge of party affairs and appointed legal consultant to the **prime minister** when the MLP won the general election of 1996. He has also served as director of the Central Bank of Malta for a number of years, was executive director for the Bank of Valletta, and was a member of the Electoral Commission in 1987. Representing the MLP, he was an active member of the Malta-EU Steering and Action Committee (MEUSAC), both before and after Malta's joining the **European Union (EU)**. Abela is married to Margaret née Cauchi, and they have two children, Robert and Maria.

ACQUIS COMMUNAUTAIRE. A French expression without a good English equivalent [approximately: "community patrimony"], it is usually shortened to "the *acquis*" and refers to the entire body of **European Union (EU)** laws, treaties, regulations, or directives agreed on by the EU institutions, including judgments handed down by the European Court of Justice. Any country wishing to join the EU must adopt, implement, and enforce all of the *acquis*. This often requires changes in existing national law and/or administrative and judicial structures and practices. Based on negotiations before joining, some candidate countries are granted derogations, meaning that they are temporarily or permanently excused from adopting a particular part of the *acquis*.

At the time Malta was preparing to join the EU, it had to translate into Maltese language and law over 80,000 pages comprising the *acquis*, a monumental task. Malta was given derogations, allowing it more time to make some of the more difficult adjustments, such as reducing state aid for shipbuilding and repair activities of the **dockyards**, regulating **bird hunting**, and applying the Common Customs Tariff to imports of certain textile products over a transitional period, which expired on 31 December 2008.

AGRICULTURE. Given Malta's size, location, poor soil conditions, and scarcity of water, supplying food to the inhabitants has always been a struggle for the Maltese. The hilly and uneven terrain necessitates the construction of many terraces, resulting in small, inefficient plots of land. These small land holdings number approximately 11,000, of which three-fourths are less than one hectare (2.5 acres) in size. Landholdings are further reduced by the tradition of dividing up land evenly among siblings when passing it on to offspring and are often not adjoined, making farming them even less efficient. Not only are the small plots of land labor-intensive, they often result in over-application of fertilizer, putting pressure on the ecosystem.

Based on evidence found in the **Ghar Dalam** (Cave of Darkness), the earliest inhabitants of Malta grew barley, wheat, and lentils. The **Carthaginians**, **Arabs**, and **Normans** are credited with introducing and refining farming and irrigation techniques important to the dry conditions of Malta. Under the **Roman** occupation, a significant olive oil production was developed, and the Normans introduced citrus fruits and cotton. The latter became a major crop, prized for its quality in producing sails and a valuable good traded for food and other necessities. Cotton was also an important crop, especially for making sails. By the beginning of the 15th century, Maltese cotton had replaced **Turkish** suppliers to the cloth makers of Genoa, Barcelona, and Montpelier. That the cotton crop became an important source of revenue is evidenced by the 2 percent tax levied on cotton exports by the **Universita** in 1472. When sails were replaced by steam engines, the cotton crop disappeared from Malta. The hand-made lace, itself a dying art, currently lingers as the only trace of the once important cotton **trade**. When the **British** arrived in Malta, they introduced the potato as a more efficient crop than wheat in alleviating the widespread malnutrition on the island. The Maltese potatoes have become the most significant agricultural export.

Today, Malta is even more dependent on trade as over 95 percent of its net cereal consumption is imported. Agricultural production represents less than 3 percent of GDP generated by approximately 14,000 farmers, many of them part-time. The number of full-time farmers has declined by over 65 percent in the last 20 years, and nearly 12 percent of agricultural land has been lost to other uses. However, farming is still an important aspect of the islands' economic and cultural activity. It consists of three types: intensive farming of fruits and vegetables requiring irrigation; dry farming; and livestock production, including rabbits (a traditional meat dish of Malta), poultry, and dairy and beef cows. Except for egg production, in which Malta is self-sufficient, poultry and meat production is supplemented by imports. In addition to potatoes, major crops include tomatoes and wine grapes.

When the British troops departed, the government was again concerned about food security and implemented farm subsidy schemes to support agricultural production. These subsidies amounted to 21 million **euros** in 2006 and continue to be a challenge for Malta (as well as the **European Union** generally) because they have resulted in maintaining inefficient production.

A growing interest in eco-**tourism** has created a new focus on traditional crops and foods. Although olive oil continued as an important ingredient of Maltese cuisine, its local production had almost completely disappeared until a recent effort to reintroduce olive trees. *See also* ECONOMY.

ALTERNATTIVA DEMOKRATIKA (AD). One of the two more recently organized of Malta's four **political parties**, the AD came into existence in 1988–89 after two members of the **Malta Labour Party (MLP)**, Wenzu Mintoff and Party President Toni Abela, challenged the party to change some goals and practices. When their moves were not accepted, the two left the MLP to organize their own party. This new "democratic alternative" attracted those who have become disenchanted with the traditionally harsh, adversarial politics of Malta. It has emphasized concerns about the **environment**, corruption, the debasement of culture, and similar matters. Although it has been unable to secure a single seat in **Parliament** in any of the national **elections** to date, it did gather enough votes to cause some concern for the two major parties and has managed to elect about a dozen local councilpersons. Probably frustrated at the party's lack of success, Mintoff and Abela both quit the AD and returned to the MLP.

Increasingly, the AD has focused on environmental issues and is commonly known as the "green party." It consistently supported Malta's bid to join the **European Union (EU)**, hoping, like many Maltese, that membership would force Malta to raise its environmental standards. In 2004, one of AD's founding members, Arnold Cassola, was a candidate for the EU Parliament. He garnered a surprising 9.33 percent of first preference votes, just short of gaining a seat. Cassola later ran as a candidate in **Italy**'s Parliament and was elected. The AD is currently led by Dr. Harry Vassallo, an articulate and outspoken critic, whose editorials frequently appear in the local papers.

During the 2008 national election campaign, Vassallo stated that the AD was seeking to enter into a coalition with whichever of the two main parties was interested in doing so, provided it was willing to uphold the AD's priorities for the electoral campaign. These were:

1. Respect of all EU environmental directives, including the abolition of spring hunting.
2. Malta Environment and Planning Authority (MEPA) reform, including the elimination of the extended Development Zones.
3. Rent reform, including the reduction of income from rent from 35 to 15 percent.
4. Public transport liberalization.
5. Extension of maternity leave from 13 to 26 weeks paid by the government.
6. Reduction of income tax from 35 to 30 percent, while tax on the income of banks will be increased from 35 to 40 percent.
7. Electricity surcharge to be based on consumption.
8. Introduction of divorce and a law to regulate cohabiting couples.
9. A more transparent governance, with a Freedom of Information Act, a Whistleblower Act, and a law regulating party financing.

In the national election of 2008, the AD again failed to win a single seat in Parliament, receiving only 3,810 votes or 1.3 percent of the 291,000 votes cast, putting it in third place of the nine parties on the ballot but far behind the PN and MLP. As a result, Vassallo stepped down as party leader, and Dr. Arnold Cassola was elected at a special meeting on 14 June 2008 to replace him.

ANGEVIN RULE. Although there were **Swabian** heirs to the Sicilian throne, Pope Clement IV achieved his objective of eliminating German influence in the region by crowning Charles of Anjou as King of **Sicily** in 1266. After fierce battles with the other claimants, Charles emerged victorious and gained complete control of Sicily and Malta. The Angevins imposed a rule that was both firm and tight and stationed a garrison of French soldiers on Malta. The Maltese were given a measure of local government plus the appointment of a notary public resident in the islands (prior to that time, it was necessary to travel to Sicily for such services). Offsetting these benefits was the burden of extremely high taxes.

French rule was not very popular in Malta and even less so in Sicily. In 1282, there was an uprising known as the "**Sicilian Vespers**." Malta, still held by the Angevins, became the place for the regrouping of a large Angevin fleet for a counterassault on Sicily. In 1283, an Aragonese fleet appeared, and Grand Harbour was witness to the first major battle to be fought in its vicinity. The Angevin fleet was defeated, much to the joy of the Maltese, and the rule of the **Aragonese** had begun. Although Angevin rule over Malta was of relatively short duration, it was during this period that Malta began to be absorbed into the Latin and European systems of laws and government.

ARAB RULE. In less than 100 years after the death of Muhammad in 632, the Arabic Muslim Empire had spread east of Syria and west into North Africa. By 832, the Aghlabid Arabs of North Africa invaded **Sicily** and captured Palermo. These excellent desert horsemen had become seasoned sailors and had built a fleet, which controlled the central Mediterranean. Some think that the Aghlabids began raiding the Maltese islands as early as 836. In 869, they attempted a siege but were driven off by the local population. Then, in 870, a stronger fleet was sent and, despite strong resistance, Malta fell to Arab rule.

It was a rule that was to last for 220 years and exert great influence on the local population, culturally as well as economically. Not only does the Maltese language retain evidence of Arab rule, but also evidence can be seen in some artifacts in the National Museum, most of the place names in Malta, and many Arabic agricultural techniques. It is also likely that the Maltese gained from the maritime influence of their rulers. Unfortunately, little exists in the form of written evidence to inform us about this time. Although the Arabs did not attempt to impose their **religion** upon their subjects, they did impose the payment of a tribute on those who wished to retain their own faith. There is evidence that Christianity became a minority among Malta's religions, but this was probably caused as much by the immigration of Muslims as by the defection of Christians.

ARAGONESE RULE. After the defeat of the **Angevin** fleet in 1283, the Maltese gave the victorious Aragonese a joyous welcome in their happiness over the delivery from **French** oppression and their anticipation of improved economic circumstances. It wasn't always to be so. Too often the tiny islands were to become political pawns of the powerful. Between 1283 and 1350, the kings of Aragon granted political (including taxing) authority to a succession of Sicilians, awarding them the titles of marquis or count of Malta. In 1350, the Maltese petitioned King Lewis of Aragon to cease granting such authority and to place the island under his own domain. When he acted positively on the petition, these hardships abated for a while.

Later, when King Frederick III died in 1377, he was succeeded by his daughter, Maria. Because of the unrest in **Sicily,** Maria, a minor, was sent to live with her uncle, King Martin of Spain. In 1391, she married the king's son, Martin the Younger. In his gratitude to Guglielmo Raimondo Moncada for bringing the couple together, the king gave him the title and privileges of marquis of Malta. In 1393, Moncada renounced the title, and it was awarded to Don Artale D'Alagona, ushering in a period of severe hardship for the Maltese.

The period 1393–97 has become known by historians as the Time of the Tyrants because of the harsh and competitive rule of four Sicilians claiming authority over the populace. Late in 1397, the islands were again made part of the Royal Domain of Sicily through a deed, signed at Catania, which praises the Maltese for their loyalty and bravery.

In 1398, King Martin I called all representatives of the cities of Sicily to a general meeting. Malta and **Gozo,** as part of the Royal Domain, were included. One of the rulings of this "parliament" was that the islands of Malta and Gozo were never again to be granted out in fee and that they were to continue to be a part of the reigning monarch's dominion. Obviously, there was great rejoicing by the Maltese over this recognition. News of Martin's death in 1409 was received by the Maltese with deep sadness, as there was a general feeling that he had been the one responsible for giving them the national recognition they felt they deserved. He was succeeded by Martin II, who in turn was succeeded in 1412 by Ferdinand I, the first of the Castilian line of rulers. *See also* CASTILIAN RULE.

ARCHEOLOGY. Malta is full of significant archeological sites covering an estimated seven millennia and including **megalithic temples** that are the oldest man-made structures known to exist anywhere, yet an examination of major reference works on archeology reveals surprisingly sparse references to Maltese sites. It was not until 1988 that archeology was added as a field of study at the **University of Malta** as part of the Department of Classical Studies. As the Malta government began to realize their importance to **tourism**, it has increased support for the excavation and conservation of archeological sites, especially since the availability of **European Union** funding.

Unusual stone monuments on Malta had been attracting curious visitors for many centuries. Jean Quintin d'Autun, a cleric who spent six years on Malta, published *Insulae Melitae Descriptio* in France in 1536. It is the earliest known work referencing archeological sites in Malta. Over a century later, Giovanni Francesco Abela (1582–1655) published *Della Descrittione di Malta* in which are found the first detailed references to archeological artifacts such as **Punic** and **Roman** coins, lamps, and jewelry, which he collected. Included is a pair of short decorative stone columns engraved with a dedication to the god Melkart in Greek and Phoenician. One of these was later given to the king of France and provided a French scholar with a key to deciphering the Phoenician alphabet. Abela describes some of the **neolithic** temples in detail, observing that, because of the immensity of the stones with which they are built, they must have been built by giants. He also references some catacombs and Roman temples.

A number of Maltese and foreign writers in the 17th through 19th centuries provide descriptions and or illustrations of archeological sites on Malta. Notable among these are Count Giovanni Antonio Ciantar's *Malta Illustrata* (1780), Agius De Soldanis's study of Gozo *Gozo Antico-Moderno e Sacro-Profano* (1745), and Jean Houel's *Voyage Pittoresque des Isles de Sicile, de Malte et de Lipari*, published in the 1780s, which offered the best descriptions and detailed illustrations of Maltese and Gozitan sites, thus giving modern archeologists an idea of the state of the temples before any excavations.

The first significant and methodological excavations were begun by A. A. Caruana, Albert Mayr, and Father Magri in the late 1800s. But Dr. **Themistocles Zammit**, considered the "father of Maltese archeology," was the first to carry out excavations in a scientifically careful manner. He excavated the sites of the Tarxien temples, the Hal Saflieni Hypogeum, and many others sites in the early decades of the 20th century. **Zammit** directed the **Valletta** Museum, later renamed the National Museum of Archeology (currently located in Republic Street, Valletta), where many of the original artifacts from various sites are preserved and protected.

After Zammit's death in 1935, serious archeological research was not resumed until the 1950s when Professor J. D. Evans was able to establish a chronology of prehistoric eras through the dating of various styles of pottery. In 1960, David Trump excavated the Skorba temple sites. *See also* DOMUS ROMANA; GHAR DALAM.

ARCHITECTURE. Few places on earth can claim as locally concentrated and broad a span of architectural history as is found on the islands of Malta. From the **neolithic** temples to **Punic** caves, from **Roman** villas to Baroque churches, from fortified bastions to modern high-rise buildings, Maltese architecture features significant examples of the influences of the various cultures that ruled the archipelago. However, only a few examples of the architectural structures preceding the arrival of the **Knights** of the Order are still standing. The Knights brought with them the art and culture of continental Europe along with abundant riches to support a new, lavish style of building, the Baroque.

The scarcity of trees on the islands has dictated that most of the structures are made of local stone. The traditional globigerina limestone used as building material dominates the islands, giving it a distinctive golden patina while limiting most structures to a height of between four or five stories. Although in recent decades the limestone has given way to concrete and steel structures, globigerina is still a highly preferred decorative surface treatment. The hot climate with scarce rainfall has influenced building styles and features: flat roofs on most buildings (except churches and some public structures) serve as terraces for drying clothes in the daytime, catching evening breezes, and collecting water during infrequent rains. Loggias and porticos providing shade and air circulation are commonly found architectural features in Malta. Many buildings, especially homes, are long and narrow because the lack of timber meant that stone slabs were used for ceilings as well. The maximum span achievable was about two meters, which necessitated supporting arches, which became an important design component of Maltese architecture. Typically Maltese are also the stone or wooden gallerias, enclosed porches, that adorn the upper floors of most multistory buildings, allowing their occupants to witness what is happening in the street below without being too publicly exposed.

In a country that served as "an island fortress" for much of its history, military architecture was naturally of great importance, and most of the early architects brought to Malta by the Knights were military engineers. Francesco Buonamici from **Italy** and Mederico Blondel of France were brought in to serve as the Order's resident engineers but also built churches and palaces, transforming **Valletta** and **Mdina** into baroque cities. In the early 18th century, fearing another invasion by the Turks, the Knights appealed to the king of France for assistance. He sent a design team to aid in bolstering Malta's defenses. It was led by one of the most experienced military engineers of France, Brigadier René Jacob de Tigné. His assistant, Charles François de Mondion, took over as chief engineer after Tigné's departure and supervised construction for 18 years, a period in which many of the fortifications were completed. Both were under the influence of the most famous French military strategist and designer of fortification, Sébastien le Prestre de Vauban.

Among the most extensive and admired fortifications in the world (almost 25 kilometers in length), they included barracks, hospitals, and warehouses constructed by the Order of the Knights and further developed by the **British**. Many ornamental gates and other decorations were added in later years to make the massive bastions more appealing to the eye.

The first native Maltese architect was **Gerolamo Cassar**. Born circa 1520, he fought against the Turks during the **Great Siege**. After the defeat of the Turks, Cassar worked under **Francesco Laparelli** who was brought to Malta to design the new city, **Valletta**. When Laparelli left, Cassar took over becoming the architect responsible for many of the new **auberges** relocated in Valletta.

The Italian Renaissance found its expression in the layout of Valletta with straight streets and large public spaces The British influence is also quite evident in the many monumental and austere colonial public buildings, schools, military barracks, and hospitals mostly built in the neoclassical style. The Bighi Naval Hospital, completed in 1832, is generally acknowledged as the best example of this.

The most prominent Maltese architect of the second half of the 19th century, Emanuel Luigi Galizia (1830–1907), was influenced by 19th century Romanticism. Galizia garnered his greatest recognition for two of the more unusual structures still standing in Malta: one is the Catholic Addolorata Cemetery in neo-Gothic style; the other is the Muslim Cemetery, originally built by the Order, which had to be relocated to make way for a new road. Galizia's Ottoman Turkish Muslim Cemetery in Paola is designed in a "flamboyant and exotic oriental style that had absolutely no architectural precedence on the island (Thake and Hughes 2005, 80).

Other than the lone high-rise Portomaso Tower, no structures dominate the horizons on the island more than the churches of Malta. They represent a physical manifestation of religious piety that required a tremendous amount of resources. Although the Baroque style is dominant for so many of Malta's public structures, especially churches, there are also examples of classical, neo-Gothic, and modern styles, including some mixtures, such as the 1844 St. Paul's Anglican Pro-Cathedral, a landmark of Valletta, which features a neoclassical facade, and a Gothic spire, the first use of the Gothic style in Malta. Another neoclassic landmark is the **Mosta Dome**, featuring one of the largest open spans in the world. Although constructed in the architectural styles of earlier centuries, a surprising number of the churches are of recent vintage. Many are credited to Guze Damato, whose best known work is the church at Xewkija in **Gozo** begun in 1952.

Post–**World War II** architecture has been dominated by functionality and clean lines of the "international modern style." A few contemporary Maltese architects, such as **Richard England**, have been very successful at adapting modern building requirements and techniques to the Maltese environment, using massive walls and bold circular forms to break the more monotonous honeycomb mold of so many apartment blocks. Two of his works, the St. Joseph Parish Church at Manikata and the renovation project for the St. James Cavalier are excellent examples.

Unfortunately, uncontrolled and indiscriminate building continues to scar and consume much of what little open countryside remains in Malta. This has finally begun to be brought under some control since 1992 with the passage of the Development Planning Act and the establishment of the Malta Environment and Planning Authority (MEPA) in 1993. Conflicts between developers, the government authority, and conservationists continue to intensify, however, as land for building is increasingly scarce. *See also* MANOEL THEATRE; ROYAL OPERA HOUSE; SACRED INFIRMARY; ST. JOHN'S CO-CATHEDRAL.

ARMED FORCES OF MALTA. After the departure of the **Knights of St. John**, Maltese soldiers were first organized in April 1800 as the Maltese Light Infantry, a battalion under the command of the **British** Royal Marines helping to evict the **French** from **Valletta** and Malta. The battalion was disbanded in 1802 and replaced by the Maltese Provincial Battalions, the Malta Coast Artillery, and the Maltese Veterans. The latter were experienced soldiers under the Knights who returned to Malta after being forced to serve under Napoleon in Egypt. In 1815, the forces were disbanded and reconstituted as the Royal Malta Fencible Artillery, the forerunner to the Royal Malta Artillery (RMA), which played an important role in defending the islands during **World War II**.

In 1970, the Malta government took charge of its own troops organized as the Malta Land Force and, on 19 April 1973, restructured under its current organization as the Armed Forces of Malta (AFM). It consists of a headquarters and three regiments. The 1st Regiment (infantry) is tasked with providing territorial security at the airport and other sensitive locations as well as assisting the police with drug enforcement. The 2nd Regiment is responsible for patrolling and protecting territorial waters and air space, while the 3rd Regiment provides logistical support. An Emergency Volunteer Reserve Force (EVRF), consisting of male and female part-time soldiers, is trained by and under the command of the 1st Regiment. In November 2006, the AFM underwent a reorganization, creating air and maritime squadrons as independent units no longer part of the 2nd Regiment.

ASSEMBLEA NAZIONALE. *See* SCIBERRAS, SIR FILIPPO.

AUBERGES. The **Knights of St. John** often lived elsewhere in Europe, at their homes or in lands owned and operated by the Order. When they were at the Convent (the home base in Malta), they were separated into **langues** based upon their region or country of origin. Each langue had its own auberge (dormitory). Originally, these were located in Birgu (renamed Vittoriosa after the **Great Siege of 1565**), but when the Knights moved to **Valletta** in 1566, eight new auberges were designed by **Gerolamo Cassar**. Five of these remain and are used as government offices or **museums**. The finest, the Auberge de Castille et Leon, is now the Office of the **Prime Minister**. Several of the original auberges in Vittoriosa have also been restored and are still in use.

AXIS BLOCKADE. Always a heavy importer, during **World War II**, Malta needed imports of 26,000 tons of materials each month. A blockade by the Axis powers was so successful that during the first six months of 1942, the *total* cargo imported by Allied convoys was just 26,000 tons. The islands were within a few days of being forced to surrender in August 1942 when five badly damaged Allied ships of **Operation Pedestal** were able to enter Grand Harbour, bringing 55,000 tons (49,896 metric tons) of supplies. In those first eight months of 1942, four large convoys out of Great Britain were sent to supply Malta, including 35 cargo ships. Of that number, 19 were sunk, seven had to turn back, and five were severely damaged. Losses to the escort vessels were also severe and included one aircraft carrier, two cruisers, six destroyers, and some smaller vessels sunk and one aircraft carrier, six cruisers, seven destroyers, and several smaller vessels severely damaged. The greatest loss, however, was in the heavy death toll. In Operation Pedestal alone, over 350 lives were lost. The planes, submarines, and surface ships used the islands as a base and continued to deny needed supplies to the Axis forces in North Africa. It is estimated that normally 40 percent, and often as high as 70 percent, of the enemy's supplies shipped from **Italy** never arrived where they were needed. Although vulnerable to attack and very costly to defend, Malta was crucial to the Allied cause.

– B –

BALL, REAR ADMIRAL SIR ALEXANDER (1756?–1809). As a **British** Royal Navy captain, Ball was appointed to command the squadron blockading the **French** military detachment, which had retreated into the fortified city of **Valletta** in 1799. The French finally surrendered on 5 September of that year, and Ball was placed in charge of the civil administration of the islands. At first, the British were uncertain as to the value of Malta, but Ball produced documents emphasizing the many benefits Great Britain could gain by retaining possession. Early in 1801, he was recalled to naval duty and, when that tour ended, received as a reward for his efforts a large cash bonus and was created a baronet.

In June 1802, he returned to Malta as rear admiral and with the permanent appointment as civil commissioner. During his time in office, he instituted reforms in the courts and in public health matters. He was respected during his life and sincerely mourned at his death in the San Anton Palace on 25 October 1809. He is buried in Fort St. Elmo. An impressive monument, erected through public subscription, stands to this day in the Lower Barracca Gardens in Valletta.

BAND CLUBS. The passionate rivalries that seem to permeate Maltese society find unique expression in the phenomenon of the band club (*Kazin banda*). In 2008, there were 90 such clubs, involving almost 4,000 musicians. Many of the band clubs are named after **British** imperial personages, leading to the suspicion on the part of some Maltese that band clubs were founded by the British as a means to keep the Maltese distracted and divided. Most band clubs have a place to meet, and some also serve as pubs or restaurants. While the British military bands may have provided a strong role model, in fact, the first band clubs were founded in 1860 by a Maltese, Indri Borg. They provided **music** for the *festas* and developed into focal points for rivalries among various local parishes seeking to outdo each other in all aspects of the *festas*. The volume of fireworks, the number of candles, guest bands, and the extent of street decorations are some of the factors in determining which band club has outdone its rivals. Not unlike some soccer fans of Europe and Latin America, band club members in Malta have sometimes become so fervent in their competition with other clubs that violence ensues. The Church and the police have had to intervene on several occasions to control some of the excesses.

BANKING. Over 20 banks have operations in Malta with balance sheets totaling over 11 billion **euros** and employees numbering almost 3,500. The country ranks third after Dubai and Shanghai among financial centers, which, according to a survey of bankers, are expected to gain most in importance in the coming years. The two major banks operating in Malta today are the Bank of **Valletta** (BOV) and the Hong Kong and Shanghai Banking Corporation (HSBC). Both are descended from a long lineage of banks in Malta. The BOV lays claim to being the oldest, tracing its beginnings to 1809, while the HSBC, currently the largest bank in Malta, has its origins in the Anglo-Egyptian bank from 1864. Smaller institutions with significant numbers of Maltese clients include the APS Bank and the Lombard Bank. When Malta adopted the euro on 1 January 2008, the Central Bank joined the European Central Bank System and the European Central Bank (ECB). Its primary function now is to maintain price stability, maintaining inflation at about 2 percent.

Before the arrival of the **British** in 1800, banking in Malta was carried out on an ad hoc, private basis by totally unregulated money lenders. An exception was a fund called Massa Frumentaria, which was managed by the **Universita** to ensure a sufficient supply of grain to the islands. The **Order of Knights of St. John's** "Commun Tesoro" (the order's "sacred treasury") also served as a kind of bank dealing with extensive export and import trading transactions, determining exchange rates, collecting and distributing funds from various sources, and paying for supplies and services. Two other institutions that functioned as quasi banks were the Monti di Pieta and Monte della Redenzione degli Schiavi. The latter was a fund used to ransom slaves captured by the Muslims, and the former served as an early form of bank, lending money to the poor against items pledged as collateral, thus helping citizens in financial distress avoid the usury rampant at the time. These two funds were merged shortly before the **French** evicted the Knights from Malta. On 1 April 1977, the funds were vested with the Maltese government and continue, albeit in

greatly diminished capacity, to this day as Monti di Pieta. The Massa
Frumentaria was finally wound up on 24 June 1994.

The first institution in Malta to actually call itself a bank was the
Anglo-Maltese Bank, established on 23 June 1809, nine years after
the British took control of Malta. Competition was not long in coming as the Banco di Malta opened its doors on 1 May in 1912, and in
the same year, a family of successful Italian immigrants from Genoa,
the Tagliaferros, who operated in shipbuilding and grain trade, established the first private merchant bank in Valletta.

Another prominent pioneer in banking of the era was the Marquis
Joepf Scicluna, whose bank, Joseph Scicluna et fils, was established
in 1830 and by 1890 had three offices in Valletta, the first example
of bank branches in Malta. Scicluna was the first banker to introduce
checks to Malta, which were called "cisk" by the Maltese. Cisk
became the nickname of the family and was used to name the beer
still sold today, in which the Scicluna family had considerable investment. The stately home Scicluna built and occupied on a spit of
land protruding into the sea at St. Julians has become the landmark
site of a casino today. The Scicluna name lives on as an investments
management company, Scicluna Estates Ltd.

Another banking institution with a long history in Malta was the
Anglo-Egyptian Bank, founded in 1864. In 1925, it became part of
the English Barclays Bank, which, in turn, the government of **Dom
Mintoff**, eager to gain more control over the **economy**, nationalized
in 1975 as the Mid-Med Bank. When it came to Malta in 1999, the
HSBC took over the Mid-Med Bank.

A similar fate befell the oldest banks of Malta in 1946 when
the Anglo-Maltese Bank and Banco di Malta merged to form the
National Bank of Malta (NBM). In 1949, Scicluna et fils affiliated
with the group as did Tagliaferro and Sons two decades later. On 6
December 1973, a run began on the NBM. The Central Bank, ap-
parently on instructions from Mintoff, refused to come to the bank's
assistance, and the NBM was taken over by the government without
compensation to any of its shareholders. The government then set up
a new bank, the Bank of Valletta (BOV), in 1974, which took over
the assets and liabilities of the collapsed NBM. The Mintoff government held 70 percent ownership of the BOV, selling 20 percent to a
Sicilian bank and slightly less than 10 percent to the public. In 1992,

the BOV became the first public company to be listed on the Malta Stock Exchange and in 1995, as part of the **Nationalist** government's drive to privatize state-owned entities, reduced its ownership share of the bank to 25 percent. A lawsuit filed by the former shareholders of the NBM, in hopes of being compensated for their losses from the collapse of the bank, is yet to be settled.

The only other major bank crisis in Malta involved the collapse of the Bank of Industry, Commerce and **Agriculture**, a small commercial bank set up by the Pace brothers Cecil and Henry in 1963. Known by the acronym BICAL, the bank failure in November 1972 involved fraud, resulting in numerous court cases that took over 25 years to settle. *See also* FINANCIAL SERVICES.

BARBARA, AGATHA (1923–2002). Born in Zabbar on 11 March 1923, Barbara was educated in government schools. As a young **woman** during the **World War II** Axis bombings, she served as supervisor of victory kitchens. In 1945, she became a teacher but turned to politics in 1946, joining the **Malta Labour Party (MPL)**. She was the first woman elected to **Parliament** in 1947. In 1955, she became the first woman minister when she was named minister of **education**. Five months later, she successfully introduced compulsory full-time education for all Maltese aged five through 14. She was involved in constructing or renovating over 40 schools throughout Malta and instituted special schools for handicapped children, free **health** care, textbooks and transportation for all pupils, and stipends for **university** students. Barbara has probably done more than any other Maltese to raise the educational standards and literacy rate of Malta. Active in the administration of the MLP, Barbara was a staunchly loyal supporter of **Dom Mintoff** and Malta's workers. She was sentenced to jail by the British for her participation in a national protest against **British rule** in 1958. She, along with her fellow executive leaders of the MLP, was also interdicted by the Church in April 1951.

From 1971 to 1974, Barbara was again minister of education and culture and from 1974 to 1981, minister of labor, culture, and welfare. She successfully campaigned to raise the leaving age for school to 16. Barbara served as acting president on several occasions. A skillful negotiator, she helped resolve the constitutional crisis of the mid-1980s. She successfully contested every **election** until 16

February 1982, when she was elected by Parliament as the first (and so far only) female **president** of Malta, serving in this office until 1987. President Barbara died on 4 February 2002. A monument in her honor was unveiled in Zabbar in April 2006.

BATHURST CONSTITUTION. This was not really a **constitution** at all, but only the instructions given in 1813 by the colonial secretary in Britain, Lord Bathurst, to the British **governor** of Malta. It stipulated that "the authority of the Governor is limited only by order of the King; he is responsible to His Majesty and to his country for his conduct, but his discretion is not to be shackled by any body of persons resident in Malta." At the same time, it provided for the "free exercise of religious worship to all persons who inhabit or frequent the islands." The overall effect of the instructions was to make Malta a Crown Colony and to specifically eliminate the Maltese from having a voice in the conduct of the affairs of their land. *See also* BRITISH RULE.

BATTLE OF ABOUKIR BAY. The battle, which is also known as the Battle of the Nile, took place on 1 August 1798. Napoleon planned to strike at Britain through India, and that was the primary reason for his expedition to Egypt. His stop in Malta on the way was but a chance at an added prize to be gained through a temporary detour. In Egypt, his army won the Battle of the Pyramids, but his navy lost when his fleet, crowded into the small harbor, was unable to maneuver, allowing the **British** fleet, under the command of Admiral Horatio Nelson, to destroy it without difficulty. The treasures from the ransacked palaces, churches, and other buildings in Malta had been loaded aboard Napoleon's flagship, *L'Orient*, which was sunk during the battle, taking them to the bottom of the bay. One of the items of high value, which somehow did not end up at the bottom of the Nile Delta, was **Jean Parisot de la Valette**'s sword with its jewel-encrusted, gold hilt. It was taken back to France and remains to this day in the possession of the Louvre Museum in Paris. Suggestions that it is a national treasure of Malta and should be returned have so far gone unheeded.

BATTLE OF LEPANTO. Just six years after the **Great Siege of 1565** came another major military action against the Ottoman **Turks**. This naval battle occurred on 7 October 1571 and became celebrated throughout Europe as evidence that, together with the victory at Malta, the seemingly irresistible force of Turkish expansion could be contained. The combined European fleet was under the command of Don John of Austria, son of Charles V. It consisted of the Spanish Mediterranean fleet, a squadron each from the Papal States, Genoa and Venice, and three galleys of the **Knights of St. John**. Together the fleet consisted of six galleasses, 212 galleys, and 24 transports under sail. The Turkish fleet was composed of 250 galleys plus various support vessels.

The battle began with the Turks in an excellent defensive position, but they failed to follow up their early success, and the Europeans slowly began to destroy their center. The Ottoman flagship, under the command of Ali Pasha, was taken after a fierce hand-to-hand fight. The three galleys of the Knights were to hold the right wing of the attack and managed to do so but with heavy loss of life. At the end of the day, it became apparent that the battle was a great victory for Christian Europe, and only a few of the Turkish ships were able to retreat. Turkish losses were enormous: 50 ships lost and 20,000 men taken prisoner or killed. A secondary outcome was the release of tens of thousands of Christian slaves from the oar-boards of the Turkish galleys.

Serving aboard a Spanish ship during the battle was Miguel de Cervantes, considered by many to be the greatest figure of Spanish literature, the author of *Don Quixote*. He was wounded twice in the chest by gunshot, and his left hand was maimed, probably by a sword wound. Although the victory at Lepanto marked the end of Turkish attacks in the western Mediterranean and Europe, the central and eastern Mediterranean continued to suffer from smaller attacks for several years. Historians identify the Lepanto battle as the last major action in which the oared galley was the predominant attacking vessel.

BATTLE OF THE NILE. *See* BATTLE OF ABOUKIR BAY.

BERTIE, FRA' ANDREW (1929–2008). A Scot and descendent of Mary, Queen of Scots, Andrew Willoughby Ninian Bertie was born 15 May 1929 in London. He was educated at Christ Church, Oxford, and spent two years in the Scots Guards before being admitted to the **Order of St. John** in 1956. Since 1981, Bertie was involved in the government of the Order. He was elected the 78th **grand master** in 1988, its only **British** head to date. Bertie lived in Malta for 20 years, so he was also the first grand master to have a real connection with the island nation since the Order's embarrassing capitulation to Napoleon in 1798. The **University of Malta** conferred an honorary degree on him in 1993, and Bertie presided over the Order until his death on 7 February 2008, age 78.

BIRD HUNTING. Because the Maltese islands are a main stopover point for many species of European migratory birds on their way to and from the African continent, the trapping and hunting of birds has become a source of passionate debate in Malta and the **European Union (EU).** The islands' limited space, about half of which is open to hunters, also causes frequent conflicts of interest between hunters and hikers (known as "ramblers").

A survey conducted by the *Malta Times* revealed that two-thirds of the Maltese population oppose bird hunting, considered an important Maltese tradition by its proponents. The Maltese political situation, so evenly and fiercely divided between **Nationalists** and **Malta Labour Party** adherents, has enabled the estimated 16,000 hunters' lobby to hold the country hostage, preventing stricter laws against their sport. In 1972, support from an active group of bird enthusiasts helped achieve the passage of the Benelux Convention on the Hunting and Protection of Birds. Many Maltese and their supporters from outside Malta are hoping that EU membership will give the government the necessary clout to better regulate hunting.

In June 2005, a formal complaint was filed with the EU by nongovernmental organizations BirdLife International and BirdLife Malta, charging the Maltese government with failure to transpose into Maltese law the EU Birds Directive banning spring hunting. Just when the EU Commission was preparing to start formal infringement procedures, the Maltese government reluctantly changed its laws to meet some of the EU requirements but continues to insist that it negotiated an exemption from the Birds Directive that permits hunting of turtle doves and quail in the spring. In the spring of 2008, the EU initiated infringement proceedings, and the EU court ruled against

Malta's position, forcing limits on bird hunting. Passions run high on both sides of the issue, which is likely to remain contentious for some time since enforcement continues to be lax.

BIRGU. *See* THREE CITIES, THE.

BLOOD COMMISSION. Chaired by Sir Hilary Blood, the commission was appointed by the **British** government to examine the political needs of Malta and to make recommendations for a course of action. During the last three months of 1960, the commission visited the islands in order to gauge public opinion. The members agreed on two main propositions: Malta is a Roman Catholic country whose **religion** must be respected, and Malta's independence must be granted despite whatever risks seem to exist. In October 1961, Malta was given a new system of government under the so-called "Blood **Constitution**," which was to encourage **elections** and the formation of a government that could then determine the nation's political future. The "constitution" stipulated that there exist a nation called the "State of Malta" and provided for the Legislative Assembly of 50 members. This assembly was given full powers in every area except that of defense and foreign affairs, which were to be shared with the British. Even at this late date in the movement toward independence, the colonial **governor** was specifically given the power to override the Cabinet and the Legislature in such matters.

BLOOD CONSTITUTION. *See* BLOOD COMMISSION; CONSTITUTION.

BOFFA, SIR PAUL (1890–1962). Born in Vittoriosa (Birgu) on 30 June 1890, Boffa joined the tiny **Malta Labour Party** in 1922, was elected to its governing board in 1924, and became leader in 1927. In the **elections** of 1932, he was the only member of the party to gain a seat on the Council. A likable person, he was a physician by profession who served with distinction as a medic in **World War II**. Boffa had pro-**British** and antisocialist leanings. He supported his political opponent, **Lord Strickland**, when the latter was the target of the bishops' pastoral letter, and this branded him as anti-Church. In the elections of 1947, the Malta Labour Party won an overwhelming victory, and Paul Boffa took the positions of **prime minister** and minister of justice. However, **Dom Mintoff**, the deputy leader of the party, led all candidates in the number of votes received.

At a Labour Party Conference in October 1949, a resolution was offered thanking Boffa for his service to the party but also stating that he was lacking in the necessary qualities to lead either the party or the nation. It passed by 244 votes to 141. A few days later, Boffa and a number of his followers resigned from the party "as now constituted" and took action to form the Malta Workers Party, which lasted just six years on the political scene.

In the short time he was in office, Boffa's government accomplished much. It improved housing, stimulated an increase in **emigration** (viewed positively at the time), implemented full-time and compulsory **education**, and placed teacher education with two capable religious orders. In addition, public **health** standards were improved. Unfortunately, Boffa's political career was undercut by one of the most charismatic politicians on Malta's political scene, his successor as prime minister, Dom Mintoff. Boffa died on 6 July 1962 without seeing his beloved country become a free and independent nation.

BORG, SIR GEORGE (1887–1954). On 10 June 1940, the chief justice and president of the Court of Appeals, Sir Arturo Mercieca, was summoned to appear before General **Dobbie** and told either to resign his positions or face forced removal. He chose voluntary resignation and was later **interned and deported** as a suspected Italian sympathizer. He was succeeded in both positions by Sir George Borg. As the highest-ranking Maltese civilian during the war years, he was often called upon to represent the general population.

Borg was slightly wounded in an air raid during the ceremony to welcome General Dobbie's replacement, **Lord Gort**, to Malta. It was also Borg who, on behalf of Malta, accepted the **George Cross** on 13 September 1942. On 3 September 1943, the Royal Air Force presented to the Maltese people the last survivor of the three **Gloster Gladiator** aircraft, the one named *Faith*. As nine Spitfires dipped low over the Palace Square, Sir George Borg accepted the historic relic amid the cheers of the assembled crowd.

His most significant action, however, came on 4 May 1942, when he and two other appeals judges reversed the judgment of a lower court and found the deportation of all the internees, including Sir Arturo Mercieca, to be illegal. Even with that decision, two years passed for some and three for others before the deportees were permitted to return to Malta

BORG COSTANZI, EDWIN J. (1925–). A brilliant student, Borg Costanzi was only 18 years old when he was awarded a Bachelor of Science degree in mathematics at the **University of Malta**. He continued on to qualify as an architect and civil engineer. He was only 20 years old in 1945 when he received the first postwar Rhodes scholarship to Oxford University to attend Balliol College and was awarded a master's degree after achieving outstanding results on his examinations. He then returned to Malta to begin teaching mathematics at the university in 1949. He was named vice chancellor and rector magnificus in 1964 at the age of 39 and began the push to modernize the curriculum and the facilities. He was the driving force behind the construction of the new campus at Tal Qroqq, Msida, which opened in 1967. As evidence of the high regard in which he was held, he was elected chairman of the Association of **Commonwealth** Universities in 1976–77.

BORG OLIVIER, DR. GIORGIO (1911–1980). The man who, as **prime minister**, led Malta to independence from Great Britain was born in **Valletta** on 5 July 1911. While pursuing his law studies at the **University of Malta**, Borg Olivier was elected president of the Students' Representative Council, the beginning of his political career. He earned the LLD in 1937 and became a notary public in 1938. In 1939, he was elected as one of three **Nationalist Party** members of the Council of Government. In May 1940, when the leader of the Nationalist Party, **Dr. Enrico Mizzi**, was first interned by the **British** and later deported to Uganda because of suspected **Italian** sympathies, Borg Olivier became interim leader. After his return in 1945, Mizzi regained his post and made Borg Olivier his right-hand man. He became deputy leader of the party in 1949 and was appointed minister of education, public works, and reconstruction. He successfully contested all **elections** from 1947 until his death.

When Mizzi died in December 1950, Borg Olivier was unanimously appointed leader of the Nationalist Party by the Executive

Committee and became prime minister. His shrewdness as a politician enabled him to use the **religion** issue and the archbishop to his advantage, even though his relations with the archbishop were usually tense. Nevertheless, he worked toward, and was able to gain, a reduction in the clerical and episcopal influence in the politics of Malta. After the election of 1962, he guided passage of the Independence **Constitution** and was, in great measure, responsible for Malta's gaining independence while maintaining good relations with the British both before and after the event. Although he continued to use the given name Giorgio in all official circumstances, after **World War II**, he used George in the informality of the political arena. After the Nationalists lost the election of 1976, he resigned the party leadership and was succeeded by **Eddie Fenech Adami**. Borg Olivier died on 29 October 1980.

BORG PISANI, CARMELO (1914–1942). Born in Senglea in 1914, Borg Pisani attended schools emphasizing the use of Italian, and it became well known that he held strong pro-**Italy** views. He attended a school in Italy and later joined a number of Italian fascist organizations with branches in Malta. In 1936, he accepted a scholarship to study art in Rome. With a strong desire to see Malta as a part of Italy, he wrote a letter to Benito Mussolini in 1940 in which he offered his services. Borg Pisani served in the Italian army in Greece in 1941 and then, when the plans were being made for the invasion of Malta, he was selected for special training. He was to land in his homeland to gather information on all aspects of the military situation and civilian attitudes. Although he was intelligent and well trained, everything went wrong. The bulk of his equipment was lost during his landing, and he was discovered clinging to a cliff near where he had been put ashore, unable to make his way to the top.

After his capture, Borg Pisani was brought to Mtarfa where several persons recognized him. He quickly divulged the nature of his mission and was taken to prison. His trial began on 12 November 1942 in a criminal proceeding before three judges, headed by the chief justice, **Sir George Borg**. Two lawyers were appointed to defend him. The trial was conducted under wartime rules and took place behind closed doors. The court found him guilty and on 19 November sentenced him to death by hanging. Several pleas for reversal and others for clemency were rejected, and on 28 November the sentence was carried out. A short time afterward, a drawing was carried in the Italian newspapers depicting Borg Pisani being put to death while calling "Viva Italia!" He was awarded Italy's highest medal for bravery, posthumously, and continues to be recognized in Italy as one of the war's heroes.

BRIGUGLIO, LINO (1944–). Born in St. Venera, Malta, on 27 January 1944, Briguglio was educated at St. Aloysius College, St. Michael's College of Education, and the Royal **University of Malta**, where he graduated with BA (Hons.) and MA degrees in economics. He earned the PhD in economics at the University of Exeter. Briguglio was active in politics as a member of the National Executive Committee of the **Malta Labour Party (MLP),** but in a clash with **Dom Mintoff's** leadership style, was expelled from the party in 1977. A cofounder and first general secretary of the Partito Demokratika Maltese (PDM), he failed to get elected to **Parliament** in the general **elections** of 1987.

As an economist, Briguglio devised a "vulnerability index," gaining an international reputation in the measurement and analysis of economic challenges particular to small island economies. He has served on several national commissions and as advisor to the United Nations on small island economies. He is the head of the Department of Economics and the director of the Islands and Small States Institute of the Foundation for International Studies at the University of Malta, where he has been on the faculty since 1976. Professor Briguglio has edited and published several books and numerous articles on small developing island economies.

BRITISH RULE. The British and the Maltese began their relationship by seeing it from quite different perspectives. Because the British helped drive the **French** from Malta in 1800, they believed that "to the victor belong the spoils." In contrast, the Maltese believed that they had "invited" the British to help evict the French from **Valletta** and, thus, had become a part of the British Empire of their own free will. They expected a strong voice in the governance of their land. The British viewed the islands as a military outpost; protecting and extending the interests of their nation and from 1814 until their departure in 1979, a minimum of 4,500 British servicemen were stationed on the island. A Royal commission appointed to fully investigate all matters concerning civil government of the islands in 1812 reported that the Maltese were not fit to be involved in any political power. The result was that the so-called **Bathurst Constitution** of 1813 vested all authority in the British **governor**, and he was not "to be shackled by any body of persons resident in Malta."

In 1835, letters patent from London granted Malta the authority to create the Council of Government to advise and assist the governor; however, only two of the eight members were to be Maltese appointees. It was probably the closest to the decision-making level of government that any Maltese had ever been permitted. Because the letters required that only the governor listen to the Council's opinions, one-man rule remained. New letters patent, given in 1849, completely changed both the structure and the authority of the Council. It was to be a legislative body and could enact laws, provided these were not contrary to either United Kingdom laws or Colonial Orders. It had 18 seats, consisting of 10 appointed and eight popularly elected officials. At least five of the appointees were to be Maltese, giving local citizens the majority. Still, the Crown reserved the power to disallow any actions of the Council.

In 1881, letters patent created an executive council of three senior officials who were to advise and assist the governor. Two years later, new letters redefined the powers of the Council of Government with the effect of reverting to the situation of 1835. A new constitution formulated in 1887 created a dual system of government, combining popular control of the Legislature with Crown control of the administrative function. It did not function well and was changed in 1903 by the creation of a structure similar to that of 1849. The severe government control created a troubled political scene, which lasted until **World War I**.

In 1921, the British attempted, within limits, to recognize Maltese demands for self-government while still retaining control in the hands of the governor for matters of military and other interests. A new constitution created two distinct governments, each with both legislative and executive powers in its own defined area. The "Maltese government" was, in effect, controlled by a British governor who consulted with a nominated council. This constitution was suspended in May 1930 because of a dispute with the Vatican regarding local political activity. The suspension lasted until June 1932, when the dual government system again became active. The Constitution was suspended again in November 1933, when the British grew increasingly fearful of the political influence of fascist **Italy**. In 1936, another new constitution vested full authority in the governor. This was relaxed slightly in 1939 with the establishment of a Council of Government similar to that of 1903.

Due to the events of **World War II**, the Colonial Office exhibited a more positive attitude toward Maltese self-government. In 1947, a new constitution, similar to that of 1921, created a unicameral rather than a bicameral legislature. The Maltese considered it inadequate and proposed a series of reforms. In April 1958, the majority **Malta Labour Party** resigned from government, and the leader of the opposition **Nationalist Party** refused to form a new government. As a result, the governor took absolute control. Shortly thereafter, Royal instructions again made Malta a Crown Colony with all authority vested in the governor. Pressure for home rule continued, including demands for **independence**. In 1952, large concessions toward home rule were made, and actual movements towards independence were begun. The Independence Constitution was approved in London on 1 August 1963. Malta became an independent nation within the British Commonwealth on 21 September 1964. British troops were still based there until they finally departed on 31 March 1979, but British influence remains a dominant feature of Maltese life and culture.

Malta still exhibits many of the signs of a former British colony: a population largely fluent in English, driving on the left side of the road, its legislation mainly based on that of Great Britain. Furthermore, ties to the British mainland, cultural as well as economic, continue to be very strong. Many Maltese get tertiary **education** in Great Britain, and Malta is a popular destination for British tourists as well as retirees. *See also* BLOOD COMMISSION; LANGUAGE QUESTION.

BROTHER GERARD (BLESSED GERARD). *See* KNIGHTS OF ST. JOHN.

BRUCE, SURGEON MAJOR DAVID. *See* MALTA FEVER.

BUHAGIAR, DR. FRANCESCO (1876–1934). Born in Qrendi on 7 September 1876, Buhagiar studied at the **University of Malta**, earning a law degree in 1901. After 20 years spent in the practice of law, he ran for the Legislative Assembly as a candidate for the Unione Popolare Maltese (UPM) and was elected in 1921 and 1924. He served as minister of justice for a year before becoming the second **prime minister** of Malta on 13 October 1922, completing the term of **Joseph Howard**. Buhagiar resigned on 22 September 1924 because the coalition government with the **Malta Labour Party** had fallen apart on 2 January, and only 10 UPM members had been reelected to Parliament. He was appointed a Superior Court judge and died in 1934.

BUSUTTIL, DR. SIMON (1969–). Born on 20 March 1969, Dr. Busuttiil was educated at St. Aloysius College and the **University of Malta**, where he earned a Diploma of Notary Public and a Doctor of Laws degree in 1993. He continued his studies in Great Britain, completing an MA in European studies at the University of Sussex in 1994 and returned to the **University of Malta** to earn a Master of Jurisprudence in international law in November 1995.

After a brief stint practicing law, Busuttil became active as an advisor and speechwriter on **European Union (EU)** affairs, serving numerous ministers of the Maltese government. During the EU accession process, he served as a member of Malta's negotiating team. In 1999, he was appointed head of the Malta-EU Information Center (MIC), tasked with communicating the EU accession process to the Maltese public. His work in writing a voluminous body of explanatory pamphlets, speeches, newspaper columns as well as several books on EU membership issues deserves much of the credit for the "yes" vote on the EU **referendum** in March 2003. In December 2003, he was recognized for his service to Malta by becoming the youngest person to be appointed a Member of the National Order of Merit (MOM).

Gifted with an exceptional ability to put his **Nationalist Party** affiliation aside when explaining complex issues to a general public in an evenhanded, lucid manner, Busuttil has become one of the most respected young political figures in Malta. This was best demonstrated by his **election** on 12 June 2004 on the first count as the first

Member of the European Parliament (MEP) gaining almost 60,000 votes.

As an MEP, Busuttil serves on the Budget Committee and was elected vice president of the **Parliament's** delegation to Maghreb countries. He is active in EU-Mediterranean issues, was appointed group negotiator for the center-right group of the EU Parliament on the proposed European Asylum Support Office, which the EU plans to establish by 2010, and has succeeded in getting EU assistance for Malta to deal with **illegal immigration** and was reelected by an overwhelming margin to a second five-year term as MEP on 6 June 2009.

BUTTIGIEG, DR. ANTON (1912–1983). The second **president** of Malta, Buttigieg was born in Qala, **Gozo**, on 12 February 1912. He earned a law degree from the **University of Malta** in 1940 and shortly thereafter entered politics as an active worker for the **Constitutional Party**. However, in 1953, he chose to join the **Malta Labour Party (MLP)** and was elected to **Parliament** in 1955. Buttigieg served the MLP as editor of the party's newspaper, as party president, and deputy leader from 1962 to 1976. He ran and was successful in every parliamentary **election** until 1976. In 1971, when Labour carried the election, Buttigieg was named minister of justice and deputy **prime minister**. Although he was in the number two position of government, he and Prime Minister **Dom Mintoff** were often in disagreement. In June 1976, Buttigieg sent a secret letter of resignation to Mintoff, who promised him the presidency if he would also resign from Parliament. He did so and, as a result, was without a salary until being sworn in as president on 27 December. As president, he desired to put aside his party affiliation and to act as the head of state for all citizens, saying, "we are all brothers and have Maltese blood in our veins."

Buttigieg's greatest accomplishment was the easing of tensions relating to the withdrawal of the **British** forces from the islands in 1979. Rear Admiral O. N. A. Cecil, the commander of the British Forces at the time, gave full credit to Buttigieg, saying, "I do not think many realize the long term effects had 1979 been a departure with bad grace." Buttigieg and Cecil were good friends. Buttigieg was a published poet and Cecil an excellent pianist. They collaborated on

"The Parting Song," which became the main feature of a final concert performed by the combined bands of the British Royal Marines and the **Armed Forces of Malta**. In part, the hymn words read,

Now the hour has arrived for our sad adieu,
Not with hate in our hearts,
But like lovers let us part,
Linked in a kiss and embrace,
Sincere and true.

When Buttigieg, in failing health, relinquished the presidency in December 1981, he did so without any fanfare or congratulatory messages from either party. He died of cancer on 5 May 1983. *See also* FREEDOM DAY.

BYZANTINE INFLUENCE. Constantine I was the first **Roman** Emperor to grant full rights and freedom to the Christian Church. He transferred the capital from Rome to Byzantium and renamed it Constantinople. After his death in 337, the Empire was divided among his three sons, Constans, Constantine, and Constantius. When Constantine was killed in battle in 340 and Constans murdered in 350, the Empire was reunited under Constantius. In 395, Emperor Theodosius I divided the Empire between his two sons, Honorius and Arcadius. Honorius reigned over the west (**Italy**, Africa, Spain, Gaul, and Britain), and Arcadius reigned over the east (Thrace, Asia Minor, Syria, and Egypt). Although no real evidence exists one way or the other, it is commonly assumed that Malta was included in the eastern portion at that time. Those were troubled times for both Rome and Byzantium, and it is likely that Malta suffered as well. *See also* VANDALS.

– C –

CALLEJA, JOSEPH (1978–). Born on 22 January 1978 in Attard, Malta, Calleja is a young tenor, a rising opera sensation, who studied under noted Maltese tenor Paul Asciak and made his debut in 1997 as McDuff in Macbeth. The following year, at age 19, he won first prize in the Caruso Competition in Milan. He has already, by the age of 30, gained an international reputation performing leading roles at major theaters throughout Europe and the United States. His first solo album, *Tenor Arias* (2004), was very well received. The second solo album, *The Golden Voice* (2005), was also highly acclaimed. Calleja is married to Tatiana Lisnic, a soprano opera singer from Moldova. They have two children.

CAMILLERI, CHARLES (1931–2009). Born on 7 September 1931 in Hamrun to a musical family, Camilleri is the most accomplished and internationally recognized of all Maltese composers. He began his career composing works in his teens, including the Malta Suite, composed when he was only 16 years old, which was strongly influenced by Malta's folk legends and **music**. Camilleri was a talented musician, self-taught on a variety of instruments as well as an author on musical subjects. He composed over 300 works for orchestra, ensemble, solo instrument, and voice. Camilleri's compositions have been performed worldwide, and over half of them have been recorded commercially. His books on improvisation are widely used. He appeared as a conductor and lecturer in many different countries and held the rank of professor at the **University of Malta**. Camilleri died on 3 January 2009.

CARAVAGGIO (1573–1610). Born Michel Angelo Mersi in 1573, the artist became known by the name of his birthplace, Caravaggio, and used it as the signature on his paintings. After a series of brawls in **Italy**, including one in which he was accused of murder, he made his way to Malta, arriving in July 1607. He had several relatives and friends who were **Knights of the Order of St. John**, and there is strong evidence that he also hoped to become one. His first commission was to do a portrait of **Grand Master** Alof de Wignacourt. The grand master's pleasure over the portrait is evidenced by the compensation awarded: a collar of gold, two slaves, and some other items of esteem. The major compensation, however, was that Caravaggio was made a Knight of the Order of Obedience. He was then given the most important commission the Order could offer: to do a painting of John the Baptist to hang as the altarpiece of a large oratory off the right aisle of the conventual church of the Order, **St. John's Co-Cathedral**. It is the largest painting he ever did and was probably done in appreciation of his knighthood. His faint signature, "Fra Michel Angelo," is proof that he was already a Knight and proud of it. *The Beheading of John the Baptist* became one of two world-renowned masterpieces he painted while in Malta, the other being *St. Jerome.* He painted a few others of lesser quality, including *Sleeping Cupid.* After living in Malta for just over a year, Caravaggio attacked and killed a Knight of Nobility and was thrown into prison. It is assumed that he had inside assistance and made his escape, leaving Malta. Because he had become an embarrassment to the Order when the charge of murder became known, the grand master expelled him in early December 1608; although, Caravaggio continued to pass himself off as a Knight to the end of his days. In October 1609, he was severely wounded in another brawl. His face had been cut to the extent that it was unrecognizable, and his recovery was slow. Some of his friends petitioned for his pardon from the murder charge. Before dying of a fever on 18 July 1610, he received a pardon from Pope Paul V. In spite of a rather short 37 troubled years of life, Caravaggio left behind lasting evidence of his exceptional artistic talent. *See also* CARAVAGGIO INCIDENT; PRETI, MATTIA.

CARAVAGGIO INCIDENT. From the time they were completed in 1608, the two masterpieces painted by **Caravaggio** were on display in the conventual church of the Order, **St. John's Co-Cathedral.** In 1957, they were sent to **Italy**, where their restoration was funded by the Italian government prior to their becoming the central part of an exhibition in Rome. Upon their return to Malta, they were taken by government agents not to their long-time home in the Co-Cathedral but to the National Museum for display. The explanation given by the government of **Dom Mintoff** was that these paintings were national treasures and should be on display where all the people could benefit from seeing them. The archbishop, claiming ownership, submitted the dispute to authorities in the Vatican. Under Canon Law, the finding was in favor of the archbishop, and the Mintoff government was ordered to return the paintings. The order was ignored. However, in April 1958, the paintings were returned to the Co-Cathedral without preliminary notification. A few days later, Dom Mintoff released a statement which said, in effect, that mutual understanding between the government and the ecclesiastical authorities was necessary for the welfare of the people.

CART TRACKS (CART RUTS). These are parallel grooves or ruts in the hard surface rock (upper coralline limestone) that exist in several places throughout Mediterranean countries; although, the greatest number, more than 100 sites, have been found in Malta and **Gozo**. They are usually situated the same distance (an average 55 inches or 140 centimeters) apart, sometimes V-shaped and sometimes U-shaped. Like railroad tracks, they often merge into one another. In one area between Dingli and Rabat, so many cross and merge that the site has been named "Clapham Junction" after the London Railway Station.

These tracks are an **archeological** enigma. Several theories attempt to explain what they were used for and how they came into existence. It is most likely that they were tracks on which sledges, pulled by men or animals, were used to move heavy loads. Carbon dating places them at 2500 BCE, too late for the moving of stones for the huge **Megalithic Temples**. One theory asserts that they were used to move topsoil from the valleys to the hills in order to make terraces and thus expand the amount of tillable land. Some tracks end in the sea, making for an even greater mystery. More recent research has identified 31 sites throughout Malta and Gozo that are closely associated with nearby quarries so that the tracks were most probably connected to the quarrying of stones used in road and building construction. The ruts were most likely chiseled by human hands and their continued use probably contributed to their unusual depth. Although the surface rock today is as hard as granite, it was probably much softer living stone when it was used for transporting materials, whatever they might have been.

CARTHAGINIAN RULE. A city-state located on the Bay of Tunis in North Africa, Carthage was founded in the 9th century BCE by **Phoenicians** from Tyre. As the Phoenicians in the eastern Mediterranean began to diminish in strength and authority after their defeat in Tyre and Sidon by the Assyrians and Babylonians, the Carthaginians assumed the vacant leadership in the central and western parts of the Mediterranean. About 480 BCE, they assumed possession of the Maltese Islands and created a form of partial home rule, including a senate and an Assembly of the People as well as the authority to mint local coinage. Elsewhere, the wealth, power, and authority of Carthage continued to expand. In the silver mines of Spain alone, Carthage employed over 40,000 men. In the world of commerce, the Carthaginians developed the use of insurance and using ships as collateral ("bottomry") to raise funds, among other practices stimulating trade. They were to be a positive influence in Malta until the end of the **Punic Wars** in 219 BCE.

CASSAR, GEROLAMO (1520–1592). In 1568, he succeeded **Francesco Laparelli** as chief architect of the fortified city of **Valletta**. A native of Malta, Cassar was described as a man of perfect morals. As a boy, he fought in the **Great Siege of 1565**, learning some things about fortifications through working with the details of men assigned to their rebuilding after battle damage. He was sent by the **Order** to Rome for formal architectural study and became its chief military engineer prior to being named Laparelli's assistant. He later fought in the Venetian-Turkish War of Cyprus from 1570 to 1573. His greatest accomplishments are the tangible, visual record in his designs of the eight **auberges**, the Grand Master's Palace, **St. John's Co-Cathedral**, and many lesser buildings in Valletta. It is said that Laparelli made Valletta a fortress, and Cassar made it what Benjamin Disraeli called "a city built by gentlemen for gentlemen." *See also* ARCHITECTURE.

CASTILIAN RULE. Martin II of **Sicily** and Aragon died in 1410 without any children as heirs. According to his will, his successor was to be elected from among his relatives by the nobles of Aragon and Sicily. In 1412, Ferdinand de Antequera, husband of Martin's sister, was elected King of Aragon, Castile, and Sicily. He took the crown as Ferdinand I, the first Castilian ever to occupy the throne. For a number of years, the Maltese increasingly had been subjected to raids by Saracen pirates, so in 1416, they petitioned Ferdinand's son Juan, who had been named Viceroy of Sicily, for assistance. They requested a number of improvements, particularly in the defense system. Juan was sympathetic and agreed to the improvements plus a reduction in the duties on imports from Sicily. The reforms never happened because Ferdinand died in the same year and was succeeded by his son, Alphonso V.

With the change in the Crown came an almost continuous state of warfare against the **Angevin** princes and the Republics of Pisa and Genoa. The North African pirates also increased the frequency of their attacks on Alphonso's realm. The result of all of this military activity was heavy taxation of the people, including the Maltese. In 1419, the king used Malta and **Gozo** as collateral when he borrowed 30,000 **Aragonese** gold florins from Don Antonio Cardona. As a part of the contract, Cardona became governor and rector of the islands with full jurisdiction over them in all matters, both civil and criminal. He was also granted the right to receive and retain all monies from taxation and other revenues. Soon, Cardona transferred his rights to Don Gonsalvo de Monroy. The Maltese suffered from two devastating raids by Saracens from North Africa in which a large portion of the population was either killed or taken into **slavery**. Then the main crop, cotton, failed, and famine gripped the islands.

All of these calamities, on top of the severe and arbitrary taxation, caused the Maltese to revolt. Everything belonging to Monroy was pillaged and destroyed, and his wife fled to one of the fortifications at the harbor against which a siege was set. For a short time, Malta was in the control of the Maltese. The Sicilian government, in support of Monroy, prohibited Maltese vessels from entering any of its harbors. The result was equivalent to a blockade of Malta, as most grain and other essential foods came from Sicily. The fervor of the revolt soon died down, and the leaders had second thoughts. The realization that Malta needed the aid and protection of Sicily brought about an alternate plan of action. It was decided to redeem the island by paying off the amount of the loan.

With supreme effort, 20,000 florins were raised. The Monroys demanded hostages as guarantees for the remaining 10,000. A Maltese nobleman, Antonio Inguanez, offered his two sons as hostages. As part of the contract, the Maltese demanded certain political rights plus a clear, unequivocal promise that the islands must never again be ceded by the Crown. Reluctantly, Alphonso agreed and in 1428 gave formal ratification. Early in 1429, Monroy died, leaving a surprising will in which he renounced the 10,000 florins, which had remained unpaid, and awarded 10,000 more to King Alphonso for the defense of his realm, especially the islands of Malta and Gozo. He returned the remaining 10,000 to the Maltese and, in so doing, called Malta "the bulwark of Christianity, and worthy of defense from the Saracens." Alphonso was influenced by events and especially by Monroy's will and again returned Malta to the Royal Domain as a free country.

The joy over these events was short-lived. Within a year, the Hafsid Saracens of Tunisia invaded and laid siege with a force of 18,000. Again, a great many Maltese were killed or taken into slavery. In spite of the severe hardships, the defenders were victorious. However, the **economy** was left in ruin, and for many years there was a struggle to raise ransom monies to free those enslaved. In order to replace the diminished population, foreign immigration was openly encouraged. Another change was that, for economic reasons, the Maltese increasingly turned to piracy.

CATHEDRAL. *See* ST. JOHN'S CO-CATHEDRAL.

CATHOLIC CHURCH. There are few, if any, countries besides Malta in which the Roman Catholic **religion** has had as strong and pervasive an influence on every day life. Article 2 (i) of the Maltese **Constitution** states that "The Religion of Malta is the Roman Catholic Apostolic Religion." According to a survey conducted in 2006, 95 percent of Maltese claim to be Catholic. Over 350 large ornate churches dominate the skyline, and religious statues are found everywhere. By tradition, the first official visit of the **president** of Malta is with the pope, and official ceremonies for installing government officials include kissing a cross.

Maltese tradition asserts, and the majority of Maltese firmly believe, that St. Paul's shipwreck described in the Bible (Acts 28:1–12) took place on Malta's shores and that the Catholic Church was founded by **Paul the Apostle** and **St. Publius** during the first century CE. The Maltese faithful, who revere St. Paul as their patron saint and St. Publius as Malta's first bishop, like to assert that only Rome has a longer reigning Apostolic See. The earliest documented evidence of a cleric's presence on Malta dates from 451 CE. Equally well established is the fact that since the **Norman** invasion displaced the **Arab** rule in the late 11th century, Roman Catholicism has been the dominant religion in Malta. By the time of the arrival of the **Knights of St. John** in 1530, there were already over 430 churches and chapels on Malta and **Gozo.**

In 1561, the Vatican asserted its power against the government in Palermo, Sicily, when the Holy Office in Rome conferred upon Mgr. Cubella the fullest power to investigate and prosecute all acts of heresy in Malta. This created a situation in which there were three persons of virtually equal authority. The **grand master** of the Knights was officially an equal of all the monarchs of Christendom, but the Holy Roman Emperor maintained the right to nominate the local bishop, who was then given a voice in the Knights' affairs, while **Inquisitor** Cubella also tried to assert his power as a representative of the pope. A similar three-way struggle for power and influence continued, albeit with different antagonists, for more than four centuries.

While the Order of the Knights controlled the islands against foreign invaders, the Church, with its own laws, operated in Malta as a quasi state within a state. In the villages and countryside, the priests served as de facto local governments. Native Maltese were not permitted to become members of the Order because it feared the Church's influence on the local population. It was a priest who led an **uprising** against the Knights of Malta in 1775 (which was brutally squashed), and it was priests who organized the revolt against the **French** occupiers. Initially welcomed as liberators from the oppressive Knights, the French troops committed a major error when they moved against the Maltese churches, looting silver and valuables and closing down convents.

After the Maltese had invited the **British** in to help evict the French, they wanted to establish clear guidelines for their new occupiers. On 15 June 1802, the Maltese issued a "Declaration of Rights" which included the assertion that "His Majesty the King is the protector of our holy religion, and is bound to uphold and protect it as heretofore; and without any diminution of what has been practiced since these Islands have acknowledged His Majesty as their sovereign to this day."

The British rulers, while denying the Maltese political control, learned from the French experience and did their utmost to avoid interfering in the Church's domain, so long as the strategic military and foreign policies of the islands were not involved. However, given the power that the Church exercised over the Maltese, appointing the bishop of Malta returned as a source of controversy. Whether wisely or cunningly, the British chose to negotiate with the Vatican directly, rather than with the Maltese ecclesiastics. The British government knew that Great Britain and the Vatican had broader interests at stake, involving many other colonies besides just Malta, and decided to use that to negotiate an agreement with the pope in regard to appointing bishops of Malta. The Vatican agreed to allow the British to veto its appointments before announcing them publicly.

In 1828, the British negotiated three concessions from the Catholic Church concerning the relationship between the colonial rulers and Roman Catholic Church in Malta: the jurisdiction of ecclesiastical courts was restricted to spiritual matters only; the right of sanctuary in criminal cases was eliminated; and all clergy, except bishops, could be made subject to court proceedings.

In late 1930, then **Prime Minister Lord Strickland**, although himself a Catholic born in Malta of an English father and Maltese mother, caused a major confrontation between the Church and government when he attempted to interfere in the removal of a Catholic priest. The Vatican resented Strickland's authoritarian style in this matter, but the incident was part of a more general dissatisfaction in Malta concerned with "the **language question.**" Strickland was accused of trying to promote the English language and culture to the detriment of the Italian-speaking professional class and the Maltese-speaking clerics and their parishioners. On 1 May 1930, a pastoral letter to the Clergy, signed by the Archbishop of Malta and the Bishop of Gozo, was distributed saying, in effect, that it was a grave sin to vote for Lord Strickland or any of his candidates in the **elections** of 1930 and that priests were forbidden to administer the sacraments to those who refused to obey the instructions. The British protested the action to the Vatican, but the protest was rejected. Then, the **governor** of Malta, with the full approval of London, refused to allow the elections to be held and withdrew the Constitution. Lord Strickland remained as prime minister in an advisory capacity. In May 1932, he addressed a letter of apology to the pope, which was accepted. Early in June, it was declared that, since the pope had accepted the apology, the pastoral letter was rescinded.

A similar conflict between Church leaders and politicians occurred in 1961 when the **Archbishop Michael Gonzi**, angered by **Dom Mintoff's** attacks on the Church and Church schools, issued an interdict against him and stated that anyone voting for **Malta Labour Party (MLP)** candidates was committing a mortal sin and would be denied the sacraments and a Christian burial.

The same democratizing influences of **World War II** and the acceleration of globalization in recent decades that have led Malta to assert its independence have had an impact on the Maltese attitudes concerning the Catholic Church in Malta. While over 90 percent of the Maltese population still claim to be Roman Catholic faithful, results of a survey released in August 2006 indicated that attendance at Mass has fallen to approximately 50 percent, down from 72.7 percent in 1982 and declining one percent per year. In Gozo, a much more conservative population, over 80 percent still attend mass regularly.

Malta is the only European country in which divorce is still illegal, but divorces granted to Maltese in other countries are now recognized, and although over half still oppose it, 60 percent of the population surveyed in 2008 think that divorce will be legalized within 10 years. Despite these changes, the Catholic Church, with its schools, societies, *festas*, and **band clubs**, still dominates everyday life in Malta. *See also* JESUITS; JEWS OF MALTA; PRIVILEGIUM FORI; XERRI, DUN MIKIEL.

CECIL, REAR ADMIRAL O. N. A. *See* BUTTIGIEG, DR. ANTON.

CENTRAL BANK OF MALTA. *See* BANKING; FINANCIAL SERVICES.

CHURCH. *See* ARCHITECTURE; CATHOLIC CHURCH; INQUISITION; JESUITS; RELIGION.

CHURCHILL, SIR WINSTON (1874–1965). Although his military service in **World War I** was as a lieutenant colonel in the army at the front in France, Churchill's political actions were always supportive of the Royal Navy, probably dating back to his appointment as First Lord of the Admiralty in 1911. His service in the Colonial Office in 1921 made him well aware of Malta and the aspirations of the Maltese.

When Churchill became **British** prime minister in May 1940, he was almost alone in recognizing the importance of holding and strengthening Malta. Paul Reynaud, **prime minister** of France, proposed that an offer be made to **Italy** that if it stayed out of the war, it would be awarded Gibraltar, Malta, Corsica, and Nice at war's end. When the five-man War Cabinet voted on whether to accept the proposal, Churchill voted "no." He was joined by Clement Attlee and Arthur Greenwood. The two favorable votes were cast by Neville Chamberlain and Lord Halifax.

In late spring 1942, Churchill worried about the failure of so many convoys to get through to the islands. He told General Claude Auchinleck, commander in chief of Middle East operations, that he must create a military diversion to help ease the attacks on the convoys, for to lose Malta would be a "disaster of the first order." When Auchinleck showed some reluctance, Churchill threatened to relieve him of his command if he did not act. Churchill's tenacious support of Malta helped save it from surrender or defeat.

If Churchill's actions showed him to be pro-Malta, the Maltese responded by being pro-Churchill. No Maltese air raid shelter was without some kind of a religious shrine. What made them unusual is that Churchill's picture was usually present along with a crucifix and a picture of Our Lady. *See also* AXIS BLOCKADE; ROOSEVELT, FRANKLIN DELANO.

CIVIL COMMISSIONER. *See* GOVERNORS OF MALTA.

COMMONWEALTH. The **British** Crown, which once reigned over an empire "on which the sun never sets," gradually relinquished control over its various colonies. Beginning with Canada in 1867, Australia in 1900, New Zealand in 1907, South Africa in 1910, and Ireland in 1921, one by one the former British colonies were given a newly created status known as "dominions." They were independent nations yet bound together by a common past, culture, and interests, a grouping once described as a "Commonwealth of Nations." In 1926, the **prime ministers** of these countries adopted the Balfour Report, which highlighted the new reality, describing the dominions as "autonomous Communities within the British Empire, equal in status, in no way subordinate one to another in any aspect of their domestic or external affairs, though united by a common allegiance to the Crown." Allegiance to the Crown was no longer a requirement when the Commonwealth prime ministers met in 1949 to admit India as a republic and drop British from the name of their organization.

Today, the 53 heads of nations, including Malta, still belong to the Commonwealth and meet every other year to discuss common goals and resolve contentious issues. Malta hosted the Commonwealth Heads of Government Meeting (CHOGM) on 25–27 November 2005.

CONSIGLIO POPOLARE. A forum for discussing matters relating to the well-being of the islands, the Consiglio Popolare, or "popular council," was originally part of the **Universita**. An early form of representative government, the members were elected from among the **Maltese nobility**, the members of the various professions, the clergy, and certain artisans. The electors were the heads of families. The Consiglio Popolare was abolished by **Grand Master** Rohan of the **Knights of Malta** in 1790. There was agitation to permit its reorganization when the **British** took over from the **French**, but permission was refused. An attempt to reconstitute a *consiglio popolare* in the early 20th century failed as **political parties** emerged and divided the organizers.

CONSTITUTION. Malta was granted numerous constitutions by the **British**, who revoked them several times during their rule over the island. The various constitutions are known by the name of the particular British official who led the negotiations. The first was the **Bathurst Constitution** of 1813, which was not a true constitution but merely orders that essentially left all decisions under the control of the governor. The same was true of the 1835 Constitution, the Ponsonby orders, but they allowed for the appointment of a seven-person advisory council. Letters patent in 1849 provided for a council with the first elected majority. By 1887, the first representative government was achieved due to the efforts of **Gerald Strickland** and **Enrico Mizzi**, but in 1903, the Chamberlain Constitution was a step backward to the conditions of the 1849 Constitution, under which the council only served as an advisory body.

Following the bread riots of 1919, the Amery Constitution was granted in 1921, creating a diarchy under which the British government was responsible for foreign affairs and defense matters but left local issues to be decided by a bicameral legislature elected by Maltese. It was suspended in 1930, reinstated in 1932, and suspended again in 1933, eliminating any participation by Maltese until 1936, when members were nominated to the executive council. An amendment to this constitution recognized **Malti** as an official language along with English. The MacDonald Constitution of 1939 restored an elected council of government, but the governor led the country through the turmoil of **World War II**. In 1947, self-government was restored. From 1955 to 1964, Malta was rocked by political upheaval that again caused constitutions to be granted, only to be withdrawn again. In 1961, the Blood Constitution was the first to mention the "State of Malta."

The Independence Constitution of 1964, which is in force today (as amended), is divided into four parts. The first contains information concerning the national anthem, the **flag**, **religion**, and language. The second deals with questions of principle, such as the right to work, compulsory and free primary **education**, social assistance, and insurance. The third covers citizenship and the fundamental rights and freedoms of each individual. The fourth concerns the head of state, the **Parliament**, including its powers, composition, procedures and all **election** matters, the Judiciary, finance, public, and other miscellaneous matters. *See also* CONSTITUTIONAL AMENDMENTS.

CONSTITUTIONAL AMENDMENTS. Several major acts have altered the 1964 Independence **Constitution**. The first of these was adopted on 13 December 1974 and provided that Malta would cease to be a monarchy and would instead become a democratic republic. This meant that the executive authority ceased to be vested in the British queen (or king). Those powers were henceforth assumed by the **president** of the Republic. **Election** is by the **Parliament** for five years. The act further provided for a reduction in the voting age from 21 to 18.

A second act, which went into effect on 14 February 1987, came about through a bit of political "horse-trading" between the **Nationalist** and Labour parties. In the preceding election, Labour had carried a majority of the seats in Parliament even though the Nationalists obtained a higher total of the popular vote. Of course, the Nationalists were anxious to change that defect for the future. The **Malta Labour Party** wanted to ensure that the nation would never again be a base for any foreign military forces. Each gained its objective in this act. It provided that Malta is to be neutral and that no foreign military base will ever be permitted. Its second provision gave assurance that any **political party** receiving more than 50 percent of the valid votes cast in the first count of an election but having a total number of elected members of Parliament amounting to less than 50 percent shall have its total number of seats increased so that its total will be one seat greater than that of the other party or parties.

An act in 1989 provided for the allowance of dual citizenship in certain limited cases, which in February 2000 was considerably broadened, permitting dual citizenship for most Maltese citizens. In 2003, as part of joining the **European Union (EU)**, the Constitution was amended to prevent Malta's laws from conflicting with EU laws. Recently, Parliament has been debating an amendment that would extend protection to unborn fetuses.

CONSTITUTIONAL PARTY (CP). The CP had its origins in a merger of Dr. Augusto Bartolo's Constitutional Party and **Gerald Strickland**'s Anglo-Maltese Party. The new party kept the name of Bartolo's party, but the leadership passed to Strickland. Although the party's positions were based upon the pragmatic needs of the moment, a few major ones remained unchanged over the years. The party was staunchly pro-Great Britain. In the **language question** it was pro-English; although from time to time, mild support was given to the idea of equality between it and Italian. There usually was general agreement with the **Malta Labour Party** on social reforms. Direct taxation and any increase in succession duties (inheritance taxes) were always opposed. Instead, the party supported the position that government revenues should come from indirect taxes. The party was dissolved in February 1946 due to a dispute among many of its leaders. *See also* POLITICAL PARTIES; STRICKLAND, MABEL EDELINE.

CORONATION INCIDENT. An event that united all of the diverse political factions in Malta occurred in the spring of 1953. It was learned that Malta's **flag** was not to be included with those of other members of the British **Commonwealth** in coronation ceremonies of Elizabeth II as queen. To make matters even worse, **Prime Minister Giorgio Borg Olivier** had not been invited to participate. On 13 May 1953, the Legislative Assembly took unprecedented unanimous action in protest against these official slights and canceled any local celebrations of the event. On 22 May, it was announced that Malta's prime minister would be on the invitation list and would be treated in a way similar to the prime ministers of Northern Ireland and Southern Rhodesia. The announcement also stated that the Maltese flag would be carried during the event. The motion cancelling Malta's own celebrations was rescinded, again by a unanimous vote. The prime minister and flag participated in the festivities in London, and a merry celebration was held in Malta.

COUNCIL OF EUROPE. Not to be confused with the European Council—the organ of the **European Union (EU)** composed of the heads of state and foreign ministers of the EU—the Council of Europe consists of two statutory organs: the Committee of Ministers and the Assembly. The council was founded on 5 May 1949 by the Treaty of London, which was signed by the 10 original member nations. The idea of an organization that would evolve into a "United States of Europe" was proposed by **Winston Churchill**. Its goal was to promote unity and common action among those states that practiced pluralistic democracy, the rule of law, and respect for human rights. Malta joined the Council of Europe as its 18th member on 25 January 1965. The Council currently represents 47 members and regularly meets in Strasbourg, where it has its secretariat. Its most important contribution has been the establishment of the European Court of Human Rights. The flag of the European Council as well as its anthem, Beethoven's "Ode to Joy," later became the flag and anthem of the European Union.

CREMONA, MONSIGNOR PAWLU (1946–). Born in **Valletta** on 25 January 1946, Cremona attended the Lyceum in Hamrun before joining the Dominicans in September 1962. He was ordained a priest in 1969 by Mgr. **Michael Gonzi**, then archbishop of Malta. He taught moral philosophy and theology for many years at the Dominican Studium in **Rabat** and earned a doctorate from the Pontifical University of St. Thomas Aquinas in Rome, then served as Dominican provincial until 1989 when he was called as parish priest serving Our Lady of Fatima in Guardamangia and, later, the parish of Jesus the Nazarene Church in Sliema. He has held numerous administrative offices and authored books and commentaries on theological issues while continuing to educate Dominican novices. Cremona was ordained as archbishop by his predecessor, His Excellency Mgr. **Joseph Mercieca**, on 26 January 2007. Shortly after his installation, he raised some eyebrows in Malta, where divorce is still illegal, when he expressed his support for laws to protect cohabiting couples.

– D –

DE BONO, DR. EDWARD (1933–). Considered one of the world's leading authorities in creative thinking, Dr. De Bono has written numerous books in which he developed the concepts of "lateral thinking," "Six Thinking Hats," and other techniques for teaching thinking as a skill. De Bono was born on 19 May 1933 in Malta, studied at Oxford as a Rhodes scholar, earning an MA in psychology and physiology and a doctorate in medicine from Cambridge. In 1969, he established the Cognitive Research Trust (CoRT), which has developed into commercial training programs, teaching business problem solving for major corporations. In 1992, he founded the De Bono Institute for the Design and Development of Thinking at the **University of Malta**, offering master's degrees in creativity and innovation, and four years later, a similar institute in Melbourne, Australia. De Bono's latest creation, launched in 2004, is the World Centre for New Thinking, housed in a compound in Fort Ricasoli, Malta. De Bono envisions a physical location where governments, corporations, and nongovernmental organizations paying a membership fee can send representatives to engage in creative problem solving.

DE MARCO, GUIDO (1931–). Professor Guido de Marco served as **president** of Malta from 1999 to 2004. He was born in **Valletta** on 22 July 1931 and educated at St. Aloysius College and the **University of Malta**, earning a Bachelor of Arts in 1952 and a Doctor of Laws degree in 1955. He began his legal career as a lawyer for the government and contested his first **election** in 1962 as an unsuccessful candidate for the Democratic Nationalist Party (Partito Democratico Nazionalista). De Marco was named Crown counsel in 1964 and elected to Parliament as a candidate of the **Nationalist Party** in April 1966, a post he retained in every election until resigning to become president. He lectured in criminal law at the University of Malta, where he was promoted to professor in 1989. He served as secretary general of the Nationalist Party until 1977, when he was elected deputy leader of the party.

In 1987, upon the Nationalist Party's return to power, de Marco was appointed deputy **prime minister** and minister of the interior and justice. He introduced bills in **Parliament**, adopting the European Convention on Human Rights into domestic law and is credited with the founding of the Police Academy and modernizing the police force. Appointed minister of foreign affairs in May 1990, de Marco's extensive knowledge of international affairs, speaking skills, and personal charm made him one of Malta's most popular politicians and a prominent representative for Malta in the **United Nations**. On 18 September 1990, he was elected president of the United Nations General Assembly (45th Session). As president of the UN General Assembly, de Marco initiated reform of the body after the fall of communism. As a result of his visits to North and South Korea, both countries became members of the UN. His proposal for revising the role of the UN Trusteeship Council is still under discussion today. De Marco actively represented Malta in other international organizations, such as the **Council of Europe**, the Organization for Security and Co-operation in Europe (OSCE), and the **Commonwealth**.

After completing his term as president of Malta, de Marco was chosen to be the new chairperson of the Commonwealth Foundation, the intergovernmental body of the Commonwealth, which works with civil society organizations. On 25 October 2000, Queen Elizabeth honored de Marco by bestowing upon him the title of Knight

Grand Cross of the Most Distinguished Order of St. Michael and St. George (GCMG). He, in turn, honored the queen by presenting her with the Maltese Companion of the Order of Merit. In 2006, de Marco was awarded the Shuman Prize. His autobiography, *The Politics of Persuasion*, was published in 2007.

DIMECH, EMMANUEL (1860–1921). A challenger of the Church as well as the colonial government, Dimech was influenced by **Fortunato Mizzi's** anti-**British** ideas. But he substituted Mizzi's pro-Italian stance with Maltese Nationalism. He was born on 25 December 1860 to an impoverished family. His mother died when he was only 13, and he began a life of crime. Dimech spent 20 years in and out of prison, initially for robbery but later on complicity in murder and charges of counterfeiting currency. While in prison, he read every book he could get his hands on and, thus, more than made up for his lack of formal **education**. Upon his final release from prison in 1897, he traveled throughout Europe and, in so doing, became aware of the various new revolutionary doctrines being talked about there.

Upon his return to Malta, Dimech set up foreign language instruction for the lower classes, wrote language textbooks, founded a self-help organization for the poor, and attempted to form a **trade union**. Because of these activities and because of his socialist leanings, he was viewed as an agitator and opposed by both the **governor** and the archbishop. In October 1911, he was excommunicated for, among a variety of other charges, advocating equal rights for **women**, for being a socialist, publishing a radical newspaper, and being a Protestant (a charge that was never substantiated). At the same time, all his supporters were condemned. Dimech was too far ahead of his time and never successful in politics. He was arrested again, deported to **Sicily** in September 1914, where he became a prisoner of war and was transferred to a concentration camp in Alexandria, Egypt. After being moved between various prisons, an insane asylum, and concentration camps in Egypt, he died on 17 April 1921.

Dimech's ideas, however, did not die with him and were picked up by others. He has become a hero to the **Malta Labour Party**, and his statue stands in what has to be the most prestigious location in **Valletta**, just in front of the Prime Minister's Office, the **Auberge de Castille**. He is also featured as the "prisoner hero" on the website of Mid-Dlam ghad-Dawl (from Darkness to Light), a prisoners' advocate organization founded in 1995.

DINGLI, SIR ADRIANO (1818–1900). Born in **Valletta** in 1818, Dingli was the son of a **Gozo**-born judge who became chief justice. He was awarded the Doctor of Laws degree from the **University of Malta** in 1837, at the age of 19. For the next five years, he studied a variety of subjects at several European universities. He was elected to the Council of Government as the member from Gozo in 1849, and in 1854, he was appointed Crown advocate. In 1880, like his father before him, Dingli became chief justice and president of the Court of Appeals. With that title, he served on several significant diplomatic missions to Great Britain and several nations around the Mediterranean. Probably his most significant contribution to Malta was his work in constructing a reformed Code of Civil and Commercial Law.

A powerful and articulate person as Crown advocate, he was equally fluent in English, Italian, and Maltese. He personally favored the use of English—his wife was English—but he opposed the forced imposition of the **language** upon the people by the colonial authorities. He was often a person of reason between the **British** authorities and the Maltese patriots. Dingli retired from public life in 1895 and died on 25 November 1900.

DIN L'ART HELWA. Din l'Art Helwa ("This Fair Land") is a nongovernmental organization founded through the initiative of Judge Maurice Caruana Curran, meeting with other like-minded citizens at the **Manoel Theatre** in **Valletta** on 9 July 1965. Over the past four decades, its prime objective has been and continues to be safeguarding Malta's cultural heritage and natural **environment**. The organization has maintained a watchdog role, lobbying the authorities for the protection of the landscape and the rich **architectural** legacy of the Maltese Islands. The organization receives no direct government support, being solely funded by contributions and sponsorships. It has restored many historical buildings and structures on the islands, especially chapels and the numerous watchtowers that line the Maltese coast. *See also* HERITAGE MALTA.

DOBBIE, LT. GENERAL SIR WILLIAM GEORGE, KCB, CMG, DSO (1879–1964). Appointed acting officer of administration of the colonial government of Malta on 24 May 1940, Dobbie was named **governor** and commander in chief on May 19 1941. A professional soldier who stood six feet, four inches tall, Dobbie commanded attention. He, his wife, and his daughter were members of the Plymouth Brethren, and their strong faith led them to lead simple, pious lives. Dobbie was hard working, without humor, and devoid of the ability to tolerate anything frivolous. He was frequently seen on his knees in prayer, even in public circumstances. He would always end meetings by saying, "the Lord has spoken and so it shall be." He seemed to be totally without fear and would often appear in the middle of a bombing raid or some other catastrophe. As the raids continued at increased intensity, he would speak to the people over **Rediffusion Radio**, a radio system wired into most homes and the larger bomb shelters. The Maltese, a people of faith, were comforted by his religious broadcasts. His concern for them and his messages endeared him to the great majority of the population.

At the same time, there were those who were highly critical of what they saw as his lack of leadership, pointing to a failure to instruct the public through air raid drills or even to dispense information about the warning signals of such raids. Dobbie was faulted for his failure to have adequate bomb shelters constructed soon enough and then for the lack of any measure of comforts such as lighting, ventilation, any kind of seating, handrails on the stairs, and the like. Another serious complaint was the failure to develop a plan for quickly getting cargo ships unloaded between the bombing raids (in March 1942, 16,000 tons of supplies entered Grand Harbour from one convoy and, after three nights, only 807 tons had been taken off before the ships were sent to the bottom). Early in his appointment, he urged the home government not to use Malta as a base for offensive operations against the Axis convoys to North Africa, fearing that such action would provoke even greater bombardment in retaliation.

On 7 May 1942, Sir William was abruptly relieved of his duties and he, his wife, and his daughter left Malta on the same plane that had brought his replacement, Lord **Gort**. The plane arrived and left in the middle of an air raid. Poor health was given as the reason for the sudden departure, and most accepted that explanation, though some thought it due to administrative weakness. After the war, a story became public that Dobbie was on the verge of surrender and had managed to notify **Winston Churchill**, who acted immediately to change the leadership. People who can remember those times are still divided: was Dobbie exactly what Malta needed in those difficult days, or was he just the opposite? *See also* AXIS BLOCKADE.

DOCKYARDS. At one time, about 20 percent of the Maltese workforce (14,000) was employed at the British naval dockyards. They were a major force in bringing industrialization to Malta, helping it to develop a highly skilled workforce. The reduction in employment began slowly after **World War II** and continued until 1959, when the colonial administration published a five-year plan for a more rapid diminishing of the dockyard workforce. The entire rundown was unpopular not only because of the obvious unemployment it created but also because of a sense of betrayal. It was the dockyards and the **Three Cities** area surrounding the yards that were most heavily bombed during the war. The matter became a major political issue and source of great financial losses in the years leading up to **independence** and continued to be so until 2009.

A naval dockyard is geared to the rapid repair of damaged ships, regardless of cost, so that they may be returned to active duty, especially during wartime. A yard that is devoted to the repair of commercial vessels, however, must give primary concern to the costs incurred. The reduction of the workforce was a natural, though painful, necessity as the change from a naval to a commercial yard was being made. After Malta gained its **independence**, the dockyards added shipbuilding and **yacht** repair and maintenance to the other services previously provided. In 2003, the government added a "super-yacht" service and repair facility to attract higher value customers in a niche market.

A series of restructuring initiatives involving lengthy negotiations with the General Workers' Union began in 2001 and led to the 5 November 2003 merger of Malta Drydocks with Malta Shipbuilding to form a new company, Malta Shipyards. The workforce was reduced from 2,600 to 1,700, but the government agreed to reassign surplus workers to other entities and almost half (46 percent) of the 900 management staff took early retirement. The government is leasing the dockyard facilities to Malta Shipyards.

Although the yards became more efficient, added new functions, downsized the workforce, and greatly increased revenues, they accumulated a debt of over 640 million **euros** (US$900 million) and were still incurring millions of euros in annual operating losses. A five-year transition period to phase out subsidies for the yards was negotiated with the **European Union**. This meant that all subsidies to the yards had to end by 2008. In 2009, the dockyards were split into three entities (shipbuilding, super-yacht servicing and repair, and the Manoel Island ship servicing and storage facility), each offered for sale, and its employees offered retirement packages. The government expects to have fully divested itself of these companies by the end of 2009. *See also* ECONOMY; PRIVATIZATION; YACHT MARINA.

DOMUS ROMANA. The remains of the Domus Romana, or Roman House, were discovered in 1881 near the fortification walls of **Mdina**. The multiroom layout and decorative elements of the house, which is estimated to date from the early part of the first century BCE, indicate a very wealthy Roman owner. The most remarkable features of the site are the sophisticated mosaics that rival in beauty and richness those of Pompeii and Piazza Armerina in **Sicily**. Fortunately, the early discoverers of the ruins managed to restore some of its architectural features and protect the mosaics from the elements. **Sir Themistocles Zammit**, Malta's first director of **museums**, further excavated and studied the site from 1920 to 1924. In 1925, he expanded the facility to include more exhibiting space and added a neoclassical facade and garden. Totally overhauled and modernized with the help of **European Union** funds, a project that took several years, the Domus Romana museum was reopened for public visits on 26 February 2005. *See also* ARCHEOLOGY.

DRAGUT'S RAID. In July 1551, the Barbary corsair Dragut (Torghoud Rais) took his fleet to Malta with the intention to invade the islands by overpowering the **Knights of St. John**. After he had seen how they had been able to strengthen their fortifications in the area of the two harbors, he moved on to lay siege on **Mdina**, the ancient fortified capital of the Arabs. Frustrated there by the strength of the fortress, he took his force to **Gozo**, where it easily overpowered the few defenders, taking almost the entire population of the island into **slavery**. It is thought that Dragut's observations during these raids led to the preparations for the **Great Siege of 1565**, which the by then 80-year-old corsair led in the service of Suleiman the Magnificent and in which he was killed by a cannonball fragment.

DU PUY, RAYMOND (10??–1160). Raymond du Puy de Provence was a French knight and was **Grand Master** of the Order of St. John of Jerusalem (**Knights** Hospitaller) from 1121? to 1160. As the second grand master, he developed Knights Hospitallers into a strong military power. He was a relative of Adhemar of Le Puy, the papal legate during the First Crusade. He accepted the eight-pointed Amalfi cross as an official symbol of the Order, which later became known as the Maltese cross after the establishment of the Order on Malta. Raymond divided the Order into clerical, military, and serving brothers and established the first significant Hospitaller infirmary near the Church of the Holy Sepulchre in Jerusalem. *See also* SACRED INFIRMARY.

– E –

E-BOAT ATTACK. A very daring attempt to penetrate Grand and Marsamxett Harbors was carried out on 26 July 1941 by elements of the **Italian** Navy. The attack had the dual purpose of paralyzing the submarine base and destroying the ships of a convoy that had arrived a few days earlier. The assaulting "armada" consisted of a wide variety of small vessels, such as motor torpedo boats, baby submarines, and E-boats. The latter were manned boats carrying a high explosive charge in all spaces except for the engine and the ejector seat for the driver. The "armada" contained the experienced elite of the Italian Navy with a well-prepared battle plan. Fortunately for Malta, the Italians possessed outdated information on defenses, and worse yet, the expected simultaneous air attack was poorly timed and misdirected. The result was a disaster for the attackers. The most they were able to accomplish was the destruction of part of the breakwater viaduct at the entrance to Grand Harbour. The victorious defenders captured 18 prisoners and recovered 15 corpses. There was great heroism on both sides. A monument was placed at the port of Augusta, **Sicily**, from which the attackers departed, commemorating "the enterprise, unlucky and glorious." *See also* WORLD WAR II.

ECONOMY. As an island nation with few resources except for its limestone, warm, sunny climate, and well-educated, English-speaking workforce, Malta has always been heavily dependent upon **trade**, especially in services, and very vulnerable to external economic shocks, such as recent surges in **energy** costs. It has to import almost 80 percent of its food and nearly 100 percent of its energy inputs, 95 percent in the form of oil and 5 percent in coal.

Before the arrival of the **British** in 1800, most of Malta's inhabitants engaged in **agriculture** or service to shipping. There was little manufacturing industry on the islands except for tobacco and cotton processing, and poverty was widespread. Under the British, Malta became a major transit point for trade between Great Britain and its colonies in Africa and Asia, a key stopping off point for refueling (coal) and ship repair, especially after the opening of the Suez Canal in 1869. In times of war, Malta's economy experienced stronger spurts of growth.

In the last three decades, Malta's economy has undergone two major transformations: the first after the British troops departed and the second when the **Nationalists** returned to power in 1987 and propelled the country toward membership in the **European Union (EU)**.

At the time of their departure, the British forces were contributing about 30 million pounds annually to the Maltese economy. The loss of revenue from the departure of the British military required an urgent and radical restructuring of the economy. Consultants from the **United Nations** and Great Britain, as well as from other countries and agencies, provided expertise for the effort to ease what all knew was to be an abrupt change for the infant nation. Six development plans were initiated from 1959 to 1986. There was general agreement that **tourism**, light industry, conversion of the **dockyards** to commercial use, and expansion of the servicing of yachts would be the major areas in which Malta could become economically viable.

These have, in fact, played an important role in Malta's economic development. The **Malta Labor Party** government, under the forceful leadership of **Dom Mintoff**, adopted a socialist, state-controlled economic strategy, which was primarily concerned with creating jobs and protecting workers. The state took an active role in the economy of Malta, owning and operating businesses in the manufacturing, **banking**, and other service sectors, including the dockyards. Part of the government plan to reduce unemployment relied on the **emigration** of a significant number of Maltese citizens to other countries. At the same time, citizens of other nations were enticed to settle in Malta by a promise of low taxes in exchange for a promise not to seek gainful employment. Soon after Malta gained independence from Britain, a variety of proposals for the creation of a **free port** together with offshore banking were put forward and implemented. Construction expanded rapidly in the 1960s and tourism in the 1970s. High tariffs and quotas protected local businesses against competition from foreign suppliers.

The second major transformation of Malta's economy began when the Nationalist government under **Edward Fenech Adami** returned to power in 1987. It recognized the vulnerability of the small island economy to external shocks, especially as its main trading partner, Great Britain, was likely to join the EU. Malta feared being excluded and pinned its hopes on joining the EU as well. Achieving this required a totally different approach from that of the Mintoff era. The requirements of membership necessitated a major liberalization of Malta's economy, new laws, and improvements in infrastructure that are still continuing after Malta joined the EU on 1 May 2004. Dependence on a socialist, state-run economy developed under the Mintoff regime, one that guaranteed jobs at the expense of bad roads and economic stagnation, has been replaced by a more open, globally competitive spirit of entrepreneurship. Once a protected economy seeking local substitutes for as many imports as possible, something that may have been necessary under the harsh conditions at the time, Malta now needs to face the forces of globalization head on.

The changes brought about by the economic liberalization under the Nationalist government in the final years of the 20th century have helped the economy expand greatly: **privatization** of most state-owned loss-making companies and entities is well under way, and economic growth has averaged more than 3 percent in the last five years. Annual GDP has risen from 53 percent of the EU average in 2001 to 80 percent in 2008, amounting to 5.7 billion **euros** or about 14,000 euros per person. The manufacturing sector surged, growing from 17 percent to over 30 percent in 15 years. Tourism, attracting almost 1.3 million annual visitors, has grown to represent more than one quarter of the economy. The government has moved away from offshore banking, strengthening laws and regulations governing financial services, which have grown 30 percent from 2005 to 2008, employing over 7,000 workers and contributing 12 percent of GDP. An infusion of funds from the EU has helped the country to upgrade infrastructure, especially its roads, and expand **education** and job training.

Malta joined the Organisation for Economic Co-operation and Development (OECD) in 2005 and by bringing its inflation, debt, and deficit down to EU requirements, was able to adopt the euro on 1 January 2008, providing a greater economic stability that has begun to attract even more foreign **investment**. The information technology center called **SmartCity**, which is already in the process of being established, plans to employ 3,500 highly skilled workers to make Malta an information technology center of the Mediterranean region.

As part of the 2008 electoral campaign, the government of **Lawrence Gonzi** laid out its "Vision 2015." The **prime minister** identified seven sectors that the government would continue to develop in order for Malta to gain a comparative advantage by the year 2015. These include further expansion of financial services and ICT; improvements in infrastructure for tourism, education, and health care; incentives to attract more manufacturing (especially higher value-added industries, such as pharmaceuticals); and plans to make **Gozo** a model of environmental sustainability.

There are, however, some economic storm clouds on the horizon. A public debt totaling 3.5 billion euros is growing as a spending deficit for 2009 is projected at 3.8 percent of GDP, exceeding the EU limit of 3 percent. Unemployment, although averaging under 5 percent in the last five years, has recently risen to almost 8 percent. Competition from Asia, especially China, threatens Malta's main electronics manufacturer employing 2,500 workers. Public sector employment is still too high as are water and energy costs, and funds from the EU that have been helping with infrastructure development will be considerably reduced by 2013. Although great strides have been made, an island nation with no natural resources except for its location and people will continue to walk a tightrope of economic challenges. *See also* FILM PRODUCTION IN MALTA; FINANCIAL SERVICES.

EDUCATION. By law, education is compulsory from age five to 16 for a total of 11 years. However, the minister of education has the authority to extend the age in certain courses whenever deemed necessary. Education is free in the public schools. Approximately 33 percent of students are in private schools. State kindergartens begin at age three, and by age four, almost 100 percent are enrolled. Primary education is for six years and secondary for five. After that, students sit for the GCE (London or Oxford) examination plus the Malta matriculation examination, both at the ordinary level. Upon securing the required number of "O Level" passes, the student is eligible to enter the "Sixth Form" to prepare for the advanced level examinations ("A Levels"). A pass in each of these examinations is transferred as the equivalent of 10 credit hours to a college or university in the United States.

Tertiary educational opportunities are available locally at the **University of Malta (UM)** as well as the **Malta College of Arts, Sciences and Technology (MCAST)**, which caters to many specialized technical fields. Additionally, a wide variety of evening adult education courses ranging from **music** and dramatic arts to business subjects and chef's training are available. Since **European Union (EU)** membership, Maltese citizens also have access to European educational institutions through various EU-funded programs, especially the eductation programs for youth, which focus on funding vocational training, formal, and informal education respectively.

EISENHOWER, DWIGHT D. (1890–1969). After the successful invasion of **Sicily**, which was directed from deep within the limestone tunnels of the Lascaris War Rooms below **Valletta**, the supreme Allied commander returned to Malta. One of the first things he did was to compose a statement of congratulations to the Maltese. It was printed on the front page of every newspaper on 5 August 1943. He wrote, "The epic of Malta is symbolic of the experience of the **United Nations** in this war. Malta has passed successively through the stages of woeful unpreparedness, tenacious endurance, intensive preparation and the initiation of a fierce offensive. It is resolutely determined to maintain a rising crescendo of attack until the whole task is complete. For this inspiring example the United Nations will be forever indebted to Field Marshall Lord **Gort**, the fighting services under his command and to every citizen of the heroic island." The Lascaris War Rooms are preserved as a **museum** open to the public where Eisenhower's spartan office and desk can be viewed. The jeep used by Eisenhower on Malta is on exhibit at the War Museum adjacent to Fort St. Elmo.

ELECTIONS. The number and variety of **political parties** contesting the national elections changed almost continually until independence. Since that time, however, the **Malta Labour Party** and the **Nationalist Party** have dominated. Election results, according to the number of seats in the legislative bodies gained by party, are:

- 1921. Legislative Assembly: Unione Politica Maltese 14, Constitutional Party 7, Labour Party 7, Partito Democratico Nazionalista 4. Senate: Unione Politica Maltese 4, Constitutional Party 1, Labour Party 2.
- 1924. Legislative Assembly: Unione Politica Maltese 10, Constitutional Party 10, Labour Party 7, Partito Democratico Nazionalista 5.
- 1927. Legislative Assembly: Constitutional Party 15, Nationalist Party 14, Labour Party 3. Senate: Constitutional Party 3, Nationalist Party 4.
- 1932. Legislative Assembly: Nationalist Party 21, Constitutional Party 10, Labour Party 1. Senate: Nationalist Party 5, Constitutional Party 2.
- 1939. Council of Government: Constitutional Party 6, Nationalist Party 3, Labour Party 1. Executive Council: Constitutional Party 2, Nationalist Party 1.
- 1945. Council of Government: Malta Labour Party 9, Jones Party 1. Executive Council: Malta Labour Party 3.

- 1947. From this date on there was only the single legislative body, the **Parliament**: Malta Labour Party 24, Nationalist Party 7, Democratic Action Party 4, Gozo Party 3, Jones Party 2.
- 1950. Nationalist Party 12, Malta Workers Party 11, Malta Labour Party 11, Constitutional Party 4, Democratic Action Party 1, Independent 1.
- 1951. Nationalist Party 18, Malta Labour Party 14, Malta Workers Party 7, Constitutional Party 4.
- 1955. Malta Labour Party 23, Nationalist Party 17.
- 1962. Nationalist Party 25, Malta Labour Party 16, Democratic Nationalist Party 4, Christian Workers' Party 4, Progressive Constitutional Party 1.
- 1966. Nationalist Party 28, Malta Labour Party 22.
- 1971. Malta Labour Party 28, Nationalist Party 27.
- 1976. Malta Labour Party 34, Nationalist Party 31.
- 1981. Malta Labour Party 35, Nationalist Party 31.
- 1987. Nationalist Party 34, Malta Labour Party 31.
- 1992. Nationalist Party 34, Malta Labour Party 31.
- 1996. Malta Labour Party 35, Nationalist Party 34.
- 1998. Nationalist Party 35, Malta Labour Party 30.
- 2003. Nationalist Party 35, Malta Labour Party 30.
- 2008. Nationalist Party 35, Malta Labour Party 34.

In order to give citizens more control over local matters, the Parliament passed a local councils act in 1993, creating 68 local councils with from 5 to 13 council members, depending upon the population of the community. Since November 1993, local elections for council seats have been held in rotation so that every year, one third of the local councils hold elections based on a schedule.

Since 2004, when Malta joined the **European Union (EU)**, elections are held every five years for representatives to the European Parliament. Malta was given five seats initially. If the Lisbon Treaty is ratified, Malta will receive a sixth Member of the European Parliament (MEP), thus in the 6 June 2009 elections, six MEPs were elected. *See also* CONSTITUTION; CONSTITUTIONAL AMENDMENTS; REFERENDA.

EMIGRATION. The **British** colonial government began encouraging emigration as early as the late 19th century. The high birth rate of the Maltese at that time was causing increasing economic pressures, which in turn caused social unrest. In addition, the colonial administrators were concerned with the impact of the growing civilian population upon the military capabilities of the naval base. In 1812, even before the islands had been formally incorporated into the British Empire, a commission commented favorably upon the general standard of living but inserted a word of caution concerning the size of the population. It was noted that the Maltese lived long and had large families.

Emigration from the islands occurred over the years in spurts, depending upon the condition of the local **economy** as compared with those in other countries. Early emigration was to other countries around the Mediterranean as well as to Great Britain. After **World War I**, the largest movements were to the United States, Canada, and Australia. The emigrants were not always well received in their new homelands. In 1916, 214 Maltese emigrants were refused entry into Australia despite having legal visas and British passports. Australian union members were protesting, worried that immigrants would take away jobs. The Australian government, facing reelection, denied entrance to the Maltese. The ship carrying them, a French liner, was diverted to New Caledonia, and the emigrants were only allowed into Australia six months later, when the controversy had died down. After 1920, marriages by proxy were permitted. This allowed a groom who had already emigrated to marry a **woman** left behind in Malta, permitting the new bride to join her husband abroad, saving the couple a round-trip journey of two months.

Following **World War II**, Australia became the primary recipient. At its peak in 1952, 11,200 citizens left Malta. Some of the emigration involved children, estimated to have numbered somewhere from 3,000 to 10,000, 310 of which were documented as sent by the Church to Australia, while the vast majority ended up in Great Britain.

At present, emigration has become negligible, and many of the earlier emigrants have returned to the islands to retire with their hard-earned savings. It is said that a major source of income for **Gozo** arrives each month in the form of American and Canadian Social Security checks.

After 10 February 2000, Maltese emigrants were permitted to have dual citizenship. On 1 March 2008, a monument in the shape of a folded paper boat was inaugurated at the **Valletta** Waterfront Cruise Terminal as a memorial to the many Maltese who left their homeland.

ENERGY. Malta is almost totally dependent on imported fossil fuels for its energy supply and imports about one million tons of petroleum products per year, half of it consisting of fuel oil. Several attempts at locating oil on the islands and in its territorial waters have not been successful.

For electricity, Malta relies on two power stations with a total capacity of only 571 megawatts serving the three inhabited islands on a single electricity grid. The two plants are powered by heavy fuel oil with a high (up to 3.5 percent) sulfur content, adding to an already serious air pollution problem. Demand for electricity has increased so that brownouts and even complete power failures have occurred several times in recent years. In addition, almost 60 percent of Malta's water supply is derived from three desalination plants that consume approximately 6 percent of total electricity production.

The Maltese government owns and controls Enemalta, the company responsible for all energy generation and distribution on the islands. Although it is against **European Union (EU)** rules for such a monopoly situation to exist, Malta received a derogation because of the size of its market, which does not make competitive systems feasible. It is planning to install an undersea direct current electrical cable connecting it to a power grid in **Sicily**. Expected to be operational by 2012, it will allow Malta to tap into cleaner, more efficient electricity generation. One hundred megawatts of generating capacity are scheduled to be added in Malta. Negotiations to tap into an undersea gas pipeline from **Libya** have not been successful to date. Enemalta imports gas, which it distributes in bottles to residences and businesses throughout the islands.

For a country that has sunshine 85 percent of the daylight hours and an abundance of wind, it is surprising that Malta has not been more active in harvesting solar and wind energy. This is beginning to change. The EU Commission has proposed a new set of renewable energy targets for Malta. By 2020, the country should be producing 10 percent of its energy needs from renewable sources.

In anticipation of obligations to be incurred upon joining the EU regarding energy production, transmission, and consumption, the government set up the Malta Resources Authority in 2000. Its duties include, among others, overseeing the energy sector. In August 2006, the government released a draft of an energy policy. This policy establishes targets for 2010 to achieve three main goals: security of supply, at reasonable cost, and with limited harm to the **environment**. It identified wind, solar, and biomass waste as viable renewable energy sources to pursue. Geothermal, hydropower, tidal, and biomass from crops were rejected as not feasible for Malta.

Wind energy is estimated to be capable of replacing up to 9 percent of 2003 levels of electricity generation. Although the government has rejected the viability of land-based wind turbines, it is currently exploring deep-sea installations of wind turbines. Another 9 percent potential electricity generation is expected from solar (photovoltaic) systems and almost 6 percent from solid waste treatment. The government has recently introduced schemes to subsidize up to 25 percent of the cost of installing photovoltaic electricity and solar water heating systems.

The first solid waste treatment center being upgraded at St. Antnin amidst great controversy but with almost 17 million **euros** in funding from the EU, will convert about 35,000 tons of organic waste into electricity for 1,400 households. Not only will this renewable energy source cut carbon dioxide emissions but also it will reduce pollution that would have occurred from the prior practice of dumping the waste into landfills and or the sea.

The government still faces a significant challenge in the **transportation** sector. It needs to increase the quality and utilization of public transport, reducing the number of cars on the island. Currently there is one car for every two residents of Malta, consuming a quarter of the fossil fuel imports.

There is no doubt that EU membership, with its imposition of rules and regulations as well as considerable financial support, has brought about a huge change in Maltese attitudes and practices regarding energy. In June 2001, a group of concerned citizens formed the Malta Energy Efficiency and Renewable Energies Association (M.E.E.R.E.A.), a nongovernmental organization that, according to its charter, seeks to "promote discussion on energy related issues among energy actors including consumers and energy decision makers in Malta."

A draft national energy plan was issued by the Malta Resources Authority in April 2009, aimed at meeting EU targets that call for a 20 percent reduction in greenhouse gas emissions by 2020, an increase of renewable sources to 20 percent of energy consumption, and a reduction of energy consumption also by 20 percent. To attain these targets, six key areas are identified by the plan: energy efficiency, reducing reliance on imported fuels, stability in energy supplies, reducing emissions, effective and efficient delivery of energy supplies, and support to the energy sector. Over one billion euros are to be spent to update the energy sector, including an intensified search for oil, the installation of an electricity cable between Malta and Sicily, a new electricity plant at Delimara, and investment in renewable energy sources. The urgent need for this was dramatically highlighted in mid-June 2009 when a complete power outage paralyzed the country for an entire day. *See also* ECONOMY; TRADE.

ENGLAND, RICHARD (1937–). Malta's best-known contemporary architect, England was born on 3 October 1937 in Sliema. He studied **architecture** and civil engineering at the **University of Malta**, receiving a bachelor's degree in 1961. After a year of studying interior design at the Polytechnic in Milan, he spent two years working for an architectural firm there before returning to Malta to join his architect father in private practice.

England has designed numerous hotels, villas, office buildings, churches, and public structures all over Malta. His best known work includes the Church of St. Joseph at Manikata, the Central Bank of Malta Annex, the Millennium Chapel, the St. James Cavalier Centre for Creativity in **Valletta,** and his proposed Master Plan for the Entrance to the Island's capital city, Valletta. He has won many international awards, including six International Academy of Architecture Awards, two **Commonwealth** Association of Architects Regional awards, and the Grand Prix of the International Academy of Architecture in 2006.

In addition to being a very successful architect, England is an accomplished painter, poet, photographer, and sculptor, who has written several books containing his creations and ideas on aesthetics. England has lectured as a guest professor in universities all over Europe and North America and is himself the subject of four books and numerous articles.

Probably his most controversial work to date is a three-meter-high sculpture in stone letters, spelling the word "love." The letters are upside down so that the word "love" is reflected right side up in the waters of Spinola Bay, at the tip of which it was erected in 2005. England was also asked to submit a design using the space currently occupied by the ruins of the bombed-out **Royal Opera House** for a new chamber for **Parliament**. The public outcry opposing the idea put those plans on hold.

ENGLISH-LANGUAGE SCHOOLS. *See* TOURISM.

ENVIRONMENT. Malta faces serious challenges covering the entire gamut of environmental issues: waste disposal; sewage treatment; **energy** generation and consumption; air, water, and soil quality; as well as destruction of habitat through overdevelopment, littering, hunting, and soil erosion. These problems are compounded by the seasonality of **tourism**, which further stresses the islands' carrying capacity.

As the fourth most densely populated political entity in the world (over 1,298 inhabitants per square kilometer), Malta must continually chose between conflicting pressures of providing housing and preserving green space. Due to the Maltese love of cars, compounded by an inefficient public transport system, there are, as of 2009, almost 290,000 vehicles registered for a population estimated at just over 410,000. Some 75 percent of the vehicles are private passenger vehicles, which translates to an average of 1.4 persons per vehicle or 700 cars for every 1,000 persons. On hot, stagnant summer days, it is possible to witness an inversion, trapping exhaust gases over the island, so that even on this relatively tiny archipelago in the middle of the Mediterranean, one can experience a smog cover. A seasonal population surge, brought about by 1.2 million tourists annually, on which the **economy** is increasingly dependent, greatly compounds Malta's environmental challenges.

Conservation promises the most significant benefits to the energy-starved country. Mater Dei Hospital, the largest complex of its kind in the world, completed in 2008, is the first building in Malta to feature fully insulated external walls and specially insulated glass in its windows. In addition, rainwater is collected, stored, and used for irrigation. Low flush toilets and environmentally adapted refrigerants as well as polypropylene piping were included in the state-of-the-art facility. The design also includes means to reduce electromagnetic fields at the hospital. Still, as with most public buildings, its wide expanses of roofs lack solar panels, and the consumption of electricity for this gigantic complex is equal to that of the entire population of **Gozo** (almost 40,000 inhabitants).

Based on per capita consumption, Malta is the ninth thirstiest nation in the world, yet less than half of its water comes from the natural aquifers below ground. Seawater treated by osmosis, an energy-intensive process, provides most of the rest. Illegally drilled wells (boreholes) have become a serious issue recently, especially as the water service charges have been raised and water subsidies are no longer permitted under **European Union (EU)** law after 2011. In spite of this, treated sewage water is thrown into the sea instead of being reused as second class water.

EU funds have helped to initiate a system by which drivers can text message the license plates of polluting vehicles to the inspection authorities. With significant financing from the EU, the (literal) mountain of garbage accumulating at the Maghtab landfill on the northeast side of the island is being redeveloped into a recreational park. Tax breaks have been instituted for those installing solar and photovoltaic energy alternatives in their homes.

Although Malta obtained a transition period until 2013 to implement the new recycling and recovery targets for packaging waste, a recycling program with separation of different waste types has been instituted to the surprise and amazement of many skeptical observers. The many laws of the EU, which Malta has had to adopt as a condition of membership, and the significant financial support that this membership brings with it are helping to bring about a change in attitudes, raising awareness of the enormous environmental challenges facing a small island nation such as Malta. **Alternattiva Demokratika**, Malta's "green" **political party** since 1989, has never succeeded in gaining sufficient support for environmental protection. Recently, however, several very active environmental groups have formed, such as **Flimkien ghal Ambjent Ahjar**, Friends of the Earth Malta, and BirdLife Malta, among others, that are gaining more grass roots support for changes in the way Malta treats its environment. *See also* ZAMMIT DIMECH, DR. FRANCIS.

EURO. As a requirement of joining the **European Union (EU)**, Malta, along with the nine other candidate countries, joined the Economic and Monetary Union (EMU) but with a derogation. This meant that the new member states would not have to adopt the euro as their national currency until ready to do so. They must, however, be making continuous progress toward having their **economies** converge with the 12 other member countries already using the euro. The degree of convergence is measured by the inflation rate, budgetary deficit, and national debt, which may not exceed prescribed limits based on the average of the three best performing countries.

Before adopting the euro, candidate countries are required to join the European Exchange Rate Mechanism (ERM II) for a trial period of no less than two years. Participation in ERM II binds members to manage their interest rates and money supply in coordination with the European Central Bank, keeping the exchange rate of their currency vis-à-vis the euro within a range of plus or minus 15 percent of an agreed fixed rate.

In a surprise announcement on 2 May 2005, **Prime Minister Lawrence Gonzi** declared that Malta was ready to join the ERM II and to adopt the euro in place of the Maltese lira "as soon as feasible." A notional exchange rate of 0.4293 liri per euro was established and a National Euro Changeover Committee (NECC) set up, tasked with formulating an action plan to organize and manage the implementation of the euro, including, critical to success, the **education** of citizens about the process.

The Maltese public voiced a number of concerns about adopting the euro. The foremost worry was that adoption of the euro would cause significant inflation as merchants "rounded up" the prices in euros. To address this concern, retailers and the service industry were, as of 1 January 2007, required to display prices in both euros and liri. Another issue was the question as to which images should be used on the currency to represent Malta. After two rounds of consulting public opinion in early 2006, three images were selected: the

Maltese cross with the most votes, followed by the Maltese coat of arms, and in third place, an image of the Mnajdra Temple.

What to call the new currency was also controversial. The National Council for the Maltese Language favored the use of a Maltese spelling, but the EU requires that all official languages of its member states use the term "euro." (Greece is the only exception since it does not use the Roman alphabet). The cabinet decided that the word "euro" should be used in all Maltese legislation and official documents; although, it encouraged the use of Maltese spelling "ewro" in other circumstances.

On 16 May 2007, the commissioner for economic and financial affairs of the EU, Joaquín Almunia, recommended that Malta be permitted to adopt the euro, and on 1 January 2008, the euro replaced the Maltese lira as the official currency of Malta.

EURO-MEDITERRANEAN PARTNERSHIP. At a conference held in Barcelona on 27–28 November 1995, ministers of the **European Union (EU)** and other countries of the Mediterranean region formed the Euro-Mediterranean Partnership and issued the Barcelona Declaration, establishing a "Barcelona Process," an initiative to promote regional cooperation. The three main objectives of the Partnership are maintaining peace and stability through dialogue among the countries participating, creating and sharing regional prosperity through financial assistance, and ultimately establishing a free **trade** area, promoting cultural understanding and exchanges between civilians of the region. These goals are to be promoted through Partnership-wide, multilateral agreements as well bilateral agreements between the EU and other members of the Partnership.

"Conscious of its unique geographical position—at the North of Africa and the Arab States and at the South of Europe—as well of its make-up, a kaleidoscope of European and Arab cultures, . . . the only nation that has a Semitic language written in Roman letters," Malta is uniquely positioned to further the Barcelona Process. An example of Malta's involvement in this process is the launching on 4 May 2007 of the European-Mediterranean Initiative for Technology and Innovation (EuroMedITI), a platform for cooperative research and innovation headquartered in the Mediterranean Conference Center in **Valletta**. Its goal is "to establish a more enhanced and structured dialogue between the Union and the League of Arab States so that closer Euro-Arab relations and understanding is achieved."

EUROPEAN ECONOMIC COMMUNITY (EEC). *See* EURO-PEAN UNION.

EUROPEAN UNION. Aside from **World War II** and gaining **independence** from Great Britain, the most significant event in Malta's history during the last century is joining the European Union. The EU was originally called the European Economic Community (EEC), which was formed in 1957 by the Treaty of Rome. The major European combatant powers of World War II sought closer economic cooperation to avoid future wars. Through a series of treaties, the EU has forged a common market promoting free **trade**, including the free movement of capital, labor, and services among its member countries. The EU has enlarged its membership to include 27 European countries as of 2009 and, in 1999, created a common currency, the **euro**, currently used by 16 of the member states.

In 1961, Great Britain applied for membership in the EU (the EEC at the time) but was rebuffed by France under Charles de Gaulle. Malta, heavily dependent upon trade, a large portion of it with Great Britain, sensed the growing importance of the EU bloc. Afraid of being shut out of Europe, the continent, and culture it had identified with most closely over the centuries, Malta negotiated an association agreement with the EU on 5 December 1970. Britain eventually became a full member in 1973.

On 16 July 1990, the Maltese government led by **Prime Minister Fenech Adami** submitted its application to become a full-fledged member of the EU. In order to qualify for membership, a candidate country must show that it is able to adopt the ***acquis communautaire***, the entire body of EU laws and regulations, in addition to meeting certain requirements concerning its economic performance. This was quite a challenging task for a country like Malta with limited resources and burdened by debt and poor infrastructure. As part of convergence with the EU economies, Malta was required to institute a new system of value added taxation (VAT). The VAT proved so unpopular with the electorate that it was widely blamed for costing the **Nationalist Party (NP)** the **election** of 1996.

On 23 November 1996, the newly elected **Malta Labour Party (MLP)** government of **Alfred Sant** withdrew Malta's application for EU membership. However, it was reactivated less than two years later on 10 September 1998 when the Nationalists regained control. The government instituted a "National Programme for the Adoption of the Acquis," outlining its strategy to meet requirements for membership by the target date of 1 January 2003. As a member of the EU, Malta would gain much freer access to a huge and growing market; its citizens could seek employment or study and travel freely in EU member countries. Malta also stood to gain access to EU structural funds for improving its infrastructure and economic competitiveness.

Realizing the importance of popular support for EU membership to become a reality, the government undertook several important measures to inform and involve the public. It established the Malta-EU Steering and Action Committee (MEUSAC) to engage a broad spectrum of citizens in the process. MEUSAC membership included the core negotiating team as well as technical experts and representatives from the business organizations, unions, **political parties**, and various other nongovernmental organizations. MEUSAC was the key public body that coordinated and reviewed negotiations between Malta and the EU. The Malta-EU Information Centre (MIC) was also set up, tasked with informing the public on the various processes and many issues related to EU membership.

Formal accession negotiations between Malta and the EU were opened on 15 February 2000. These negotiations involved the timetable for adoption of the *acquis*. Each of its 35 chapters, devoted to aspects such as **agriculture**, competition, employment, and so forth, was examined to see how easily Malta could adapt to its requirements. Malta was able to obtain 76 special arrangements (derogations) concerning its adoption of the *acquis*. The main arguments for special treatment were Malta's small population and island status, which make it more vulnerable to external shocks and less able to avoid monopoly situations. Of particular concern was a potential market distortion from an influx of competitive labor (especially from the former Soviet Bloc), which could displace Maltese workers. Another concern was the threat of investors from other EU countries buying up scarce land and displacing local residents.

Malta obtained special guarantees that its antiabortion laws would not be challenged, that a 25-mile fishing conservation zone around Malta would be maintained, that **Gozo** would be considered a separate region eligible for extra assistance, and that Malta's neutrality would be preserved. Malta was also given additional transition time to eliminate subsidies for the **dockyards** and agriculture, while it preserved the right to use protective measures in case of severe economic impacts. A derogation allowing Malta not to charge VAT on food and medicines was made permanent in 2009.

The MLP continued voicing its opposition to Malta's joining the EU. Sant argued for an alternative agreement he called "partnership," a sort of free trade agreement that lacked many of the greater benefits and responsibilities of full membership. Other Labourites, led by former Prime Ministers **Dom Mintoff** and **Mifsud Bonnici**, organized a group named Front Maltin Inqumu (Front Maltese Awake), opposing EU membership. They proposed an alternative association agreement, reviving an earlier Mintoff proposal that proposed Malta as the "Switzerland of the Mediterranean."

A **referendum** was held on 8 March 2003, asking a simple question: "Do you agree that Malta should become a member of the European Union in the enlargement that is to take place on 1 May 2004?" Fifty-four percent voted in favor, 46 against. In a curious twist, both sides claimed victory! Sant tried to argue that the no vote had won because only 48 percent of eligible votes were cast in favor whereas 52 percent (following the MLP's recommendation) either voted "no," abstained, or destroyed their ballots! Prime Minister Fenech Adami called for general elections in the following month in which the NP gained 35 seats versus 30 for the MLP, thus sealing the victory for Malta's joining the EU, which it did formally on 1 May 2004.

As a member, Malta currently has five representatives serving in the European Parliament and is represented on the EU Commission by Joe Borg, European commissioner for fisheries and maritime affairs. The EU Commission in Malta is represented by Joanna Drake. Malta has qualified for access to EU funding in excess of 900 million euros, which, along with matching funds from the government, has begun to bring about significant improvements in the lives of Maltese citizens. On 1 January 2008, Malta successfully adopted the euro, replacing the Maltese lira as its national currency. *See also* LISBON AGENDA; SCHENGEN AGREEMENT.

– F –

FARRUGIA, LOUIS A. (1951–). Louis Farrugia received his education in Great Britain and qualified as a Fellow Member of the Institute of Chartered Accountants of England and Wales in 1973. He returned to Malta in 1974 after working for a brief period with the public accounting firm Pricewaterhouse in **Italy**.

In 1980 Farrugia was appointed managing director of Simonds Farsons Cisk, one of Malta's largest companies. Founded in the 1920s by his father, Lewis Farrugia, after his family's flour mill was burned down during riots over the increased price of bread, it is Malta's major brewery, engaged in the brewing, production, and sale of branded beer and beverages. The group also operates a number of well-known quick-service food franchises (TGIF, Pizza Hut, Burger King, and KFC) and imports major brands such as Danone, Quaker, and Tropicana.

Like his father before him, Louis Farrugia is a prominent member of the business community who has served as chairman of the Malta Chamber of Commerce (1998–99) and as an officer on the Council of the Malta Federation of Industries. He was appointed a director of the Malta Development Corporation in 1987 and served as deputy chairman (1988–91). He was reappointed as a director a decade later and served for a two-year period.

Farrugia played an active part in the setting up of the Foundation for Human Resources, an organization jointly launched by the government and private industry in September 1990 to provide training and support in human resources. He served as its president until May 1994.

Between March 2000 and September 2006, he served as a nonexecutive director of HSBC Bank Malta and in November 2003 became a director of the London-based Commonwealth Business Council. In recognition of his contribution to Malta's industry and enterprise on a national level, the **president** of Malta nominated Farrugia a member of the Order of Merit in November 2004.

In November 2006, Farrugia was appointed as a nonexecutive director of Malta Venture Capital, a newly established venture capital fund, and also serves as chairman of two other family-owned businesses: Multigas and Farrugia Investments. He is married to Monica née Galea and has two sons.

FENECH ADAMI, DR. EDWARD, KUOM, LLD (1934–). Born on 7 February 1934 in Birkirkara, Dr. Edward (Eddie) Fenech Adami studied economics and law at the **University of Malta**, becoming an attorney in 1959. He joined the **Nationalist Party**, was elected to **Parliament** in 1969, and was reelected in every general **election** that he contested thereafter. In 1977, he succeeded **Dr. Giorgio Borg Olivier** as leader of the Party and served as **prime minister** from 1987 to 1996. Under his resolute leadership, Malta dismantled much of the socialist legacy of **Dom Mintoff**, instituting major changes in preparation for joining the **European Union (EU)**.

Improvements in infrastructure, **privatization** of state-owned corporations, and streamlining of government services were launched. Malta submitted its formal application to join the EU on 16 July 1990, only to have it frozen by the Malta Labour Party when it returned to power for 22 months (1996–98). As soon as Fenech Adami and the Nationalists were back in control, the process of integration with the EU was resumed, and membership negotiations concluded in December 2002. Prime Minister Fenech Adami signed the EU Accession Treaty on 16 April 2003, and on 7 April 2004, his 70th birthday, he announced that he was stepping down as party leader. He resigned from the office of prime minister on 23 March and was elected **president** of Malta on 4 April 2004 and served until **George Abela** succeeded him on 4 April 2009.

FESTAS. Distinctly Maltese celebrations, which have their roots in similar traditions in **Sicily**, *festas* take place annually in the towns and villages between the beginning of May and the end of September. The celebrations are family events to be anticipated by members of all ages and involve great quantities of locally made fireworks and numerous marches by **band clubs**. They are part religious, part political, and part festive carnival. Originally, these celebrations were held on a day commemorating the patron saint of the local parish, but in recent years, the government has decreed that they be held during the closest weekend. The statue of the saint is brought out of the parish church and carried in the parades. In many of the towns and villages, rival band clubs have evolved, generally with different political leanings. As each will have its own patron saint, each will hold its own *festa*. On occasion, the rivalries have become so intense that the parish priests have had to cancel some *festas*, fearing brawls and fistfights.

The entire funding for these events comes from private donations. Heavy competition is involved in fund-raising so as to have the "best *festa*," meaning the most numerous, expensive, and loudest fireworks. Over 1,300,000 **euros** are spent each year on fireworks in Malta.

The task of preparing these elaborate fireworks displays usually takes the entire year and involves some risk. In the last 30 years, 36 workers have been killed in accidental explosions during the manufacture of fireworks. It was thought that contemporary changes, such as television, would erode the *festas*' popularity, but on the contrary, enthusiasm for them seems to have become stronger than ever. They have also become important events on the tourist calendar. *See also* CATHOLIC CHURCH; MUSIC; RELIGION.

FILFLA. One of the uninhabited islands of the Maltese Archipelago, Filfla is but a rock jutting out of the sea. It has no harbors or inlets and is visited only with great difficulty. It was used as a safe haven by some Maltese to escape the 1813 plague and, at various times over a period of two centuries, as a target for naval gun practice by **French**, **British**, **Italian**, and American forces. This reduced the island's size considerably and made it even more dangerous to access because of a shoreline littered with large rock fragments and unexploded shells. The Malta government banned the bombing in 1971 and declared the island a nature preserve in 1989. Its isolation has made it a living link with the distant past. It is home to a dark green lizard identified as *Lacerta muralis* var. *filfolensis*, which is found nowhere else on earth.

FILM PRODUCTION IN MALTA. To help Malta's **economy** survive the departure of the **British** forces, the government decided to attract filmmakers to the islands. Malta's predictably sunny weather, its centuries-old yet well-preserved fortifications and buildings, a remote location, relatively low wages, and an English-speaking population all combine to make Malta a destination popular with filmmakers. In the last 50 years, over 40 major films, including several James Bond titles, *The Gladiator* (2000), *The Count of Monte Christo* (2002), *Troy* (2004), and Steven Spielberg's *Munich* (2005), were filmed in part or entirely in Malta.

In 1964, the government established the Mediterranean Film Studios (MFS) on the peninsula by Fort Ricasoli as a state-owned company, offering a unique feature at the time: two large tanks for shooting underwater scenes.

In 1993, the MFS company was **privatized**, first leased and subsequently bought by Catalyst Entertainment Inc. of Toronto. In 1999, the company was bought by German businessman Jost Merten, who has undertaken the restructuring and cost-cutting steps necessary to keep the business competitive.

The government introduced financial incentives in 2005, offering a rebate of up to 20 percent of most of the local expenditure. As a result, an estimated 18 million **euros** were injected into the economy by the film industry over a 12-month period (2005–6) as 12 productions were filmed on the islands, including Spielberg's *Munich* and *The Da Vinci Code*, a rather controversial film for predominantly **Catholic** Malta. *Agora*, shot in 2009, was the first major film produced entirely in Malta.

FINANCIAL SERVICES. One of Malta's strategic goals has been to increase the quality and size of its financial services sector. By reducing bureaucracy, lowering fees, and simplifying procedures, the government hoped to attract foreign **banking** operations to Malta. This would enable banks to take advantage of Malta's lower cost structure, well-educated work force, and location as a bridge between Europe and the Mediterranean south.

In anticipation of **European Union (EU)** membership, many changes in Malta's banking laws were introduced, beginning in January 2000, to harmonize them with EU regulations and bring Malta into line with international best practices in financial services. Government ownership of banks was greatly reduced, and the Central Bank of Malta, which had been established in 1968 after

independence, was given greater independence from government interference. Several foreign banks set up operations in Malta, most notably the Hong Kong and Shanghai Banking Corporation. In 1994, Malta stopped issuing offshore licenses, the last of which expired in September 2004. Malta was among the first six countries in the world to reach an advanced accord on financial practices with the Organisation for Economic Co-operation and Development, assuring that it does not serve as a tax haven country.

On 23 July 2002, the Malta Financial Services Centre, governed by the Malta Financial Services Authority, was established by an act of **Parliament** as an autonomous public institution to become the sole regulator of banking and other financial services, such as **investing**, insurance, and the Malta Stock Exchange, all duties previously carried out by the Central Bank. Originally developed to serve retail funds sold to the local market, Malta's fund administration sector now includes almost 100 European funds and more than 150 hedge funds, attracting global investors.

The conclusion of double tax treaties with many of the largest free market economies of the world, including with the United States in April 2008, has made Malta an attractive site to set up investment and trading subsidiaries. The financial services sector of the **economy** has grown considerably in the last decade. It now represents about 12 percent of Malta's GDP, a share that is expected to double in another decade.

FLAG OF MALTA. Tradition has it that the red and white colors of the Maltese national flag were given to Malta in 1091 by Count Roger of **Sicily**. He supposedly tore off a portion of his own flag, which was checkered in red and white. There is no historical evidence to support this. The national flag of Malta is prescribed in the **Constitution** as consisting of two equal vertical stripes, white in the hoist and red in the fly. The width of the flag is one and a half times its height. The **George Cross** is represented in the upper right corner of the white field.

FLIMKIEN GHAL AMBJENT AHJAR (FAA). One of the newest nongovernmental organizations in Malta, Flimkien ghal Ambjent Ahjar (FAA, literally translated from Maltese as "together for a better environment") is a grassroots movement growing out of a general public outrage about the destruction of cultural **heritage** and a decline in the natural **environment** caused by overdevelopment of the islands.

FAA was set up by Helen Caruana Galizia and **Astrid Vella** in the Spring of 2006, following a drive to prevent the demolition of one of the oldest buildings in the locality of Sliema dating back to the Baroque period. FAA quickly organized two public rallies, bringing together a large number of different NGOs in an unusual show of unity, gaining significant public support. The organization's sense of urgency was heightened by rationalization plans that were being proposed by the Malta Environment and Planning Authority (MEPA) that would have redrawn development zones, opening more of the countryside for building speculation. Public protest led by FAA and other environmental groups caused MEPA to cutback the proposal.

These and subsequent initiatives on subjects as diverse as overdevelopment, planning legislation reform, water issues, air pollution, alternative **energy**, and heritage protection have helped FAA to raise the profile of environmental issues in Malta in both the public and political consciousness. FAA's efforts have also succeeded in helping to block development on several other projects: in **Gozo**, at Ramla al Hamra and Ta Cenc and in **Valletta**, a proposed underground **museum** addition to the **St John's Co-Cathedral** that some experts feared threatened the integrity of the cathedral's foundations.

FONDAZZJONI PATRIMONJU MALTI. In 1992, a group of individuals with support from the government and numerous corporate donors established a foundation with the goal of preserving and promoting Malta's cultural heritage. The Fondazzjoni Patrimonju Malti (Maltese Heritage Foundation) organizes exhibitions, research projects, and publications highlighting Maltese antiques, art, and culture. Its main publication is *Treasures of Malta*, a highly acclaimed magazine appearing three times a year. Because it is so widely and highly respected, the foundation is able to gain access to valuable private collections (of which there are many in Malta), making them accessible to the public in Malta and abroad. Its largest project to date is the painstakingly complete restoration of the **Palazzo Falzon** (Norman House) in **Mdina**, which it opened to the public as a **museum** in the spring of 2007. *See also* DIN L'ART HELWA; FONDAZZJONI WIRT ARTNA; HERITAGE MALTA.

FONDAZZJONI WIRT ARTNA. Organized to help preserve Malta's national heritage, Fondazzonji Wirt Artna (FWA) is a nongovernmental organization that relies on many volunteers in addition to a paid staff. The FWA owns and operates several historical sites, such as the Malta War **Museum** in Vittoriosa (Birgu), featuring a complex of underground bomb shelters, and Fort Rinella, at which it performs reenactments and occasionally fires a 100-ton gun, the largest in the world, featuring a 45-centimeter caliber barrel. FWA also performs the traditional canon salute at the Upper Barrakka Gardens, which was used to mark high noon in earlier times. *See also* DIN L'ART HELWA; FONDAZZJONI PATRIMONJU MALTI; HERITAGE MALTA.

FONSECA, EMMANUEL PINTO DE (1741–1773). The longest serving **grand master**, Pinto brought the **Order of St. John** to its zenith in international recognition and diplomacy. He considered himself the equal of any reigning monarch of Europe and acted accordingly. He did not hesitate to challenge (and to bluff) larger states toward his own ends. He was arrogant and autocratic. Fond of pomp, Pinto insisted on royal protocol at all ceremonies. He expelled the **Jesuits** from Malta and converted their college into a recognized **university**. The beautiful **Auberge** de Castille was completed during his reign. In 1749, there was an uprising of slaves attempting to murder Pinto and seize control of the island of Malta. The attempt was crushed, and Pinto had more than 60 of the slaves put to death in what became known as the "carnival of cruelty." He died at age 92, leaving the Order in a state of unsteady finances. *See also* SLAVE UPRISING; SLAVERY AND SLAVE TRADE.

FOREIGN POLICY. Independence in 1964 required the new nation to develop, for the first time, its own foreign policy. Even before independence, **Prime Minister Borg Olivier** had to decide which of the two Chinas Malta would recognize. He opted for the United States' position, that Taiwan represented the true China as opposed to the **British** position, which urged recognition of mainland China. Malta sought to emphasize its newly independent stature further by adopting a policy of nonalignment. In June of 1971, **Dom Mintoff** was returned to office as prime minister. He immediately began negotiating with Great Britain to completely withdraw its forces from Malta and, in 1973, led Malta to join the nonaligned movement in pursuit of a policy of neutrality. On 15 December 1980, Malta signed an agreement with **Italy** to guarantee neutrality between the two nations and in 1981, published a "Declaration Concerning Neutrality," which barred foreign troops from Malta's soil. U.S. warships were banned from entering Maltese waters for resupply and/or repairs.

Malta under Mintoff turned away from the Western powers, such as Great Britain and the United States, seeking, instead, closer relations with the **Arab** states of **Libya**, Egypt, Syria, and Tunisia and communist states such as the People's Republic of China and North Korea. He hoped to have Malta become a bridge between Europe and North Africa.

When the **Nationalist Party** returned to power in 1987 and **Fenech Adami** was elected prime minister, he made it clear that Malta would continue its policy of nonalignment yet seek closer relations with the United States and other Western powers. However, the two main priorities of the new administration were to have Malta gain membership in the **European Union (EU)** and to improve Malta's finances.

Since 2004, Malta's foreign policy continues within the framework of its obligations to fellow members of the EU. Malta's strategic goals include making the best of EU membership, while strengthening ties to surrounding Mediterranean neighbors; working for peace and development in the Middle East, especially Palestine and Israel; and maintaining a focus on key issues such as climate change, **energy** supplies, and the particular problems of small island economies. Malta continues actively to seek strengthened bilateral relations with key partners and to promote Malta and Maltese customs through its embassies and consulates around the world.

FRAZIER, VANESSA (1969–). Born on 24 May 1969, Vanessa Frazier earned a BA from Luther College (U.S.) and an MA in diplomatic studies from the University of Malta. She joined the diplomatic corps of Malta in 1994 and served embassies in Rome, Washington, and London. As consul general in Washington and London, she represented Malta at the International Maritime Organization, among many other international organizations, and served as political officer in London, representing the CHOGM 2005 Task Force to set up and organize the **Commonwealth** meeting in Malta. In 2006, Frazier was appointed director of defense matters in the Office of the Prime Minister, serving as liaison for the **Armed Forces of Malta**.

FREEDOM DAY. Established to celebrate the departure of **British** forces from Malta, the first Freedom Day occurred on 31 March 1979. The ceremonial activities were held at Senglea at a new monument erected to commemorate the event. President **Anton Buttigieg** was to have had a major part in the important historical event but was upstaged by **Libya**'s head of state, Colonel Muammar al-Qaddafi. The two arrived at the monument site at the same time. The difference was that the Qaddafi contingent consisted of several hundred Libyan students who were studying in Malta plus over 500 other Libyans who had traveled to the island on a passenger ship for the event. The continued orchestrated shouts of "Qaddafi! Qaddafi!" dominated the event even as the British flag was lowered and the Maltese **flag** was raised at midnight. The president had to watch, powerless, as this major event in his small nation's history was overpowered by the actions of the leader of a neighboring nation.

Whether Qaddafi had received an "official" informal invitation to the event or came on his own has never been really determined, but the suspicions continue. The morning of the next day, the HMS *London* departed Grand Harbour, taking with it the final remnants of the British forces. President and Mrs. Buttigieg stood in the wind and rain on the highest roof of Fort St. Angelo at the mouth of the harbor in order to wave farewell. They did this so that the final symbolic event of the leaving of the British forces would not be tarnished by the embarrassment of the preceding evening.

FREE PORT. In order to attract foreign businesses to Malta, the government established the Malta Freeport Corporation in January 1988. A free port consists of a cargo handling facility with duty-free enterprise zones that enable products to be landed in Malta without officially entering the country. After the products have been further processed (through some value-adding operations), they are shipped on to other countries without having to pay Maltese duties. The manufacturers save money, and Maltese workers get more jobs.

Taking advantage of Malta's location and deep harbors, the Freeport has become a major transshipment hub in the Mediterranean, especially for goods from Asia on their way to Europe. Currently, about 1.5 million 20-foot containers, to and from 115 foreign ports, pass through the facility annually. An oil terminal, storing and transferring crude oil, fuel oil, jet fuel, and gasoline, operated by Oiltanking Malta, a German subsidiary, is also located at the free port. Since **privatization** on 5 October 2004, the free port is operated by a company under a 30-year lease.

FRENCH INVASION. After the French Revolution, the attitudes in France toward the **Knights of St. John** shifted definitely toward the negative. In the prevailing circumstances, an organization with aristocratic and religious foundations was unlikely to be very popular. In 1792, all of the Order's possessions in France were confiscated by the government. This loss of wealth and income plunged it into a state of financial instability. Of necessity, it began negotiations for alliances with Russia, the Kingdom of the Two Sicilies, Austria, and Great Britain. Because the French had cultivated subversive elements in Malta, there was a strong pro-French attitude on the part of the Maltese. Many French Knights, including the commander of fortifications, were in sympathy with what was happening in France.

The French fleet, on its way to Egypt, stopped in Malta on 9 June 1798. Napoleon requested permission to have his ships enter Grand Harbour in order to take on water. His request was denied. The next day his armed troops were put ashore. A combination of surprise, poorly manned defenses, and pro-French factions among the Knights and the Maltese caused the meager resistance to crumble. **Grand Master** Ferdinand von Hompesch asked for an armistice on 11 June 1798. Napoleon's terms were harsh indeed. The Order was to give up all claims to the Maltese Islands and to all its property located there, real and personal. Within a few days, the grand master and other Knights left the islands (although the Knights of the French **Langue** were permitted to stay). Napoleon moved his command ashore to take control and to set about applying French revolutionary principles to the lives of the Maltese. The influence of the Church was reduced significantly, and the **Inquisition** was abolished. All valuables of the Knights that could be removed were transferred to the French fleet. A new legal code was instituted. The initial response of the Maltese citizenry was extremely positive. *See also* BATTLE OF ABOUKIR BAY; FRENCH OCCUPATION.

FRENCH OCCUPATION. The Maltese found the revolutionary concept of equality, encouraged by their new French rulers, a most acceptable one after the autocratic reign of the **Knights of St. John**, which had lasted over 250 years. However, this positive feeling slowly began to erode. The French refused to pay the debts of the Knights, leaving the local suppliers to suffer the losses. The feeling of unfairness was heightened as they watched the wealth of the Knights being loaded onto the French ships. The new rulers also refused to honor the pensions promised to loyal servants and other employees of the Order. Interest rates were raised, new taxes imposed, and the terms of leases on public lands were arbitrarily altered. On 17 June 1798, Napoleon left Malta, resuming the movement with his fleet toward Egypt, his primary objective. He left behind 4,000 soldiers as a garrison to control the islands.

Gradually, the negative opinions about the new rulers began to harden. When it was learned that Napoleon had suffered a defeat to the **British** Navy in Egypt, the status of the French occupying force in Malta was tenuous at best. The most serious mistake committed by the French, however, was the pillaging of the churches' silver and other valuables. This aroused the anger of the Maltese, which finally erupted when the French attempted to strip ecclesiastical buildings in **Mdina**. The small force of French soldiers in the old city was massacred and, in a short time, all of Malta rose up against the occupiers. The remaining French forces withdrew into the fortifications of **Valletta**. When several brave attempts to storm the fortifications failed, the decision was made to deny supplies to those in the city. It was, in essence, a blockade against the French by the Maltese on their own island.

The Maltese created a sort of national assembly and sent messengers seeking help to **Sicily** and Naples. The king of Naples responded by sending a squadron of Portuguese ships. Additionally, a British squadron under the command of Captain **Alexander Ball** joined the blockade, and Ball became the overall commander. After a while, it was decided that a land campaign was needed as well as the blockade, and Brigadier General Thomas Graham was given the responsibility of raising a local regiment of volunteers. He was very successful, and the unit became the Maltese Light Infantry, a part of the British Army. Eventually, the French gave up because of the effects of the blockade and the threat of a land-based assault. Unfortunately, history repeated itself, and the Maltese were given no voice in the surrender negotiations, which permitted the French to leave the island with all of their possessions. The Maltese could only look on as the departing soldiers left in defeat, taking with them a great amount of items really belonging to Malta. On 5 September 1800, the British flag was raised over Malta. *See also* FRENCH INVASION.

FRENDO, DR. HENRY (1948–). Born on 29 August 1948, Frendo studied the Maltese and English languages in addition to history at the **University of Malta**, earning a BA and an MA in history with a thesis on the language-culture clash in Malta. He chaired a student organization leading a national campaign called Djar ghall-Maltin (Houses for the Maltese), which sought to ease the housing crisis for lower income Maltese. In the early 1970s, Frendo served as editor of a daily newspaper, *Il Hajja*, before earning a PhD in 1976 at Oxford with a dissertation on the formation of Maltese **political parties** under **British rule**, which was later published as a book under the title *Party Politics in a Fortress Colony: The Maltese Experience*. Before becoming a full-time faculty member, Frendo served as a program officer with the **United Nations** High Commissioner for Refugees (UNHCR) in Mozambique, Zimbabwe, Egypt, and Papua New Guinea.

Since 1992, Frendo has been a professor of modern history at the University of Malta and a leading authority on Malta's contemporary political history, authoring numerous books on Maltese political parties and personalities, including *The Origins of Maltese Statehood: A Case Study of Decolonization in the Mediterranean*. From 1993 to 1997, he chaired the Malta branch of the European Cultural Foundation and from 1994 through 1998, was the mayor of Attard. In 1994, he was elected president of the Local **Councils** Association and served as head of delegation to the Congress of Local Councils association in Strasbourg.

Since 2001, Frendo has served as chairman of the Refugee Appeals Board and as vice president of the Council of Europe's committee of experts on local government. Frendo is married to Margaret née DeBono, and they have three children.

FRONTEX. *See* ILLEGAL IMMIGRATION.

– **G** –

GALEA, VICTOR (1960–). Victor A. Galea was born on 24 September 1960 in Sliema, the oldest child of Anthony Galea and Anna née Salomone. He graduated with a BA in management from Luther College in 1983. In 1996, he earned the MBA from Brunel University after a course of study at Henley Management College.

Galea joined his family business in Malta in 1983 as a third generation manager of the V. J. Salomone Group, a company founded in the 1920s and still a leading distributor of fast-moving consumer goods in Malta.

An active promoter of Maltese **trade** and commerce, Galea was first elected to the Council of the Malta Chamber of Commerce in 1989 and has remained active in Chamber business, serving as vice president in 2004 and 2005. In 2006, he was elected to a two-year term as president of the Chamber, during which time he helped to strengthen the organization by engaging in discussions with the Malta Federation of Industry to engineer a merger. In December 2007, the merger memorandum of understanding was signed. Galea holds directorships in several other group companies. He is also a director of Middle Sea Insurance as well as Malta Enterprise. He is married to Rita née Cachia, and they have three children.

GAMES OF THE SMALL STATES OF EUROPE. These games, a sort of mini-Olympics, have been held in odd-numbered years since 1985 at different locations. Eligible are those nations that by geographical area or population below one million citizens (or both) qualify as "small." Currently included are Andorra, Cyprus, Greenland, Iceland, Liechtenstein, Luxembourg, Malta, and San Marino. Malta entered into an ambitious series of construction projects of athletic facilities prior to hosting the Fifth Games in 1993. It hosted the games again in 2003, placing fourth in the overall medal count with 44, 11 of them gold. Currently, 12 sports are contested, including athletics, basketball, judo, tennis, lawn bowling, and volleyball.

GANADO, DR. HERBERT (1906–1979). As editor of a Maltese-language newspaper that favored **Nationalist Party (NP)** positions, Ganado was one of those detained and then exiled to Uganda soon after the outbreak of **World War II**. Upon his return after the war's end, he became active again in the political and social life of the islands. Soon he became president of Catholic Action, an organization of laymen of the Church. In 1956, he became a member of the Executive Committee of the NP. In 1958, he joined a number of other party members in a breakaway group that founded the Democratic Nationalist Party. This new party had objectives not very different from those of the parent party, except that the attitude toward the Church and the clergy was much more positive. In the **elections** of 1962, the new party gained 9.3 percent of the votes, while the parent party gained 42 percent. In 1966, its percentage dropped to 1.3 percent, and after that, it ceased to exist as a **political party**.

GENERAL WORKERS' UNION (GWU). *See* TRADE UNIONS.

GENOESE INFLUENCE. When King Roger II of **Sicily** and Malta died in 1154, his successor was William I. He became known as William the Bad because of his personal lifestyle and his disinterest in the affairs of governance. The main beneficiaries of his rule were the Genoese, who were granted a number of substantial privileges, especially in Sicily. His successor was his son, William II, who became known as William the Good, probably both because of his close relationship with the Church and the contrast of his reign with that of his father. When William II died childless in 1190, a dispute arose over his successor. The rightful heir was Constance, the daughter of Roger I, married to Henry VI, son of the emperor of Germany. However, the pope feared the possible German influence in the area and gave his support to Tancred, of illegitimate birth and **Norman** descent, who was crowned King of Sicily in 1190. He elevated a Genoese pirate, Margarito of Brindisi, to the position of royal admiral of Sicily and count of Malta. He was succeeded by another Genoese corsair named William Grasso.

He, in turn, was succeeded by his son-in-law, Henry Pistore, an ambitious, colorful person, who became Count of Malta in 1203. In 1205, Pistore and some Maltese sailors in two galleys captured two additional Venetian galleys and, with the four, attacked Tripoli in **Libya**. They were welcomed as heroes upon their return to Malta. Pistore continued to use Malta as a base for his operations throughout the Mediterranean, most likely with a positive impact upon the economy. Genoese influence attained its highest level at this point. A strong Genoese fleet sailed from the islands in 1205 to successfully attack Syracuse, Sicily, after it had been seized by Pisans. After that point, Pistore's connections with Malta diminished and disappeared.

GEOLOGY. The Maltese archipelago was formed between 25 and five million years ago through the uplifting of sedimentary layers that once were below the sea. The lifting action resulted in fissures along several fault lines caused by forces that gave Malta steep cliffs and deep natural harbors. Its terrain slopes from a high point in the southwest, site of the Dingli cliffs, to the lower lying shores of the northeast. Five major layers of geological deposits, mainly limestone and clay varieties, make up the islands. Sandwiched between the upper and lower coralline limestone layers are (from top to bottom) a layer of green sand, a layer of blue clay, and a layer of globigerina limestone.

The globigerina layer is about 20 to 100 meters (65 to 338 feet) thick. It derives its name from the planktonic globigerinid foraminifera, the skeletons of which form most of its sediment. Fossils of crocodiles, turtles, and seals are also found in this layer. Locally known as "franka," Globigerina is a very soft, honey-colored limestone, which has been quarried from deep pits around the islands. Abundant, soft, and easily sawed into blocks, it represents Malta's main natural resource and is the traditional material used to build and decorate most of the buildings in Malta. The harder, dense, crystalline coralline limestone was used to build the **Megalithic Temples**. The green sand layer is soft, porous, and only one to 10 meters thick. It lies on top of the impermeable blue clay layer, which acts as a sort of reservoir collecting water underground. The blue clay layer, on average one meter thick, is the most fertile but also very soft and subject to erosion. *See also* ARCHITECTURE.

GEORGE CROSS (GC). The endurance of the Maltese people through the horrors of the incessant bombings of **World War II** and the severe hardships they caused was heroic. That heroism was recognized on 15 April 1942, when a message was received in **Valletta** from King George VI. In his own handwriting it said, "To honour her brave people I award the George Cross to the Island Fortress of Malta to bear witness to a heroism and devotion that will long be famous in history." The George Cross is the highest award that Great Britain can bestow on civilians. The award to Malta was the first time that a collective group received this award (the only other being the Royal Ulster Constabulary in 1999). The **flag of Malta**, divided vertically into a white field on the left and a red field on the right, was soon changed to include the depiction of the George Cross in the upper left corner of the white field.

In a ceremony amid the ruins of Valletta on 13 September 1942, the **governor** and military commander, **Lord Gort**, said,

> On my appointment as Governor of Malta, I was entrusted to carry the George Cross to this island fortress. By the command of the King, I now present to the people of Malta and her dependencies, the decoration which his Majesty has awarded to them in recognition of the gallant service which they have already rendered in the fight for freedom. How you have withstood for many months the most concentrated bombing attacks in the history of the world is the admiration of all civilized peoples. Your homes and your historic buildings have been destroyed and only their ruins remain as monuments to the hate of a barbarous foe. The Axis Powers have tried again and again to break your spirit but your confidence in the final triumph of the United Nations remains undimmed. What Malta has withstood in the past, without flinching, Malta is determined to endure until the day when the second siege is raised. Battle-scarred George Cross Malta, the sentinel of Empire in the Mediterranean, meanwhile stands firm, undaunted and undismayed, awaiting the time when she can call 'pass friend, all is well in the island Fortress.' Now it is my proud duty to hand over the George Cross to the people of Malta for safekeeping.

He closed by reading the citation written by King George VI and handed the case to the chief justice, Sir **George Borg**. A plaque displaying the citation was mounted on the wall of the **Grand Master's** Palace in Valletta.

In 1988, the George Cross Island Association (GCIA) was organized and began holding annual reunions, featuring commemoration ceremonies of the granting of the GC. Recently, these festivities have occasioned criticism by some Maltese, who resent the addition of the GC to the Maltese flag as an arbitrary act on the part of the colonial administration and another symbol of the **British** domination of the island.

GEORGE VI (1895–1952). His Majesty King George VI, the **British** monarch, showed his respect and affection for the people of Malta in many ways, but chief among them were the following: On 3 April 1942, he assumed the title of colonelcy-in-chief of the royal Malta Artillery Regiment, an unusual honor to be given to a non-British military unit. His message to the regiment included his "admiration for the stout-hearted resistance of all in Malta, Service personnel and civilians alike, to the fierce and constant air attacks of the enemy." He concluded by saying, "Please convey my best wishes to all ranks of my new Regiment, and assure them of the added pride with which I shall follow future activities." On 15 April 1942, he awarded the **George Cross** to the people of Malta. On 20 June 1943, he arrived in Grand Harbour aboard the HMS *Aurora*. He stood on a special platform built on the ship's bridge, saluting the joyously boisterous crowds that filled every available space around the harbor. *See also* WORLD WAR II.

GERADA, BISHOP EMMANUEL. In March 1966, Mgr. Gerada was appointed auxiliary bishop. From the beginning, it seemed certain that he had been promised the coadjutorship with right of succession to the archbishopric. Born in Malta, he was a Vatican diplomat with an excellent reputation and extensive experience. His main charge with the appointment was to settle the problem between the **Malta Labour Party (MLP)** and the Church. As a beginning gesture of conciliation, he invited all members of **Parliament** to his consecration service. **Dom Mintoff**, together with his followers, declined the invitation, giving as their reason the fact that so many of them continued to be denied the sacraments of the Church through the interdict because of what was interpreted as political activities against the Church.

It was not until 13 December 1968, that Gerada's diplomatic skills succeeded in getting Archbishop **Michael Gonzi** to remove the religious restrictions. At the same time, he pledged that he would work hard to reach an agreement with the party. The relationship between Gonzi and Gerada was always tense, with each attempting to outmaneuver the other. In early 1969, Gerada prepared a draft of a Church/MLP agreement, which, when revised, was approved by Mintoff. He then sent it to the Vatican for approval. The return letter raised several objections and urged slower progress. Gerada never showed the letter to anyone else but did proceed with the negotiations.

Finally, on Good Friday, 4 April 1969, a statement was issued bearing the signatures of Mintoff and Joe Camilleri of the MLP and Archbishop Gonzi, Bishop Gerada, and Bishop Cauchi of the Church. It provided that a distinction be made between the political community and the Church and included the promise that the Church would not interfere in politics. In addition, it recognized the duty and right of the Church to teach its principles. The Church also promised not to impose mortal sin as a censure. Many observers believe that this agreement paved the way for the MLP victory in the **election** of 1971 and for Mintoff to become **prime minister**. After this success, Gerada lost his chance to become archbishop through excessive meddling in both political and Church affairs, while Gonzi was not yet retired. The local priests became polarized, and he then lost credibility among them. The Vatican reacted to all the cries against him in November 1973 by naming him apostolic nuncio in Guatemala and El Salvador. *See also* CATHOLIC CHURCH; LIGUTTI, MONSIGNOR LUIGI.

GHAR DALAM. This cave, called the "Cave of Darkness," is located near the village of Birzebugia along the southeast coast of the island of Malta. It is one of the most important paleontological and **archeological** sites in Malta. This is because discoveries made inside give tangible evidence that the archipelago was once part of a land bridge between Europe and Africa. The fossil and skeletal remains of a variety of roaming animals of both continents have been found in the cave and are now on display in the **museum** at the same location. Included are dwarf hippopotamuses and elephants from the south and wild boar, red deer, and antelopes from the north. It is presumed that these animals where driven southward by the advancing ice age and roamed freely until the coming of the great floods of about 700,000 years ago. It was then that the archipelago became separated from the two continents, stranding the animals on Malta where they eventually became extinct.

The cave also contained evidence that it was used by humans in the Stone Age and again in the Bronze Age. Teeth found in the cave were once believed to have belonged to contemporaries of Neanderthal man, but this was later disproved. In 1991, a new species of wood-louse (*Armadillidium ghardalamensis*), only found in Ghar Dalam and a neighboring cave, was identified. The cave and its museum were declared a "Special Area of Conservation" under the **European Union**'s Natura 2000 framework and are currently administered by **Heritage Malta**, the national agency responsible for museums and conservation of cultural heritage. *See also* GEOLOGY.

GLOBIGERINA. *See* ARCHITECTURE; GEOLOGY.

GLOSTER GLADIATOR. At the outbreak of **World War II** in 1939, there were three dozen airports on **Sicily**, all within a 15-minute flight of Malta. Based throughout them were 350 bombers and 200 fighters of the Italian Regia Aeronautica. These were fast, modern aircraft manned by experienced pilots. Against this powerful force, there were on Malta just four obsolete biplanes, and these were there only by accident. When the **British** carrier HMS *Glorious* hurriedly departed the islands for duty in the defense of Norway, eight crated naval fighter planes, called Gloster Gladiators, were left behind. Although designed for use aboard aircraft carriers, a compromise decision was made, and four of the planes were assigned to the RAF defense of the Maltese Islands. The official quota of aircraft for that defense was to have been two squadrons of bombers and reconnaissance planes and four squadrons of fighters. They were never assigned because of the severe needs elsewhere. Thus, the defense was entrusted to four sturdy but outdated naval aircraft converted for land use. The pilots were all volunteers from air force administrative staff, none of whom had been trained in fighter aircraft. Of the 12 volunteers, seven were selected. The ground crews to service the aircraft also came from an array of Maltese and RAF volunteers. Knowing that it was inevitable that **Italy** would declare war soon, the small air force practiced all aspects of fighter tactics and the required land support.

At 6:57 a.m. on 11 June 1940, shortly after Italy officially declared war, the first wave of bombers approached Malta, expecting no opposition. Instead, they were met by the four converted fighter planes. That first day, the Italians mounted eight raids, using well over 150 bombers. The first raids were without fighter support, but from then on, all raids carried such additional protection. After that first day, one of the Gladiators was retired to a hangar as a source of repair parts. The remaining three, named *Faith*, *Hope*, and *Charity*, raised the morale of the garrison of 30,000 British and Maltese and the 225,000 civilians by their highly visible air actions. Benito Mussolini had boasted that his forces would be in Malta in a few weeks. He was proved to be very wrong. The three Gladiators shot down 30-plus enemy aircraft. Only one Gladiator was lost to enemy action. Even more important was their disruption of the precision bombing runs. With the arrival of Hurricane fighters in August, the Gladiators gained a well-earned retirement.

Currently, the body of *Faith* (without its wings) is on exhibit in the National War **Museum** in **Valletta**. However, in May of 2007, the newly organized Malta Aviation Museum in Ta Qali requested permission to take possession of the aircraft as part of its exhibit. In exchange, it promised to restore the craft to its original state by adding a pair of wings recently donated for that purpose by the RAF. Moving the airplane to the larger new facilities of the Malta Aviation Museum is supported by 66 percent of the Maltese citizenry, but **Heritage Malta**, the organization overseeing the National War Museum, has so far refused to release its prized artifact. *See also* BORG, SIR GEORGE.

GONZI, DR. LAWRENCE, KUOM, LLD, MP (1953–). Lawrence Gonzi was born on 1 July 1953 in **Valletta**. He studied law at the **University of Malta**, graduated in 1975, and began his law career as an attorney in private practice. He later joined the Mizzi Group of companies as a corporate lawyer and rose to group chairman, a position he held from 1989 to 1997. A strong commitment to the **Catholic** faith led him to join the Malta Catholic Action Movement, for which Gonzi served as general president from 1976 to 1986. The political and religious turmoil of the 1980s motivated him to become involved in politics when he contested the 1987 **election** as a **Nationalist Party (NP)** candidate. He was elected speaker of the House of Representatives on 10 October 1988, serving the Sixth Legislature (1988–92) and was unanimously reelected speaker for the Seventh Legislature on 5 April 1992.

Reelected to **Parliament** in October 1996, Gonzi continued to earn respect for his calm but forceful leadership, serving as opposition party whip, secretary to the Parliamentary Group, and shadow minister for social policy. He was elected as NP general secretary in the following year and led the Nationalists to victory over a **Malta Labour Party (MLP)** government that had been in office less than two years. Reelected to Parliament in 1998, Gonzi was appointed minister for social policy and leader of the House of Representatives. His business and negotiating experience served him well as he helped to restructure Malta's **economy** in preparation for membership in the **European Union (EU)** by reforming employment and industrial relations, especially in the case of restructuring at the **dockyards**. He also introduced a stringent policy of zero-tolerance toward benefits fraud.

When **Guido de Marco** was appointed **president** of the Republic, Gonzi was elected to replace him as deputy leader of the NP. **Prime Minister Edward Fenech Adami** chose him as deputy prime minister. After Fenech Adami had successfully led Malta to a point at which membership in the EU was assured, he stepped down, paving the way for Gonzi to be chosen and sworn in as prime minister on 23 March 2004.

Since becoming prime minister, Gonzi has been a determined leader, taking many steps required of membership in the EU that involve major changes and short-term pain for long-term gain. Despite the cost to his popularity and chances for reelection, he has continued to push through reforms, seeking to take maximum advantage of EU funds available to new member states. Gonzi was reelected on

8 March 2008 in a hotly contested election, which the NP won with the slimmest of margins, garnering only 1,500 votes more than the rival MLP.

GONZI, ARCHBISHOP MICHAEL, KBE (1885–1984). Gonzi was born in Vittoriosa on 16 November 1885, the youngest of eight children in a working class family. After gaining a degree in philosophy from the **University of Malta**, he did further theological studies and became ordained as a priest in 1908. After serving in several parishes, he was appointed **Roman Catholic** chaplain to the **British** forces on Malta during **World War I**. For a time, Gonzi was a professor of holy scripture at the University, and in 1919, he was appointed secretary to the archbishop. At the same time he was given the title of monsignor. One of the cofounders of the **Malta Labour Party (MLP)**, he was elected to the Senate in 1921. In 1924, at the age of 39, he was appointed bishop of **Gozo** and had to relinquish his Senate seat.

As bishop, Gonzi was in a position of authority to advocate the Church against the government, regardless of the party in power. Because Gonzi considered the Church itself to be above any civil authority, both he and the Church came into almost continual conflict with the government. He also feared that Protestantism was making inroads among the Maltese. Although he was never anti-British, the colonial authorities feared him. As bishop of Gozo, he joined with the archbishop of Malta in the issuance of the pastoral letter against the followers of **Lord Strickland**. During **World War II**, Gonzi allayed British fears about him when he declared that hoarding food was a mortal sin, causing the Gozitans to send their surplus wheat to Malta, helping with the shortages there.

After a long period of negotiation among the Colonial Office in London, the Holy See in the Vatican and various factions in Malta, Gonzi became archbishop in December 1943 and was immediately awarded the KBE. He issued an order that forbade priests from becoming candidates for any political office. Although he favored the MLP under **Paul Boffa**, when **Dom Mintoff** took over as leader, the antagonism between the two eventually prompted Gonzi to issue a pastoral letter against him. His opposition to **Giorgio Borg Olivier** was more subtle, but it was there. Gonzi's working class background bought him considerable popularity among the masses. Among the clergy, he gained a loyalty through patronage. In a strange way, it was the colonial authorities that supported the political strength of the Maltese Church.

When **independence** came, that support was gone. After a lengthy series of confrontations, debates, and negotiations, Gonzi was forced to agree to a lessening of Church authority in civil matters and to lift the pastoral interdict. Just prior to his resignation as archbishop in 1976, he declared that "Malta is spiritually and morally sick." A small man, Archbishop Michael Gonzi played a big part in the modern history of Malta. He died on 22 January 1984. *See also* CREMONA, MONSIGNOR PAWLU; GERADA, BISHOP EMMANUEL; LIGUTTI, MONSIGNOR LUIGI.

GORT, LORD, VC, GCB, DSO, MVO, MC, ADC, (1886–1946). General John Standish Surtees Prendergast Verecker Viscount Gort became **governor** and military commander in chief in Malta on 7 May 1942, relieving General **William Dobbie**. He had been commander of the **British** Forces in France early in the war and, in that capacity, had to suffer the military indignity of the Dunkirk evacuation. Early on, it was feared that he had been brought to Malta to oversee a similar disaster, namely a surrender. However, he was slowly able to gain the respect of both the civilian and the military populations as he led them through the darkest days of the war. He kept a lower profile than did his predecessor, even as he paid more attention to the physical needs of the two populations.

As the war in the Mediterranean became more favorable to the Allies, Lord Gort had to act as host and guide to a long list of visiting dignitaries, including King George VI, **Winston Churchill, Franklin D. Roosevelt, Dwight Eisenhower**, and many of the other top officers of the Allied military forces. He was a member of the official party accepting the official surrender of the Italian fleet in Malta.

To show their gratitude and respect for Gort, the Maltese held a public event in his honor on 12 March 1944, in Zebbug. On behalf of the Band and Allied Clubs of Malta and **Gozo**, he was presented with an elaborately decorated and inscribed "Sword of Honour" as a token of "the People's admiration, gratitude, devotion and love." Another large public gathering was held on 5 August 1944, in **Valletta**, a goodbye celebration as Lord Gort left Malta for his new post as high commissioner and commander in chief, Palestine. *See also* GEORGE CROSS; WORLD WAR II.

GOVERNORS OF MALTA. The first **British** administration was led by Captain **Alexander Ball**, who was appointed civil commissioner, followed by three others. Lieutenant-General **Sir Thomas Maitland** was the first of a total of 34 governors who served as chief administrators of Malta under the **British**. Upon Malta's gaining its **independence** in 1964, then ruling governor Sir Maurice Dorman continued representing the British government as governor general for seven years until **Dom Mintoff** requested that a Maltese should hold the post. Dorman resigned, whereupon Sir **Anthony Joseph Mamo** became the first Maltese to hold the post, until 1974, when Malta became a Republic and he was elected **president**.

Civil Commissioners of Malta

Captain Alexander Ball	1799–1801
Major-General Henry Pigot	1801
Sir Charles Cameron	1801–2
Rear-Admiral Alexander Ball	1802–9
Lieutenant-General Sir Hildebrand Oakes	1810–13

Governors of Malta

Lieutenant-General Sir Thomas Maitland	1813–24
General the Marquess of Hastings	1824–26
Major-General Sir Frederic Ponsonby	1827–36
Lieutenant-General Sir Henry Bouverie	1836–43
Lieutenant-General Sir Patrick Stuart	1843–47
Richard More O'Farrall	1847–51
Major-General Sir William Reid	1851–58
Lieutenant-General John Gaspard Le Merchant	1858–64
Lieutenant-General Sir Henry Storcks	1864–67
General Sir Patrick Grant	1867–72
General Sir Charles Van Straubenzee	1872–78
General Sir Arthur Borton	1878–84

General Sir Lintorn Simmons	1884–88
Lieutenant-General Sir Henry Torrens	1888–90
Lieutenant-General Sir Henry Smyth	1890–93
General Sir Arthur Freemantle	1893–99
Lieutenant-General Lord Grenfell	1899–1903
General Sir Mansfield Clarke	1903–7
Lieutenant-General Sir Henry Grant	1907–9
General Sir Leslie Rundle	1909–15
Field-Marshal Lord Methuen	1915–19
Field-Marshal Viscount Plumer	1919–24
General Sir Walter Congreve	1924–27
General Sir John du Cane	1927–31
General Sir David Campbell	1931–36
General Sir Charles Bonham Carter	1936–40
Lieutenant-General **Sir William Dobbie**	1940–42
Field-Marshal Viscount Gort	1942–44
Lieutenant-General Sir Edmond Schreiber	1944–46
Sir Francis Douglas	1946–49
Sir Gerald Creasy	1949–54
Major-General Sir Robert Laycock	1954–59
Admiral Sir Guy Grantham	1959–62
Sir Maurice Dorman	1962–64

Governors General of Malta

Sir Maurice Dorman	1964–71
Sir Anthony Joseph Mamo	1971–74

GOZO. The sister island to Malta, Gozo is 67.3 square kilometers in area and has a population of approximately 32,000. The closest of the Maltese islands to **Sicily**, it was probably the first of the archipelago to be settled and has been inhabited for over 7,000 years. Gozo's name has changed over the centuries. The **Phoenicians** called it Gwl, probably because its shape was reminiscent of their ships of that name. The **Greeks** called it Gaulos, their name for the same kind of ship. To the **Romans** it was Gaulus, and to the **Byzantines**, Gaudes. When the **Arabs** arrived, they called it Ghawdex (pronounced "Aw-desh"), the name still used in Maltese today. In medieval times, a

Latinized version used by church scholars was Gaudisium, synonymous with the Latin word for "joy." The **Castilians** used their own word for "joy" and called the island Gozo, the name still used by non-Maltese to this day.

The inhabitants of Gozo are, of course, Maltese, but they also believe they have a higher distinction—they are Gozitans. History supports their opinion; there have been more persons from Gozo gaining high national offices than the size of the population would suggest. If one were to characterize the two islands by color, Malta is light beige, and Gozo is green. Legend has it (with the support of many scholars) that Gozo is Ogygia, the island where Odysseus was held captive by Calypso for seven years. It is possible to visit "Calypso's Cave," and most tourists do.

Gozo, which suffers from "double insularity" (an island that is mainly accessed from another island), has benefited since Malta's accession to the **European Union (EU)** from EU funds as a "special region."

GRAND MASTERS OF THE ORDER OF ST. JOHN (IN MALTA). The original title of the person chosen to lead the **Knights of the Order of St. John** was "Master of the Hospital and the Custodian of the Poor of Christ," which was shortened to "grand master" in 1267. The grand master, elected for life, was an absolute ruler. Elections to choose a replacement were held almost immediately upon the death of a grand master in order to avoid the possibility that the pope might interfere in the selection process. Twenty-eight of the 78 Knights elected grand master served the Order while it was in Malta. They are as follows:

Fra' Philippe Villiers de L'Isle-Adam (France)
    13 November 1521–21 August 1534
(elected in Rhodes)
Fra' Pierino del Ponte (Italy)
    26 August 1534–17 November 1535
Fra' Didier de Saint-Jaille (France)
    22 November 1535–26 September 1536
Fra' Juan de Omedes (Aragon)
    20 October 1536–6 September 1553

Fra' Claude de la Sengle (France)
11 September 1553–18 August 1557
Fra' Jean Parisot de la Valette (Provence)
21 August 1557–21 August 1568
Fra' Pietro del Monte (Italy)
23 August 1568–26 January 1572
Fra' Jean Levesque de la Cassiere (Auvergne)
30 January 1572–31 December 1581
Fra' Hughes de Loubens de Verdalle (Provence)
12 January 1582–4 May 1595
Fra' Martin Garzes (Aragon)
8 May 1595–7 February 1601
Fra' Alof de Wignacourt (France)
10 February 1601–14 September 1622
Fra' Luis Mendez de Vasconcellos (Castile)
17 September 1622–7 March 1623
Fra' Antoine de Paule (Provence)
10 March 1623–9 June 1636
Fra' Jean Paul Lascaris de Castellar (Provence)
13 June 1636–14 August 1657
Fra' Martin de Redin (Aragon)
17 August 1657–6 February 1660
Fra' Annet de Clermont-Gessan (Auvergne)
9 February 1660–2 June 1660
Fra' Rafael Cottoner (Aragon)
5 June 1660–20 October 1663
Fra' Nicholas Cottoner (Aragon)
23 October 1663–29 April 1680
Fra' Gregorio Carafa (Italy)
2 May 1680–21 July 1690
Fra' Adrien de Wignacourt (France)
24 July 1690–4 February 1697
Fra' Ramon Perellos y Roccaful (Aragon)
7 February 1697–10 January 1720
Fra' Marcantonio Zondadari (Italy)
13 January 1720–16 June 1722
Fra' Antonio Manoel de Vilhena (Castile)
19 June 1722–10 December 1736

Fra' Ramon Despuig (Aragon)
  16 December 1736–15 January 1741
Fra' Emmanuel Pinto de Fonseca (Castile)
  18 January 1741 –23 January 1773
Fra' Francisco Ximenes de Texada (Aragon)
  28 January 1773–9 November 1775
Fra' Emmanuel de Rohan (France)
  12 November 1775–13 July 1797
Fra' Ferdinand von Hompesch (Germany)
  17 July 1797–12 May 1805
  (evicted from Malta in June 1798)

See also AUBERGES; DRAGUT'S RAID; GREAT CARRACK
OF RHODES; GREAT SIEGE OF 1565; KNIGHTS AFTER
RHODES.

GREAT CARRACK OF RHODES. It was probably the largest ship
in the Mediterranean at the time and was the flagship of the **Knights
of St. John.** Named the *Santa Maria*, it had eight decks and could
stay at sea without resupply for six months, a lengthy time considering that it carried over 700 men, including crew members, Knights,
soldiers, and **slaves.** One feature, unusual for the time, was that it
had ovens for baking bread. The two forward masts carried square-
rigged sails, and the two aft were lateen rigged. It was armed with
over 70 cannons of various sizes. The *Santa Maria* carried the **grand
master** of the Order to Malta after the surrender at Rhodes. In 1532,
an accident caused an explosion, which resulted in its total destruction in Grand Harbour. A new, even larger carrack, named the *Santa
Anna*, was built as a replacement. Both carracks (sometimes called
carracka) presented a beautiful and fearsome sight. Soon, however,
the expense of operating the huge ships, coupled with their reduced
effectiveness against newer and faster ships, made them obsolete. In
1548, the *Santa Anna* was dismantled and the salvage used to create
the major portions of three more modern fighting ships.

GREAT SIEGE OF 1565. The Great Siege of 1565, in which an attacking force of Ottoman **Turks** numbering approximately 40,000
were successfully repelled by the vastly outnumbered defenders of

Malta, is one of the two most celebrated heroic events of Maltese history (the other being the siege of **World War II**).

Suleiman "the Magnificent," under whom the Ottoman empire had reached the peak of its military, economic, and cultural power, was determined to conquer the Order of the **Knights of St. John** to put an end to their marauding attacks on merchant ships in the Mediterranean. As a young ruler in 1522, he had made the mistake of allowing the Knights to leave their stronghold on the island of Rhodes after having defeated them.

Forewarned about the intentions of the Turks to invade the islands, the Knights brought to Malta one of the foremost of European military engineers, Bartolomeo Genga, to design a new fortress on the Sciberras peninsula, the hilltop where the city of **Valletta** was later built. Genga died in Malta before any work could be started, and the work was stopped in 1563 to concentrate efforts on the strengthening existing fortifications instead.

As soon as the Turkish fleet was sighted on 18 May 1565, the preparations for the coming battle intensified. Against this tremendous force of arms, **Grand Master Jean Parisot de la Valette** had approximately 8,500 men under his command. This included 592 Knights, not all of whom were physically fit for battle; 5,830 Maltese militia and irregulars; 1,230 mercenary soldiers, mostly from Spain; several hundred Italian volunteers; and a small group of galley slaves released under pledge of faithful service. All buildings outside Birgu and Senglea were razed to the ground to avoid their being used as cover for sharpshooters. The farmers were ordered to bring all animals and crops inside the walls of Birgu, **Mdina**, and the Citadel in **Gozo**. Everyone was ordered to take refuge within the fortified cities of Birgu, Senglea, and Bormla. A few Knights plus cavalrymen were sent to Mdina. There is no record of the **Maltese nobility** participating in either the preparations or the battles. They stayed within their homes in Mdina, probably out of resentment that the Order did not consider them qualified to become members and because they had not been consulted about battle plans and defenses.

The Turkish invading force consisted of almost 200 ships, including 138 war galleys commanded by Admiral Piali Pasha, grandson-in-law of Suleiman. The ships carried about 40,000 of the best soldiers Suleiman could muster, including Janissaries reared from

The Ggantija ("Geegahnteeyah") Temple is from 3500 BCE and the Xewkija ("Showkeejah") Church is from 1953 CE.

Balluta Bay with the only skyscraper in Malta, the Hilton Tower.

Classic Malta Bus.

Florianna, a town just outside of Valletta, seen from the Barrakka Gardens inside Valletta. The parish church of Florianna, dedicated to St. Publius, one of three patron saints of Malta, is seen in background.

The Azure Window in Dwejra Bay, Gozo.

View of Valletta from Ta' Xbiex ("Tasch Beesch").

View of Auberge de Castille, the Office of the Prime Minister in Valletta.

Cart ruts nicknamed "Clapham Junction."

A globigerina quarry in Gozo. Most buildings in Malta are constructed using this soft, honey-colored stone.

The Grand Harbor and Fort St. Angelo viewed from Valletta.

Valletta, St. Paul Street.

Mnajdra Temple.

infancy for fighting, and Layalars, religious fanatics seeking death in a "holy cause" whom the Turks used to spearhead all their battles. In command of the army was Mustapha Pasha, a veteran of the Turkish defeat of the Knights at Rhodes.

On 21 May, an assault on Birgu was made despite Sultan Suleiman's order to wait for the arrival of **Dragut**—a Turkish corsair fighting on behalf of the Suleiman, he knew the islands well. He would have devised a more successful strategy, had he been there in time. A fierce hand-to-hand fight outside the walls of Birgu raged for six hours, repelling the attackers with heavy loss of life on both sides.

The Turks next attacked Fort St. Elmo on the tip of Sciberras peninsula, estimating that it would fall in four or five days. Great cannons were placed on the hilltop above the fort to begin pulverizing the walls. But because much of the defensive works had been cut into the solid rock, the defenders remained mostly unscathed. On 29 May, another 250 defenders were sent across the harbor from Fort St. Angelo, bringing the total in Fort St. Elmo to 1,500.

Soon after these reinforcements arrived, the first mass assault started, led by the Janissaries. They were beaten off with a variety of weapons, including fire and hot oil. The sweltering heat and humidity of Malta's summer made fighting difficult for both sides but especially for the Knights in their heavy armor. St. Elmo was under continual cannon bombardment. Massive waves of attacks on 10 and 16 June left piled up dead bodies in the ditches by the ruined walls. On 23 June, Fort St. Elmo finally fell, killing all defenders except for five Maltese soldiers, who managed to escape by swimming across Grand Harbour.

The invaders took no prisoners and went so far as to behead the dead Knights and send the bodies floating on wooden crosses past Fort St. Angelo. Enraged, Valette had all his Turkish prisoners decapitated and sent their heads as cannon balls fired across to the Turkish lines. The fall of St. Elmo had cost the invaders dearly. Dead were Dragut and several other top officers plus over 8,000 soldiers. A few days later, the invaders lost another 3,000 men in two separate attempts to take Birgu. On 2 August, a tremendous bombardment of St. Angelo began.

Five more days of fierce fighting followed, but just when a Turkish victory in Senglea seemed certain, Mustapha Pasha sounded the retreat. The cause of this amazing turnaround was the action of the small force of the Order's cavalry, which came out of Mdina at the peak of the battle. They attacked the huge, minimally defended Turkish camp at the harbor, killing thousands of sick and wounded soldiers, burning stores, stampeding horses, and creating a general panic.

When he heard of the attack, Mustapha mistakenly thought that a large relief force from Sicily was preparing to surround him and, thus, sounded the retreat. Discovering the truth, he became enraged and called for two additional assaults. During the first, the 70 year-old Valette, led a charge, which rallied a victory from what seemed to be certain defeat. In a second assault, on 23 August, the defense won a fragile victory thanks in large part to the sick and wounded who joined in the fighting. Although minor skirmishes continued, the invaders were badly demoralized.

On 7 September, promised Sicilian reinforcements arrived at the northern end of the island, and Mustapha ordered a hasty retreat. By the next day, the remaining 15,000 Turkish soldiers departed Malta. When word of the victory spread throughout Christian Europe, there was great rejoicing, which resulted in an outpouring of wealth and riches upon the Order of St. John as a thank offering. *See also* GREAT CARRACK OF RHODES; KNIGHTS AFTER RHODES; LANGUES.

GREEK PRESENCE. About 600 BCE, the **Phoenicians** controlled the North African coast and the west and north of **Sicily**. Greece was in control of southern **Italy** and the eastern and northeastern shores of Sicily. That there were no hostilities between the two powers seems to indicate that they had entered into some kind of agreement of peaceful coexistence. As Malta was part of the Phoenician area of domination, it was spared any Greek attempts to change the status. However, there is evidence of **trade** with Greece, and there are even some Greek temple building ruins.

– H –

HAPSBURG DYNASTY. The marriage of Ferdinand II to Isabelle of Castile in 1479 politically reunited Spain. Phillip, archduke of

Austria and duke of Burgundy, married their daughter, Joanna. Their firstborn son became Charles V, the Holy Roman Emperor. Their youngest son, Ferdinand, married Anna, sister of Louis II of Hungary and Bohemia. A series of favorable marriages such as these brought to the dynasty an empire "over which the sun never set." In 1530, at the urging of Pope Clement VIII, Charles V granted to the **Order of St. John** the islands of the Maltese Archipelago with the added obligation to maintain the defenses of Tripoli in North Africa. In exchange for all of this, the Order was made responsible for the payment of an annual rent of one falcon to be paid to the Holy Roman Emperor.

HEALTH AND HEALTH CARE. Based on the **British** system, Malta's public health care is comprehensive, equitable, and fully integrated at the national level under the regulation of the Ministry of Health. Funded by general taxes and national insurance, it is available free of charge to all Maltese (and European Economic Area citizens with **European Union** health identity cards). All drugs used during in-patient treatment and for the first three days after discharge are free of charge for the patient. Maltese citizens who qualify because of low income or selected chronic diseases are entitled to free drugs dispensed at government-run pharmacies. In 2001, almost 9 percent of GDP was spent on health care, 70 percent paid by the government and 30 percent privately. Routine dental care is provided by licensed private practitioners and paid out of pocket by the patient.

A recent survey determined that the Maltese are not very physically active. They are the least likely of all EU citizens to take a 10-minute walk. The survey also found that over a third claimed to have been on a diet in the past year, and 78 percent of respondents claimed to be in "good" health.

Life expectancy in Malta (2002) is 72 years for men and 76 years for **women**. The main causes of death in Malta are circulatory disease and cancer—the former being almost twice as common as the latter. The most frequent cancers are nonmelanoma skin cancer, lung cancer, colorectal cancer, and breast cancer in women. In all but the skin and breast cancer, the Maltese incidences are below the EU average. Diabetes is among the top five most significant diseases in Malta and is expected to increase by about 50 percent from 39,000 cases in 2000 to 57,000 by 2030.

New laws against smoking in restaurants and bars, while not yet strictly enforced, should discourage smoking and reduce the incidence of lung cancer. Meanwhile, binge drinking, especially among youth, seems to have become a problem in recent years. The percentage of 11-year-olds responding to a survey that they got drunk within the last 30 days rose from almost 0 percent to 10 percent among boys and 5 percent among girls. For 15-year-olds, that percentage climbed to 29 and 15 percent respectively, the highest in the EU.

The Ministry of Health is responsible for funding, managing, and regulating all health care in Malta. Over 6,000 workers are directly employed in the system, which includes seven public and three private hospitals in addition to a 1,000-bed facility for the aged. Nine public health centers, distributed throughout Malta and **Gozo**, serve self-referred patients seeking general, noncritical care.

Planning to supplement the main hospital on Malta, St. Luke's, with a state-of-the-art acute care, teaching, and research facility began in early 1990. The project's ballooning size and cost led to considerable political controversy, delaying completion several times. Originally intended to include 650 beds, its capacity was increased to 800 beds and 8,000 rooms when the **Malta Labour Party (MLP)** briefly came back into power. A no-confidence vote in **Parliament** in 2004, triggered by cost overruns, failed by only four votes to dislodge the **Nationalist** government. The hospital was scheduled to open in 2005. In fact, it was opened in November 2007 at a total cost of over 600 million **euros**, more than three times the original estimate. Christened "Mater Dei," it is one of the largest hospital buildings in the world, and its operating costs are currently estimated at about 10 million euros per month, a strain on the government's finances that is sure to continue, causing great controversy in the nation. One year after Mater Dei's opening, a shortage of beds was already being lamented. In an attempt to decentralize government, providing more transparency and oversight, legislation was enacted in 2003, establishing an independent Medical Council to regulate standards of ethics and practice.

Health care has a long history in Malta, beginning with the temple builders. Evidence of pottery forms depicting diseased body parts has led some to conclude that these were offerings to the gods in hopes of a cure the for the donors' afflictions. The **Romans** left more convincing evidence of medical practice: carvings of surgical instruments on a stone slab in the catacombs at **Rabat**. A tombstone found near Mdina is inscribed in **Greek**, identifying a Christian physician named Domesticus.

The earliest hospitals in Malta were established around the middle of the 14th century, certainly by 1372 when a Franciscan friar was recorded as being in charge of a hospital named Santo Spirito in **Mdina**. Beginning in the 16th century, with the arrival of the **Knights of St. John**, whose origins as Hospitallers to the crusaders made them eminently knowledgeable in medicine, health care got a significant boost. The knights founded a hospital called "The **Sacred Infirmary**" in Birgu where they first settled. Their skill in surgery and knowledge about the importance of sanitary procedures (such as the use of silver plates and cutlery) are credited with helping them defeat the attacking **Turkish** forces, who, lacking such care and regard for a sanitary environment, suffered far greater losses due to injury and infections. In 1574, the Sacred Infirmary was relocated to a larger facility in **Valletta**. A separate hospital for women called the "Casetta," was opened in Valletta in 1659 by **Grand Master** Martin de Redin. Health care was also available in the towns and villages via special services provided to poor women.

In 1815, after the **plague** outbreak of 1813–14, the **British** established a quarantine facility, the Lazzaretto on Manoel Island, and united all hospitals in Malta under common management. Sir **Themistocles Zammit**, a medical health officer, pushed to introduce chlorination of the water supplies and, in 1887, helped to discover the cause of "**Malta fever**," a disease spread by the thousands of milk goats running free in Valletta.

In 1936, the Public Health Department was established, taking charge of all hospitals, including charitable hospitals initially established to serve the poor, which were from then on used by the general public needing medical care.

The British greatly expanded hospital capacity on the islands due to the large number of casualties of **World War I** and **World War II**. Malta continued the tradition of the Order as a place of healing for sick and wounded, becoming a center for treatment of thousands of wounded soldiers, earning Malta the nickname "nurse of the Mediterranean."

In 1980, under the socialist government of **Dom Mintoff**, hospital admission and treatment was made free of charge. Doctors went on strike in 1977 when Mintoff forced them to work at public clinics and capped their wages. He tightened the control of the government over health care by moving the authority to license doctors from the **president** to a minister. Many doctors fled the islands, mainly to Great Britain. The strike lasted 10 years, ending in 1987 when a Nationalist government was returned to power. There was a silver lining to the strike: many doctors who had left Malta to practice medicine in other developed countries returned in 1987, bringing with them new skills and knowledge to the benefit of medical care on the islands. Recently, a serious brain drain of doctors leaving Malta has been occurring again: over half of doctors educated in Malta have left for Great Britain and America where salaries and working conditions are significantly better. The socialized medicine has also created bottlenecks involving excessive waiting periods for patients seeking medical treatment For example, in June 2008, a backlog of over 9,000 patients waiting up to two years to see an optometrist was reported in Parliament.

In a 2007 report by an independent rating agency that evaluated 29 countries, including all EU members, Malta ranked 20th in the overall rankings, just ahead of Slovenia and Greece. *See also* PLAGUE.

HERITAGE MALTA. Recognizing the importance of its national cultural heritage sites to **tourism** and eager to tap into **European Union (EU)** funds, the Maltese government passed the Cultural Heritage Act in 2002, establishing Heritage Malta as the national agency responsible for the "management, conservation, interpretation and marketing" of Malta's numerous national **museums** and sites. Thirteen museums and seven UNESCO World Heritage Sites are some of the 36 sites under its management, including Fort St. Angelo, the **Megalithic Temples**, chapels, caves, and catacombs.

The head office of Heritage Malta is located in **Valletta** in a building that itself has an extensive history. Built in 1533, it originally housed the Collegium Melitense, which later evolved into the original campus of the Royal **University of Malta**. Heritage Malta has the following museums and sites under its responsibility:

Museums:

Archaeology Museum, Citadella at Victoria, **Gozo**
Folklore Museum, Citadella at Victoria, Gozo
Ghar Dalam Cave and Museum, Birzebbuga
Inquisitor's Palace, Birgu
Malta Maritime Museum, Birgu
National Museum for the Maltese Language, Birgu
National Museum of Fine Arts, Valletta
National Museum of Archaeology, Valletta
National Museum of Natural History, **Mdina**
National War Museum, Valletta
Natural Science Museum, Citadella at Victoria, Gozo
Old Prison, Citadella at Victoria, Gozo
Palace Armoury, Valletta
Domus Romana, **Rabat**

Temples and Catacombs:

Abbatija tad-Dejr catacombs, Rabat
Borg in-Nadur temple, near Birzebbuga
Ggantija Temples (UNESCO World Heritage Site), Gozo
Hagar Qim Temple (UNESCO World Heritage Site), near Qrendi
Hypogeum of Hal-Saflieni (UNESCO World Heritage Site), Paola
Mnajdra Temples (UNESCO World Heritage Site), near Qrendi
Skorba Temples, near Zebbiegh in Mgarr
St. Paul's Catacombs, Rabat
Salina Catacombs, near Naxxar
Ta' Hagrat Temples, near Zebbiegh in Mgarr
Tal-Mintna Catacombs, Mqabba
Tarxien Temples, Tarxien
Tas-Silg Temples, near Marsaxlokk

Other sites:

Roman Baths, Ghajn Tuffieha
San Pawl Milqi, Roman villa, Burmurrad
State Rooms, **Grandmaster's** Palace, Valletta
Ta' Kola Windmill, Xaghra, Gozo

HMS *ILLUSTRIOUS*. Late in the evening of 10 January 1941, the new aircraft carrier HMS *Illustrious* limped into Grand Harbour, listing badly and steering only with the engines. While guarding a convoy for Greece about 80 kilometers (50 miles) west of the Maltese Islands, it was attacked by 87 German dive-bombers and sustained six serious hits. This was the first major attack by the German Fliegerkorps X in the Mediterranean area. Lost were 126 dead and 91 wounded, and the ship itself seemed to be mortally wounded with a caved-in flight deck and all aircraft elevators out of commission. First estimates were that it would take many months just to get it ready to put to sea and over a year to have it ready to fight again. Repairs were started immediately by over a thousand Maltese **dockyard** workers of every specialty. The ship was quickly painted yellow to blend in with the surrounding limestone bluffs. A bombing raid was expected at any time, but none came. In the meantime, all of the guns around the harbor and on the ships in the harbor were directed to form a blanket pattern in an attempt to disrupt low-level bombing attacks.

Six days later, in the early afternoon, 70 German bombers, escorted by several dozen **Italian** fighters, arrived to begin the attack. At the same time, the most intensive antiaircraft barrage ever in the defense of a single ship was begun. RAF Hurricane fighters managed to down five of the attackers. The result was a failure for the Axis force, which returned for a second try in the afternoon. That was no more successful than the first. Three days later, on Sunday morning, an even heavier attack was made, but again, the ship escaped serious damage. That evening, under the cover of darkness, the *Illustrious* left Malta and one and a half days later was in Alexandria. After additional repairs, it sailed to the United States for a complete overhaul. It was later returned to duty in the Mediterranean.

HOWARD, JOSEPH (1862–1925). Malta's first **prime minister**, Howard served from 1921 to 1923. Although his **Unione Politica Maltese** Party gained 14 seats in the Legislative Assembly in the 1921 **elections**, that number still fell short of a majority in the 32-seat Assembly. As a result, a government had to be formed through a coalition with the **Malta Labour Party**, which had seven seats. Howard's selection as prime minister was unusual in that his personal views were very close to those of the **Constitutional Party**, which also gained seven seats. The first act passed by the new government was the **Religion** of Malta Declaration Act, proclaiming Roman Catholicism as the official religion of all of Malta. Its passage was not without controversy and was but a preliminary to many later debates over the Church-state relationship.

HYZLER, DR. ALBERT V. (1916–1993). Born on 20 November 1916, Hyzler studied medicine at the Royal **University of Malta** and became a doctor, like his father (leader of the Democratic Action Party), as well as followed in his father's footsteps into politics. Elected to **Parliament** in 1947, he served as minister of health in the government of **Paul Boffa**. Hyzler had to resign his ministry position because of constant disagreements with **Prime Minister Borg Olivier** and joined the **Malta Labour Party** in 1953. He successfully won subsequent **elections**, spent a month in jail after being arrested during the 1958 riots against the **British**, and retired in 1976. He served as acting **president** from 27 December 1981 to 15 February 1982.

– I –

ILLEGAL IMMIGRATION. In recent years, Europe has witnessed a significant increase in the flow of economic and political refugees from Africa, causing a major immigration crisis. As the southernmost and smallest country in the **European Union (EU)**, Malta has been experiencing particular difficulties in dealing with this problem. Almost 13,000 illegal migrants have landed in Malta in the seven years since 2002. In 2005 alone, 48 boats arrived, carrying 1,822 persons. Lacking proper facilities, Malta houses the refugees in military barracks and tents under primitive conditions.

On several occasions, migrants in confinement escaped by knocking down flimsy fencing but were quickly recaptured. In January 2005, a group of detainees denied asylum and in the process of being deported, rebelled at the Hal Safi detention center. Maltese police, brought in to quell the uprising, were accused of using excessive force. An official investigation into the matter, while admitting that one policeman had struck a detainee who was on the ground, declared that the police were justified in their actions and blamed poor supervision and inadequate facilities. The incident was widely carried in the **media**, putting Malta in an unfavorable light. An inspection team sent to Malta by the **United Nations** High Commissioner for Refugees (UNHCR) to investigate the situation complained of deplorable conditions.

Which country is responsible for dealing with illegal immigrants is a question that has caused friction between Malta, **Italy**, and Spain, the three EU countries most severely affected. On 26 October 2004, the EU Commission created FRONTEX as a specialized and independent body headquartered in Warsaw to coordinate border security operations of member states. In April 2006, the European Parliament passed a resolution to address the immigration crisis, pledging to give Malta financial aid to cope with illegal migrants. Malta spent over 5.8 million **euros** on over 1,800 illegal immigrants arriving in 2006 alone. About 1,000 of these remained in detention at the beginning of 2007.

The EU Parliament also pledged to revise the Dublin II Regulation, which holds the country of first entry responsible for dealing with illegal immigrants and asylum seekers.

In July 2006, a Spanish ship carrying 51 refugees was denied access to Maltese shores because the refugees had been picked up in Libyan waters. Malta transported three persons needing hospitalization to shore but forced the ship to remain at sea for eight days until Spain agreed to take the refugees. In May 2007, 27 shipwrecked Africans spent several hours clinging to a Maltese-owned tuna pen that was being towed by Maltese fishermen in the Mediterranean. The fishermen would not let the refugees board their ship, leaving them in the water clinging to the pen until they were rescued by an Italian vessel and taken to the Italian island of Lampedusa.

These incidents and numerous others like them have caused a major international uproar, putting Malta on the defensive. The issue has caused a rise in anti-EU sentiment among the Maltese and is partly to blame for the emergence of a new right-wing party, Azzjoni Nazzjonali, formed in June 2007. Illegal immigration is certain to continue as a major problem for Malta and the EU for a long time.

INDEPENDENCE. For centuries, Malta enjoyed intermittent periods of limited independent control over its internal affairs as various rulers appointed bishops, the **Universitas**, or consuls to represent the Maltese to the **Romans**, **Aragonese**, or later the **British** government. Had the uprising against the **French** succeeded, or the Treaty of Amiens been accepted, Malta might already have gained its independence at the beginning of the 19th century with the expulsion of the French. Certainly, the Maltese, who invited the British to Malta, must have had a sense of being independent at the time, but this too quickly proved to be an illusion.

Freedom from foreign rule came in fits and starts as the British granted constitutional rights only to have them withdrawn and replaced by others. **World War II** had a great democratizing effect: it built self-confidence in its survivors, especially the **women** who had been called to take over the jobs of men away at war, and its aftermath revealed the weaknesses of political institutions. The result was an increased demand for political freedom. The time had come for the powers of Europe to disentangle themselves from their colonial past by granting independence to their colonies. Malta, like many others, had outlived its usefulness to Great Britain, which could no longer afford to support it, neither financially nor militarily. In 1947, a new **constitution** was granted by Britain, restoring the sharing of rule (first introduced in 1921), under which the Maltese could decide local issues, leaving defense and foreign policy decisions to the British. This newest constitution gave women the right to vote, abolished the Senate, and replaced it with an enlarged Legislative Assembly of 40 democratically elected members.

The Maltese citizens were divided about the future of their islands. Not all were in favor of the push for independence: **Dom Mintoff**, leader of the **Malta Labour Party (MLP)**, pursued integration with Great Britain. He thought Malta should become a part of the United Kingdom and envisioned three Maltese as elected members of the British Parliament. This was opposed by the **Catholic Church**, which was concerned about its possible status in a predominantly Protestant country, while others, worried about losing their jobs, also preferred the status quo. The **Nationalist Party (NP)** leaders wanted dominion status for Malta.

Meanwhile, the British government, seeing the division among the Maltese, decided against integration, so independence became the most widely agreed solution. Achieving it took a decade and a half.

Finally, on 21 September 1964, Malta and Great Britain signed the Anglo-Maltese Mutual Defense Agreement, and Malta became a sovereign nation within the British **Commonwealth.** The "Mintoffians," upset that this had occurred during the time the NP was in power, steadfastly maintained that true independence was not achieved until Mintoff had renegotiated the final withdrawal of British troops, which occurred on 31 March 1979. Others thought that independence was achieved on 13 December 1974, when Malta became a republic. Even today, the debate among the Maltese continues as to which day should be celebrated as the one "real" independence day.

"INNU MALTI." In 1923, Maltese poet Mgr. Dun Karm Psaila wrote the lyrics to accompany music composed by Dr. Robert Sammut, and the piece became known as "Innu Malti." Originally written primarily for school pupils, the piece gradually began to be played and sung at a variety of public events. With the passage of time, its popularity increased, and it was officially recognized as the national anthem at the time of **independence** in 1964. A short but beautiful melody coupled with words of equal beauty, "Innu Malti" stirs strong emotions in the Maltese people. *See also* PSAILA, MONSIGNOR DUN KARM.

INQUISITION. Tribunals of the Inquisition differed in method and purpose from nation to nation. In Malta, the primary objective was that of reforming morals among the Knights, clergy, and the religious. Flirting with the opposite sex or with adolescents was only one of the vices it sought to correct. A secondary role of the inquisitor was protecting the public from the dangers of heresies, mainly those brought to Malta by outsiders militating against the Roman **Catholic** faith. Such heresies included the failure to accept the teachings or the authority of the Church, studying or teaching a publicly dishonored **religion** (for example, Lutheranism or Calvinism), reading forbidden books, necromancy with the dead, or sorcery with the devil to gain worldly goods. The penalties were wide ranging and included spiritual penance, confiscation of property, confinement to village or domicile, imprisonment, hard labor, and, in extreme cases, death. The goal of the Inquisition was penitential, aiming at the persuasion of those accused to confess their heresy and submit themselves to the Church.

The earliest records in Malta list a regional or proinquisitor in 1433, but the Tribunal came into greatest authority in 1561 when the Holy Office in Rome conferred upon Mgr. Cubella the fullest power to investigate and proceed against all acts of heresy. The result was the creation of an unusual situation at the highest level of ecclesiastical authority—three persons of virtually equal authority. The **grand master** of the **Knights of St. John** was officially an equal of all the monarchs of Christendom. But by granting Malta to the Knights, the Holy Roman Emperor had reserved the right to nominate the local bishop, who was then given a voice in the Order's affairs. With Cubella as inquisitor, a three-way struggle for authority and deference began to take place. Each attempted to shelter his own followers from the actions of the others, thus creating a climate that weakened rather than strengthened the Catholic faith.

A building located in Vittoriosa (Birgu) originally served as the Court of Justice before it was renovated and expanded into a palazzo with courtyard in 1574 to serve as the office and residence of the first inquisitor. It was further modified by the 61 inquisitors who served over the following three centuries until the inquisition was abolished by Napoleon in 1878. The jail cells located on the first and second floor contain numerous carvings of historical interest made by prisoners in the soft limestone walls. Today the three-story structure houses a **museum**, which often serves as a venue for special exhibitions and is now under the control and management of **Heritage Malta**.

INTERNMENT AND DEPORTATION. At the outbreak of **World War II**, the **British** began taking into custody all those suspected of being dangerous because of nationality or political sympathies. The first were those of German, Austrian, or **Italian** birth, including a number of female "artistes" from the Strait Street cabarets. In May 1940, a number of Maltese were interned without due process, particularly those leaders of the **Nationalist Party** known to be or alleged to be Italian sympathizers. Included were **Dr. Enrico Mizzi**, the leader of the party, and several business leaders and other professionals. In June 1940, the chief justice and president of the Court of

Appeal, Sir Arturo Mercieca, received his summons. The internees were kept in Fort Salvatore in the Cottonera Lines, briefly confined in the Corradino prisons, and later moved to the St. Agatha convent in **Rabat**.

In early February 1942, the British government decided to exile 43 (the majority) of the group including Mrs. Mercieca and two of their children. A court ruling found the internment illegal on the grounds that no crime had been committed, so a change in the law to legalize the deportation was debated on 9 February in the Council of Government. Arguing against the change, Council Member Sir **Ugo Mifsud** made such an impassioned speech defending his fellow Maltese's human rights that he suffered a heart attack and died two days later. The change in law was voted for anyway, and shortly before an appeal was to be heard that would ultimately be decided in their favor, the detainees were deported to Uganda on 13 February 1942. Many contracted malaria, though all were ultimately returned to Malta in March 1945. In retrospect, it appears to have been an unnecessary and expensive measure, for the deported group of Maltese proved to be anything but subversives in later years once they reentered full political life. *See also* BORG PISANI, CARMELO; BORG, SIR GEORGE; ITALIA IRREDENTA.

INVESTMENT. Prior to Malta's **independence**, most investment in the islands went to military infrastructure. The **Knights of St. John**, and later the **British**, were preoccupied with building fortifications, harbors, hospitals, and barracks. After 1964, the newly independent country was focused on restructuring the **economy** for manufacturing and **tourism**. Hotels, factories, and warehouses sprang up, albeit on a limited scale. The government took businesses under its control and became the major investor. The economy was tightly regulated, imports restricted, and high taxes and tariffs put in place. These conditions tended to discourage investment and held back economic growth.

The **Nationalist Party** took control of the government in 1987 and ushered in a significant change in economic policy, favoring a more liberal, market-driven economy. The Malta Investment Management Company Limited (MIMCOL) was set up and registered on 21 April 1988 as a limited liability company with the primary objectives to manage, restructure, and selectively divest from the portfolio of state-held investments, those businesses, mostly in the manufacturing and service sectors, which, in addition to being loss-making enterprises, competed unfairly with the private sector. Malta formally applied for membership in the **European Union (EU)** in 1990, hoping to gain access to EU funding, new markets, and investment opportunities. The prospect of membership also enabled the government to justify much needed economic and legal reforms, opening the country's markets for more competition. Tax and other incentives were put in place to encourage foreign businesses to invest in Malta.

In 1994, legislation was introduced to modernize the regulations and laws governing **financial services** provided from and through Malta. This has attracted a number of foreign banks such as the Hong Kong and Shanghai Banking Corporation (HSBC), resulting in a rapid growth of financing and investment activity. The value of aggregate assets of banks based in Malta has doubled since 2004, growing to 42 billion euros in 2009. Malta's insurance business has grown from 116 million euros in premiums to 508 million euros from 2004 to 2007. Similarly, the number of investment funds has increased by 33 percent from 2008 to 2009, this in spite of the recent global financial crisis.

The Maltese have substantial business contacts and investments in North Africa. They speak a Semitic language in addition to English, so Malta, a member of the EU and the "bridge of the Mediterranean," is particularly well positioned to serve the relatively new and growing niche market of Islamic finance. Malta is seeking to become a center of Islamic banking, serving North Africa and Islamic populations in Spain and Italy. Changes in tax and banking laws are being instituted to accommodate the specific needs of Islamic *Sharia* laws.

EU membership in 2004 and adoption of the euro in 2008 have boosted Malta's economic stability and, therefore, its attractiveness to foreign investors. The World Economic Forum's Competitive Index for 2008–9 ranked Malta as the 10th soundest banking system in the world out of 134 countries. In a recent executive survey, Malta ranked fifth as the most likely foreign site for new foreign direct investment. The country's well-educated, relatively low-cost, English-speaking workforce will continue to be a positive factor in attracting foreign investment to Malta. *See also* BANKING; TRADE.

ITALIA IRREDENTA. Translated as "unredeemed **Italy**," the movement became prominent in Italy in 1878 and advocated the incorporation into Italy of neighboring regions having a primarily Italian population. The movement gained a good deal of support in Malta, particularly among the educated classes, the same group that supported the early **Nationalist Party**.

ITALY. Consisting of a long peninsula extending from the Alps over 1,127 kilometers (700 miles) south to the Mediterranean Sea, the large islands of **Sicily** and Sardinia, plus several smaller Italian islands, Italy is Malta's closest neighbor. For much of its history, Italy has been Malta's main model for things artistic and intellectual. Even during the **British rule**, the majority of the cultural presentations in Malta's **Royal Opera House** were from the neighboring nation.

In the 8th century BCE, the Etruscans settled in the north and the Greeks along the coasts in the south. In the 5th century BCE, a Celtic invasion drove the Etruscans south until they were defeated by the Samnites. They, in turn, were defeated by the **Romans** in several wars spanning the years 326–290 BCE. From the 5th century BCE to the 5th century CE, Italy witnessed the rise of Rome and the Roman Empire. Even so, firm control was never established over southern Italy and Sicily. The land remained fragmented into independent entities, such as the Kingdoms of Sicily and Naples, under continually changing political control. Napoleon remade the map of Italy several times. When Victor Emmanuel II became king in 1861 under a unification movement called the Risorgimento (resurgence), Venice and Rome remained outside. In 1866, Venice joined the united Italy and, in 1870, Italian troops annexed Rome by force. Even so, the dispute with the papacy was not finally resolved until 1929.

From 1861 until 1922, Italy was ruled by Victor Emmanuel II, Humbert I, and Victor Emmanuel III. It expanded by the addition of Somaliland, Eritrea, and **Libya** as colonies. In the early 1920s, political unrest led to the rise of fascism and Benito Mussolini, creator of the totalitarian "corporate state." He conquered Ethiopia (1935–36) and seized Albania in 1939. On 11 June 1940, Italy declared war and very soon thereafter dropped the first bomb on Malta. By 1943, it had lost in North Africa to the Allies, and Sicily had been invaded and lost. Italy surrendered to the Allies, who later recognized it as a cobelligerent against Germany. A referendum in 1946 made it a republic, and in 1949, it was accepted as a member of **North Atlantic Treaty Organization** (NATO). Mussolini's speeches called Malta a part of Italy's natural domain, and, until the hostilities of **World War II** began, a sizable portion of the population of Malta agreed with him. Agreement quickly changed to anger once the bombs began to fall.

After the war, the U.S. Marshall Plan helped to rebuild its economy, and Italy joined the **European Union (EU)** as a charter member, signing the Treaty of Rome in 1957. Beginning in late 1969, Italy suffered more than a decade of great political upheaval known as the "lead years," when right-wing and left-wing factions—most notorious among them the radical communist faction known as the Red Brigade—were involved in bombings, kidnappings, and killings. It was the Red Brigade that kidnapped and executed **Prime Minister** Aldo Moro, a member of the Christian Democratic Party.

Since Malta gained its **independence**, Italy has concluded numerous bilateral, regional, and multilateral agreements with its neighbor on common issues, working hard to restore a bond that had been severed by World War II. Access to Italian television programs helped, but financial assistance was even more effective. Beginning in 1979, Italy has signed five financial protocols, giving Malta grants and loans in excess of 500 million **euros** to help with restructuring its **economy**, building roads, power stations, and other infrastructure. Italy also donated several ships and helicopters for Malta's use in combating drug trafficking. The latest Italo-Maltese protocol agreement covered the period 2004–7 and amounted to 75 million euros.

Most recently, the two countries, along with Greece and Spain, have worked hard to win EU assistance in dealing with **illegal immigration** from North Africa. Relations between Italy and Malta were temporarily strained in April 2009, when a dispute arose over which country was responsible for a boatload of refugees. *See also* BORG PISANI, CARMELO; E-BOAT ATTACK; ITALIA IRREDENTA; LANGUAGE QUESTION.

– J –

JESUITS. The Fathers of the Society of Jesus were always active in the political, educational, and religious life of the islands. The order came to Malta to set up a college (approximately at the level of today's high school) in 1592 in **Valletta**. The wide interests of the members plus their activist conduct often brought them into the center of controversy. In 1639, some young **Knights of St. John** were disciplined by the **grand master** and blamed the Jesuits for their punishments. In youthful anger, they created a disturbance at one of the pre-Lenten carnival celebrations, an action not well received by the local population. In anticipation of the possibility of a popular uprising on behalf of the Jesuits, the grand master forced them to leave for **Sicily**. After the anger had subsided, they were permitted to return but only after promising to lead more sedate lives.

A much more serious event occurred in 1768. When Charles V expelled the Society from Portugal, Spain, and France, Grand Master Emmanuel Pinto de Fonseca, wanting to be rid of the Jesuits and hoping for financial gain, seized the opportunity to do the same. He expelled the Jesuits from Malta and confiscated all of their property. After lengthy discussions and negotiations, Pinto was able to gain papal approval for the conversion of the Jesuit college into a **university** in 1769, taking over the original building constructed by the Jesuits. The structure was renovated in 2003 to house the administrative offices of **Heritage Malta**.

JEWS OF MALTA. Recent evidence indicates that a population of about 500 Jews lived in Malta and **Gozo** during the 15th century. About one-fourth to one-third the population of **Mdina** was Jewish, estimated to be 300 persons. It is likely that most came to Malta from England and the European continent to escape persecution. There is little evidence that they experienced the same sort of bigotry in their new homeland. In addition, the Jews were comfortable linguistically in Malta, for their own Semitic language was very similar to Maltese. Some of the families lived in Malta for several generations.

The comfortable life for Malta's Jews came to an abrupt end in 1492. Ferdinand II of Spain signed a decree on 31 March calling for the expulsion of all Jews from his kingdom, including **Sicily**, Malta,

Gozo, and Pantelleria. The only exceptions were to be those who had converted to Christianity. However, even those who converted after the decree were permitted to stay. A short time was allowed for the deportees to take care of their personal affairs. After extinguishing all debts, they were permitted to depart with their wealth. All the Jews from Malta and Gozo were transported to Messina, Sicily, where they joined their coreligionists from that large island. The only remaining evidence of a Jewish presence in Malta during that era is a few place names and some family names of those who converted. Today, approximately 125 followers of the Jewish faith live in Malta. *See also* RELIGION.

– K –

KARM, DUN. *See* PSAILA, MONSIGNOR DUN KARM.

KNIGHTS AFTER RHODES. After their defeat by the **Turks**, the **Knights of St. John** left Rhodes on 1 January 1523 and sailed to a variety of Mediterranean ports for a year. In January 1524, the pope granted to the Order a temporary base at Viterbo, and the search for a permanent base began. The next six years involved a great deal of political manipulation and intrigue. After Pope Clement VIII exerted considerable pressure upon the Holy Roman Emperor, Charles V, the Maltese islands were awarded to the Order as their new home, which the Knights, hoping for a much grander location, accepted reluctantly. In October 1530, their fleet moved into Grand Harbour and dropped anchor.

The reluctance of the Knights was more than matched by the disappointment of the Maltese, who resented the fact that they had not been consulted. The action was considered a breach of the promise given to them by King Alfonso, that the islands would never be separated from the Royal Estate. Official protests by the Maltese went unanswered. Although the **Maltese nobility**, fearing a loss of their authority and privileges, were the most angered, it is likely that the other citizens looked upon their new overseers with guarded optimism, hoping both for increased protection against the Saracens as well as a substantial increase in their economic well-being. **Grand**

Master L'Isle-Adam took quick action to attempt to calm the fears of the nobility. It is likely that the Knights thought of Malta only as a temporary base until something better could be arranged. In the original grant by the Holy Roman Emperor, Tripoli in North Africa was included as part of the Knights' defense responsibility. When Tripoli fell in 1551, any hopes of gaining a better home were also lost. All energies and resources were turned to strengthening the meager fortifications of Malta. The Maltese, with their extensive knowledge of the sea, became an important addition to the Knights' sea warfare capabilities.

Although the local economic situation was booming because of all the construction, the Order's finances were unstable. The Protestant Reformation had resulted in a massive loss of valuable church property. The Church of England's break from papal authority did the same and also resulted in the loss of the English **Langue**. Nevertheless, the Knights attempted to maintain a hospital at Birgu and a fleet of eight war galleys in addition to all of their defensive constructions. Furthermore, the fear of an expected invasion by the Turks required the purchase of a stockpile of supplies and munitions. As these financial pressures continued to increase, a remarkable man was elected grand master—**Jean Parisot de la Valette**, who turned out to be a person of great vision and leadership ability. He proved to be the man for the time. *See also* GREAT SIEGE OF 1565.

KNIGHTS OF MALTA. *See* KNIGHTS OF ST. JOHN.

KNIGHTS OF ST. JOHN. The Order began as a brotherhood for protecting the poor and sick in the Christian hospital in Jerusalem who had journeyed as pilgrims from Europe to the holy city. The founder and first leader was Brother Gerard (later referred to as "Blessed Gerard"), who used the title of rector. The hospital and adjoining church were dedicated to St. John the Baptist. When the first Crusade captured Jerusalem in 1099, the hospital was already in full operation. Fourteen years later, Pope Paschal II gave his approval to the hospital, placing it under the protection of the Holy See. The Papal Bull changed the Brotherhood into a Holy Order of the **Roman Catholic Church** with sole right to freely elect the rector's successors without interference from any other authority, ecclesiastic or lay. This has been confirmed and expanded by successive pontiffs.

Succeeding Rector Gerard was **Raymond du Puy**, who was given the title of master of the hospital. Late in the 13th century, the title became **grand master**. Under Raymond du Puy, the Order expanded to include military and chivalric duties as well. It became the Sovereign Military Hospitaller Order of St. John of Jerusalem (later the words "of Rhodes" and "of Malta" were added to the official name). The grand master also introduced the white, eight-pointed cross (the Maltese cross), which has remained the symbol of the Order to this day. The **flag** of the Order, red with the eight-pointed cross in white, received Papal approval in 1130. After the Crusades failed and Jerusalem fell to the forces of Islam in 1187, the Knights of the Order moved to Cyprus and added what was to become an equally important element to its military capability, a naval force. The time in Cyprus was difficult as the Sovereign Order was there only as a guest of the king.

In 1310, the Order gained absolute control of the island of Rhodes and began the task of fortifying it. The grand master and his council took on all of the duties of nationhood, including the minting of coins, maintaining diplomatic relations with other states, and so forth. While in Rhodes, the Order became a major power of the eastern Mediterranean, using that power for the defense of Christendom as well as to harass the forces of Islam whenever possible. In 1522, the **Turkish** forces, under the leadership of Suleiman the Magnificent, attacked Rhodes, laying siege to the fortifications. After six months, the Knights were forced to surrender.

Impressed with their bravery, Suleiman was generous in setting the terms of the surrender, a generosity he would later greatly regret. The Order was permitted to leave in its own ships with its arms and other movable property. It then moved from place to place for seven years without a home base until, in 1530, the Holy Roman Emperor, Charles V, ceded to the Order in sovereign fief both the islands of the Maltese Archipelago and Tripoli in North Africa (the latter was lost to Islam in 1551). The Knights ruled Malta until 1798, when they surrendered to Napoleon's forces without giving any opposition, leaving the island in disgrace. In the later years of its rule in Malta, the Order had become decadent and the Knights' lavish lifestyle a drain on the Maltese **economy**. Thus, the Maltese population was only too glad to see them leave.

Today, the Knights are headquartered in Rome, located at 68 Via Condotti, a building that houses the smallest nation in the world. It contains the headquarters of the Sovereign Order, descended from that original brotherhood in Jerusalem and known in Rome as the Sovrano Militare Ordine di Malta. Larger than ever, it concentrates its activities on providing funds for the operation of hospitals, an ambulance service, halfway houses, and the like. It provides medicines, equipment, and medical volunteers worldwide. Although the Order retains a fondness for the trappings of nobility, it continues to emphasize its original goals. It also continues as a sovereign order, maintaining diplomatic relations with 95 other nations, holding its own courts of law, and issuing its own passports, postage stamps, and even coins. The Order returned to Malta in 1964, after **independence** was gained, in the form of an ambassador to the new nation. In 1989, the Order held an international gathering of Knights in Malta for the first time since their departure in 1798. On 24 August 1994, the Order was granted observer status in the **United Nations**. *See also* AUBERGES; GREAT SIEGE OF 1565; KNIGHTS AFTER RHODES.

– L –

LABOUR PARTY. *See* MALTA LABOUR PARTY.

LANGUAGE QUESTION. When the **British** arrived in Malta in 1800, they found two languages in place—Italian, used by the intellectual and higher business classes, and Maltese, used by everyone else. Unlike Italian, however, Maltese (**Malti**) existed only as a spoken form of communication. Subtle, and eventually not so subtle, actions were taken by the British to encourage the learning and use of English while discouraging the same for Italian. These attempts were usually less than successful because of several factors, primarily the fact that English was looked upon as a Protestant language while Italian was felt to be **Roman Catholic**. In addition, Italian carried positive cultural acceptance, particularly for the educated.

In 1880, the colonial **governor**, following the recommendations contained in several reports of royal commissioners, began a series of changes designed to encourage the learning and use of the English language. Not only was English to be the official language of the schools and the **university** but also proficiency in English was to be of primary importance in all Civil Service appointments. At the same time, the colonial government encouraged the use of Maltese, especially in the teaching of English, as a weapon against the entrenched Italian. By 1934, Maltese and English had become the official languages of the law courts, and Italian had lost all such standing. In the past, Italian had been the symbol of Maltese nationalism, but that language quickly lost such support when **Italy** became an enemy in **World War II**, and its air force began bombing the islands. In its place, the Maltese language became a rallying point of nationalist feelings.

More recently, the English language skills of the Maltese have given the nation a major economic advantage as globalization drives Europeans to Malta to learn English in a sunny climate. A number of very successful English-language schools have become a niche industry, contributing to Malta's **economy**. Meanwhile, the requirement that any student seeking admission to the University of Malta pass a proficiency examination in Maltese was dropped because of concern that it excludes many foreigners from studying in Malta. However, the Maltese also perceive globalization as a threat in the form of **illegal immigrants** from Northern Africa and cheap goods from Asia, among others, which has heightened nationalist feelings and concern about preserving Malta's identity, its culture, and language. The successful insistence on including Maltese as an official language of the **European Union** and the debate over the spelling of the **euro** are recent examples.

LANGUES. French for "tongues" or "languages," the langues were a practical way of grouping the different languages (and, therefore, political and cultural heritages) of the **Knights of St. John**. In the early years of the Order, this was necessary in order to facilitate quick communication. Each langue had its own quarters, or **auberge**, as can be seen by the side chapels in the **St. John's Co-Cathedral**, each dedicated to a different langue. This grouping continued throughout its history while it remained a fighting order. The langues were Aragon, including Catalonia and Navarre; Auvergne; Castile, including Leon and Portugal; England; France; **Italy**; Germany; and Provence. Each langue developed specialized expertise and was given particular responsibilities. For example, the langue of Italy was in charge of the navy, while the French managed the hospital (**Sacred Infirmary**), and the English were responsible for the cavalry.

The English Langue virtually ceased to exist as a result of the breach between Rome and King Henry VIII. After the Order's departure from Malta, there were attempts at the creation of a Russian Langue but with little success. *See also* GRAND MASTERS OF THE ORDER OF ST. JOHN; ST. JOHN AMBULANCE BRIGADE.

LAPARELLI, FRANCESCO (?–1570). A former pupil of and, later, assistant to Michelangelo, Laparelli became an expert in military **architecture** and had been involved in a number of Vatican commissions when he arrived to assist the **Knights of St. John** in December 1565. Within three days, he had a plan ready for the **grand master** and his advisors. His first proposal was to strengthen the defenses of the **Three Cities** area in anticipation of a quick return of the **Turks**. He next proposed using the Sciberras peninsula for a totally fortified city. He also gave full support to Grand Master **Jean Parisot de la Valette**'s idea that Malta itself was a natural fortress with marvelous deep-water harbors. Because of that, it was a perfect home for the Convent of the Knights. Laparelli stayed at his task for only two years before requesting and getting permission to leave the islands. Laparelli left Malta in 1569 and died of the **plague** at Candia on the island of Crete in 1570. *See also* ARCHITECTURE; CASSAR, GEROLAMO; VALLETTA, CITY OF.

LIBYA. The first embassy opened by a newly independent Malta in 1964 was in Libya. Because it is one of its closest neighbors to the south and controls an abundance of oil, Malta viewed Libya as an important partner for **trade**. Five years later, Muammar Qaddafi, a soldier in the Libyan army, took control of the country to establish "the Great Libyan **Arab** Socialist Jamahiriya" (Arabic roughly translated, "rule by the masses"), leading a coup that deposed the Libyan king.

In 1971, when **Dom Mintoff** was elected **prime minister** of Malta, he used the threat of closer relations with Libya as a bargaining chip in negotiations with Great Britain for continued rent of Malta's naval base. Qaddafi was viewed by the Western powers with suspicion, and Mintoff went so far as to have the Libyans arrive with a planeload of crates, suggesting that the Libyans were prepared to take Great Britain's place, supplying the Maltese with weapons. The strategy was successful, causing the **British** to pay more for the right to extend their stay until 1979.

Nevertheless, Mintoff shared the Libyan colonel's socialist leanings. He developed a closer rapport with Qaddafi, who supplied Malta with funds to cushion the impact of the British troop departure, the ceremony for which was attended by several hundred Libyans shipped in by Qaddafi for dramatic effect. Meanwhile, several hundred Maltese made good money working in Libyan oil fields, and Libya agreed to sell Malta oil at a discounted rate.

Mintoff, for his part, sought to convince his people that the Arab neighbors, whom the Maltese for centuries had reviled as the arch enemy of Christianity, the "Saracens," who had invaded Malta, were in fact "blood brothers." Qaddafi contributed funds to build the national sports stadium and a mosque in Malta (to date, the only one on the islands). He also established two Arab cultural centers. In return, the Maltese government briefly made the study of Arabic a prerequisite for admission to the university. History books were rewritten, depicting Malta as culturally closer to North Africa than Italy and Europe. This was a tough sell that the Maltese populace never fully bought. In a 2009 editorial, a Maltese journalist wondered whether Mintoff's efforts actually reinforced rather than eased Maltese popular prejudice against Arabs.

In 1984, pressured by Qaddafi, who was seeking greater international support, Malta signed a treaty of "Friendship and Cooperation" with Libya, which agreed to train and arm Maltese forces. In April 1986, when United States' President Ronald Reagan ordered a bombing attack on Qadaffi's living quarters, Maltese air controllers warned the Libyans about approaching unidentified aircraft, thus reducing the element of surprise the Americans had sought.

Maltese-Libyan relations were not always smooth, however. In 1980, Libyan gunboats confronted the Maltese navy in a dispute over oil field exploration. Because the Maltese were (and still are) buying oil from Libya at a special discount, the Malta government retreated.

The **Nationalist Party** returned to power in 1987 and began reversing many of Mintoff's policies, adopting a distanced approach to relations with Libya while seeking to rebuild ties with the West and join the **European Union (EU)**. The 1988 bombing of Pan Am flight 103 over Lockerbie, Scotland, later proven to have been instigated by Libyan agents based in Malta, did not help Maltese-Libyan relations nor did the 1995 assassination of the Palestinian leader of Islamic Jihad, Fathi Shqaqi, which was carried out by Israeli agents in Malta.

In 1992, the **United Nations (UN)** imposed sanctions against Libya because it refused to hand over the agents accused of arranging the bombing of the Pan Am flight. Although Malta and Libya had considerable mutual investments at risk, Malta supported the UN sanctions by shutting down the only flights serving Libya. However, it maintained service by sea between the two countries, the main remaining transit point for passengers and cargo to and from Libya.

In 1999, Maltese authorities intercepted crates containing Scud missile parts bound for Libya, which were returned to Great Britain. In 2004, Malta joined the EU and reinstated visa requirements for Libyans traveling to Malta. This, in addition to a significant increase in **illegal immigration**, mostly via Libya, continues to complicate relations between the two countries. *See also* FOREIGN POLICY; FREEDOM DAY.

LIGUTTI, MONSIGNOR LUIGI (1915–1984). In 1969, when serving as the Vatican's representative to the Food and Agriculture Organization of the United Nations in Rome, Ligutti was appointed apostolic visitor to Malta. This came in response to a request to the Vatican by Archbishop **Michael Gonzi**. Ligutti was to act as a consultant, assisting in the reorganization of the administration of the property of the **Catholic Church** in Malta in accordance with the reforms of the Second Vatican Council. To assist in the challenging assignment, the McKinsey firm of management consultants was engaged. That firm hired two British Roman Catholic priests who were finance and administration experts to assist in the task. The report of the consultants was completed in September 1970 and was sent to every priest in Malta. The report was approved and signed by the Archbishop, Mgr. Ligutti, and **Mgr. Emmanuel Gerada** to certify that it was to become official policy. It contained a number of specific recommendations with the goal of improving the use of Church property and other capital toward the maximization of income and its use. Of major interest to the priests was the recommendation that their salaries be brought at least to the level of teachers' salaries. In all of the meetings and consultations, Ligutti acquired a great admiration of Gonzi but, according to his biographer, came to suspect the actions of Gerada. He left the islands feeling that the problems of the Church, which he had been sent to solve, were going to continue and most likely intensify.

LISBON AGENDA. In March 2000, **European Union (EU)** ministers, concerned about the EU's lagging economic performance, met in Lisbon, Portugal. The meeting resulted in the adoption of a goal for the EU to become "the most dynamic and competitive knowledge-based **economy** in the world, capable of sustainable economic growth with more and better jobs and greater social cohesion and respect for the **environment** . . . by 2010." To achieve such an ambitious goal, EU members were to "step up the process of structural reform by completing the internal market . . . investing in people . . . [and] applying an appropriate macro-economic policy mix."

Labeled the "Lisbon Agenda" (also "Lisbon Strategy"), the EU leaders' summit intended to signal a turning point for EU business and innovation by promoting more research (spending at least 3 percent of GDP), entrepreneurship, and information technology by increasing spending and reducing red tape.

A November 2004 progress report submitted by the former prime minister of the Netherlands, Wim Kok, complained that "(an) overloaded agenda, poor co-ordination and conflicting priorities" were preventing the EU from achieving its Lisbon targets. The report puts the main blame, however, on the "lack of political will of the member states." Matters were not helped by a slowdown in the global economy that hit Europe especially hard. Undaunted, the EU Commission relaunched the Agenda in 2005 but chose to focus only on the economic aspects, abandoning its social and environmental goals.

A London-based think tank, the Centre for European Reform (CER), presented a progress evaluation of the Lisbon Agenda in the spring of 2005, which ranked Malta as a "villain" in last place (27th of 27 EU members) with regard to achieving the Agenda targets. While praising Malta's high level of public access to the Internet ("e-readiness") and the lowest tax burden on low-wage earners (15.8 percent), the report was critical of the country's total lack of renewable **energy** sources (versus the EU 2010 goal of 20 percent), total reliance on landfills for waste disposal, lowest secondary school completion rate (47.9 percent versus the EU goal of 85 percent), second lowest female employment rate (33.6 percent), and the highest level of subsidies. Clearly, many of these shortcomings relate to Malta's particular geographic location, size, and population density and will remain difficult challenges for years to come. *See also* EDUCATION; PRIVATIZATION; WOMEN.

LITERATURE. Two factors have severely limited the development of Maltese literature: the size of the audience and its linguistic diversity. The Maltese population, which has never exceeded half a million, was largely illiterate (80 percent in the 1860s). Also, over the centuries, Maltese writers have written works using six different **languages**: Arabic, Latin, Sicilian, Italian, Maltese, and English. Rooted in the Semitic language of the islands' Arabic occupiers, the Maltese language (**Malti**) was limited to everyday usage among the common populace, while Latin and later, with the arrival of the **Knights**, Italian were elevated to languages of the privileged, educated, and ruling class of Malta.

The earliest known literature written in Maltese is a poem attributed to Pietro Caxaro, a notary public born in **Mdina**. Caxaro died in 1485, and scholars assume that he wrote the poem shortly before his death. A copy of the poem, which was included in notarial documents dating from the 1530s, prepared by a descendant of Caxaro, was discovered in the archives of Mdina by Godfrey Wettinger and Michael Fsadni in 1966.

The second oldest work of Maltese literature known to exist is a 16-line poem, the "Sonetto," composed in the 1670s by Giovanni

Francesco Bonamico to eulogize **Grand Master** Nicholas Cottoner. A doctor by profession, Bonamico mainly wrote in Latin, producing several collections of poetry, numerous treaties on medical and scientific topics as well as memoirs of his travels throughout Europe from 1657 to 1676. Except for these two works, Italian was the language of Maltese writers while Maltese was the language of everyday conversation. The first book printed in Malta in 1643 was in Italian, and it was not until the mid-1800s, under the influences of the Romantic movement, which fostered nationalism and a return to cultural roots, that Maltese became a primary language of Maltese literature. The presence of Italian exiles from the Risorgimento affected Maltese literature as well as politics.

Mikiel Anton Vassalli in his *Vocabolario Maltese* (1796) introduced the notion of the Maltese language as a national cultural inheritance to be valued as a key symbol and delineator of a country. Pride in a national consciousness was further stoked by Italian writers of the Risorgimento, who fled **Italy** and (ironically) encouraged the Maltese to free themselves of foreign influences. Giovanni Antonio Vassallo (1817–1868), is considered the first major Maltese poet to actively promote the use of Maltese in his writing.

A shortage of resources, coupled with the boom and bust cycles of war inflicted on the **economy** of an island fortress, forced so many Maltese to leave Malta, making the theme of **emigration** a main topic of Maltese literature.

The 1960s witnessed the beginning of a period of rebellion against traditional forms and confining social norms. Lino Spiteri, one of the most celebrated authors in modern Malta, wrote *Rivoluzzjoni do minore* in 1980, a fictionalized account of the conflict between the government and the Church. Reality intruded with a greater focus on the individual confronting his or her **environment** in a "love hate relationship . . . characteristic of some modern Maltese novels and short story collections such as Alfred **Sant**'s . . . *The First Palms of the Prickly* Pears (1968), Frans Sammut's . . . *The Cage* (1971) . . . and Oliver Friggieri's . . . *The Lie* (1977)." This represented a shift from creating a national identity to finding meaning in a personal identity, ironically at a time when Maltese were, to a much greater extent, being exposed to the wider world. "The island itself is perhaps going through such a process of self appraisal" (Henry **Frendo** and O. Friggieri 1994). *See also* "INNU MALTI."

LOCAL COUNCILS. Given Malta's small territory, its foreign masters felt they could sufficiently govern through a single centralized institution. Local issues of the various towns and villages were not well understood or much considered by the ruling powers. Control in a more democratic manner by a local government did not exist until very recently. Except for the relatively elitist **Universita** and **Consiglio Popolare** bodies that existed for a few centuries before the **British** took control, official government existed only at the national level. The parish priest was the closest to any kind of local official. It was he who saw to it that the town or village received its share of road repairs, police protection, and similar services.

In February 1993, the government published a bill calling for the setting up of local councils. On 30 June, the **Parliament** approved the Local Councils Act (Act no. XV of 1993), modeled on the European Charter of Local Self-Government, which the Maltese government, as a member of the **Council of Europe**, had signed and ratified.

In November 1993, the first local **elections** were held with a 63 percent turnout. Currently, there are 68 local councils—54 in Malta and 14 in **Gozo**. There are no intermediary governing structures between the councils and the national government. Elections are held every year for one-third of the councils, which serve a three-year term. The number of councilors representing each locality is determined by population: communities with fewer than 1,000 elect five, whereas communities with 20,000 or more elect the maximum of 13. Councils receive grants from the national **Parliament** and have reasonable authority to spend the amounts for local community needs, roads maintenance, parks, and other services. In 2000, local wardens were appointed to enforce laws on a local level. Such local control is an entirely new experience for the Maltese. On 24 April 2001, Act no. XIII of 2001 amended the **Constitution** to more firmly implant local councils in Malta's governance structure.

– M –

M.U.S.E.U.M. *See* ST. GEORGE.

MAITLAND, LIEUTENANT GENERAL SIR THOMAS, GCB, GCH (1759–1824). Malta's first colonial **governor**, Maitland was appointed both governor and commander in chief in 1813 and served until his death in 1824. He was a reformer and an efficient but autocratic administrator. When he arrived in Malta, the **plague** was raging, and the **economy** was in a very serious recession. He promptly attacked both problems, gaining eventual success. In retrospect, his accomplishments were many. He not only reorganized the court system, bringing in trial by jury, but also separated the executive, legislative, and judicial powers of the colony and abolished the **Universita**. Although he declared that English would replace Italian as the official language of government, in this he was much less successful. Because of his stern, strong will, he was known as "King Tom" by one segment of the population at the same time as other segments approved of his actions. He died in Malta in 1824 and is buried in the Upper Barakka Gardens overlooking Grand Harbour. *See also* BRITISH RULE; LANGUAGE QUESTION.

MALTA COLLEGE OF ARTS, SCIENCE AND TECHNOLOGY (MCAST). Established and mostly financed by the government as a community college, MCAST was launched in 2001 to provide vocational and technical training needed to establish a knowledge-based society capable of coping with global competition. MCAST has nine institutes: Agribusiness, Art and Design, Building and Construction Engineering, Business and Commerce, Community Services, Electrical and Electronics Engineering, Information and Communication Technology, Maritime, and Mechanical Engineering.

The college currently serves about 4,000 full-time and 5,000 part-time students at various sites, including a center in **Gozo**. MCAST has become a priority for Malta as the shift from manufacturing to service jobs intensifies, especially in light of the **Lisbon Agenda** of the **European Union (EU)**, the planned **SmartCity** development, and increasing investments in Malta by the **financial** sector. Consequently, the government recently issued a strategic plan for 2007–9 that seeks to grow the student body at MCAST and encourage more adult participation in retraining. On 27 May 2007, Prime Minister **Lawrence Gonzi** announced the Malta government's intention to spend Lm50 million for a new campus that would combine the various institutes currently scattered about the island in one central location and allow enrollment to grow to 10,000. The completion of this ambitious expansion project is expected around 2015. *See also* ECONOMY; EDUCATION.

MALTA ENVIRONMENTAL PLANNING AUTHORITY (MEPA). *See* ENVIRONMENT; FLIMKIEN GHAL AMBJENT AHJAR.

MALTA-EU STEERING AND ACTION COMMITTEE (MEUSAC). *See* EUROPEAN UNION.

MALTA FEVER. Malta fever is so named because the microbe that causes the disease was discovered there in 1886 by Surgeon Major (later Sir) David Bruce. The microbe was named in his honor, *Brucella melitensis*. The severity of the disease among **British** servicemen caused a financial burden on the British government, and in an effort to determine the cause and eliminate it, a medical commission was set up in cooperation with the government of Malta. The commission included one Maltese in its membership, Dr. **Themistocles Zammit**. After the testing of a wide array of substances without success, Dr. Zammit began experiments with milk goats. At the time, large herds of these animals were driven into the towns and cities to supply milk directly to the people living there. The goats were then milked right on the doorstep of the family or military personnel making the purchase.

On 25 June 1905, Zammit discovered the microbe in the blood of some goats, as many as 5,000 of which were said to be wandering in the streets of **Valletta** at the time. The microbe was transferred to humans through the consumption of the milk from infected goats. The method of testing the milk is still known as "Zammit's Test." The medical profession as well as the government of Malta carried out a series of protests about the use of a geographical location in the name of a disease, urging the use of the term "undulant fever" instead. The abandonment was slow until the introduction of the term *Brucellosis* in honor of the discoverer of the microbe. *See also* HEALTH AND HEALTH CARE.

MALTA FUNGUS. A black fungus so well accepted that it has a Latin name, *Fucus coccineus melitensis* grows on the top of a very tiny island close to the west coast of **Gozo**. This island, called Fungus Rock, was considered so important to the **Knights of St. John** that a permanent guard was kept in the tower on Gozo overlooking the island. At some point early in the time of the Knights, it was learned from the locals that the fungus had curative properties for dysentery and blood matters, such as hemorrhages and wounds. Although the curative powers of this fungus were accepted for hundreds and possibly thousands of years, a scientific analysis at Bighi Naval Hospital in 1968 failed to find any basis for this acceptance other than a mildly anesthetic effect. *See also* HEALTH AND HEALTH CARE.

MALTA LABOUR PARTY (MLP). The first Labour Party was formed prior to the 1921 **elections**. The first leader was Lieutenant Colonel William Savona. For that election, the electoral program called for the reform of the system of taxation with the abolition of the bread tax and greater emphasis on the use of direct taxation. Compulsory **education,** coupled with improvement in the elementary curriculum, was an additional part of the program. The **language question**, always a major factor in elections at the time, came in through advocacy of Maltese as the language of instruction with English the only other language to be studied up to the fourth standard. After that, English and Italian were to be studied "pari passu" (on an equal basis). The party also called for the terms of enlistment of Maltese in the **British** military to be the same as for British enlistees. As a final nod to its constituency, the platform called for improved housing for the labor force.

In 1921, the party was successful in gaining 22 percent of the seats in the Legislative Assembly and 29 percent in the Senate, a reasonable result for a newly organized party. However, both party membership and electoral support continued to decline until the outbreak of **World War II**.

In 1945, the name was changed to the Malta Labour Party (Partit tal-Haddiema in Maltese). It won 90 percent of the seats in the Council of Government and 100 percent of the Executive Council. With elections under the new 1947 **Constitution**, the party gained 65 percent of the seats available. However, a series of disputes among the party leaders caused what had been a powerful political force to become fragmented. It again gained majority control in 1955, holding it until 1962. During that period, the party favored integration with Great Britain, but a **referendum** on the subject brought less than conclusive results. The party advocated voting rights for all over the age of 18. It also opposed self-government until the colonial government had created a sound economic situation in the islands. In the elections of 1962, the Labour Party lost to the **Nationalist Party (NP)**, which then presided over the **Independence** Day events.

After gaining majority control of **Parliament** in 1971, the MLP maintained that control until 1987. During that time, under the forceful leadership of **Dom Mintoff**, abrupt changes were made in both the educational system and the **university** structure, private medical service was virtually abolished, and strict controls were placed on imported products. Constant pressure was maintained on the British government for increases in all forms of financial payments to Malta. On the international political scene, there was a definite leaning toward the Eastern Bloc. Cordial relations were maintained with, and economic grants received from, North Korea, the People's Republic of China, and **Libya**, among others. The party supported government control of **banks** and many enterprises and opposed membership in the **European Union (EU)**—at that time called the European Community.

The NP was returned to majority control of Parliament in 1987 and retained control in the 1992 elections. In 1997, the MLP regained control and immediately set about freezing Malta's application filed by the preceding Nationalist government to join the EU. It also replaced the VAT system instituted by the previous government with a tariff and excise tax regime. Internal party strife between **Prime Minister Alfred Sant** and Mintoff caused the former to call for snap elections, which returned the Nationalists to power after less than two years. The MLP strongly opposed EU membership for Malta, proposing a "partnership" status instead and encouraged its members to boycott the **referendum** on 8 March 2003 that was to decide the issue. In a strange twist, although the referendum decided in favor of joining the EU by a 53.6 percent majority, MLP leader Sant claimed victory on the dubious basis that fewer than half of the eligible voters had voted in favor of joining. More recently, the MLP has accepted membership in the EU as generally the best option for Malta, but continues vigorously attacking the incumbent NP government's every move.

Several controversial remapping scandals involving development zones and building permits, a decline in the **tourism** industry, high **energy** prices, and a flood of **illegal immigrants**, among other issues, have caused significant voter dissatisfaction with the current NP government. This gave the MLP high hopes that it would be returned in the general elections of 2008. Party leader Sant, once again the MLP candidate for prime minister, was a familiar face to voters who were looking for change, and the MLP offered little in the way of fresh alternatives. Nevertheless, the MLP lost the election by only 1,500 votes. As a result of losing a third general election in a row, Sant resigned, and a new leader, Joseph Muscat, was elected party leader. The MLP won 4 out of 6 seats in the June 6 elections for the European Parliament. *See also* BARBARA, AGATHA; BOFFA, SIR PAUL; BUTTIGIEG, DR. ANTON; DIMECH, EMMANUEL; MIFSUD BONNICI, DRS. CARMELO; POLITICAL PARTIES.

MALTA RAILWAY. From the beginning, the Malta Railway was an unusual venture: a narrow-gauge railroad on a small island with little distance between stations to service a very poor population. It seemed obviously doomed to failure from the very start. Yet the necessary capital was obtained outside of Malta, and construction began in early 1879. After several delays, the Malta Railway opened to the public in early 1883 with a route running from **Valletta** to **Mdina**. Because the locomotives were too small for the abrupt grade changes along the route, repair and maintenance costs proved much higher than anticipated. As a result, the venture was never able to cover its operating costs, much less give a return to its investors. In 1889, the line was forced to shut down for 29 days while extensive repairs were made to the locomotives. In final frustration, the Malta government seized the property under the forfeiture provisions of the original concessions agreement.

Immediately, the government repaired the old equipment, purchased some upgraded new equipment, and made improvements in the right of way. In 1900, a short but expensive extension was made from Mdina to Mtarfa, where a new **British** military barracks and hospital were under construction. Although the railway finally began to show a profit, it was short-lived. In 1903, a new concession for the construction and operation of a tramway from **Valletta** to neighboring towns was granted by the government. This diminished the use of the railway. A spurt of increased usage occurred during **World War I** when wounded soldiers were transported to the hospital at Mtarfa. After the war, motorized buses were imported, and another change in public **transportation** caused the demise of the tramway at the end of 1929 and the railway in early 1931.

Although the railway ended as a financial failure, it was a social success. For the first time, the lower classes were able to afford to travel to the countryside for Sunday outings or the chance to join the religious *festas* of other towns. They took advantage of these opportunities, which before had been available only to the wealthier classes.

MALTA SHIPYARDS. *See* DOCKYARDS.

MALTA SUMMIT. *See* UNITED STATES–SOVIET SUMMIT.

MALTA WORKERS PARTY. *See* BOFFA, SIR PAUL.

MALTESE CROSS. *See* KNIGHTS OF ST. JOHN.

MALTESE LANGUAGE. *See* MALTI.

MALTESE NOBILITY. Titles of nobility date back to the **Norman** conquest of the islands in 1090. The ancestors of many of the current noble families arrived in Malta with Count Roger, or shortly thereafter, and were granted parcels of land. A bit later, the kings of **Sicily** granted several titles. After 1530, when the **Knights of St. John** came to rule over Malta, a number of Maltese were awarded titles by various monarchs of Europe, which were recognized by the **grand masters**. The nobility was abolished in 1798 during the **French occupation** but reestablished under the **British rule** a few years later. In 1889, the Committee of Privileges of the Maltese Nobility was founded and continues functioning to this day. It maintains a website listing 30 Maltese titleholders. On 23 June 1975, the **Dom Mintoff** government withdrew all official recognition of titles of nobility. Nevertheless, their use continues today, though only informally. **Mdina**, known as the *Citta Notabile*, is still home to a large number of the Maltese noble families.

MALTI. The first and daily language of the island nation, Malti was long thought to have its roots in **Phoenicia** and Carthage. More recent scholarship has concluded that it stems from North African Arab dialects. Although its construction is obviously Semitic, it is a living language filled with words originating from **Sicily**, **Italy**, Spain, France, and England. Malti was strictly a spoken language until early in the last century, despite attempts at creating a written form dating back to the time of the **Knights of St. John**. The Roman alphabet, with a few adaptations, is used rather than Arabic script. Recently, scholars have been more successful in standardizing spelling and other aspects so that books, newspapers, signs, and other written usages are very extensive. Still, occasional debate has surfaced in the Maltese press about the spelling of loan words.

At one time, Italian was the primary language of the educated class. English was used to a far lesser extent. The colonial authorities constantly applied pressure to increase the use of English, and in the 1930s, it began to supplant Italian. **World War II** caused an even faster decrease in the use of Italian, the language of the enemy. Today, English is recognized as an official language along with Malti. However, Italian is rapidly regaining its earlier strength through the popularity of Italian television, which is easily available to the entire populace. As a result, a high percentage of Maltese are trilingual, at least to some degree.

In seeking to join the **European Union (EU)**, the Maltese government successfully negotiated to have Malti included as an official language of the organization. This means that all official documents and debates need to be translated into Malti (as well as all 22 of the other official languages). This created an immediate demand for translators and interpreters of Malti and the other languages.

EU membership prompted another interesting debate—how to spell "**euro**" in Malti. In June 2004, the Maltese **Parliament** passed the Maltese Language Act, establishing a National Council for the

Maltese Language. The council was given the sole authority to determine the correct spelling of words and phrases that enter Maltese usage from other languages. After careful study of various options, the Council chose *ewro* as the correct word to use at about the same time the secretary of the Maltese Parliament, Tonio Fenech, was quoted as saying that "euro" would be the spelling in all legal documents and in the public information campaign leading up to the adoption of the euro on 1 January 2008. *See also* LANGUAGE QUESTION.

MAMO, SIR ANTHONY J., Kt., OBE, QC (1909–2008). As the culmination of a long and distinguished career, Mamo became the first **president** of the Republic serving from 1974 to 1976. Born in Birkirkara on 9 January 1909, his entire **education** through the Doctorate of Laws was in Malta, first at the Archbishop's Seminary and then at the Royal **University of Malta**, graduating with a BA in 1931 and a Doctor of Laws in 1934. Mamo served as crown counsel from 1943 to 1952, as legal advisor to four **prime ministers**, and as attorney general from 1955 to 1957. At the university, he was professor of criminal law from 1943 to 1957. In 1957, Mamo was named chief justice and president of the Court of Appeal. He held those positions until 1971 when he became the first Maltese citizen to be named **governor** general by the **British** Colonial Office, and he carried that title until the ties to the British Crown were severed in 1974. Although elected to the presidency by a **Labour** government, Mamo was highly respected by persons of all shades of political opinion. Mamo died on 1 May 2008, the oldest living head of state in the world at the time.

MANOEL THEATRE. It was financed by and opened by **Grand Master** Manoel de Vilhena, who gave it his name. At the opening celebration on 9 January 1732, he specified that it was to be "for the honest recreation of the people." The horseshoe-shaped construction was completed in 10 months with an interior entirely made of wood. For almost 130 years, the Manoel Theatre was the main performance venue in Malta for operas and dramas. Renamed the Royal Theatre under the **British rule**, it fell into disuse after the newly constructed **Royal Opera House** was inaugurated. The theater experienced a revival of fortunes and was renamed the Manoel Theater when the

Opera House burned in 1873. When the Opera House was reopened, the Manoel Theater again fell into decline and was used as a dance hall and cinema. During **World War II**, it served as a refuge for homeless people. After the war that had completely destroyed the Opera House, Manoel Theater was taken over by the government, which spent 10 years restoring it to its former glory and reopened it in 1960.

Like most buildings in Malta, the theater has a bland exterior without any distinguishing **architectural** features. The inside is another matter. An ornately decorated paneled ceiling is highlighted by a large crystal chandelier, and the dark green color of the hall is offset by 22-carat gilded ornamentation. There are 45 boxes plus the Presidential Box, reserved in past years for the grand masters and later for the British king or queen.

Manoel Theatre continues to be the scene of concerts, recitals, ballet, opera, and theatrical productions. The theater has its own orchestra and operates the Manoel Theatre Academy of Dramatic Arts. In 1993, the government allocated funds for the renovation of what is not only a major **tourist** attraction but also a major historical treasure, one of Europe's oldest theaters still in use.

MDINA. This Maltese city has had many different names over its long history. The **Arabs**, who used it as their capital city, called it Medina. To the **Romans**, it was Melita. Early on, the **Knights of St. John** called it Città Notabile. But after the completion of **Valletta** in the 16th century, Mdina became known as Citta Vecchia, or the "old city." To the Maltese, it has always been Mdina and was the capital until the arrival of the Knights. Because of its easily defended location on a 152-meter (500-foot) ridge, evidence exists of settlements on the site dating at least as far back as the Bronze Age. A sister city located outside the fortifications named **Rabat** has a history almost as long.

Tradition holds that Publius, the Roman governor, welcomed **Paul the Apostle** to this area in 60 CE. Tradition also holds that St. Paul lived in a cave in Rabat during his stay in Malta. The ruins of a Roman villa (**Domus Romana**), located at the edge of these two cities, have become part of a **museum**. Mdina has been the home to many of the **Maltese nobility** and remains so to the present. It is an excellent example of a medieval walled city that is still inhabited. It is also commonly referred to as the "silent city" because its narrow, curved alleyways muffle sound and because automobile traffic is highly restricted. *See also* PALAZZO FALZON.

MEDIA. Although Malta is a tiny country with only 410,000 inhabitants representing a small audience further divided by the usage of several **languages**, it has a surprisingly high number of media outlets: four daily and 10 weekly newspapers, half of them published in Maltese (**Malti**) and the other half in English, all available on the Internet as well as in print; about a dozen radio stations covering the nation, mostly in Maltese; and six television channels broadcast by four stations in Maltese, English, and Italian. Such diversity poses a serious challenge to the commercial viability of popular print and audio-visual media. Limited resources make them more dependent on financing and, therefore, more susceptible to influence by the government and/or other powerful institutions with certain agendas.

This might partly explain a peculiarity of the Maltese media: much of it functions as direct organs of the **political parties**, the **trade unions**, or the **Catholic Church**. Thus, in addition to state-run media, the **Nationalist Party (NP)**, the **Malta Labour Party**, the General Workers' Union (GWU), and the Church each have their own newspapers as well as radio and/or television stations. The four daily newspapers are the *Independent* and the *Times of Malta* in English and two Maltese dailies, *L-Orrizont* (The Horizon) and *In-Nazzjon* (the Nation), published by the GWU and the NP, respectively. Although circulation numbers are not publicly revealed, the *Times of Malta*, a conservative leaning paper, is the most widely read with an estimated circulation of only 30,000.

Since the license to own a printing press was strictly controlled by the government under the **Knights** and even into the first four decades of **British** occupation, the earliest newspaper in Malta was published by the **French occupation** in 1798. The *Journal de Malte* was printed in French and Italian, the latter being the language of the educated in Malta at the time, but only in 500 copies. It ceased publication after several months when the French occupiers were forced to retreat into the walled city of **Valletta**. The French departed after two years, and the only newspaper, the *Gazetta del Governo* (Government Journal), was published by the British from 1813 on, albeit in Italian. However short their stay, the French left a lasting imprint: the Maltese word for newspaper today is still *gurnal* (pronounced like the French), instead of the Italian *gazetta*.

Freedom of the press was finally granted in 1939, and various supporters of the Italian Risorgimento, the Catholic Church, and others founded newspapers—some in Italian, others in English—promoted their particular perspectives and causes. The four daily papers were all published in Italian until the late 1870s. *Lehen is sewwa* (The Voice of Truth), a paper published by the Church in Maltese without interruption since 1928, is the oldest surviving newspaper.

Radio was first provided by the British occupiers in the mid 1930s over cable through a system called **Rediffusion**, which served until 1970. Television broadcasting first came to Malta from Italy in 1957 and soon after from the island itself. However, licenses were tightly controlled and became political pressure tools as the government of **Dom Mintoff** refused to grant the NP a broadcasting license. This was changed in 1991 when a new broadcasting law was adopted that permitted competition from private television broadcasters in Malta.

Satellite and Internet technology have completely changed access to media in Malta as elsewhere. On 10 October 2003, Finance and Economic Affairs Minister John Dalli announced that Malta had a higher rate of Internet users per 100 inhabitants than countries such as Greece, Spain, and France. From the beginning of 2000 to the end of 2001, Malta's Internet users per 100 inhabitants doubled from 13.3 to 25.4.

MEDITERRANEAN CONFERENCE CENTER. The **Sacred Infirmary** was built in 1574 by the **Knights of St. John**. Although not in use at the time, it was badly damaged by bombs during **World War II**. In the period 1950–60, there were plans for restoration, which were not carried out due to a lack of funds. Finally, in the late 1970s, new plans and the necessary funding were put together for the project. The restored Infirmary was inaugurated on 11 February 1979 and renamed the Mediterranean Conference Center. The restoration was called "superb" and won the Europa Nostra Award. Severely damaged by fire on 25 March 1987, the facility was rebuilt and reopened on 4 October 1989.

This state-of-the-art conference center boasts a main conference hall capable of seating 1,400 and five other rooms seating from 70 to 450. Each room also contains simultaneous interpretation facilities and the latest in audio-visual equipment. The La Vallette Restaurant on the premises is available to serve and seat 1,000 persons at one time. A series of exhibits displaying the history of the building as a hospital under the Knights was opened in its subterranean passageways in 2005.

MEGALITHIC TEMPLES. According to carbon dating, these are the oldest freestanding, human-made structures known to still exist anywhere in the world. Constructed between 3600 and 3000 BCE, they are older than the pyramids of Egypt, Stonehenge in England, or any structures from ancient Greece or Rome. The word "megalithic" comes from the Greek *mega*, meaning "big," and *lithos*, meaning "stone." Although megalithic temples can be found elsewhere in the world, there are 23 sites on Malta, representing an unusually high concentration, especially for such a remote land. They are built without the use of any mortar. The oldest of the temples is a pair called Ggantija (The Maltese word for "giant" because it was presumed that only giants could have moved such huge stones) and is located in **Gozo**. They consist of limestone slabs standing 6.67 meters (20 feet) above the earth, each weighing many tons. It is a source of amazement that the people who constructed the temples were able to move these slabs, much less to stand them up vertically in positions that have remained little changed for over 5,500 years. The later temples on Malta contain beautiful and intricate carvings on the stonework. Three are especially interesting in this regard—Hagar Qim, Mnajdra, and Tarxien. They are typically on high ground with two, three, or more elliptical chambers connected by passageways.

Another, the Hypogeum (from the Greek *hypo*, "below," and *geo*, meaning "earth") of Hal Saflieni was constructed below ground level and was carved out of the living globigerina limestone. Although its layout is similar to the other temples, it was constructed on three different levels, each containing a number of circular chambers with vaulted ceilings. The site, situated in a residential area of Paola, was accidentally discovered as builders were digging a foundation while constructing a new home. Although they attempted to hide the find from the authorities, word leaked out, and the site was saved for the public to explore instead of being cemented over. Created about 3000 BCE, it was like the other temples in that it was first a place of worship and later used for burial of the dead. The most impressive of the rooms architecturally, called "the holy of holies," was probably used for the sacrifice of animals. Another unusual room is the oracle chamber, which contains a 61-centimeter circular opening into an adjoining echo chamber. Interestingly, it will resonate a male voice but not a female one. A number of female figurines were discovered in the temples and are on display in the **Museum** of **Archaeology** located in the former **Auberge** de Provence in **Valletta**. The Hypogeum and the Ggantija temples were designated **World Heritage Sites** by the **United Nations** Educational, Scientific and Cultural Organization in 1980, and five other temples, including Hagar Qim and Mnajdra, were added to the list in 1992.

In the run-up to joining the **European Union (EU)**, Malta has begun to better appreciate the importance of the sites to **tourism**. A major incident of vandalism at the Mnajdra site in April of 2001 caused a public outcry and demonstrations, motivating the government to use some of the EU funding to better protect the sites. This includes a protective roof being installed over several of the temples in order to shield them from the elements. *See also* ARCHITECTURE; ZAMMIT, SIR THEMISTOCLES.

MERCIECA, SIR ARTURO. *See* BORG, SIR GEORGE.

MERCIECA, MONSIGNOR JOSEPH (1928–). Born in Victoria, **Gozo**, on 11 November 1928, Mercieca attended the Gozo Seminary and was ordained in March 1952. He earned the BA (London) plus the S.Th.D. from Gregorian University and the JD from Lateran University. He served as rector of the Gozo Seminary from 1959 to 1969, when he was called to Rome. While at the Vatican, he served in several responsible positions, including judge of the Roman Rota and consulator of the Sacred Congregations of Sacraments and of Doctrine of the Faith. In 1974, Mercieca was named auxiliary bishop of Malta and on 29 November 1976, consecrated as the archbishop of Malta upon the resignation of Archbishop **Michael Gonzi**. Although bishops are normally required to tender their resignation upon turning

75, which Bishop Mercieca did in 2003, the Vatican asked him to continue serving until the installation of Archbishop **Pawlu Cremona**, which took place on 26 January 2007.

MICELI-FARRUGIA, DAME LILIAN (1924–). A prominent philanthropist, a model of volunteerism, known in Malta for her extensive involvement in charitable work, Dame Miceli-Farrugia was born Lilian Bartoli on16 December 1924 to a businessman and politician. She was educated at the Convent of the Sacred Heart in St. Julians, Malta. On 12 January 1956, she married Anthony Miceli-Farrugia, KM, managing director and chairman of the Simonds Farsons Cisk Brewery, and they raised six children.

She served as chairman of the Co-Workers of Mother Teresa for 16 years. The well-known nun from India praised her for creating and editing a newsletter for the Youth Co-Workers called "I Thirst," which was circulated in 72 countries. Miceli-Farrugia and Mgr. Philip Calleja cofounded SOS Albania in 1991, a committee established in Malta to provide humanitarian aid to Albania. In addition to sending 53 containers of supplies, founding a clinic and a home for handicapped children in Elbasan, Albania, they equipped the first Roman **Catholic Church** and parish center and established an English-speaking middle school in Korce, Albania, run by a Maltese lay teaching society. They also provided humanitarian assistance to the Kosovar refugees in Albania and Malta, establishing playgrounds for deprived children in Kosovo.

Miceli-Farrugia chairs the board of SOS Malta, a nongovernmental organization that has aided earthquake victims in Pakistan and tsunami victims in Sri Lanka as well as supported charitable work in Malta. She has organized numerous fund-raisers for local hospitals, orphanages, schools, churches, and nursing organizations. She served as president of the Friends of the Sovereign Military Order of Malta (FMOM) in 2002–3 and for 20 years chaired the board of the Convent of the Sacred Heart.

Her years of leadership in charitable work have earned her many honors. In 1993, she was named Dame of the Sovereign Military Order of Malta (DM) and was the first **woman** to serve on its council in Malta. Her country honored her with the Medal for Service to the Republic in 1994. She received the title Dame of Magistral Grace of the Order of St. Lazarus in 1995, was chosen Senior Citizen of the Year in 1999, and given the title Dame of Magistral Grace in Obedience in the SMOM in 2006.

MICELI- FARRUGIA, MARK (1950–). Born on 23 July 1950 in St. Julians, the son of a prominent Maltese family in the beer brewing business, Mark Miceli-Farrugia attended the **University of Malta** and graduated from the London School of Economics in 1976 with an MS in Management Studies. Miceli pursued a career marketing beverages in Malta, Canada, and **Italy.**

Convinced by a French oenologist that Malta had all the prerequisites for producing quality wines, Miceli founded Meridiana Wine Estate in 1994 in partnership with Marchese Piero Antinori, descendant of one of the world's oldest vintner families (whose Giovanni di Piero Antinori founded the Florence Guild of Winemakers in 1385). Meridiana pioneered in Malta the production of quality wines to internationally recognized standards from grapes grown exclusively on Maltese soil. Like his father before him, who introduced the uniquely Maltese soda drink, "Kinnie," Miceli-Farrugia developed and marketed a new aperitif, "Leila," in 2004.

In 1992, Miceli-Farrugia graduated from the Mediterranean Academy of Diplomatic Studies at the University of Malta and in 2003 was appointed as nonresident ambassador to the Baltic states of Estonia, Latvia, and Lithuania. He has served on various public and private boards, including the Malta Chamber of Commerce and Enterprise, Malta Enterprise, L. Farrugia and Sons Ltd., and the Farsons Group of Companies. He was elected president of the Maltese-American Chamber of Commerce, serving from 2005–7. On 25 July 2007, he presented his credentials as ambassador to the United States. He also serves as high commissioner designate of Malta to Canada and the Bahamas. Miceli-Farrugia is married to Josette, a solicitor, and they have a son, Christopher.

MIFSUD, SIR UGO P. (1889–1942). Malta's third **prime minister** and the first to serve a full term, he was born in **Valletta** on 12 September 1889. He graduated from the Royal **University of Malta** in 1910 with a degree in law and pursued a successful career in international law based in Brussels. Mifsud was elected secretary to the

National Assembly committee drafting a **constitution**. In 1921, he was elected to the Legislative Assembly as a candidate for the Unione Popolare Maltese (UPM) party. On 24 September 1924, he became the youngest prime minister in the **British** Empire. When the UPM merged with **Enrico Mizzi's** Partito Democratico Nazionalista (PDN) to form the **National Party**, Mifsud became co-leader of the new party. He was part of the delegation that traveled to London in 1932, submitting Malta's petition to be granted dominion status. Mifsud headed five different ministries at various times in his political career, including finance (1924–26) and justice (1926–27 and 1932–33). On 9 February 1942, he suffered a heart attack after delivering an impassioned speech against the plan to deport several Maltese citizens viewed as Italian sympathizers and died on 11 February 1942. *See also* PANZAVECCHIA, MONSIGNOR IGNAZIO.

MIFSUD BONNICI, DRS. CARMELO. So numerous are the members of the Mifsud Bonnici family involved in Malta's politics that the clan could be considered the Maltese equivalent of the Kennedy family in the **United States**. There are, in fact, three persons from the same family named Dr. Carmelo Mifsud Bonnici, each of them having earned the LLD degree at the **University of Malta** and each of them having served or currently serving as representatives in Government! A fourth relative, **Dr. Ugo Mifsud Bonnici**, son of the first Dr. Carmelo and (like his brother, Giuseppe, a professor of philosophy of law and an emeritus chief justice) also holder of the LLD, served as **president** of Malta (1994–99).

The first Dr. Carmelo Mifsud Bonnici was born in 1897. He served as minister of the treasury in the **Nationalist Party** governments of 1924 and 1932. He was a respected professor of criminal law at the University of Malta and served on the Elected Council under **British rule**. He died in 1948 after a long illness.

The second Dr. Carmelo Mifsud Bonnici, LLD, nephew of the first, was born on 17 July 1933. He received his BA and LLD at the Royal University of Malta and did additional study in industrial law at London University. Unlike the rest of his clan who were Nationalists, he made his mark with the Labourites when, as one of their legal advisors, he helped to prevent the Nationalist Government from passing an Industrial Relations Bill that had included provisions for criminalization of striking workers. He became deputy leader of the **Malta Labour Party** in 1980, minister of labour and social services in 1982, and senior deputy prime minister and minister of **education** in 1983. Mifsud Bonnici gained the nickname of "Doctor Zero" because he was not elected but rather appointed (coopted) to replace another MP who did not complete his term. Similarly, upon the resignation of **Dom Mintoff** on 22 December 1984, he became **prime minister**, hand-picked by Mintoff himself, who had the political influence to get Mifsud Bonnici elected, many think as a defensive move to preclude election of another candidate less desirable to Mintoff. Although Mifsud Bonnici was given most of the blame for the party's loss in the 1987 election (it was said that his heart attack was caused by that blame), he was made leader of the opposition and held that title until the party again lost in the **elections** of 1992. He was succeeded as leader of the party and leader of the opposition by **Dr. Alfred Sant**. In 2005, Mifsud Bonnici briefly made headlines with his strong opposition to the MLP support for the newly drafted constitution of the **European Union**.

The third Dr. Carmelo Mifsud Bonnici, LLD was born in Floriana on 17 February 1960 and was named after his grandfather, first mentioned above. He earned his LLD from the University of Malta in 1984. A Nationalist, like his father Ugo, he was elected as a Nationalist MP in 1998 and 2003. He was appointed parliamentary secretary for the Ministry of Justice and Home Affairs in 2003 and reappointed in 2004. Mifsud Bonnici is also a senior lecturer in Roman law at the University of Malta. *See also* MIFSUD BONNICI, DR. UGO.

MIFSUD BONNICI, DR. UGO (1932–). Born in Cospicua, Dr. Mifsud Bonnici received the BA in 1952 from the Royal **University of Malta** and the LLD in 1955. He was editor of *Malta Letteraria* from 1952 to 1962 and *Il Poplu* in 1966. Although Cospicua, where he still resides today, is a stronghold of the **Malta Labour Party**, he was successful as a **Nationalist** candidate for Parliament in every **election** beginning in 1966. In 1987, he was named minister of education and held that position until his selection as **president** in 1994. During his tenure as minister of **education**, Mifsud Bonnici became known for his continued encouragement of the fine arts, appearing personally at most concerts, recitals, and art exhibitions. During the same period, he served as president of the General Council and the Administrative Council of the **Nationalist Party**. *See also* MIFSUD BONNICI, DRS. CARMELO.

MINTOFF, DOMINIC (DOM) (1916–). Born in Cospicua on 6 August 1916, as one of 11 children, Mintoff completed the Lyceum in 1933 and received the BS degree in engineering and **architecture** from the **University of Malta** in 1937. A Rhodes scholar at Oxford, he was awarded the MA in engineering science in 1939. Mintoff served as an architect in Malta and civil engineer in Great Britain. He had joined the **Malta Labour Party (MLP)** in his youth and became secretary general upon his return to the islands in 1943. After being elected to membership on the Council of Government and the Executive Council in 1945, he was elected to **Parliament** under the new **Constitution** in 1947. Mintoff was named deputy prime minister and minister of works and construction in the new government. After resigning from Parliament in 1949, he was chosen leader of the MLP at age 33, its youngest leader to date. A combative politician, he served as **prime minister** from 1955 to 1958, when he resigned in protest against Britain's firing of several dockworkers.

The **British** government declared a state of emergency in the wake of the ensuing riots of April 1958, which were instigated by Mintoff's supporters. The MacMichael Constitution was abrogated. Mintoff is blamed by many because of his strident opposition to the British and the **Catholic Church**. In 1962, Archbishop **Michael Gonzi** issued a letter stating that any one voting for Mintoff and the other Labour candidates was guilty of a mortal sin. Mintoff was reelected, but the **Nationalist Party** candidates got more votes, so he served as leader of the opposition from 1962 to 1971. He was returned to Parliament in every **election** he contested until the end of his last term in 1997. Although he resigned a total of three times in his political career, once in conflict with Malta's government, once when the British declared a state of emergency, and in 1984 to let a younger man take over, Mintoff served his government with only minor interruptions for over 50 years, including two terms as prime minister.

More than mildly influenced by the Fabian Society during his days at Oxford, Mintoff's socialist leanings were evident as he nationalized the Malta **Dockyards, banking,** shipping, and many other industries. He courted Muammar Qaddafi of **Libya** and the communist regimes of Cuba, Russia, and China. He was forced often to state publicly "I am not and never was a Communist," a label his opponents attempted to attach to him. Tremendously popular among the working class, he seldom wavered in his anti-British and anticlerical policies. His proposals for the relations between Church and state became known as Mintoff's "Six Points" and were the center of continuing tension between the MLP and the Church. The principles of the "Six Points" were eventually achieved by agreement between the two.

Among Mintoff's other accomplishments was a painful reorganization of the university along more contemporary lines and the transformation of Malta into a Republic headed by a **president.** He forced the reduction of fiscal reliance on the military expenditures of other nations together with a nonaligned status. He had the hospitals that were previously owned by the Church brought under government control and helped to establish a greater commonality among public, private, and Church-run schools. These changes did not happen easily and were accompanied by corruption and often by violence.

Mintoff was (and is) abrasive, disputatious, and impatient. He is used to having his way, and several times there were vague suggestions that violence might be directed at those who opposed him. A contemporary member of the Foreign Service recently published his experience of Mintoff's berating a minister in front of his colleagues for suggesting an idea that Mintoff called ridiculous but several days later himself proposed and claimed as his own.

This contrarian aggressiveness caused a split in the MLP when Mintoff voted against a project championed by the MLP members. Mintoff's vote against his own party caused the collapse of the government and ended the Labour Party rule of Prime Minister **Alfred Sant** after less than two years. In 2006, at age 90, Mintoff sued the government and received a settlement because his property was adversely affected by a nearby recycling plant. He was (and is) both loved and hated. It can be said, without fear of contradiction, that he brought more changes to this small nation, and in a shorter time, than any leader in all of its modern history. *See also* PRIVILEGIUM FORI.

MIZZI, DR. ENRICO (1885–1950). Mizzi was born in 1885, shortly after his father, **Dr. Fortunato Mizzi**, had formed Malta's first political party. Like his Maltese father (his mother was Italian), he was educated in law. By upbringing and **education**, he was Italianate through and through, and this was a root cause of his anti-**British** and Maltese nationalist sentiments. He looked to **Italy** as Malta's "mother country," saying that the Maltese and Italians are united in fact and should be united in law. Mizzi was first elected to the seat from **Gozo** in 1916 and promptly stated that he was the representative for the Italian nationality of Malta. He was soon arrested and condemned to a year of imprisonment. The **governor** reduced the penalty to a reprimand. However, in May 1917, Mizzi was arrested and court-martialed for sedition during wartime. He was found guilty of all charges and sentenced to another year of imprisonment. Although this sentence was also reduced, this time to a severe reprimand, Mizzi lost the right to practice his profession as well.

In the late 1920s and early 1930s, Mizzi's newspaper, *Malta*, published high praise for Benito Mussolini and Italian fascism. He strongly suggested that Italy and Great Britain enter into a trade of colonies, Malta for Eritrea, but only if Malta were granted "the dignity of a free people." Politically, he was able to bring several other parties together under the banner of the **Nationalist Party**. When **World War II** began, Mizzi was **interned** by the British and then deported to Uganda. After the war, with Italy as a **North Atlantic Treaty Organization (NATO)** partner, his rehabilitation hastened. A cultured and intelligent man, he was a true patriot. He died in 1950.

MIZZI, DR. FORTUNATO (1844–1905). Educated in law, Mizzi was first elected to the Council of Government in 1880. He consistently opposed the colonial government because its elected members were always in the minority. In the **election** of 1883, he was courted by the Partito Anti-Reformista because he was both a man of principle and a champion of Italian culture and **language**, which he called "the tongue given to the Maltese by mother nature." The party placed primary emphasis upon the retention of Italian as the language of commerce, **education**, and government. Mizzi was returned to Council in that election, only to resign in 1886, an action that became his antigovernment practice throughout his political life. He joined his voice with that of **Gerald Strickland** to advocate a return to the **Consiglio Popolare**. This agitation resulted in the **Constitution** of 1887. As editor of his own newspaper, the *Gazzetta di Malta*, Mizzi was unwavering in his opposition to government policy and in his support of Maltese nationalism and all things Italian. He once said the Maltese were attached to "the British Flag, the language of **Italy** and the **religion** of the pope." Strickland's strong pro-British stance eventually caused a severe rift between the two. Mizzi was also a bitter foe of **Sigismondo Savona**.

Eventually the Partito Anti-Reformista became the **Partito Nazionale** with Mizzi as leader. In turn, that Party was the ancestor of the contemporary **Nationalist Party**. Fortunato Mizzi died on 18 May 1905, and his son, **Enrico Mizzi**, succeeded him as leader of the Partito Nazionale. *See also* POLITICAL PARTIES; ITALIA IRREDENTA.

MOSTA DOME. Malta is a land of over 350 churches, and the St. Marija Assunta parish church in Mosta is one of the most impressive among these. The phrase "parish church" usually denotes a humble structure without any particular **architectural** significance, but this is not true in Malta, where ordinary churches can resemble the cathedrals of other nations. Built in neoclassical style and featuring one of the largest domes in the world, it is a close imitation of the Pantheon in Rome, including a colonnade entrance. Construction was begun in 1883 and completed 27 years later.

On 9 April 1942, at about 4:40 p.m., a German bomber was attempting to hit the Ta' Qali airfield located just west of Mosta when his bomb release mechanism malfunctioned. The bomb drop was delayed by several seconds so that instead of striking the airfield, a bomb plunged through the dome, hit the marble floor, bounced off a wall, and skidded the entire length of the church. It not only did not explode, but not one of the 350 worshippers in the church was injured. About the same time, two other bombs fell just outside the church, also without exploding. The people of Mosta have no difficulty accepting that they received divine protection that day. Today, the bomb that fell through the roof is still on display for visitors to the church.

MUSEUMS. Recognizing the increasing importance of **tourism** to the **economy** and that Malta needed to expand its offerings for tourists beyond "sun and sand," the country has dramatically increased both the quality and number of Malta's museums in recent decades. As of 2009, there were 30 museums and historical sites, 21 on Malta and nine on **Gozo**. Many of these are under the management of the national **Heritage Malta** Trust, others are privately owned, such as the Casa Rocca Piccola, a residence with a 400-year history that is still partially occupied by its owner, the Baron Nicolas de Piro. Others are run by nongovernmental organizations, such as Palazzo Falzon. The oldest public museum is the National Museum of **Archeology**, first opened in 1905 as the Museum of **Valletta** and later reopened as the National Museum of Archeology in 1924 through the dedicated direction of **Dr. Themistocles Zammit**. Many of the collections in Malta are eclectic, for example, the Cathedral Museum in **Mdina** contains the second largest collection of Albrecht Durer prints in the world, along with an extensive coin collection.

Some installations may not really qualify as museums, as for example the "Infirmary Museum" located in the underground passageways of the former infirmary, now Malta's main conference center. It is not a museum; other than some pharmacy jars, it doesn't house many artifacts but rather numerous life-size figures depicting scenes from the time when the caves were used as a hospital. Similarly, the Fort Rinella 100-ton canon exhibit might also not qualify as a museum, although of great historical interest. Other "museums," such as the one housed in **Jean Parisot de la Valette**'s chapel in Vittoriosa, contain a hodge podge of very interesting church artifacts (in addition to Valette's hat!) that document various periods of history but are displayed without professional organization or proper preservation techniques. Much of this is due to lack of funds in the face of such an abundance of rich heritage. *See also* DOMUS ROMANA; GHAR DALAM; INQUISITION; MEGALITHIC TEMPLES; PALAZZO FALZON; SACRED INFIRMARY; ST. JOHN'S CO-CATHEDRAL.

MUSIC. It is safe to assume that the prehistoric **neolithic** temple builders had rituals that involved some singing or chanting, yet aside from the mention of various cantors such as Guido Anselmi (1112), Philippus (1124), and Willelmus (1234) and reference to nine musicians employed by the militia at **Mdina**, the earliest written records documenting the existence of music in Malta date from 1600. The **Knights of St. John** brought with them from the various houses of Europe a new level of cultural and artistic sophistication. This included music, especially that used in church services for which the knights and their bishops established "cappellas" in **Valletta** and **Mdina**. At first they hired musicians from **Italy**, which became important training grounds for Maltese musicians such as Pietro Gristi (1696–1738) and Girolamo Abos (1715–1760), both sent to Naples as young men to study music. Abos never returned to Malta and traveled extensively, becoming a conductor and composer well known throughout Europe. Gristi did return and was appointed *maestro di cappella* at the cathedral in Mdina in 1717.

Giuseppe Balzano (born in Valletta, 19 September 1616), the *maestro di cappella* at the cathedral in Mdina, is credited with the earliest work by a Maltese composer. Written in 1652 and entitled "Beatus Vir," the composition is a motet for two tenors, bass, and continuo in the early Italian Baroque style. Although it is Balzano's only signed and complete work known to exist, recent research has identified seven other hymns and cantatas as likely composed by him.

In the middle of the 17th century, a new form of music, the opera, was introduced to Malta from Italy. In 1664, *Annibale in Capua*, probably written by Sicilian composer Vincenzo Tozzi, was performed in Valletta. A libretto by Enrico Magi, *Dafne, ovvero La Vergine Trionfante* (circa 1650), is the earliest Maltese opera text known to exist; although, there is no evidence of who, if anyone, composed music for the text nor whether the work was ever performed. The enthusiasm in Malta for the new form of music is evidenced by the construction of the **Manoel Theater** in 1732. A venue well suited for opera performances, it remains one of Europe's oldest such theaters still in use.

Mikiel Ang Vella (1715–1792) was born and died in Bormla, where he is credited with being the first to introduce the secular cantata to Malta, another musical development that originated in Italy. He also started the first school in Malta that was modeled on those of Italy and devoted to training musicians. His students included Azopardi, Isouard, Burlo, and Magri, all significant musicians and composers in the middle to late 18th century.

Nicolo Isouard (1773–1818), who in later life preferred using the name Nicolo de Malthe, brought Malta to the attention of music lovers throughout Europe. Like most Maltese composers before him, he left Malta to study in Naples, where he soon made a name for himself by composing a highly successful opera, *L'Avviso ai Maritati*, which had its debut in Florence in 1794. **Grand Master** Emmanuel de Rohan called him back to Malta to serve as *maestro di cappella* at **St. John's Co-Cathedral** in Valletta for several years, but Isouard, a Francophile, left Malta when the French were evicted from the islands. He settled in Paris, where he became an instant success with operas in the opéra comique style, such as *Jeannot et Colin, Joconde*, and *Cendrillon*, which were well received throughout Europe. He never returned to Malta and died in 1818.

Two families, creating music in Malta for almost two and a half centuries, deserve particular mention. These were a remarkable five generations of the Nani family and a contemporary four generations of the Bugeja family. Angelo Nani (1751–1844), a contemporary of Isouard, was a violinist from Venice hired to play for the Order by Grand Master de Rohan. Angelo's son, Emanuele Nani (1768–1860), was also a violinist and musical director (*maestro di capella*) who performed throughout Europe. He conducted a concert in honor of **Alexander Ball** upon the latter's arrival to govern Malta. Emanuele's son, Dr. Paolo Nani (1814–1904), was the most prolific composer of the family. He took over his father's position upon the latter's death. Paolo's son, Antonio Nani (1842–1929), became a popular *maestro di cappella* as well and composer of church music still popular today. Antonio's son, Paolo Nani (1906–1986), was the last musician of this impressive lineage, who studied in Rome and, like his father and grandfathers before him, served as a popular *maestro di cappella*.

A similar family dynasty, lasting almost two centuries, began with Pietro Paolo Bugeja (1772–1828), for whom Angelo Nani (mentioned above) served as first violinist. A successful composer, Bugeja served as *maestro di cappella* in Naples for five years before returning to Malta to become musical director at the Teatro Reale (Manoel Theater). He succeeded Francesco Azzopardi as *maestro di cappella* at St. John's Co-Cathedral in 1809, a position he handed down to his son, Vincenzo Bugeja, 19 years later in 1828. In addition to replacing his father as musical director in numerous churches, Vincenzo wrote an opera, *Lodoviska*, funeral masses, antiphons, and six symphonies.

His younger brother, Filippo (1808–1891), was an organist, pianist, and musical director, as was Vincenzo's oldest son, Riccardo Bugeja. The great grandson of Pietro Paolo, Vincent Bugeja (1910–1967), founded and directed the Malta Amateur Theatrical Company after the Italian opera company departed Malta because of the approach of **World War II**. Although Italian operas were still on the program, the performers were entirely Maltese.

The most noteworthy Maltese composer of the late 19th century is Paolino Vassallo (1856–1913), whose symphonic poems, concert overtures, and symphonies used advanced harmonic language and French structures, breaking away from the Italian forms and structures that had dominated Maltese music for centuries. Vassallo was a leader in the *motu proprio* effort of Pope Pius X to make church music less florid and more dignified and sacred.

In the twentieth century, four composers have achieved international recognition: Carmelo Pace (1906–1993), **Charles Camilleri** (1931–2009), Pawlu Grech (1938–), and Joseph Vella (1942–).

The most significant form of Maltese folk music is the *ghana*, a musical narration usually in rhyme and accompanied by guitar. Other musical instruments used for folk music in Malta are those common to the Mediterranean region, including flutes, pan flutes, tambourines, and drums, among others. Unique to Malta is a form of bagpipe called *zaqq*, which is traditionally made from a dog skin and held under the arm. Since with the feet stretched upward, it still closely resembles the animal from which it is made, this instrument is offensive to modern sensibilities and likely to disappear. Music in Malta has also been promoted over the centuries by the many **band clubs** in towns and villages, which participate in feast days and other communal celebrations. *See also* ROYAL OPERA HOUSE.

– N –

NATIONAL ANTHEM. *See* "INNU MALTI."

NATIONAL HOLIDAYS. Five days are celebrated in Malta as official national holidays: **Independence** Day, 21 September, celebrates Malta's gaining its independence from Great Britain in 1964; Republic Day, 13 December, celebrates the change from monarchy to republic in 1974; **Freedom Day**, 31 March, commemorates the departure of the last **British** military forces from the islands in 1979; **Sette Giugno**, 7 June, remembers the deaths of four young Maltese in the bread uprising of 1919, considered the birth of nationalism in Malta; finally, the Feast of Our Lady of Victories (Il Victorja) on 8 September has triple significance for the islands—it celebrates the birth of Our Lady, the defeat of the Turks to end the **Great Siege of 1565**, and the collapse of fascism in **Italy**, ending the assault on Malta during **World War II**. The day is commemorated with a traditional wreath-laying ceremony at the Great Siege Monument in Floriana.

Because independence was achieved while the **Nationalist Party (NP)** was in office, its celebration is favored by that party, whereas Republic Day and Freedom Day occurred while the **Malta Labour Party** held office, and the celebration of these receive particular encouragement from that part of the political spectrum. In addition to the official national days, there are no fewer than nine other public holidays on which workers get time off, including Christmas, New Year's Eve, Workers' Day (1 May), and religious holidays such as Good Friday and several feast days. In 2006, the ruling NP government, in an attempt to improve Malta's productivity, moved to reduce the number of holidays workers get by ending the practice of granting a day off in the following week whenever a holiday falls on the weekend.

NATIONAL LIBRARY. Known locally as the Biblioteca, the library's origins go back at least to 1555 when the books of deceased **Knights of St. John** were automatically bequeathed to the Order. In 1763, 9,700 volumes were given by a Knight, L. Guerin de Tencin, for the purpose of turning the total collection into a public library. In 1776, the Order declared these volumes a public library in perpetuity. In 1785, the design and construction of a new building was commissioned. However, because of the **French invasion** and subsequent **British** occupation, the building was not truly used as a library until 1813.

It was not until the 20th century that the collection gained major importance when, under Head Librarian Sir Hannibal Scicluna, the archives of the Order were acquired. After **World War II**, an equally important part of the collection became devoted to items of Melitensia. With the opening of a new public library in 1974, it remained solely a research library and, in 1976, became in name what it really had been for so many years, the National Library of Malta, a major cultural asset for so small a nation.

NATIONALIST PARTY (NP). In the 1921 **elections,** the **Unione Politica Maltese,** led by **Mgr. Ignazio Panzavecchia,** topped all others in votes received. At the same time, the weakest showing was by **Dr. Enrico Mizzi**'s Partito Nazionalista Democratico. In the 1924 elections, the relative positions of the two parties changed little, but they did join together to form a minority government. As a result of this coalition, the Partito Nazionalista was formed on 26 January 1926, largely through the political skill of Dr. Mizzi. The program for the 1927 elections promised to protect the use of the Italian **language** in **education** and the courts. Although English and Italian were equally accepted for educational purposes, the party remained adamant that Italian remain the sole language of the courts. The Nationalists barely lost the 1927 election for the Legislative Assembly, but they did gain control of the Senate. After taking office following the elections of 1932, the Nationalists proceeded on a blatant pro-**Italy** course, encouraging the use of the Italian language and disseminating fascist propaganda. Official warnings to the party went unheeded, and the colonial **governor** suspended the **Constitution** in 1933.

After the end of **World War II,** the political appeal of the Italian language and culture had ceased to exist, and the NP dropped any mention of Italy from its program. Even the party name was changed from the Italian "Partito Nazionalista" to the Maltese "Partit Nazzjonalista," the name it uses today. Instead of its old platform, it began to champion other matters of political concern, primarily the drive to gain dominion status within the **Commonwealth.**

The party's leanings were for **independence,** a mild form of democratic socialism coupled with a probusiness attitude, and an international position favoring the Western Bloc of nations. The drive to join the **European Union (EU)** was successfully led by the NP, which has remained in power since 1987, except for the 22-month interlude when the **Malta Labour Party (MLP)** took over. Recently, the process of adopting EU laws, norms, and standards, along with some controversial development projects and a general slowdown of the **economy**, caused popular dissatisfaction with the NP in government among Maltese voters. Victories for the MLP in **local council** elections of 2008 and 2009, in addition to the results of EU parliamentary elections in June 2009, indicate dissatisfaction with the Nationalist government and its leader, **Prime Minister Lawrence Gonzi**. The NP managed to win the general election of 2008 by only 1,500 votes, thanks in part to the personal charisma of Gonzi and a poorly managed campaign by the opposing MLP candidates. *See also* BORG OLIVIER, DR. GIORGIO; DE MARCO, GUIDO; FENECH ADAMI, DR. EDWARD; GANADO, DR. HERBERT; GONZI, DR. LAWRENCE; LANGUAGE QUESTION; MIZZI, DR. ENRICO; POLITICAL PARTIES; TABONE, DR. VINCENT "CENSU".

NATO. *See* NORTH ATLANTIC TREATY ORGANIZATION.

NEOLITHIC SETTLEMENTS. Although Malta can be seen from **Sicily** on a very clear day, the actual movement of humans across the 100-kilometer (60-mile) span of the Mediterranean came relatively late, probably about 5000 BCE. When neolithic tribes finally arrived, they found fertile land, abundant animal life, and a surrounding sea filled with fish. Evidence indicates that they brought some livestock with them. This would mean that in addition to farmers, they must have been skilled sailors as well, capable of building and sailing fairly large vessels. The numerous caves on both Malta and **Gozo** also provided natural shelters. Later, simple huts, grouped into small villages, were erected, the remains of which were discovered at Skorba, just outside the village of Zebbieh on Malta. Artifacts discovered at this location span the period of about 4000 BCE to 2500 BCE, well into the Copper Age. *See also* ARCHEOLOGY; MEGALITHIC TEMPLES.

NOBILITY. *See* MALTESE NOBILITY.

NONGOVERNMENTAL ORGANIZATIONS. *See* FLIMKIEN GHAL AMBJENT AHJAR; FONDAZZJONI PATRIMONJU MALTI; FONDAZZJONI WIRT ARTNA.

NORMAN CONQUEST. Near the beginning of the 11th century, Normans returning from a pilgrimage to the Holy Land passed through southern **Italy**. While there, they were invited to stay and become employed as mercenary soldiers. Over the years, they were joined by other Norman fighters and became very powerful. Gradually, they began to rule over their former employers. The first Norman leaders were the sons of Tancred, a Norman knight. After gaining control of Calabria in the foot of Italy, the Normans turned their attention to **Sicily**, invading it in 1061 under the leadership of Tancred's youngest son, Roger. The **Arabs** controlling Sicily put up fierce resistance, and it was not until 1090 that it fell. That same year, Roger and his fleet, using a ruse, took the island of Malta from the Arabs without bloodshed on either side. Roger gained a revered place in the history of Malta, a place which has, it seems, grown with the passage of time. Tradition holds that it was Roger the Norman who gave Malta its **flag** by tearing off a portion of his own flag.

Malta still remained a backwater, however. While many art treasures and examples of fine **architecture** of that time were left in Sicily, almost nothing remains in the Maltese Islands except for a few homes in **Mdina** and a series of lookout towers along the seashore. There is some evidence of a Muslim presence until about 1122. In that year, the Arabs refused to pay their annual tribute and secretly plotted to massacre the Maltese as a first step toward regaining the islands. By accident, the plot was discovered, and the slaughter turned the other way. Word of the situation was sent to Sicily, and Roger's son and successor, Roger II, mounted a second conquest. The leaders of the uprising were put to death, and many Arabs were deported.

NORTH ATLANTIC TREATY ORGANIZATION (NATO). Never itself a member of NATO, except by proxy through the **British**, the Malta government had accepted the stationing of a NATO command post and continued to work closely with Great Britain and other NATO member countries after Malta achieved **independence**. This changed abruptly when the government of **Dom Mintoff** came into power in 1971, strongly advocating a **foreign policy** of nonalignment. Mintoff envisioned Malta as a "Switzerland in the Mediterranean," a neutral and peace-promoting nation. As a result, the subheadquarters that NATO had maintained in Malta were forced to close and moved to Naples, Italy, where it remains today. The British forces were allowed to remain until 1979, but only after Malta had negotiated greatly increased financial contributions from the United States, Great Britain, and other NATO members. U.S. warships ceased making liberty calls until 1992, after the **Nationalist Party (NP)**, with a decidedly more pro-Western stance, had been returned to power. Malta is still very proud of its posture of neutrality but in 1995, opted to join the Partnership for Peace program (PfP), which had been created in 1994 for nations wanting a more limited relationship with NATO that did not necessarily require committing troops.

When the government of **Alfred Sant** came to power in 1996, it suspended Malta's participation in the PfP, stating that it ran counter to Malta's neutrality. In 2003, workers at the **dockyards**, who initially balked at being asked to work on the U.S. warship *LaSalle*, ultimately gave in to financial realities. The NP government softened its stance towards NATO, which was asked to and did provide security during the high profile **Commonwealth** Heads of Government meeting in November of 2005. On 4 April, at the NATO Bucharest Summit, Malta announced that it was rejoining the PfP as well as joining the Euro-Atlantic Partnership Council, a forum for NATO allies and PfP partners.

– O –

OMBUDSMAN. On 25 July 1995, the **Parliament** adopted a bill creating the Office of the Ombudsman, a Swedish word meaning "representative." The ombudsman's primary duty is to investigate complaints by individual citizens about administrative actions of their government. Although the existence of such a representative has been noted as early as the Qin dynasty in China, the modern version of an ombudsman was established in Sweden by an act of Parliament at the beginning of the 19th century. The **European Union** and much of the rest of the world have adopted the office along with the Swedish word for it. The ombudsman of Malta is appointed by the **president**, but the appointment must be approved by a two-thirds vote of the Parliament. The term of the ombudsman is currently set at five years and can be extended by reappointment for another five years. The first ombudsman, Joe Sammut, was appointed in 1995 and served two five-year terms. On 12 December 2005, Parliament unanimously approved the appointment of former Chief Justice Joseph Said Pullicino as ombudsman.

OPERATION HERKULES. When Crete was invaded by the Germans on 20 May 1941 and surrendered on 1 June, the Maltese expected to be next on the Nazi hit list. Field Marshal Albert Kesselring, commander of all the German forces in southern **Italy** and **Sicily**, had suggested the possibility of such an invasion to Adolf Hitler as early as February 1941. After strong urging from Kesselring, he had agreed to the proposal. However, as time went by, Hitler's reluctance to give real consideration to such an invasion remained. Nevertheless, Kesselring went forward with the planning and preparations under the code name of "Herkules." It was to be a joint invasion with the **Italians**, who called it "Operazione C3: Malta." By May 1942, three airstrips for gliders near Catania, Sicily, were being used for training. The invasion was to be by amphibious landings, by parachute drop, and by troop-carrying gliders. Almost 100,000 well-trained German and Italian soldiers and their equipment were poised for the main event set for the early morning hours of 10 July. But a call to action never came. After the capture of Tobruk, **Libya**, on 21 June, the invasion date was postponed in the euphoria of that success. It turned out that this postponement was final. In his published memoirs, Kesselring said that two major errors were committed by the Axis powers in the conduct of the war. The first he listed as Italy's failure to occupy Malta at the beginning of the war. The second was Hitler's refusal to invade the islands later on. *See also* WORLD WAR II.

OPERATION PEDESTAL. Although Malta had long been a net importer of almost every commodity, additional demands for imports were brought on by its military response to German and Italian bombardments during **World War II**. Estimates indicate that the islands needed 26,000 tons of supplies (23,587 metric tons) each month—the balanced cargo of three large merchant ships. In 1942, **British** air and submarine forces became increasingly successful in destroying Axis cargo ships en route to North Africa in support of the campaign there.

In an effort to eliminate this serious threat to its success, the **Italian and German** air forces greatly increased the bombing attacks. During March and April, the tonnage of bombs dropped on Malta was twice the amount dropped on London during the entire year of its worst air raids. Special attention was given to denying any resupply by hitting the convoys often and hard on their way to Malta from either the eastern or western ends of the Mediterranean Sea.

During the first six months of 1942, a total of less than 26,000 tons landed at Malta and that at a cost of 29 Allied ships either sunk or badly damaged. In spite of severe rationing for both civilians and military personnel, great shortages were occurring. Because of the scarcity of food, some calculated that the islands would be forced to surrender between 31 August and 7 September 1942. Aviation fuel and antiaircraft ammunition would be fully depleted even before that time, forcing an end to almost all military activity against the enemy. It was decided that a massive effort be made to get critical supplies to the beleaguered islands.

A huge convoy under the name of Operation Pedestal was ordered to escort 14 merchant cargo ships to Malta. These ships were to be protected by two groups of escorts: Force Z with two battleships, four aircraft carriers, three cruisers, and 12 destroyers; and Force X with four cruisers, 12 destroyers, and a fleet tugboat. Accompanying was Supply Force R, consisting of two tankers, four corvettes, and a tugboat to refuel the convoy at sea. Following behind the main convoy was another aircraft carrier escorted by eight destroyers. Aboard this carrier were Spitfire fighters to be flown to Malta. The entire convoy was to proceed through the Mediterranean to a point east-by-southeast of **Sicily**, called the Skerki Bank, where Force Z was to turn back, leaving the protection of the remaining convoy with Force X.

The Axis powers were aware of the convoy's intentions before it even left Great Britain, and they made plans to counter it with massive air, sea, and undersea attacks. They were successful in sinking nine of the important cargo ships and damaging the remaining five. However, those five did arrive in Malta to unload 55,000 tons of cargo. The last one to arrive was the tanker SS *Ohio*, which was sinking as it was brought into the harbor, lashed between two destroyers. It arrived on 15 August, the Holy Feast Day of the Assumption, known in Malta as Santa Marija Day. The convoy is still reverently referred to as "il-Convoy ta' Santa Marija." Four naval ships were sunk and six suffered major damage. Over 350 lives were lost but the strength of Malta was revived. *See also* AXIS BLOCKADE.

OPERAZIONE C3: MALTA. *See* OPERATION HERKULES.

ORDER OF ST. JOHN. *See* KNIGHTS OF ST. JOHN.

OUTREMER. From the French *outre mer* meaning "beyond the sea," it was the name used during the 11th, 12th, and 13th centuries to refer to the Latin Colonies in the Holy Land and the Levant. Hoping to recover these lands from the control of the Muslims, the Christians of Europe formed various Orders of Knights under papal sanction, including the **Order of St. John.** Loosely translated, Outremer was used to refer not only to the lands themselves but also to the efforts at their recovery. Thus, the Crusades were efforts at Outremer.

– P –

PALAZZO FALZON. One of the oldest buildings still standing in **Mdina**, it was originally a one-story house built in the first half of the 13th century. A second story was added in the 15th century. It was purchased in 1927 by Captain Olof Gollcher, OBE, who united various parts of the building into a home and renamed it "The Norman House." Born into one of the noble families of Malta, Gollcher was a philanthropist and artist. He collected an impressive number of valuable objects, including paintings, silver, furniture, jewelry, oriental rugs, armor, and a library containing over 4,500 valuable books and manuscripts. In 1943, he intended to donate the house to the Venerable Order of the Hospital of St. John of Jerusalem in the **British** Realm, of which he was a member, but the order did not feel capable of managing the property, which was handed over to the Captain O. F. Gollcher Art and Archeology Foundation. In 2001, the **Fondazzjoni Patrimonju Malti** was given control over the management and restoration of the Palazzo. A five-year restoration process was finished in 2007 when the Palazzo was opened to the public as a historic house **museum**.

PANZAVECCHIA, MONSIGNOR IGNAZIO (1855–1925). A champion of the "Catholic Cause," Panzavecchia became the leader of the **Unione Politica Maltese (UPM)**, a successor to the Partito Popolare. The UPM was pro-Church, staunchly anti-Protestant, populist, somewhat pro-English **language**, antigovernment but not anti-**British**. In the 1921 **elections**, the UPM gained the largest number of seats of all the contesting parties but still had to form a coalition government. As the leader of the majority party, Mgr. Panzavecchia normally would have become the **prime minister**, but he declined the position because of his ecclesiastical ties. After the elections of 1924, the Unione Politica merged with the Partito Democratico Nazionalista to form the Partito Nazionalista (PN). *See also* CATHOLIC CHURCH; MIZZI, DR. ENRICO; POLITICAL PARTIES.

PARDO, DR. ARVID (1914–1999). Born in Rome on 12 February 1914 to a Maltese father and a Swedish mother, Pardo was orphaned as a young child and raised by his uncle, an Italian diplomat. He earned a degree in diplomatic history at the University of Tours and a doctor of international law degree at the University of Rome in 1939. Active in the antifascist movement in **Italy**, he was arrested, first by the Italians and then by the German Gestapo. After his release at the end of the war, Pardo moved to London where he became a civil servant for the **United Nations** in a variety of capacities. In 1964, he was named Malta's first permanent representative to the UN, a position he held until 1971. During this time, he also carried, simultaneously, the responsibilities of ambassador to the **United States**, ambassador to the USSR, and high commissioner to Canada.

In 1967, Ambassador Pardo addressed the UN General Assembly concerning the questions surrounding the control and resource management of the world's oceans and seas. He made what was considered by many the radical proposal that the seabed and ocean floor "underlying the seas beyond the limits of present national jurisdiction" should be "the common heritage of mankind." His speech led directly to the UN International Conference on the Law of the Sea, which examined those questions as well as the sharing of that wealth by all of the earth's nations. Because of that speech and the activity it aroused, Dr. Arvid Pardo is generally recognized as the "father of the Law of the Sea." He served as professor of political science at the University of Southern California from 1975 to 1990 and passed away in Seattle, Washington, on 19 July 1999.

PARLIAMENT. The Parliament of Malta (Kamra tad-Deputati or "Chamber of Deputies") is a single House of Representatives, operating under rules that are modeled on the British House of Commons. Its members include the **president**, who is elected by the Members of Parliament (MPs). MPs are elected in general **elections** for five-year terms from 13 five-seat constituencies. This means that the normal number of MPs is 65. However, under a rule agreed upon as a **constitutional amendment** shortly before the election of 1987, if the party receiving the majority of the popular votes does not win the majority of seats, additional seats are awarded to give it a majority. As a result, 69 MPs, 35 members of the **Nationalist Party**, and 34 members of the **Malta Labour Party** were serving in the 13th Parliament after the election of 2008.

The Parliament's composition, powers, and procedures are laid out in Chapter VI of the **Constitution**, including "standing orders" detailing the rules and order of the Parliament's sessions. The first standing orders were granted in 1850, when the Parliament was known as the Legislative Council. The Parliament currently meets in the **Grand Master's** Palace from 5 p.m. until 9 p.m. on Mondays, Tuesdays, and Wednesdays whenever there is a quorum of at least 15 MPs. Parliamentary secretaries (currently 14) are appointed by the **prime minister**, who is in turn appointed by the **president** if elected by the Parliament. In 1995, the Parliament established five standing committees to deal with increased legislative responsibilities as Malta was preparing to join the **European Union**. Audio live broadcasts of parliamentary debates were first made available on 11 July in the same year. Since 2005, audio live broadcasts of both parliamentary debates and committee meetings have been accessible on the parliamentary website.

PARTITO ANTI-REFORMISTA. *See* MIZZI, DR. FORTUNATO; PARTITO NAZIONALE; POLITICAL PARTIES.

PARTITO NAZIONALE. The Partito Anti-Reformista (PAR) was started in 1880 in opposition to **Sigismondo Savona**'s encouraging the learning of English. The PAR was anti-British, against promotion of the English **language**, and very successful in arousing public opinion against the government. It had substantial support among professionals and gained an adept politician as leader, **Dr. Fortunato Mizzi**. Soon the party name was changed to Partito Nazionale (PN). With the return of **Lord Gerald Strickland** to the Maltese political scene, the PN had another strong supporter of English and England to battle. **Dr. Enrico Mizzi**, Fortunato's son, gradually gained the PN leadership position and set out to increase the pro-**Italy** and pro-Italian stance of the party. The name changed again, this time to Partito Democratico Nazionalista. Under this name it contested the first **elections** in 1921 and 1924 under the **Constitution** of 1921. After the latter election, it entered into a minority coalition with the **Unione Politica Maltese**. This coalition resulted in a merger of the two parties into the Partito Nazionalista, which, by 1939, became known as the **Nationalist Party**.

PARTITO NAZIONALISTA. *See* NATIONALIST PARTY; POLITICAL PARTIES.

PARTITO POPOLARE. *See* SAVONA, SIGISMONDO; POLITICAL PARTIES.

PARTITO UNIONISTA. *See* SAVONA, SIGISMONDO; POLITICAL PARTIES.

PARTNERSHIP. During the debates preceding the **referendum** on whether Malta should join the **European Union (EU)**, the **Malta Labour Party** leader, **Dr. Alfred Sant**, and his followers were strongly opposed to Malta's membership. They argued that Malta should pursue a "partnership" with the EU states, even though, as the pro-EU forces led by the **Nationalist Party** pointed out, partnership was not an option being offered by the EU.

PARTNERSHIP FOR PEACE. *See* NORTH ATLANTIC TREATY ORGANIZATION.

PAUL THE APOSTLE. Probably the most well-known event in the history of Malta is the shipwreck of St. Paul in 60 CE (the generally accepted date; although, some place the event at 58 or even 53 CE). Paul was a prisoner being taken by sea from Jerusalem to Rome in the custody of Julius, a **Roman** centurion. He was accompanied by St. Luke, who was not a prisoner and who later chronicled the events in the Acts of the Apostles. It was late in the fall, and the safe sailing season was nearing its end. Paul warned the centurion that if the voyage were continued, there would be "hurt and much damage, not only of the lading and the ship, but also of our lives." His words were not heeded, and the ship continued its journey.

Soon they were in the midst of a fierce storm, one so bad that they had to take in the sails and let the wind drive them where it chose. There were 146 persons aboard. After several days, the crew and passengers threw all of the gear overboard to lighten the ship. After a few more days, Paul admonished them for not listening to him but also told them that an angel of his god had told him that all would be saved but that the ship would be lost. After 14 nights, the sailors reported that they were fast approaching a rocky shore and that they feared breaking up. They lightened the ship to the maximum, jettisoning cargo and gear in order to stay with the vessel until they were able to run it aground. When it finally did, the forepart remained intact, but the stern broke into pieces. Those who could swim, did so, and those who could not, held on to broken pieces. In that way, all were able to reach the beach and safety.

Eventually they discovered that they were "on the island called Melita and the barbarous people showed us no little kindness." Because they did not speak Greek, the Maltese were considered barbarians, a typical prejudice of that time. Luke wrote that Paul performed several miracles early in their stay, including the healing of the ill father of **St. Publius**, the "chief man of the island." Paul stayed with Publius for three days and then moved to a cave now known as St. Paul's Grotto, located beneath the Parish Church of St. Paul in **Rabat**. The cave is reputed to be the first recognized church in Malta. It seems obvious that the first seeds of Christianity were sown by this event in what is today a strongly **religious** nation. However, it was not, as often suggested in Malta, a sudden conversion but rather a long, gradual process. Although some historians argue that the events of the biblical narrative took place on an island other than Malta, this view is soundly rejected by most Maltese.

PHOENICIAN RULE. It is generally assumed that the Phoenicians spread outward from their home in the Levant on the shores of Syria in about 1000 BCE. They moved along the **trade** routes of the Mediterranean, establishing settlements as they went. It is further assumed that the Phoenicians colonized Malta about 800 BCE as a logical stopping place between the eastern and western parts of their domain. Not only was its location of great benefit but it also possessed the best natural harbors of the region, a quality of great importance to a seafaring people. The larger island of Malta was called *Malet* by the Phoenicians, a word meaning "refuge." There seems to have been an easy transition between the Bronze Age people and the new inhabitants. The Phoenician pottery found in graves and tombs of the period is very similar to that of the Bronze Age. The Phoenicians were primarily interested in **trade** rather than conquest, and their shipbuilding and navigational skills were developed toward those ends.

A major discovery concerning this period was made in 1697 in Malta. Two stone candelabra, each containing dual inscriptions of a prayer to the Phoenician god Melkart, were discovered. The inscriptions were in both **Greek** and Phoenician. The result was that an 18th century scholar, Abbe Bartholomy, was able to use the inscriptions to decipher the Phoenician alphabet. Phoenician rule of the islands ended in 480 BCE, when the **Carthaginians** moved in with little, if any, resistance.

PLAGUE. The Maltese suffered from several major outbreaks of the plague. The first occurred in 1592–93, during the rule of the **Knights of St. John**, and lasted a whole year, killing an estimated 3,000 persons or one in nine of the entire population. The epidemic resulted in near famine for the population of the islands as merchants refused to unload grain shipments in fear of contracting the disease. The Order instituted rules of quarantine so severe that anyone coming to Malta had to first spend time in isolation, and guards had standing orders to shoot to kill anyone caught violating the quarantine. Visitors to Malta had to spend 40 days in isolation. A second epidemic, lasting only nine months, occurred in 1675–76 and claimed nearly 9,000 lives. The last major outbreak was in 1813–14. The **British** established the quarantine facility Lazzaretto on Manoel Island, which successfully contained all future outbreaks.

POLITICAL PARTIES. Political polarization has been a constant feature in a Maltese population that for most of its history was ruled by outsiders. The cultural divide between those Maltese who welcomed, or at least accepted, the laws and customs of **Roman**, Spanish, Italian, **French**, or **British** occupiers of the time and those who did not continues to this day, albeit in altered form.

Political parties in Malta had their roots in the spirit of nationalism that swept across Europe during the middle of the 19th century. Italian political refugees agitating for a united **Italy** fled to Malta and brought with them their struggles for liberalism and constitutionalism. At the same time as the opening of the Suez canal on 17 November 1869 increased Malta's strategic importance to Great Britain, causing it to value Malta more in terms of a fortress outpost than a colony, the Maltese upper classes were clamoring for more say in their local affairs. Because Italy could pose a threat to British control, the British became concerned about the Italian influence on that portion of the Maltese population that consisted of the professional class and the ecclesiastics.

Thus, political leaders in Malta saw themselves divided over "the **language question**" between those who favored the British (and, therefore, use of the English language) and those who saw their cultural roots in Italian language and customs. Should Malta become "anglicized" (Protestant and English-speaking) or remain **Catholic**, conducting business in Italian? The "modernizers" (today they might be considered the proponents of globalization) were the reformers (Riformisti). They were pro-British like the Anglophile **Sigismondo Savona**, who formed the Partito Popolare and was opposed by the Italophiles, who became staunch opponents of reform (Anti-Reformisti), the party that through various mergers ultimately became the **Nationalist Party (NP)**.

Or should Maltese be the language of an awakening nationalism? The latter was not a question until the 1930s, when Maltese orthography was standardized and pride in one's native language became, for the first time, accepted.

World War II had three important results for Malta: a strengthening of pro-British attitudes among many Maltese, a simultaneous desire for personal and national liberation among others, and a strengthened labor movement as Great Britain began to draw down its forces and related local employment. The labor movement organized as the Malta Workers Party, which later became the current **Malta Labour Party (MLP)**. The pro-British **Constitutional Party**, led by **Lord Gerald Strickland**, had merged with the Anglo-Maltese Party but dissolved shortly after World War II. The two parties that emerged as dominant after World War II were the MLP and the NP. In the 1950s, the major dispute between the two was whether Malta should become a dominion of or be integrated into Great Britain. By the 1980s and 1990s, the main issue had become whether or not to join the **European Union**.

A Communist Party was organized by a disgruntled group of former MLP members in 1969. It contested the general **election** of 1987 but won only 0.1 percent of the vote, failing to win a seat in **Parliament**. Similar fates have befallen the **Alternattiva Demokratika**, which was formed out of frustration with the leading NP and MLP, and the newest party, Azzjoni Nazzjonalista. Malta's system of "single, transferable vote" is designed to encourage multiple parties, but this has not happened in recent elections. Although seven parties contested the general elections of 2008, only two, the NP and the MLP, managed to get any seats in Parliament. *See also* UNIONE POLITICA MALTESE.

POSTWAR RECONSTRUCTION. The severe **World War II** bomb damage to the majority of buildings on both sides of Grand Harbour left Malta with a major rebuilding task. As soon as the bombing runs ceased in 1943, the reconstruction was begun. It could have been done in a quick, haphazard way. Luckily, the reconstruction was just that—an attempt to rebuild what had been destroyed to a state that it had been beforehand. As a result, **Valletta** and the **Three Cities** (Vittoriosa, Cospicua, and Senglea) appear today much as they did before the war. That is a big plus for

tourism. In contrast, the beautiful single-family dwellings, which had lined Tower Road, the coastal road in Sliema, have largely been razed to make way for modern high-rise apartment buildings, and although these are not unattractive, the beauty of a consistent style of **architecture** from the colonial era has been lost. Reconstruction continues to this day. The latest project is the restoration in 2009 of the Chapel of St. Anthony of Padua (on Manoel Island). Built in 1727, it had been three-fourths destroyed by a direct bomb strike and lay in ruins for over 65 years. Malta has yet to decide what to do about the site of the ruins of the **Royal Opera House** in Valletta, over which there have been numerous suggestions and much controversy.

PRECA, DUN GORG. *See* ST. GEORGE.

PRESIDENT. By act of **Parliament**, Malta became a democratic republic with **constitutional** authority vested in the president, who must be a citizen and is elected by the House of Representatives (the Parliament). The president is the figurehead of the nation, responsible for upholding the democratic posture of society and, although not permitted to ever take sides between the various **political parties**, is obliged to support the policies of the government in power. In addition to being the figurehead representative of Malta, the president is responsible for appointing the **prime minister** and the executive branch of the government. At the state opening of a new parliament, it is also the constitutional duty of the president to present the government's plan for the five years upcoming based on the platform presented to the voters.

By tradition, the president's first official visit is with the pope. **Election** of the president is by resolution of Parliament and is for a period of five years. Removal from office may be made by a similar resolution on the grounds of inability to perform the functions of the office or misbehavior. The first and only female president was **Agatha Barbara**, elected in 1982. Whenever the president is absent from Malta, the prime minister, in consultation with the opposition party, appoints an acting president. The flag of the president was established in 1988 and bears the seal of the republic on a dark blue field with a Maltese cross in gold at each corner. Those who have served in the office thus far are as follows:

1974–1976	**Sir Anthony Mamo**
1976–1981	**Dr. Anton Buttigieg**
1981–1982	**Dr. Albert Hyzler** (Acting, 27 December–15 February)
1982–1987	**Agatha Barbara**
1987–1989	**Paul Xuereb** (Acting, 16 February–3 April)
1989–1994	**Dr. Vincent ("Censu") Tabone**
1994–1999	**Dr. Ugo Mifsud Bonnici**
1999–2004	**Professor Guido de Marco**
2004–2009	**Dr. Edward Fenech Adami**
2009–	**Dr. George Abela**

PRETI, MATTIA (1613–1699). The Knights of St. John were the sons of the wealthy nobility of Europe, and they used their wealth to try to make Malta a place worthy of their presence. Many of the famous and near famous artists were brought to the islands to use their talents in the embellishment of the **auberges** and palaces. One of the most talented of these was the Italian painter, designer, and architect Mattia Preti. Born in Taverna, Calabria, in 1613, he developed his artistic reputation in Rome and Naples before coming to Malta in 1661, where he became known as the Cavalier Calabrese. It was **Grand Master** Rafael Cottoner who first commissioned Preti to paint the ceiling of **St. John's Co-Cathedral**. From this he went on to embellish the entire interior. He created 18 spaces within the church in which he depicted various episodes in the life of John the Baptist. It was he who did the drawings for all of the carvings and sculptures of the nave and the aisles. He also did important work on the interiors of the Cathedral in **Mdina** and St. George's Basilica in **Gozo**. He died in **Valletta** in 1699 and is buried in the Co-Cathedral under one of the ornate marble tombstones among the Knights of St. John. It can be said that Preti is the one responsible for much of Malta's artistic glory. *See also* ARCHITECTURE; CARVAGGIO.

PRIME MINISTERS. The prime minister of Malta is appointed by the **president** after the former has received a majority vote of **Parlia-**

ment. The prime minister appoints a cabinet that assists him or her in carrying out responsibilities for the executive branch of government, which include running the government and keeping the president informed of government affairs. If the prime minister is out of country or incapacitated in any way, the president may appoint another member of the cabinet as a president pro tem.

Twelve different men have served as prime minister, an office first established in 1921. Several have held the office two or more times, with **Dom Mintoff**'s terms totaling the largest number of years served. The office did not exist from 1933 to 1947 and from 1958 to 1962. Eight of the 12 current and former prime ministers have doctoral degrees. Four of them each served two nonconsecutive terms.

1921–1923	**Joseph Howard, OBE**
1923–1924	**Dr. Francesco Buhagiar**
1924–1927	**Sir Ugo P. Mifsud, KB**
1927–1932	**Sir Gerald Strickland, GCMG**
1932–1933	Sir Ugo P. Mifsud, KB
	(office abolished)
1947–1950	**Dr. Paul Boffa, OBE**
1950–1950	**Dr. Enrico Mizzi**
1950–1955	**Dr. Georgio Borg Olivier**
1955–1958	**Dominic (Dom) Mintoff**
	(office abolished)
1962–1971	Dr. Georgio Borg Olivier
1971–1984	Dominic (Dom) Mintoff
1984–1987	**Dr. Carmelo Mifsud Bonnici**
1987–1996	**Dr. Edward (Eddie) Fenech Adami**
1996–1998	**Dr. Alfred Sant**
1998–2004	Dr. Edward (Eddie) Fenech Adami
2004–	**Dr. Lawrence Gonzi**

PRIVATIZATION. As the **British** forces prepared to depart Malta, strong measures were needed to transform the country's economic base away from reliance on servicing the troops and their ships. The government had to steer the **economy** toward **tourism** and manufacturing by investing heavily in owning and operating the nation's major industries and companies. This was a necessary and positive development in the early years of **independence**. However, the **Malta Labour Party (MLP)** government of **Dom Mintoff** became so focused on creating jobs and cutting Malta's reliance on imports, that it carried the government's role in the economy too far, stifling private investment and burdening the country with many overstaffed, inefficient, heavily subsidized enterprises. By the late 1980s, approximately 42 percent of the nation's workforce was employed by the government. More than 10,000 companies in activities as far ranging as **film production**, printing, **agriculture**, tourism, shipping, and manufacturing were government owned, representing a 77 percent increase in the 11 years between 1980 and 1991.

When the **Nationalist Party (NP)** regained control of the government in 1987, it embarked on an ambitious and difficult program of privatization. The disposition through sale of assets, stock, or simply shutting down of government-owned companies was motivated in part by preparations for membership in the **European Union (EU)**, which required deficit reduction and does not permit some of the subsidies necessary to keep these companies solvent. More generally, the privatization trend is an economic and political reality imposed by the forces of global competition. This is especially important for such a small, vulnerable island economy.

In 1988, the Malta Investment Management Company (MIMCOL) was set up to manage, monitor, and rationalize government **investments**. On 22 November 1999, the government issued a white paper, laying out its plans concerning privatization. By then, over 40 companies had already been transferred wholly or in part to the private sector, including entities such as the postal service, Maltapost, the Public Lotto, the Mid-Med Bank, the Bank of Valletta, and the Malta International Airport. This process not only improves economic productivity and investment, it also generates cash for the government while reducing its deficit.

In cases where the elimination of many jobs is required, as with some of the larger infrastructure and service entities, the privatization process has been and continues to be especially difficult. A culture of guaranteed life-time employment and the half-day schedules during summer months cultivated by the MLP government led to overstaffing that in most cases now requires job cuts of 20 to 50 percent. Needless to say, the **trade unions** have strongly resisted such measures.

In 2006, a deal to sell the government-owned shipping company, Sea Malta, to an Italian firm was derailed by the General Workers' Union (GWU). When the GWU refused to agree to some of the conditions of the sale, negotiations collapsed, and a determined NP government simply liquidated the company, eliminating some 150 jobs. Given the greater government investment and number of workers involved, the situation at the **dockyards** was particularly difficult to resolve. The national airline, Air Malta, and Enemalta, the sole provider of **energy** in Malta, are among other entities the government is still in the process of transferring to private ownership. *See also* BANKING; LISBON AGENDA; YACHT MARINAS.

PRIVILEGIUM FORI. This gained for the clergy the right to be tried before an ecclesiastical judge in all civil and criminal matters. The original reasoning was that many laymen have inclinations to suppress the clergy and that it was not appropriate to have priests and nuns brought before lay judges. The abolition of the privilegium fori was one of the demands made by **Dom Mintoff**. *See also* CATHOLIC CHURCH; RELIGION.

PROGRESSIVE CONSTITUTIONAL PARTY. *See* STRICKLAND, MABEL EDELINE.

PSAILA, MONSIGNOR DUN KARM, CBE (1871–1961). Dun Karm (his pen name) was born on 18 October 1871 in Zebbug. He began writing poetry in Italian during his student days at the seminary. Ordained a priest in 1874, he became a teacher at the seminary and later an assistant librarian at the public library. It was in 1912 that he wrote his first poem in Maltese, and he continued to write more until his death. In 1923, he wrote the lyrics for a piece of **music** composed by Dr. Robert Sammut. It has become the national anthem, "**Innu Malti**." Most of Dun Karm's poems have been translated into English. His poetry covered all aspects of ordinary life in the small country. Dun Karm was a founding member of the Ghaqda tal-Kittieba tal-Malti (Writers Union of Malta), and in 1927, he was elected president and editor of the organization's journal, *Il-Malti*. Between 1947 and 1955, he compiled a three-volume, Maltese-English dictionary. In 1945 the Royal **University of Malta** conferred upon him the honorary degree of Doctor of **Literature**, and in 1956, Queen Elizabeth decorated him with the Commander of the Order of the **British** Empire. Malta honored him with the title "Poet Laureate of Malta." He died on 13 October 1961. *See also* LITERATURE.

PUNIC WARS. There were three of these wars between Carthage and Rome. Although Rome possessed a powerful army, Carthage ruled the Mediterranean Sea. As a result, each was jealous of the other's power. In 260 BCE, a **Carthaginian** galley became stranded in **Italy** during a storm. The Romans were able to seize the vessel to study its construction. In a short time, a powerful navy was built, and Rome declared war. During the first war (264–241 BCE), the Romans occupied Malta as a base for the attacks on Africa. After a naval victory, the Romans landed in Carthage. They lost the land battle, however, so a peace was arranged. **Sicily** was awarded to Rome, and Malta was awarded to Carthage. The Carthaginians proceeded to fortify the islands as an outpost for defense. In the second of the wars (218–202 BCE), Malta was again captured by the Romans. After a series of land battles across southern Europe, the Carthaginians were defeated at the Battle of Zama, and a second peace was established. Even though it had suffered a severe loss, Carthage made plans to attack again. Rome did the same. The third Punic War (150–146 BCE) began with a siege of Carthage. After four years of resistance, the city was completely destroyed, and Rome was victorious. The survivors of the siege were sold as **slaves**. Malta stayed under **Roman rule**. Eventually, some of the marble from the palaces of Carthage ended up as part of the altars of the churches of Malta.

– R –

RABAT. Situated directly outside the walls of **Mdina**, Rabat (from the **Arab** word for "suburb") is home to almost 20,000 inhabitants. It occupies much of the former site of the **Roman** town of Melita. When the Arabs took over Malta, they fortified a part of the city, which became the capital Mdina and left two-thirds of the original city as a suburb, or Rabat. Many subterranean passageways and catacombs in Rabat, originally dug out by the Romans to bury their dead, were used as secret worship sites for the early Christians. The **Apostle Paul** is believed to have occupied a grotto in Rabat during his stay on Malta. St. Paul's and St. Agatha's catacombs are now popular **tourist** sites under the management of **Heritage Malta**.

REDIFFUSION RADIO SYSTEM. This is a system of radio relay by wire, which was available to each home and business. As very few wireless radios were available, the Rediffusion system was a form of monopoly in public communication. The civilian government controlled that monopoly except in matters of civil aviation, public safety, and defense, when control passed to the **British** colonial government. Of course, after **independence**, the ambiguity of control ceased to exist. The system remained in use into the mid-1970s. *See also* MEDIA.

REFERENDA. Only five referenda have ever been held to date. Four major questions have been placed before the Maltese electorate. In 1870, the question, "Are ecclesiastics to be eligible for the Council of Government?" passed overwhelmingly with almost 60 percent of the eligible voting. On 11–12 February 1956, the question of integration with Great Britain gained an almost four-to-one favorable vote, but the results were unacceptable because of a low turnout of the eligible voters after the **Nationalist Party** and others discouraged participation. On 2–4 May 1964, the vote on the **Independence Constitution** passed with a favorable vote of 54 percent and on 8 March 2003, the country voted to approve Malta's joining the **European Union**. A fifth referendum, held on 11 November 1973, was restricted to the voters of **Gozo**, asking them to decide whether Gozo should remain a separate entity from Malta with its own civic council and taxing authority in addition to having representatives in Malta's **Parliament**. Amazingly, fewer than 200 (less than 2 percent) of the 15,621 eligible voters voted, 88 percent of which were overwhelmingly in favor. In fact, all but the 1870 referendum were decided by less than a majority of eligible voters.

In 1996, the Referenda Act of 1973 was amended to permit citizens to vote to repeal certain existing laws. Such an "abrogative" referendum requires a petition signed by at least 10 percent of the eligible voters and can be prevented from taking place if Parliament votes to amend the legislation or is dissolved.

REFORMISTI. *See* SAVONA, SIGISMONDO.

RELIGION. The Maltese **Constitution** states in Article 2 (i) that "The Religion of Malta is the Roman **Catholic** Apostolic Religion." In Article 22, it provides, among other fundamental rights and freedoms, protection from discrimination on grounds of race, color, place of origin, political opinions, or creed. Even during **Arab rule**, Malta remained a Christian nation. The Arabs did not attempt to force their beliefs upon the native population; although, there were a few subtle encouragements, such as exemption from some taxes for those professing the Muslim faith. When the **Knights of St. John** arrived, the encouragements went the other way. An example is in the operation of the **Sacred Infirmary.** It was open to persons of all faiths, but non-Catholics were not allowed to stay in the Great Ward for more than three days unless they agreed to receive religious instruction from one of the Roman Catholic chaplains. During the time of **British rule**, the Anglican church established a presence in Malta, and political battles sometimes involved the power of the Church, but there was always agreement that Malta was a Roman Catholic nation.

Although religious instruction in Roman Catholicism is required in all state schools, and the government cooperates with the Catholic Church in a foundation that provides funds to Catholic schools, freedom of religion is strictly enforced. Since the passage of the Ecclesiastical Entities Act of 1991, all kinds of churches have the same rights, such as owning property, having their ministers perform marriages, and so forth.

Approximately 350 Roman Catholic churches and chapels exist in Malta, but there are only a handful of Protestant churches (mainly serving non-Maltese residents and visitors), including two Anglican (St. Paul's Pro-Cathedral in **Valletta** and Holy Trinity in Sliema) and the Church of Scotland (in Valletta), also serving as the congregation of some Methodists. Several hundred Baptists, Mormons, Jehovah's Witnesses, and Fellowship of Evangelical Churches are also present in Malta. An estimated 3,000 Muslims, of which approximately 150 are native born, 600 naturalized, and the remaining 75 percent foreigners, are served by one mosque and two schools. There are about 125 persons of the Jewish faith and a synagogue in Ta' Xbiex. Malta is the only European country in which divorce is still illegal. A key concern of the Maltese with regard to joining the **European Union** has been whether divorce and embryonic cell research, both strongly opposed by the Catholic Church, would per force become legal upon membership.

While 95 percent of the Maltese population claim to be Roman Catholic faithful, results of a survey released in August 2006 indicated that attendance at Mass has fallen to approximately 52 percent. Nevertheless, the Catholic Church, with its schools, societies, *festas*, and **band clubs**, still dominates Maltese social life. *See also* JEWS OF MALTA; VATICAN CHURCH-STATE PROCLAMATION.

ROMAN RULE. The Romans held Malta for a time during the first of the **Punic Wars** and came into full control early in the second of the three wars. Roman troops under the leadership of the Consul Sempronius Longus captured Malta in 218 BCE, and the archipelago became incorporated into the Republic of Rome. Remains of over 30 villas, several baths, monuments, sculptures, coins, and inscriptions attest to the long history of Roman culture in Malta. The Maltese were at first granted a limited form of autonomous government, although still considered a conquered territory with primary governance from Rome. In 117 BCE, both Malta and **Gozo** were raised to the official level of "municipium" with autonomous local government vested in legislative, executive, and to a lesser extent, judicial functions.

Gradually, the **language** and culture of the Maltese became less Punic and more Roman as the lifestyle of the colonial master was emulated. Coins bearing both Latin and Punic inscriptions evidence this. The **economy** of the islands also improved as their products of textiles and honey became famous throughout the Roman world. It is likely that the name Melita, used by the Romans, came from the Latin word *meli*, meaning "honey." Immediately across the moat in front of **Mdina** is the newly renovated **museum**, **Domus Romana**, which sits on the site of a former roman villa. *See also* ARCHEOLOGY; CARTHAGINIAN RULE.

ROOSEVELT, FRANKLIN DELANO (1882–1945). In North Africa in 1942, President Roosevelt and Prime Minister **Winston Churchill** agreed to visit Malta when it was possible. They both did, Churchill in November and Roosevelt in December 1943. Roosevelt arrived at the airport and spoke to the huge crowd gathered there. He said that for some time he had wanted to pay a tribute to the people of Malta and that he was presenting it today in the form of a scroll. He read,

In the name of the people of the United States of America, I salute the Island of Malta, its people and defenders, who, in the cause of freedom and justice and decency throughout the world, have rendered valorous service far above and beyond the call of duty. Under repeated fire from the skies, Malta stood alone but unafraid in the center of the sea, one tiny bright flame in the darkness—a beacon of hope for the clearer days which have come. Malta's bright story of human fortitude and courage will be read by posterity with wonder and with gratitude through all the ages. What was done in this island maintains the highest traditions of gallant men and women who from the beginning of time have lived and died to preserve civilization for all mankind. I have signed it and dated it, December 7, 1943.

Roosevelt was able to view his words on a ceramic plaque fixed to the outside wall of the **Grand Master**'s Palace on Kingsway (now Republic Street) in **Valletta** when he and **Churchill** stopped in Malta on their way to Yalta in early February 1945.

ROUNDTABLE CONFERENCE. In 1955, Prime Minister Anthony Eden of Great Britain called for a conference to consider the proposals for a closer association between Malta and the United Kingdom, including the proposal for integration promoted by the **Malta Labour Party** and **Dom Mintoff**, which meant that Malta would be represented in the British Parliament. Malta was the only **British** colony ever considered for integration. The conference was composed of members from each of the three main parties represented in **Parliament**. It was to consider constitutional and related questions from these proposals. The conference held 12 sessions in London and three in Malta. Leaders of the three major **political parties** in Malta were invited to express their views and did so. The final report was published in December. In summary, it said that the Maltese people were entitled to political equality and, if they so chose, to representation in the Parliament of the United Kingdom.

The expectation was that a **referendum** would be held in Malta. Before that could be done, however, the archbishop of Malta and the bishop of **Gozo** issued a pastoral letter, which said, in effect, that whatever the changes, the status quo of the Church had to be guaranteed in writing. In addition, the **Nationalist Party** called for a boycott of the vote. Although the referendum passed by a vote of 67,607 to 20,177, the results were open to question because over 62,000 persons did not vote. As a result, Eden stated that the representation question would only be settled in the future by another much more positive vote in Malta. The question of integration quickly disappeared as an issue in Maltese politics as attention shifted to the matter of **independence.**

ROYAL OPERA HOUSE. Designed by the British **architect** Edward Middleton Barry, it was constructed in the years 1862–66 in **Valletta** as one of the largest and most ornate structures of Malta. Almost completely gutted by a fire on 25 May 1873, it was restored within four years and continued to serve as the cultural and social center of Malta until **World War II.** In the evening of 7 April 1942, this architectural gem was destroyed in an Axis bombing raid. Over 65 years later, a portion of the front steps and facade are all that remain, and the future of the site continues to be a political football. In 1946, German prisoners of war reputedly offered to rebuild the structure free of charge, an offer that was rejected by the **Malta Labour Party (MLP)** leader **Dom Mintoff,** who feared competition for scarce jobs.

In 1953, after failing to secure assistance from the **British** War Damage Funds, the **Nationalist Party** government planned a project to rebuild a scaled-down version of the opera house on the site, but the MLP government came into power and scratched the project in 1954 before it got under way. Shortly after the war, several small shops were established in the basement of the facade, and they remain today, while the rest of the space formerly occupied by the building is used as a parking lot. In 2005, a plan to build a new **Parliament** building on the site was being considered, but strong public opposition stopped the idea. In the summer of 2006, a cultural festival staged in the space was so well received that the government is now proposing to develop the site as a permanent open-air stage for performing arts.

ROYAL UNIVERSITY OF MALTA. *See* UNIVERSITY OF MALTA.

– S –

SACRED INFIRMARY. Although the **Order of St. John** began as a hospital organization, it soon became a fighting Order of the first rank. Even so, it never lost its concern for the Hospitaller aspect of its reason for being. Important hospitals were set up in Cyprus and then in Rhodes after leaving the original in Jerusalem. Then, when they settled in Malta, one of the first tasks was to set up a functioning infirmary in Birgu. That hospital functioned even under bombardment throughout the **Great Siege.** A few years afterward, a new hospital opened in about 1575 in the new fortified city of **Valletta.** It became the envy of the nations of Europe. Modeled after Santo Spiritu in Rome, the Great Ward was (and is) one of the largest rooms in Europe at 56.4 meters in length, 10.7 in width, and 9.4 in height (185, 35, and 31 feet, respectively).

It gained renown because of its cleanliness at a time when such conditions were not given high priority in the treatment of the ill or wounded. To protect against the transmission of disease, the patients ate off sterling silver plates. This marvelous structure was severely damaged during the bombing raids of **World War II** but has been restored and is now a center of international meetings of all kinds. In 2005, the extensive underground passageways and chambers were restored and opened as a **museum** with exhibits displaying the history of the infirmary. *See also* HEALTH AND HEALTH CARE; MEDITERRANEAN CONFERENCE CENTER.

ST. GEORGE (1880–1962). Born in **Valletta** and educated in the Lyceum, Gorg Preca developed his religious fervor at an early age, serving as an altar boy. After attending the seminary, he fell seriously ill from a respiratory disease and lost the use of a lung. His survival hung so much in doubt that his physician reportedly counseled against buying the vestments for his ordination, as Preca was not expected to live very long. Crediting the intercession of St. Joseph for his miraculous recovery, he was ordained on 22 December 1906. The following year, at age 27, Dun Gorg (Father George), as he became known popularly, realized a bold vision he had harbored for several years: in a small rented house, he established a society of lay instructors organized to help the less well educated congregants by giving instruction in the Bible and theology.

The Society of Christian Doctrine (SDC) was viewed with suspicion by the Church leaders and derision by some others. Two years after its founding, the Society had expanded into several houses when it was ordered closed down by the Curia. The bishops feared that its lay instructors were themselves too poorly trained to give proper instruction. However, because of Preca's persistent dedication and popular support, the order was soon rescinded. Nevertheless, it was not until 1932 that Archbishop Mauro Caruana officially sanctioned the organization. An avid scholar of Latin, Preca had chosen as the motto for the Society "Magister Utinam Sequatur Evangelium Universus Mundus" ("Master, may the entire world follow the Gospel"). This was shortened to the acronym M.U.S.E.U.M., which subsequently became the popular name for the organization. The SDC has spread beyond the shores of Malta and currently has a membership of about 11,000 with centers in Australia, Peru, the Sudan, Kenya, Great Britain, and Albania.

A prolific writer, Preca authored over 150 books and pamphlets in Maltese. In 1952, he was nominated as a papal secret chamberlain with the title of monsignor, but true to form, he rejected the offer to remain humbly focused on his life's work with the SDC until his death on 26 July 1962. This served to greatly enhance his popularity and made him venerated by the faithful.

In 1964, the scientifically inexplicable healing of a Maltese who had suffered from a detached retina of the left eye was attributed to the intercession of Father George Preca and declared a miracle. As a result, Preca was declared "Venerable" on the 28 June 1999, and on 27 January 2000, Pope John Paul II signed the decree officially confirming the healing. On 23 February 2007, the "Blessed George" was declared the first Maltese **Catholic** saint and now named San Gorg in Maltese. An estimated 5,000 worshippers from Malta attended the ceremony of his canonization in Rome on 3 June 2007.

ST. JOHN AMBULANCE BRIGADE. In 1831, the English **Langue** was reorganized in Great Britain but without the consent of the Grand Magistry of the Order of St. John in Rome. Nevertheless, there has always been complete and friendly cooperation between the two separate organizations devoted to the same ends. This English Priory was granted a royal charter into the British Order of Chivalry by Queen Victoria in 1888. It was this order that created the St. John Ambulance Brigade with duties and obligations virtually identical to those of the modern Knights of Malta. It is strongest in the nations of the British Commonwealth. *See also* KNIGHTS OF ST. JOHN.

ST. JOHN'S CO-CATHEDRAL. Commissioned by **Grand Master** Jean de la Cassiere in 1572, construction was begun in 1573 on the conventual church dedicated to John the Baptist, the patron saint of the Order. The **architect, Gerolamo Cassar**, designed a structure with twin towers and a plain facade concealing the heavy stone buttresses. The external appearance is very plain—even austere—but it is the interior that causes descriptions full of superlatives from all who visit it. Sir Walter Scott said it was the most striking interior he had ever seen. The walls are covered with ornate carvings in the stone, and everywhere there is a burst of color. The floor is paved with 400 memorial tombstones of deceased **Knights of St. John**, slabs of inlaid marble designs of spectacular craftsmanship. There are sculptures and oil paintings in most of the eight side-aisle chapels, each of which is dedicated to one of the **langues**.

On certain feast days, a set of 14 magnificent Gobelin tapestries is hung. These tapestries, along with many vestments and other religious artifacts, are usually displayed in a **museum** located in adjacent chambers, including the oratory where the ceremony to induct Knights into the Order were held. The Oratory houses the most famous painting in Malta, *The Beheading of John the Baptist* by **Caravaggio**. The designation "Co-Cathedral" was applied after the 1820s when the bishop of Malta, whose seat was in the old capitol, **Mdina**, was also permitted to use St. John's, which is certainly one of the nation's most important buildings both artistically and historically. *See also* PRETI, MATTIA; ST. LAWRENCE BY THE SEA.

ST. LAWRENCE BY THE SEA. When the **Knights of St. John** first arrived in Malta in 1530, they settled in Birgu (later renamed Vittoriosa). Though it was by then both a fighting and medical order, it was still primarily a religious brotherhood. As such, one of its first acts was to select a conventual church. Chosen was one of the oldest on the island, St. Lawrence by the Sea. It had been built as a small chapel in 1090 and enlarged in 1508. It remained the principal church of the Order until after the **Great Siege** and the construction of the fortified city of **Valletta**. *See also* CATHOLIC CHURCH; ST. JOHN'S CO-CATHEDRAL; THREE CITIES, THE.

ST. PAUL. *See* PAUL THE APOSTLE.

ST. PUBLIUS. Mentioned in the Bible (Acts 28:7) as the "chief of the island," Publius was a Roman governor of Malta who welcomed St. Paul when the latter was shipwrecked on Malta. Publius converted to Christianity and was consecrated as bishop of Malta. He was martyred by the **Romans** under Emperor Trajan in about 112 CE.

A biblical saint, Publius was never canonized and so is not technically the first saint of Malta; although, he is revered as one of its patron saints in addition to being the patron saint of the town of Floriana. His feast day is celebrated on 21 January. *See also* PAUL THE APOSTLE; ST. GEORGE.

SAMMUT, DR. ROBERT. *See* PSAILA, MONSIGNOR DUN KARM; "INNU MALTI."

SANT, DR. ALFRED (1948–). Born in Sliema on 28 February 1948, Sant received both the Bachelor and Master of Science degrees from the Royal **University of Malta**. He then studied in Paris at the Institut international d'administration publique, where he was awarded a Diploma in International Affairs in 1970. After five years in the Foreign Service stationed in Brussels, he took a leave for additional study, earning an MBA at Boston University with high honors in 1976 and a DBA from Harvard University in 1979. Sant returned to Malta to practice as a management consultant from 1977 to 1980 and then became the executive chairman of the Malta Development Corporation, a post he held until 1982. He then became active in politics as the chairman of the information department of the **Malta Labour Party (MLP)**, leaving the position when he became president of the party in 1984. He was elected to **Parliament** in 1987 and was chosen leader of the party in 1992 after the resignation of **Carmelo Mifsud Bonnici.**

In part due to the institution of a value added tax (VAT), an extremely unpopular but necessary step in preparing Malta to join the **European Union (EU)**, the MLP won the general **election** in 1996, and Sant was sworn in as **prime minister** on 28 October. **Dom Mintoff**, still active as an MP, was upset about a development project championed by Sant. When Mintoff voted against his own party in a closely divided Parliament, Prime Minister Sant decided to call snap elections after only 22 months in office. The Labour Party and Sant suffered a severe defeat, returning the **Nationalist Party** to power, which immediately reactivated the application to join the EU.

Sant became the leader of the opposition and strongly opposed Malta's bid for EU membership, arguing for a **partnership** with the EU instead. When the **referendum** on the EU question was held in 2003, he urged his party members to boycott it or to destroy their ballots. Although over 90 percent of eligible voters voted, with 53 percent in favor, Sant insisted that the MLP had won because fewer than half the eligible voters had voted in favor. This puzzling interpretation had the result that the streets of Malta were filled with noisy jubilation by both camps. Sant continued as a controversial leader of the opposition and the MLP until resigning after his party lost the national election of 8 March 2008.

SAVONA, SIGISMONDO (1837–1908). Savona was born to a working class family, completed the Lyceum, and enlisted in the Royal Malta Fencible Artillery. As a sergeant he was sent to a two-year course for teachers at the Royal Military School in Chelsea, England. Upon completion, he graduated with a first place on the final examination. He resigned from the military in 1865 and then opened what became the best school in Malta for the teaching of the English **language** and also started publication of an English language newspaper, *Public Opinion*. He soon became the acknowledged leader of an informal pro-**British** group known as the "Reformisti" because of their advocacy of the reform of the **educational** system to use English rather than Italian. The Colonial **governors** had been trying to encourage the use of English but without much success. Savona saw English as an important tool in helping Maltese students understand democracy and eventually be able to use democratic institutions. He was appointed as the director of education and, in that capacity, also became the rector of the **University**, even though he had never attended one.

After entering politics, his positions changed significantly. He became a populist dedicated to Maltese self-government. He was a clever debater, a charismatic leader, and, to his opponents, a completely unscrupulous demagogue. In 1891, a new party, the Partito Unionista, was formed with Savona as its leader. It lasted only two years. In June 1895, at a public meeting in **Valletta**, another **political party** was formed by the raising of hands in the gathered crowd. It was called the Partito Popolare, and Savona was elected leader in the same manner. By now he had become a patriot who identified the Maltese language **(Malti)** as the language of the nation. He had become almost anti-British, most certainly anticolonialist. In addition, he had become pro-Catholic and anti-Protestant. Savona gained the adulation of the masses and, as much as anyone, was responsible for bringing them to an awareness of their political power. He died in 1908. *See also* LANGUAGE QUESTION.

SCHENGEN AGREEMENT. One of the original goals of the **European Union (EU)** was to promote freedom of movement for citizens of its member states. A major issue was whether or not non-EU citizens should also be permitted this same freedom, which meant all border controls within the EU could be eliminated. Because the EU member states could not all agree, a meeting of five that could was held in the town of Schengen, Luxembourg. At this meeting, France, Germany, Belgium, Luxembourg, and the Netherlands agreed to create a territory without internal borders.

Signed on 14 June 1985, the "Schengen Agreement," as it became known, paved the way for other EU member states to join the "Schengen area," which grew to include 13 countries by 1997 and 30 countries in 2007. The Nordic countries, including EU members Denmark, Finland, and Sweden, already belonged to a similar agreement among themselves, which was absorbed into the Schengen

Agreement. As a result, Norway and Iceland also participate. Switzerland ratified the agreement in 2004.

In addition to the elimination of all internal borders, the agreement provides for common rules regarding visas, asylum rights, and checks at external borders as well as an electronic system to exchange information. The Schengen Agreement was incorporated into EU law as part of the Treaty of Amsterdam on 1 May 1999, which means that Malta, as a new member, was obligated to participate upon meeting certain requirements. Great Britain and Ireland obtained a derogation, allowing them to maintain their borders; although, they participate in some aspects of Schengen, such as the exchange of information. Upon approval of Malta's security system, sea border controls were lifted by Malta on 21 December 2007, its air border controls on 30 March 2008.

SCIBERRAS, SIR FILIPPO (1850–1928). On 23 November 1918, as president of the Comitato Nazionale (a committee formed to defend the rights of the Maltese), Sciberras issued an appeal inviting all legally constituted organizations to send a delegate to a representative assembly. The announced intent of the assembly was to present a united front in the request for a new **constitution** from the colonial government. The appeal emphasized that there existed an emergency situation. In February 1919, the first meeting was held under the name of Assemblea Nazionale, and Sciberras was elected the presiding officer. The original motion for a new constitution was withdrawn, and a substitute was passed unanimously. It called for the establishment of complete autonomy in local affairs. The British response was not only slow but also much less than positive.

The Assemblea was in session again on 7 June 1919 as the disastrous events, which have become known as **Sette Giugno**, erupted. Afterward, the Assemblea called upon all parties to suppress their political differences in order to present a united front toward the British. The final result of this effort was the new Constitution of 1921, the first under **British rule**, which gave any real degree of self-government to the Maltese people. The new Legislature was convened on 1 November 1921 and was opened by the Prince of Wales. The climax of the ceremony was the knighting of Sciberras for his leadership in convening the Assemblea Nazionale.

SCICLUNA, SIR HANNIBAL. *See* NATIONAL LIBRARY.

SERRACINO INGLOTT, REVEREND PETER (1936–). Malta's most internationally recognized contemporary scholar, Serracino Inglott, was born on 26 April 1936 in **Valletta**. He gained his BA from the Royal **University of Malta** in 1955 and was awarded a Rhodes scholarship to Oxford, from which he received an MA and the Chancellor's Prize for English Prose in 1958. In 1963 he was awarded a PhD from the Universita Cattolica del Sacro Cuore di Milano. From 1987 to 1988 and 1992 to 1996, he served as rector of the University of Malta.

An unusually witty and charming person, affectionately known as Father Peter to faculty and students alike, he set up his office in a refurbished traditional Maltese stone farm house adjacent to the University of Malta campus, where he still directs the university's Mediterranean Institute. He was a member of the Planning Council to establish the International Ocean Institute and president of the Commonwealth Association of Universities (1995–96). Father Peter chaired the Malta Council of Technology and Science for a decade and was a consultant of UNESCO on the Rights of Future Generations as well as Malta's representative to the **European Union's** Convention to draft a constitution, to name just a few of the major organizations he has served.

Serracino Inglott has been a member of the faculty at colleges and universities in Malta, Canada, the United States, and **Italy** and has authored several books including *Encounter with Malta* and a great number of articles on a wide variety of subjects from art and **music** to philosophy and the social sciences. He has written libretti for two operas by his countryman, the composer **Charles Camilleri**. In September 2006, the Commission of the Bishops' Conferences of the European Community (COMECE) appointed Serracino Inglott a member of the "Committee of the Wise," which has been charged with preparing a report to clarify the values on which the EU is based. He has received numerous awards, including honorary doctorates from Luther College in Decorah, Iowa (1989), and the University of Brunel (UK), the Chevalier of the Legion d'Honneur (France, 1990), the Cross of Merit (Portugal, 1995), the Cavaliere di Gran Croce (Order of Merit, **Italy**, 1995), and Kumpann ta' L-Ordni tal-Mertu (Companion of the Order of Merit, Malta, 1995).

SETTE GIUGNO RIOTS. Although the Maltese had experienced a fair amount of prosperity as a result of **World War I**, the war's economic aftermath magnified the tensions that had long existed between the **British** masters and their colonists. The lack of any significant voice in their own destiny was a constant irritant to the Maltese. The economic effects of the war's end fell most heavily upon the lower classes, whose inferior educational opportunities and poor housing conditions merely added to increasing unemployment. An additional irritant was the rising cost of living, particularly the price of bread, the major staple of the Maltese diet, which more than tripled between 1914 and 1918. A series of protests began, strangely, with an organized march by university students on 10 March 1919. They were protesting against a new system of awarding degrees. The demonstration was quickly turned into a political protest, and four students were taken into custody by the police but were later found not guilty.

On 7 June 1919, an important meeting concerning Maltese unity was held in **Valletta**. The gathering crowds quickly became unruly, throwing stones and attacking a shop that was flying a British flag. The University, the Lyceum, and the *Daily Mail Chronicle* presses were all trashed. The police were unable to control the crowds, and the acting **governor**, General Hunter Blair, brought in soldiers to regain order. The troops were inexperienced recruits without adequate training in crowd control. In the tenseness of the situation, someone fired, probably out of fear, but without orders to do so. A young man, Emmanuele Attard, was killed. A short time later, Guze Bajada from **Gozo** was shot while carrying a banner. The two killings only intensified the unruliness of the crowds. Another angry crowd gathered in a threatening way in front of the Chronicle Press. In fear, the lieutenant ordered his men to fire, and another young man bearing a banner, Lorenzo Dyer, fell mortally wounded.

At this point, a group of Maltese clergy and political leaders went out amidst the crowds in an attempt to calm their anger. They made an appeal for the removal of the soldiers, who eventually withdrew, restoring an uneasy peace. The following morning, crowds again entered Valletta to place flowers and wreaths where the dead had fallen. The British and their Maltese supporters began taunting the crowds, and numerous fights broke out. At this point, British Marines, more highly trained than the earlier troops, were called to restore order. In doing so, Carmelo Abela was bayoneted and killed. Though the four young dead Maltese men had been only marginally involved in the entire protest, they have attained the status of martyrs to the cause of Maltese nationalism, which, it is said, was born that day. From that point on, the British were forced to treat the needs and the desires of the Maltese in a different way. The 7 June is still celebrated as a **national holiday**. *See also* SCIBERRAS, SIR FILIPPO.

SICILIAN VESPERS. This is the name given to the revolt of the Sicilians against the rule of the **Angevins**. It began on Easter Monday, 30 March 1282. The immediate cause was an incident in which a Sicilian woman (many said a bride) was insulted by a French soldier outside the Church of Santo Spiritu in Palermo at the hour of vespers. The incident resulted in widespread rioting against all of the French persons in the city and quickly spread throughout the whole island. Almost the entire French population of **Sicily** was murdered. The opposition to the rule of Charles I of Anjou was strong, but also working to promote unrest was Pedro III of Aragon, whose wife, Constance, was the daughter of King Manfred of Sicily. What had begun as a popular uprising because of many grievances, particularly high taxation, was quickly channeled toward the wishes of the nobility and particularly Pedro of Aragon, who sent his ships to take advantage of the situation. His negotiations resulted in his acclamation as King of Sicily by a Palermo Parliament in December 1282. It was the beginning of the **Aragonese rule** over Sicily and, later, Malta. *See also* UNIVERSITA.

SICILY. The largest island in the Mediterranean Sea, Sicily is just 96.6 kilometers (60 miles) north of the Maltese Archipelago. It is very likely that the first inhabitants of Malta came from Sicily, probably settling first in **Gozo** and then Malta. The histories of Sicily and Malta ran in parallel ways. When the same nations dominated the two at the same time, Malta was usually made subservient to Sicily whether in legal, governmental, or ecclesiastical matters. Although the two have the same roots, they developed quite differently in social structure and especially linguistically. Sicilian evolved from its Latin roots and Maltese from its Semitic roots. Although the awarding of Malta to the **Order of St. John** diminished the association between the two, Sicily remains the primary supplier of imports to Malta. In recent years, Malta has again come under Sicilian influence through the television programs broadcast from Sicily, which can be received despite the distance. *See also* SICILIAN VESPERS.

SLAVE UPRISING. In 1749, during the reign of the Portuguese **Grand Master Manoel Pinto de Fonseca**, an attempt was made by both the house and galley slaves of the **Knights of St. John** to seize control of **Valletta** and its adjoining cities. It was a well-conceived plan and could have gained some degree of success except for a betrayal by one of the conspiracy leaders. After a disagreement with other slave leaders, the disgruntled conspirator reported the entire plot to the grand master. Pinto acted quickly to put down the uprising. More than 60 of the suspected ringleaders were hanged, and security over all slaves was tightened. Even house slaves, normally granted wide freedoms, were sent to live in the slave quarters under close observation. *See also* SLAVERY AND SLAVE TRADE.

SLAVERY AND SLAVE TRADE. During the reign of the **Knights of St. John**, slavery was an accepted part of life in Malta. The slave **trade** was also an important source of the Order's wealth and income. As their naval forces became more successful, they acquired a surplus of slaves even though their own need for them had increased. This surplus was sold to traders in **Italy** and **Sicily**, providing what we now call "current funds." Even into the 18th century, the Order had need for over 2,000 slaves both in Malta and on its naval ships. *See also* SLAVE UPRISING.

SMARTCITY. In early 2006, Dubai-based TECOM Investments announced that it would invest approximately $110 million, in a project to be called "SmartCity@Malta." This would represent the single largest private **investment** in Malta ever. TECOM is a telecommunications and information technology company set up by the Dubai government, which has already developed a strategic base for about 700 technology companies including Microsoft, IBM, Cisco Systems, and other global IT companies in Dubai, naming it "Dubai Internet

City." The idea is to provide a similar "one stop" site in Malta for companies needing IT support. SmartCity seeks to take advantage of Malta's **European Union** membership, its location between Europe and North Africa, and the Maltese "linguistic bridge" between English and Arabic. The facility will become part of a network of future SmartCities around the world, enabling businesses to get global access to markets, labor, and innovation.

Malta's government projects that, within eight years, the SmartCity project will create about 6,000 knowledge-based jobs and an additional 2,500 support positions. Located on the Ricasoli peninsula in Kalkara (across the Grand Harbour from **Valletta**), the total cost of the project is projected to be in excess of 275 million euros and cover 360,000 square meters. It will include a public park and 60,000 square meters of residential development. Site preparation began on 11 October 2007. The government has made a commitment that the bureaucratic procedures facing a new company seeking to do business at the site can be completed within 10 days. There is some concern about whether enough Maltese will be sufficiently trained to fill all of the positions required of the project. The project was officially launched on 14 June 2008, and on 20 March, Parliament unanimously approved a motion to transfer land at Ricasoli to SmartCity Malta, Ltd., a US$300 million joint venture project with TECOM Investments in which the government will own a 9 percent stake. The first occupants will begin operations in 2009, but it is not expected to be fully developed until 2020. SmartCity will provide a tremendous boost to the economic well-being of Malta. *See also* ECONOMY.

SOVEREIGN MILITARY AND HOSPITALLER ORDER OF ST. JOHN OF JERUSALEM, OF RHODES, AND OF MALTA. *See* KNIGHTS OF ST. JOHN.

STOLPER, WOLFGANG FRIEDERICH (1912–2002). Stolper, a Harvard economist, headed a **United Nations** team that arrived in Malta in 1962 to assist in the production of a plan for the economic development of the islands. He possessed great experience, having spent two years assisting Nigeria in a similar way. The team's report, called the "Stolper Report," carried proposals for encouraging light industry, **tourism**, specialized **agriculture**, and conversion of the

dockyards to civilian use. However, Stolper's greatest emphasis was on Malta's rising unemployment problem. The report urged that 10,000 Maltese each year for at least the next five years be encouraged in every possible way to emigrate to other countries in order to find work. The goal here was to reduce the size of the workforce as the nation struggled for self-reliance. In response to the urgings of the report, an emphasis upon **emigration** was a major part of the early development plans immediately after **independence**. *See also* ECONOMY; INVESTMENT; TRADE.

STRICKLAND, LORD GERALD (1861–1940). Strickland was born in **Valletta** on 24 May 1861. His father was English, a captain in the Royal Navy and a practicing Roman **Catholic**. His mother was a member of the **Maltese nobility**. At age 18, he inherited the property of his grandfather and became Count della Catena. Educated in law at the Royal **University of Malta**, he also attended the Jesuit College outside Rome and Cambridge University in England, where he excelled in debate. His professional career was unusual because he served both Great Britain and Malta. In 1888, he became chief secretary to the government of Malta, that country's highest-ranking civil service officer. Beginning in 1902, he served as the governor of a number of **British** colonies, including the Leeward Islands, Tasmania, Western Australia, and New South Wales.

In 1917, Strickland returned to Malta to become a major player on the political scene. In 1921, he founded the Anglo-Maltese Party, which merged with the Maltese Constitutional Party a few months later to become the **Constitutional Party** under his leadership in opposition until 1927. In 1924, Strickland was elected as a Conservative Member of the British Parliament from Lancaster and served until 1927. Early in 1928, he was raised to the peerage, becoming Baron Strickland of Sizergh and, thus, an automatic member in the British House of Lords. He served as **prime minister** of Malta from 1927 to 1932. An ardent imperialist, he had a dominating and aggressive personality and was a vigorous opponent of all attempts to make Malta Italian. Although he possessed a great number of strengths, his major weakness was a tendency to fiercely attack the opposition, with the result that public opinion became polarized and tempers ran hot and heavy. At one point, there was even an attempted assassination.

Strickland's pro-British stand was accompanied by an equally strong anticlerical position. Even though he was a practicing Catholic, his tenure as prime minister was one of continuing battles with the Maltese Church and even with the Vatican. It finally resulted in a pastoral letter to the clergy, signed by the archbishop of Malta and the bishop of **Gozo**, which said, in effect, that it was a grave sin to vote in the **elections** of 1930 for Lord Strickland or any of his candidates and that priests were forbidden to administer the sacraments to those who refused to obey the instructions. The British protested the action to the **Vatican**, but the protest was rejected. Then the **governor** of Malta, with the full approval of London, refused to allow the elections to be held. Lord Strickland remained as prime minister in an advisory capacity.

In May 1932, Strickland addressed a letter of apology to the pope, and it was accepted. Early in June, it was declared that since the pope had accepted the apology, the pastoral letter was rescinded. A few weeks later, the elections were permitted, and the **Nationalist Party** was the winner. However, the Nationalist's blatant pro-**Italy**, and even pro-fascism, stance caused the governor to suspend the **Constitution** in 1933. After the elections of 1939, Strickland became the majority leader in both the Council of Government and the Executive Council. He lived just long enough to see the first Italian bombs fall on his homeland. He died on 22 August 1940 and was buried in the Cathedral in **Mdina** according to his hereditary right. *See also* STRICKLAND, MABEL EDELINE.

STRICKLAND, MABEL EDELINE, OBE (1899–1988). The daughter of **Sir Gerald Strickland** and his wife, Edeline Sackville Strickland, Mabel Strickland was born on 8 January 1899 and educated in Tasmania and Australia. During **World War I**, she was a cypher officer on the staff of the commander in chief, Mediterranean, of the Royal Navy. She served as secretary and general assistant to her father, who was the leader of the **Constitutional Party** from 1921 until 1940. In 1944, she was awarded the Order of the British Empire and was elected to the Legislative Assembly as a Constitutional Party candidate in 1950 and 1951. In 1953 she was the main force in organizing the Progressive Constitutional Party (PCP) and became its leader. As a candidate for the PCP, she was elected to **Parliament** in 1962.

Whatever her party affiliation, Mabel Strickland was a respected and authoritative voice as editor of the *Times of Malta* from 1935 to 1950 and the *Sunday Times of Malta* from 1935 to 1956. Although she expected to succeed her father as the leader of the Constitutional Party, two major obstacles stood in her way: Maltese culture simply could not adapt to a female in a position of political leadership and, on top of that, she had never learned to speak Maltese. Later in her life she complained, pointing to her sizable breasts, "If it wasn't for these, I'd have been **prime minister**." Sadly, this was probably true. "Miss Mabel" died on 29 November 1988, a Maltese patriot who never spoke the **language**. *See also* WOMEN.

SULEIMAN THE MAGNIFICENT (1494–1566). *See* GREAT SIEGE OF 1565.

SWABIAN RULE. William II, King of **Sicily** and Malta, died in 1189 without an heir. Next in line of succession to the throne was the daughter of Roger I, Constance, but she was married to Henry of Hohenstaufen, the son of the Emperor of Germany. Because the Sicilian populace did not look favorably upon this shift from **Norman** to German rule, they, with the backing of the newly elected pope, Clement III, saw Tancred of Lecce crowned king in 1190. He claimed the title as an illegitimate son of Hauteville descent. His reign was a short one filled with treachery and intrigue. He died in 1194, opening the way for Henry VI, who, on Christmas Day of the same year, was made Emperor Henry VI of Hohenstaufen, King of Sicily, ending the rule of the Normans in Malta and beginning that of the Swabians.

The day after the coronation, Constance gave birth to a son. She made sure that there would never be any doubt that the child was her son and, thus, the grandson of Roger II and Frederick Barbarossa. No ordinary child, he later would become known as "Stupor Mundi" (the wonder of the world). When Henry VI died in 1197, he was succeeded as king by the three-year-old Frederick II. When Constance died in 1199, the affairs of Sicily and Malta remained in an unsettled state until Frederick II came of age in 1220. Although he had definite **Arabic** leanings in his everyday life, he did seek to evict rebellious Muslims from his domains. By 1224, he had succeeded in expelling them completely from Sicily and Malta. About the same time, the population of Celano was expelled to Malta in punishment for supporting local feudal barons against the Crown. The result was a distinct shift in the religious balance of Malta in favor of Christianity. In 1240, Frederick II sent 18 falconers to Malta, then a famous breeding sanctuary for the birds of prey. Frederick II was a patron of the arts and founder of the University of Naples.

An early supporter of the separation of Church and State, he was in constant conflict with the pope as he sought to diminish papal influence and ability to collect revenues. He died excommunicated in 1250. Although three other members of the Hohenstaufen family ruled for short periods, the end of Swabian rule in Malta came in 1268.

– T –

TABONE, DR. VINCENT "CENSU" (1913–). Born on 30 March 1913, in Victoria, **Gozo,** Tabone received a degree in pharmacy from the **University of Malta** in 1933 and an MD in 1937. During **World War II**, he was regimental medical officer for the Royal Malta Artillery and later became an ophthalmic specialist trainee at Mtarfa Military Hospital. In 1946, he gained the Diploma in Ophthalmology at Oxford University, received the Diploma in Ophthalmic Medicine and Surgery from the Royal College of Surgeons of Edinburgh, and the Diploma in Medical Jurisprudence of the Royal Society of Apothecaries of London. From 1956, he served as a member of the International Panel of Trachoma Experts of the World Health Organization and, in that capacity, was a medical consultant in 15 different third world countries. In 1954, he founded the Medical Officers Union, serving as president until 1962. That organization evolved into the Medical Association of Malta.

In 1961, Tabone became a member of the Executive Committee of the **Nationalist Party** and served as secretary general from 1962 to 1972, deputy leader from 1972 to 1977, and president of the Executive Committee from 1978 to 1985. Elected as a Member of **Parliament** at every **election** from 1966 through 1987, he served as minister of labour, employment, and welfare from 1966 to 1971. In that capacity, he made a proposal at the **United Nations (UN)** in

New York, calling that body's attention to the needs of the growing number of aged persons. It led to the establishment of the UN Institute on Aging with headquarters in **Valletta**. In 1987, when the Nationalists were returned to power, Tabone was named minister of foreign affairs and again made a proposal before the United Nations. This concerned the dangers of human influence on climate changes and led to the UN Resolution on Climate Changes. In March 1989, he resigned as minister, and on 4 April 1989, he was elected by Parliament as the fourth **president** of Malta.

THREE CITIES, THE. Situated on two peninsulas jutting out into Grand Harbor across from the capital city of **Valletta** are three adjoining towns, local councils still known by their Maltese names: Birgu, Bormla, and Isla and collectively referred to as "The Three Cities."

When the **Knights of St. John** arrived in Malta in 1530 under the leadership of **Grand Master** Phillipe Villiers de L'Isle Adam, the capital city of the time, **Mdina**, was located in the center of the island on a high hill occupied by the **Maltese nobility** and not easily accessible. The knights wanted to be closer to their ships and chose to locate on a peninsula in Grand Harbour. They built Fort St. Angelo at the tip of the peninsula by a village called Birgu (il Borgo) and encircled the area with fortifications that encompassed Birgu as well as two other adjacent villages named Cospicua (Bormla) and Senglea (Isla). The most extensive fortifications were around Cospicua, which was later given the name Citta Cottonera. The name Cottonera is often used to refer collectively to the "Three Cities." The knights built their residences or "**auberges,**" in Birgu as well as a palace and a hospital. In honor of the victory over the Turks in the **Great Siege of 1565**, Birgu was renamed Vittoriosa, but the Order moved its headquarters and residences to the newly constructed city of **Valletta** shortly afterward, and even today, Vittoriosa is still called Birgu by the locals. Because of their location close to the **dockyards**, the Three Cities were heavily bombed during **World War II** and are today still predominately working class neighborhoods, strongholds of the **Malta Labor Party**.

Recently, a new mega-**yacht harbor**, hotel, and casino have begun to revitalize the area, which includes the Maritime **Museum**, Fort

St. Angelo, and the restored **Inquisitor's** Palace among its tourist attractions.

TOURISM. At the time of Independence in 1964, there was virtually no infrastructure in place for the tourist industry. Because Malta had been a military base, tourists were obviously not encouraged to visit. Needed were hotels and restaurants, swimming pools, tennis courts, and all the other amenities desired by tourists. Also needed were the human services provided by sightseeing guides, waiters, clerks, maids, and so forth. Not only did people have to be trained in a new occupation but also in new attitudes. The methods and manners used in dealing with soldiers and sailors would not be acceptable to tourists.

Although the industry grew slowly, it now has become a major sector of the **economy**, serving well over one million visitors a year and representing about 25 percent of Malta's GNP. Its importance was underscored when, after the election of 2008, **Prime Minister Lawrence Gonzi** took tourism as part of his portfolio. The government spent 4.43 million **euros** in 2007 on improving tourism, which employs over 40,000 workers, more than one quarter of Malta's workforce. Aircraft landings are approaching an average of 1,000 per month, and 2.9 tourists per resident arrive annually. In 2008, 397 cruise liner port calls visited Malta's Grand Harbour, carrying 537,000 tourists. From 1995 to 2005, the number of five-star hotels grew from five to 15, with the number of beds in this category increasing more than fivefold, from 1,274 to over 7,000, as Malta attempts to capture a higher spending clientele.

At first the Government Tourist Board emphasized "Sun, Sea and Sand" in its literature. That has gradually changed to an increased emphasis on "visible history" and less mention of sand (there are only a few small, sandy beaches, and they are typically crowded). Fifteen government-financed **museums** exist on Malta and five on **Gozo**, in addition to a significant number of private or church-owned museums. A significant problem has been that tourism seems to be concentrated during the summer months. Membership in the **European Union** has given Malta access to structural funds that have been used to upgrade numerous tourist sites and improve or add new tourist activities, such as diving and rock climbing. By concentrating on business incentive, **health**, sport, and other cultural tourism, the Malta Tourist Authority hopes to attract more tourists in the off-season, helping to relieve pressure on the islands' infrastructure and **environment** during the summer months.

Another niche market that has grown considerably in the last two decades is that of "language tourism." At the end of 2000, there were 29 registered English language schools, serving over 35,000 students annually. By 2008, the student numbers had grown to 85,000, half of them adult learners. The language schools employ over 2,000 teachers and staff and account for 15 percent of the annual bed nights, many in four and five star hotels. The Tourist Board is also exploring the promotion of health tourism, capitalizing on Malta's relatively inexpensive yet sophisticated health care.

A number of factors, including competition from the former communist countries of Eastern Europe, a rise in incidence of global terrorism, a national airline (Air Malta) with a higher cost structure and fuel shortages, have caused significant declines in tourism to Malta in the first five years of this century. The government has responded by increasing expenditures on upgrading infrastructure, tourism promotion, and after several years of intense debate, was finally convinced to offer special conditions encouraging low cost airlines to serve Malta. Ryan Air began flights to Malta from Great Britain and the European continent in October 2006, followed by German Wings Meridiana and a number of other airlines. A new cruise terminal completed at the **Valletta** Pinto Wharf in the summer of 2005 has also helped to increase cruise liner arrivals.

Special events, such as powerboat races, fireworks competition, and the Notte Bianca ("White Night") and Notte Magica ("Magical Night") in Valletta, celebrating culture and **music**, have been organized in recent years by the Malta Tourist Authority in hopes of attracting more tourists to Malta.

Great Britain, Germany, and **Italy** have been the traditional countries of origin for tourists visiting Malta, but increased advertising campaigns and more cities served by low cost airlines have brought a growing number of tourists from Russia, Denmark, Austria, the Netherlands, and Switzerland. Malta's adoption of the euro and simplification of border controls under the **Schengen Agreement** should also help boost tourism. However, as Malta's economic reliance on tourism grows, pressures on the environment have increased as well, raising concern about the islands' tourist carrying capacity.

TRADE. As a small island nation in the middle of the Mediterranean, Malta has been very dependent on trade for most of its history. The **Phoenicians** were among the earliest to establish trading and pirating outposts on the islands, which became an important stopping point for **Greek, Carthaginian,** and Etruscan traders. By the time the **Romans** chased the Carthaginians from Malta in 218 BCE, there is evidence of a considerable volume of commerce in Maltese cloth and olive oil production. The **Arab** invaders introduced citrus fruits and developed cotton as an important crop. The earliest reference to any manufacturing on Malta is found in an 11th century Arab chronicle that mentions the building of ships from trees described as being plentiful at the time.

More detailed information about Maltese trading activity is available from the **Aragonese,** for whom Malta was an important way station in their trade with the African coast. Their records indicate that by the late 13th century, Malta was dependent on **Sicily** for wheat supplies, in exchange for which they traded Maltese cotton. By the beginning of the 15th century, the Maltese had replaced **Turkish** suppliers to the cloth makers of Genoa, Barcelona, and Montpelier. That the cotton crop became an important source of revenue is also evidenced by the 2 percent tax levied on cotton exports by the **Universita** in 1472. King Ferdinand appointed officials to maintain checks on the quality of the goods. Later, as sails were replaced by steam engines, the cotton trade disappeared from Malta.

When the **Knights of St. John** arrived in 1530, they expanded trade in Malta to a whole new level. They moved the center of Maltese politics and commerce from the old capital of **Mdina,** located high on a hill in the center of the island, to Birgu in Grand Harbour, with easier and more direct access to the sea. The Knights also provided Malta with access to a sophisticated supply chain of connections with various trading centers in Europe. Goods also were gotten from attacking passing ships, especially those of the Ottoman Turks, looting their cargo, and selling their crews into **slavery.** Piracy and the slave trade—an important source of wealth and income for the Knights— were still accepted realities of life in the Mediterranean at the time.

After the **British** arrived in 1800, Great Britain became Malta's major trading partner. The **dockyards** and harbor facilities were expanded to provide a naval recoaling station, a key outpost in the British Empire's control of the Mediterranean, from Egypt to the Strait of Gibraltar. Shipbuilding and repair facilities were greatly expanded. The importance of Malta as a trading entrepôt grew significantly with the opening of the Suez Canal in 1869. Sicily continued to be a major source of grain and other supplies.

By the time the British departed in the late 1970's, Malta's **economy** had become too reliant on the jobs and income from the occupying forces. The **Malta Labor Party** government of **Dom Mintoff** attempted to soften the economic impact of British troop withdrawal, reducing dependence on outsiders and creating jobs by raising high tariffs on imports, limiting foreign currency exchange, and nationalizing much of the country's industry. This dampened international trading activity in the 1970s and 1980s. Mintoff's anti-Western policies led to relationships and trade agreements with communist and other controversial regimes, such as **Libya**, which agreed to supply Malta with petroleum at favorable rates.

When the **Nationalist Party** regained control in1987, **Edward Fenech Adami's** administration reversed many of Mintoff's policies, reducing import tariffs, **privatizing** government-owned companies, liberalizing laws to encourage foreign **investment**, and preparing Malta for membership in the **European Union (EU)**.

As globalization gained momentum and Great Britain joined the EU, Malta's trade increasingly shifted that way as well. Two-way trade with the EU, especially in the clothing and electronics sectors, was already at 65 percent of Malta's GDP shortly before EU membership in 2004. Malta was accepted as a member of the World Trade Organization in 1995.

Given the relative openness of its economy and its limited resources, Malta's balance of trade remains very vulnerable to external economic shocks, such as recent increases in the cost of **energy**, 100 percent of which must be imported, 95 percent in the form of oil and 5 percent as coal. Approximately 80 percent of the nation's food supply is imported. Reliance on trade in services, which represent about 70 percent of the total economy, has increased in recent decades. **Tourism**, at approximately 25 percent, is still the most significant, but financial services, transshipment, online gambling, and information technology have grown significantly as competition from Asian economies has reduced exports of Malta's manufactured goods. In 1988, the government opened the Malta Freeport facility, which handles the bulk of Malta's trade and transshipment of goods. In 2004, the Freeport handled 1.5 million twenty-foot container units. It includes facilities for storage and includes an oil bunkering and offloading facility. The operation of the Freeport was turned over to private enterprise through a 30-year lease agreement in 2004, later extended to 65 years.

Total exported goods in 2008 amounted to approximately 3 billion euros. Although the value of electronic exports shrank by 200 million euros in 2008, they still totaled in excess of 1 billion euros. Meanwhile, imports amounted to about 4.6 billion euros. Malta is expected to continue running a trade deficit for some time as it adjusts its infrastructure to EU standards.

TRADE UNIONS. The first attempt at a unionlike organization in Malta occurred in 1885 with the founding of the Society of Workers in Senglea. Because the society aroused the suspicions of local segments of the **Catholic Church**, the name was changed to the Society of Catholic Workers. This did little to diminish those suspicions, however. Eventually the Society attracted the support of **Emmanuel Dimech**, an action that again caused suspicions to increase within the Church and then among the upper classes. In the face of this opposition, the Society ceased to exist about 1912. English workers, brought to Malta to work in the **dockyards** during **World War I**, encouraged the Maltese workers to organize. As a result, trade unions, especially at the dockyards, grew rapidly.

The unions were continually confronted with opposition from the Church, which feared that they were socialist organizations and, therefore, antireligion. Even the archbishop, in a letter issued in 1921, questioned the purposes and goals of unions. By 1929, the **Malta Labour Party (MLP)** was instrumental in gaining passage of the Trade Union Act, which gave legitimacy to the trade union movement. After that, the movement progressed, although with periodic reversals. In February 1943, the General Workers' Union (GWU) was formed. It included workers from the dockyards, the government, and private industry. By July 1944, it had absorbed most of the smaller unions into its membership, estimated at 35,000. Its various publications were of great value in spreading the union message. In 1986, the GWU, together with the second largest union, Union Haddiema Maghqudin (UHM), mainly a "white collar" union of clerical workers, had gained a total union membership of over 60,000, just slightly over 60 percent of the wage and salary workers.

In total, there are currently about 35 union organizations in Malta, nine of which belong to the Confederation of Malta Trade Unions (CMTU), an umbrella group. The GWU, still the largest union, representing about 56 percent of trade union membership, does not participate in the CMTU because of its strong ties to the MLP, while the UHM, which does, represents about 30 percent of the total union membership. Strong, but smaller unions include the Malta Union of Teachers (MUT), the Malta Union of Bank Employees, and the Union of Midwives and Nurses.

In the summer of 2006, the GWU leader, Tony Zarb, created a controversy when he fired two leaders of the Public Sector Union's workers. A number of members have revolted against Zarb's autocratic leadership and left the Union to form their own, causing a dispute about who actually represented the workers. Similarly, in December 2008, the MUT withdrew from the CMTU because of a disagreement about procedures in negotiations with the government about electricity prices. The need to cope with global economic competition will continue to threaten cohesion and viability of trade unions as demonstrated in the case of the dockyards.

TRANSPORTATION. Because it is an island nation, there are only two ways to get to Malta: over water or by air. Almost 1.3 million **tourists** arrive in Malta annually, most of them by air, some by ferry from **Sicily** and **Italy**, and more recently, about half a million by cruise ships. Grand Harbour, Malta's principal deepwater port for handling cruise passengers and car ferry service in addition to freight, is located along the southern edge of **Valletta**. The Marsamxett Harbor, situated on the other side of Valletta, handles some cargo and, in stormy weather, car and passenger ferries from **Gozo**. Car and passenger service between Malta and Gozo is normally operated on a daily basis between Cirkewwa on the northern end of

Malta and Mgarr on Gozo, a 20 minute ride. A less frequently used ferry service also operates between Sliema and Valletta. A traditional form of travel over water involved a boat called a *dghajsa*, a smaller version of the Italian gondola. Today, it is mainly used to transport tourists touring the harbors. A similar fate has befallen the traditional *karrozin*, a horse-drawn cart today only used by tourists for touring Valletta and surroundings.

It was not until shortly after **World War II** that commercial air service began operating from Malta at an air field in Hal Far. The first license issued in the **British** Empire to a private airline was granted to Air Malta in 1948. Since then, the state-owned airline has served the islands with regular connections to major cities in Europe and Africa from the country's lone airport at Luqa. The two other airfields, Hal Far and Ta' Qali, were used primarily during World War II and have been closed. Helicopter service between Malta and Gozo has ceased, but there are ongoing discussions about a construction of a runway for fixed wing aircraft on Gozo. A float plane service currently operates between Grand Harbour and Mgarr Harbor.

Once on the islands, the private automobile is far and away the preferred mode of transportation. As in most former colonies of Great Britain, cars drive on the left side of the road. There are 290,000 licensed vehicles and 2,550 kilometers of road in Malta, many of them still in very poor condition.

Buses first appeared on the island in 1904, serving between Valletta and St. Julians. Today, about 500 privately owned large buses operate as an association serving Malta from a central terminal just outside the Valletta gate. Many of them are 50- and 60-year-old antiques that are popular tourist attractions; although, some of their drivers are notoriously aggressive and unfriendly. Over 400 privately owned and operated minibuses (seating 14) also serve the islands, mostly for transporting school children, workers, and **tourist** groups.

A small fleet of taxis serves Malta and Gozo, mainly in the larger urban areas, but to date, they are still unregulated and without meters. The only railroad on Malta was built in 1883 from Valletta to near Mdina. It was extended to Mtarfa in 1900, but it ceased operations in 1931, succumbing to competition from a tramway that was inaugurated on 23 February 1905 and the advent of private cars on the islands. *See also* MALTA RAILWAY.

TREATY OF AMIENS. This treaty between Great Britain and France was signed on 17 July 1802. It exemplified what was to become a long-term **British** disregard of the opinions and the rights of the Maltese. Because there was no consultation with any faction in Malta, the treaty was in complete opposition to the desires of the populace. Malta was to be returned to the **Order of St. John** and placed under the questionable protection of Naples. In addition, Austria, Britain, France, Prussia, Russia, and Spain were to guarantee Malta's neutrality.

The anger of the Maltese over these terms was immediate, and a Declaration of Human Rights was drawn up by all the representative deputies and lieutenants of the villages and towns. It held that the Sovereign Lord of the Maltese was the King of Great Britain and Ireland. However, before any action was taken on the Maltese protest, both sides violated the treaty. The British finally broke with it altogether, deciding to remain in Malta. Napoleon, in his anger, gave an ultimatum for the British to leave the islands. In May 1803, war was declared again by the French. Subsequent events were to convince the British of the strategic value of the Maltese Islands, and any thoughts of allowing them to pass into the possession of any other power were quickly left behind. *See also* TREATY OF PARIS.

TREATY OF PARIS. This treaty name has been used to refer to several important treaties signed in or near Paris, France, from 1763 to 1947. The one in 1814 was between France and its foes, the main allies of Austria, Great Britain, Prussia, and Russia, at the end of Napoleon's first abdication. France paid no financial penalties and had most of its colonies returned. Great Britain was permitted to retain Malta, supporting the status quo. The Congress of Vienna in 1815 confirmed the actions of the treaty. *See also* TREATY OF AMIENS.

TURKISH THREAT. From 1000 to 1300 CE, the Turks came to accept the Muslim faith and to adopt Islamic customs and manners. To this Muslim world they brought a pride in their own military ability while retaining their own language. They embraced the concept of jihad, or "holy war." The Sultans Orkhan (1326–62) and Murad (1362–89) were the first to bring together an Ottoman State and, by the 1350s, were moving into Europe both as settlers and as invaders.

In 1453, Constantinople fell to this strengthening "oriental horde," and the Turks began building what was to become a formidable navy.

In 1520, Suleiman I (called "The Magnificent" by the Christians and "The Lawgiver" by the Muslims) succeeded his father, Selim I, as Ottoman Sultan at age 26. It was during his 46-year reign that the Ottoman Empire reached the peak of its glory, almost entirely at the expense of Christian Europe. With powerful military forces on both land and sea, it carried the jihad threat throughout Europe but especially in the Mediterranean area. *See also* GREAT SIEGE OF 1565.

– U –

UNION HADDIEMA MAGHQUDIN. *See* TRADE UNIONS.

UNIONE POLITICA MALTESE (UPM). Mgr. **Ignazio Panzavecchia** was the driving force in the recruitment of the party members in its early days. When the time came to contest the election of 1921, it had become the largest party in Malta. Because it was still not able to gain enough seats for a majority, its minority government had to look to the **Malta Labour Party** for support. Its platform included making Roman Catholicism the official **religion** of Malta and the teaching of English and Italian on an equal basis. In addition, it advocated a change in the system of taxation, adjusting the burden to the financial means of the taxpayer. In spite of the latter, the party's main supporters were from the wealthier professional, educated, and ecclesiastic classes. In the **election** of 1924, the UPM was again successful but without gaining a majority. It formed a coalition with the Partito Democratico Nazionalista, eventually resulting in a union of the two to form the Partito Nazionalista (PN). *See also* LANGUAGE QUESTION; POLITICAL PARTIES.

UNITED NATIONS (UN). On 1 December 1964, shortly after acquiring independence, Malta joined the United Nations as the body's 114th member. The new member emphasized its unique role in the Mediterranean region as a bridge between Africa and Europe and gained the General Assembly's respect by soon taking an active part in the work of the organization. Malta's first permanent representative to the UN, **Arvid Pardo**, addressed the UN General Assembly concerning the questions surrounding the control and resource management of the world's oceans and seas. He proposed that the seabed and ocean floor "underlying the seas beyond the limits of present national jurisdiction" should be "the common heritage of mankind." This led directly to the adoption of the 1982 UN Convention on the Law of the Sea, which entered into force on 16 November 1994. Malta has also pushed for the development of safeguard provisions favoring developing countries that are net importers of commodities.

As a result of Malta's participation in discussions on problems of the elderly, the UN adopted the Vienna Plan of Action under which Malta agreed to establish the International Institute on Aging in **Valletta**, which was inaugurated on 15 August 1987.

In 1990, then Deputy Prime Minister and Minister of **Foreign Affairs Guido de Marco** was elected president of the 45th UN General Assembly, serving from September 1990 through September 1991. Malta continues to actively pursue UN action on **environmental** issues of the common spaces of the world, the role of the ocean, and climate change as well as measures to deal with the particular challenges facing small island nations. *See also* TABONE, DR. VINCENT "CENSU."

UNITED STATES OF AMERICA. *See* EISENHOWER, DWIGHT D.; EMIGRATION; LIBYA; ROOSEVELT, FRANKLIN DELANO; UNITED STATES–SOVIET SUMMIT.

UNITED STATES–SOVIET SUMMIT. This was a major meeting between U.S. President George H. W. Bush and Mikhail Gorbachev, chairman of the Presidium and general secretary of the Central Committee of the Communist Party, on 23 December 1989. Although the original plans were for the meetings to be held aboard the Soviet cruiser *Slava* and the U.S. cruiser *Belknap*, high winds and generally foul weather caused a change in plans. The Soviet cruise liner *Maxim Gorky* was moored in Marsaxlokk Harbour and became the location of the meetings. Among the other major participants were Secretary of State James Baker and the USSR's Minister of Foreign Affairs Eduard Shevardnadze.

While no formal agreements were signed, the summit is viewed as a major turning point in East-West relations. The two leaders agreed to continue efforts toward weapons reduction and to jointly seek ways to end regional conflicts. Of equal importance, however, was American support of Soviet efforts at reforming the USSR's political and economic systems. Although Bush arrived in Malta early in the morning of 1 December, Gorbachev did not arrive until late in the evening. He had detoured by way of Rome where he had a private audience with Pope Paul II at the Vatican. This reconciliation ended the 70-year breach between the Soviet Union and the **Roman Catholic Church**.

UNIVERSITA. The revolt against the **Angevin rule** in 1282 resulted in political and economic instability from which a new local form of political organization known as Universita emerged. A form of town council whose members were drawn from local **nobility**, it was headed by a *hakem* or *capitano della verga*, assisted by four *imhallfin* or *giurati* and other officials. The Universita was the local administration responsible for maintaining the fortifications, the markets, and sanitation, in short, the general functioning of the town. The Universita funded itself by raising taxes. Occasionally, it sent envoys to the king in **Sicily** to present petitions or grievances known as *capituli*, requesting action or funds for a particular issue.

In the last quarter of the 14th century, Universitas were established in **Mdina** and on **Gozo** that essentially ruled these towns without much outside political interference, even after the arrival of the **Knights of St. John** in 1530; although, by 1550 a knight was appointed by the **grand master** to head the Universita in Gozo. In the late 17th century, an advisory council, which became known as the **Consiglio Popolare**, was constituted to give broader voice to the upper class. When the **British** arrived, a form of *consiglio popolare* was briefly reestablished but banned as of 1 January 1819 by a proclamation of the **governor**.

UNIVERSITY OF MALTA. The origins of the present University can be traced to 1592 when Bishop Gargallo and **Grand Master** Hughes de Loubens de Verdalle invited the **Jesuits** to Malta to organize a college. They did so in **Valletta**, receiving authority from

Pope Clement VIII to confer degrees in philosophy and theology. A Medical Faculty was started in 1647 when Grand Master Nicholas Cottoner founded the School of Anatomy in the **Sacred Infirmary** of the Order. In 1769, Pope Clement XIV gave Grand Master Pinto de Fonseca the authority to raise the college to full university status. On 5 June 1901, the University gained top recognition throughout the **British** Empire for its medical degree. In 1937, royal patronage was granted, and it became the Royal University of Malta until 1976, when an amendment to the **Education** Act eliminated the patronage, and it became the University of Malta again.

The 16-year reign of the **Malta Labour Party** from 1971 to 1987 placed great stress on the institution. Most of the Faculty of Medicine left in a dispute with the government. Then, in the 1978 amendments of the Education Act, the Faculties of Engineering and **Architecture**, Medicine and Surgery, and Dental Surgery were transferred to the College of Arts, Science and Technology (called the Polytechnic), which had been at the approximate level of an American vocational-technical junior college. It was renamed the "New University." The Faculty of Theology was transferred to the Archbishop's Seminary at Tal Virtu in Rabat. The remaining Faculties of Arts, Science, and Laws were given the name of the "Old University." Another amendment in 1980 caused the suppression of the Faculties of Arts and Science, while Law was transferred to the "New University," which then became the "University of Malta."

With the return to power of the **Nationalist Party** in 1987, the Faculties of Arts and Science were reestablished, and those who had been transferred away were returned to the University campus at Tal Qroqq, Msida. The distinction between "new" and "old" ceased to exist, as did the College of Arts, Science and Technology. Its building eventually became the home of the Lyceum. A relaxation of admission quotas for students in most faculties has resulted in a great increase in the size of the student body and required a big expansion of the physical facilities. Today, the University of Malta is recognized as the oldest university in the British **Commonwealth** outside the United Kingdom. *See also* BORG COSTANZI, EDWIN J.; JESUITS; MALTA COLLEGE OF ARTS, SCIENCE AND TECHNOLOGY.

UPRISING OF THE PRIESTS. The **grand masters** of the Order of St. John were all autocrats who ruled the Maltese citizenry absolutely. As the most **educated** group, the Maltese clergy were often the most resentful. In their position of respect, they passed this resentment on to their parishioners. The situation became especially antagonistic under Grand Master Francis Ximenes de Texada, a **Knight** of the **Langue** of Aragon. In his zeal to improve the precarious state of the Order's finances at the time, he imposed harsh and abrupt economic reforms. These had severe negative results for the people. There was high unemployment coupled with a shortage of food.

To improve the supply of fresh meat, Ximenes decided to encourage the breeding of more rabbits. As part of the plan, he ordered that hunting of any kind be outlawed. This order was received with great anger. Hunting was a major form of recreation for most males, including the clergy. To make matters even worse, he forbade the clergy from participating in secular events, particularly field sports. Shortly, some priests were caught hunting and were publicly punished, causing an even further deterioration of relations between the grand master and the bishop.

In 1775, a group of approximately 24 clerics was involved in a general uprising against the Order. In a surprise attack, they took Fort St. Elmo and other parts of the fortifications of Valletta. The expected rebellions elsewhere in the islands failed to materialize, and the priests were taken as prisoners by the Knights. Ximenes ordered the priests beheaded and their heads displayed on pikes at the entrance to **Valletta.** The others were imprisoned. Relations between the Maltese and the Order, never very cordial after the **Great Siege,** fell to a new low. This ended a few months later with the death of Ximenes. His successor as grand master, Emmanuel de Rohan, provided a stark contrast. His first action was to pardon all involved in the uprising. He went on to win great personal popularity by a series of broad reforms, which were of lasting benefit to the populace.

– V –

VALETTE, JEAN PARISOT DE LA (1494?–1568). Valette joined the **Order of St. John** of Jerusalem at the age of 20, and there is no record of his ever again visiting the family estates in Toulouse, France. A handsome man, he was fluent in Italian, Spanish, Greek, Arabic, and Turkish. By the time the Order was forced to leave Rhodes on 1 January 1523, he was 28 years old and had already been a galley **slave** for over a year after his capture by a **Turkish** corsair. He gained his freedom through an exchange of Muslim and Christian prisoners. He had also served as the captain general (admiral) of the Order's fleet, an appointment usually given to an Italian. After arriving in Malta, he was one of the very few who believed that it was exactly the right place for the Order to be located. In 1557, at the age of 63, he became the **grand master** of the Order.

A brilliant leader, Valette planned thoroughly, made sure his planning was put in place by those he was leading, and should the need arise, was quick to adjust. He was aware that the Turks were planning an invasion because of the information he had received by way of the very good espionage system the Order had developed in Constantinople. Under the circumstances, he was as prepared as any leader could have been for the **Great Siege of 1565**, and certainly the end result bears evidence to that. In the midst of the continuing battle, at one point, he did, though wounded, lead a countercharge—and this at about age 70. After the siege, he was certain the Turks would return, and he immediately set out to improve the fortifications and to gain replacements for the Knights killed or maimed during the battles. As Valette was doing this planning, there were a number of dissenting Knights who planned to leave Malta and had even gone so far as to pack the Order's religious relics and other valuables for shipment. It was always said that he did not drive, he led, and in this instance, he was able to overcome the objections with logic (combined most probably with a bit of senior officer authority), by pointing out that Malta was a natural fortress, perfectly suited for the Order's home.

Valette was as strong for the Knights' religious practices as for their military prowess. When, after the Siege, he was offered a cardinal's hat, he declined, explaining that he felt that the military side of the Order was not suitable for a cardinal and that he did not wish to leave the Order. In July 1568, he suffered a stroke, which took his life. He was buried in the new city, which bears his name. [How and when it came to be spelled with a double *l* is not clear.] A Latin inscription composed by Sir Oliver Starkey, Valette's personal secretary and a Knight of the **Langue** of England, reads as translated, "Here lies la Vallette, worthy of eternal honor. Once the scourge of Africa and Asia from whence he expelled the barbarians by his Holy Arms, he is the first to be buried in this, his beloved city which he founded." *See also* VALLETTA, CITY OF.

VALLETTA, CITY OF. After their success against the **Turks** in the **Great Siege of 1565**, the **Knights of St. John** fully realized that there would be another attempt at ousting them from Malta. The experience of the Siege showed that the high Sciberras peninsula would have to be fortified because of its command over both Grand Harbour and Marsamxett Harbour and the adjoining areas. It was decided to build a fortified city covering virtually the entire peninsula in order to provide protection both against marauding pirates and corsairs and against the anticipated second invasion by the Turks. The Vatican **architect Francesco Laparelli** was sent to be in charge of the task. He drew the plans for a rigid grid, with streets running the entire length parallel to the shoreline and with others crossing at right angles transversing the width. The original plan was to level the hills and valleys, but the urgency of the military need, plus the great cost involved, caused that plan to be cancelled, and the streets were allowed to follow the natural contours.

Laparelli's plans located the Palace of the Grand Master in the center of the city in a large square. The other major buildings, such as the conventual church and the various **auberges**, were similarly located on the drawings. In the morning of 28 March 1566, a High Mass was celebrated, and the first foundation stone was laid for the new fortified city named in honor of the **Grand Master Jean Parisot de la Valette**. After two years, Laparelli tired of the task and asked to be relieved. He was succeeded by his assistant, **Gerolamo Cassar**, who, though following the original plans, was the one who created the architectural beauty of the city. Though severely damaged in the bombings during **World War II**, it was substantially rebuilt along its original lines. Its bastion walls seem to rise from the sea, topped with rectangular buildings and domed churches. It remains one of the most important planned cities of the Renaissance, one of the first and few European cities laid out with parallel streets and right angles.

Recently, however, Valletta had become a city in decline. Full of **tourists**, shopkeepers, and government workers during the day, there was, with a few exceptions such as the **Manoel Theater** and the St. James Cultural Center, little to attract visitors at night. Over 40 percent of its buildings are unoccupied because of outdated rent control laws that prevent property from being rented out, a situation that is only gradually being addressed by the politicians. With assistance from **European Union** funds, the government has taken several measures to revive Valletta. A recent park-and-ride system, coupled with stringent restrictions on driving in the city, has greatly reduced congestion and pollution, which had been eating away at the soft limestone of Valletta's architectural heritage. Unsightly air conditioners are being removed under government pressure and repairs to many structures planned. A "White Night" street party was very successful at drawing crowds, and the buses have been convinced to schedule service later at night. Still, much remains to be done.

VANDALS. Although there is no supporting evidence, some historians believe that Malta was occupied by the Vandals in 454 and the Goths in 464. There is evidence that **Roman** General Belisarius was in Malta in 533 CE after the reconquest of Africa and on his way to **Sicily**. Some think he was there merely to rest between two hard battles. On the same minimal evidence, others believe he defeated the Goths and returned the islands to the **Byzantine** Empire.

VATICAN CHURCH-STATE PROCLAMATION. In 1828, the Vatican agreed to three major requests put to it by the **British**. These related to the relationships between the Roman Catholic Church in Malta and the colonial rulers. The first restricted the jurisdiction of Ecclesiastical Courts to spiritual matters only. The second abolished the right of sanctuary in criminal cases. The third stipulated that all clergy, except bishops, could be made subject to court proceedings. The proclamation had the effect of reducing the ecclesiastical immunities, something the **Knights of St. John** had tried to achieve but without success. *See also* RELIGION.

VELLA, ASTRID (1959–). Born in Sliema on 10 June 1959, Astrid Vella earned her BA in English and French at the **University of**

Malta and pursued further French studies at the University of Tours (France). Vella began her career as an investment promotion officer to France with the Malta Development Corporation, a government agency for the promotion of industry in Malta. She later managed an advertising agency. After the birth of her children, she worked as a freelance journalist and marketing consultant. A course in Baroque **architecture** at the International Institute of Baroque Studies in Malta was the prelude to her becoming an activist, seeking to protect Maltese heritage and **environment**.

In 2006, shocked and angered at the impending destruction of the oldest house in Sliema, which developers were being permitted to carry out despite laws and regulations to protect such heritage structures, she cofounded **Flimkien ghal Ambjent Ahjar** (Together for a Better Environment). A very petite individual, Vella has successfully combined passion, energy, and determination with experience in marketing and journalism, enabling this "small big woman" from Sliema to gain sufficient public support to successfully block several proposed development projects that threatened historic buildings and/or infringed on environmentally sensitive land. She has organized rallies at which concerned citizens are able voice their disapproval of the government's policy on the environment.

Vella has also advised residents' groups all over Malta and **Gozo** facing serious **health** problems due to overdevelopment, traffic congestion, and toxic emissions as well as loss of residents' rights, such as access to environmental information, public beaches, and gardens. Other priority issues she pursues include alternative energy, climate change provisions, and measures to protect Malta's scant water resources. In December 2008, her work was recognized by the **European Union (EU)** with the EU Voluntary Work Award presented in Strasbourg, France.

– W –

WOMEN. Although statues and figurines found in **archeological** sites of the temple period suggest that the female was worshipped as a fertility goddess, it is not clear whether a matriarchal form of governance ever existed on the islands. The figure of Mary is highly revered by the overwhelmingly **Roman Catholic** country, but it is primarily in her role as mother of Jesus that she is so honored. As the Dutch sociologist, Jeremy Boissevain, and others have pointed out, the inferior status of women, a situation common in many Mediterranean countries, has been reinforced by the two major institutions of Maltese life: the church and the government. Women were considered unclean and blamed for the fall of man. Their honor was to be protected lest the family reputation be sullied.

In the villages, traditionally distinct differences in gender roles are still reflected in terms of space: the public domain belonging to the male, the private domain being ruled by the woman. Men are comfortable hanging out in the village square while women tend to remain in their homes over which they exercise control.

However, globalization is changing Malta's social norms and values greatly. The traditional *faldetta*, a large, black, hooded cape worn by women to shield them from public scrutiny, has disappeared. Women teachers are no longer required to resign their positions in public schools upon getting married, or expectant and female **tourists** wearing bikinis are no longer arrested as they still were in the early 1960s. Since 1993, the husband is no longer the legal head of the household in Malta.

Especially since **World War II**, when women were badly needed to work in factories to replace the men who were off at war, there has been a significant shift in women's roles and concurrent demand for gender equality. Maltese women gained the right to vote in 1947. They voted in their first election on 25–27 October, in which Dr. **Paul Boffa** was elected **prime minister**. The labor movement, with its socialist ideology under the strident leadership of **Dom Mintoff**, promoted the equality of all workers, including women. On 16 February 1983, the long-time **Malta Labour Party** member, **Agatha Barbara**, was elected as third **president** of Malta, the first woman to hold the office. However, this remained a relative anomaly, and she is still the only female ever to be president of Malta. To date, no woman has served as prime minister.

Malta has ratified a number of international conventions that are designed to guarantee equal rights for women, including the **United Nations** Convention on the Elimination of All Forms of Discrimination against Women and International Labor Organization conventions on equal pay and employment discrimination. Antidiscrimination legislation was written into the Maltese **Constitution** (1964) and the civil and criminal codes as well as numerous other acts of Parliament. In 2003, in preparation for joining the **European Union (EU)**, **Parliament** enacted the Equality for Men and Women Act (EMWA), promoting gender equality and prohibiting sexual discrimination and harassment. It also established the National Commission for the Promotion of Equality for Men and Women, which came into existence in 2004.

As in many other areas, the laws and intentions are far better than their enforcement, but a benefit of joining the EU is that, in cases where Maltese legal remedies are exhausted or inadequate, the European Convention Act gives citizens the right to file an appeal with the EU Commission.

Although the current prime minister, **Lawrence Gonzi**, has made the hiring of women a priority, so far, the number of women appointed to top government posts has risen only slightly: two of eight ministries in the cabinet and less than one-third of the directorships in the prime minister's office are staffed by women. On 11 October 2006, Madam Justice Abigail Lofaro became the first woman judge ever appointed in Malta. In elected positions, the results are even less encouraging: only 81 women (compared to 1,000 men) have ever been candidates in one or more national campaigns since women gained the right to vote in 1947. While recent **elections** have shown considerable improvement with 4 of 16 female candidates elected in 1996, 6 of 24 in 1998, 6 of 23 in 2003, and 6 of only 19 in 2008, compared to other Western European nations, these results are fairly poor. Malta and Cyprus are the only two EU member countries with no women representing them in the EU Parliament.

A 1995 study analyzing results for women candidates in Maltese general elections found no bias on the part of the electorate against women candidates, who were only slightly less likely to be elected (23 percent) than their male counterparts (25 percent). The study concluded that the low number of women in Parliament was due to some other factor: it blames a party leadership reluctant to nominate women and reluctance on the part of women to run. The study also mentioned that incumbents had a significant advantage and were usually reelected, making it harder for women to gain a foothold in politics. The study also found that women were more socially than politically motivated to run and, thus, more likely to concentrate on parochial and familial issues than the larger national ones.

Although in real wages, Malta boasts the smallest gender gap among all EU member countries, on average, women in Malta are paid 23 percent less than their male counterparts performing the same work. The female employment rate in Malta of 36 percent is the lowest in the EU. The obstacles facing women at work remain the familiar ones: the lack of access to adequate child care, the "glass ceiling," which means that only 15 percent of Maltese managers are women, and the aforementioned gap in pay. In addition to a general lack of support from male partners, there is still tremendous social pressure by church and society to stay at home, taking care of the family. Since 1995, women have outnumbered men at the **university**, yet only 30 percent of female graduates enter the workforce. Those who do not, cite "personal and family" reasons. A recent report by a visiting team of International Monetary Fund advisors commented on the importance of raising female participation in the labor force, which it cited as "a major driver of GDP growth."

The National Council of Women of Malta was established in 1964 as a nonpartisan, nongovernmental umbrella organization for individual women and women's groups. It seeks to promote human rights and equality of opportunity for women. However, it was not until 40 years later, in 2004, that the Parliament passed the "Equality for Men and Women Act," a law required of EU membership, creating a National Commission for the Promotion of Equality. *See also* MICELI-FARRUGIA, DAME LILIAN; FRAZIER, VANESSA; STRICKLAND, MABEL EDELINE; VELLA, ASTRID.

WORLD HERITAGE SITES. As a result of growing international concern over threats to cultural and natural wonders of the world, such as ancient temples in Egypt threatened by the construction of the Aswan dam and the city of Venice slowly sinking into the sea, a Convention Concerning the Protection of World Cultural and Natural Heritage was adopted by **United Nations** Educational, Scientific and Cultural Organization (UNESCO) on 16 November 1972. This convention established a World Heritage Committee that uses a set of criteria by which certain cultural or natural sites of interest are selected to become official World Heritage Sites. Sites on the list, which numbered over 830 as of 2007, are eligible to receive financial assistance for preservation, management, and publicity.

In 1980, three sites in Malta were designated as World Heritage sites: the Hypogeum, the City of **Valletta**, and the Ggantija Temples. In 1992, the temples of Hagar Qim, Mnajdra, Tarxien, Ta Hagrat, and Skorba were added to create the **Megalithic Temples** of Malta.

WORLD WAR I. The "war to end all wars" began when Austria declared war on Serbia on 28 July 1914 in reaction to the assassination of Archduke Ferdinand of Austria and his wife. A week later, on 5 August 1914, Malta was mobilized after Germany, France, and Great Britain had entered the conflict. Its deepwater port located midway between the Suez Canal and Gibraltar, Malta had become a very significant base for the **British** navy as a coaling station and shipyard with **drydocks** for maintenance and repair work. The war effort would rely on Malta in additional ways: as a center for treating sick and wounded soldiers, an internment camp for prisoners of war, and a source of recruits, including soldiers and skilled support laborers.

Most important of these was the hospital function. Almost 60,000 sick and wounded soldiers were treated in Malta, earning it the nickname "nurse of the Mediterranean." At the beginning of the war, there were four small hospital facilities with a total of 278 beds. By the end of hostilities, the number of hospitals and beds had expanded to 28 and 20,000, respectively. Of particular significance was the 1915 Gallipoli Campaign, which resulted in an unusually high number of dead and wounded.

The British had further developed the islands' already impressive fortifications, and Malta was so heavily defended that it was never attacked during World War I, but the conflict had other impacts on the citizenry. When it ended, of the 24,000 Maltese who served Britain in the war, close to 600 had lost their lives. From an **economic** standpoint, the war affected Malta by creating inflation and shortages as war-related activities on Malta ramped up, followed by unemployment and poverty as the war ebbed.

WORLD WAR II. World War II began at 4:45 a.m. on 1 September 1939, when the old German battleship *Schleswig-Holstein* fired its

11-inch guns into a Polish ammunition depot near Danzig. That was quickly followed by the land and air blitzkrieg into Poland. Although there had been no declaration of war by the Germans, the **British** and French did declare war on 3 September. As a British colony, Malta was officially at war with Germany from that date. However, Malta's "real" war, the "second great siege" (after the one of 1565), started over nine months later when **Italy** made a formal declaration of war and quickly followed it with a bombing raid, the first of the many that were to occur over the next three years. Malta was to earn the dubious distinction of having received the greatest tonnage of bombs of any of the World War II targets of either side.

Because Malta had been left without any effective defense capability, the Italians could have invaded the islands with little difficulty. Only three ancient airplanes could be used against the incoming bombers. However, Malta was saved by the overly cautious and inept conduct of its enemy in those early days of the conflict and later by the nature of its terrain and sturdy building construction. The numerous caves and tunnels, particularly on the island of Malta, the major target, provided safe shelters from air bombardment. As all buildings were of stone, there was nothing to burn; a bomb hit on a single building destroyed only that building. Besides, the relentless bombing attacks served only to harden the will of the people.

A state-of-the-art tanker, the SS *Ohio*, owned by the Texas Oil Company and on loan to the British, was part of a convoy bringing oil to Malta, which was beginning to face starvation and certain defeat for lack of supplies. The *Ohio* was attacked numerous times over two days. Bombed from the air and hit by a torpedo, the ship was in imminent danger of sinking, so the order to abandon ship was given. Four other escort ships managed to maneuver alongside, barely keeping the ailing vessel afloat just long enough to bring it and its precious cargo into Grand Harbour as thousands of cheering Maltese welcomed them. Once the cargo was unloaded, the *Ohio* sank to the bottom of the harbor. Its oil and the food on the four other supply ships that made it to Malta (nine others were sunk!), enabled Malta to avoid starvation. The dramatic incident was viewed as a miracle by the devout Maltese. Such good fortune and the earlier failure of the enemy to act more forcefully when Malta was weakest gave the British time to bring in reinforcements, particularly fighters and bombers, and turn the tide of war. This not only prevented an invasion but also helped transform the islands into an offensive machine, a "stationary aircraft carrier," which became a major factor in the Allied victory in North Africa in mid-May 1943.

With the end of the North African campaign, Malta became more of a provider than a receiver of bombs and other munitions. Ships, stores, ammunition, vehicles, and all the accoutrements of the impending Allied invasion of Europe were everywhere. There was also a massive buildup of the air arm. Supreme Allied Commander General **Dwight D. Eisenhower** chose Malta as the headquarters for the initial invasion activities "because of her splendid naval communications system." In addition to Eisenhower, Bernard Montgomery, Lord Louis Mountbatten, and others of the top command were there. D-Day was 10 July 1943, and 3,000 ships and large landing craft, with 115,000 British **Commonwealth** and 66,000 American troops, were ready. Harsh weather from a freak storm made the operation much more difficult, but it proceeded successfully. Among the first to land was the 231st Infantry Brigade of the King's Own Malta Regiment, which used a white Maltese cross on a red shield as its brigade insignia. On 13 July, the supreme Allied commander first set foot on Axis-dominated Europe.

Italy surrendered on 8 September 1943, the feast day of Our Lady of Victories. Under the terms of the agreement, the Italian fleet was to surrender at Malta. The fleet sailed from various ports under the guard of parts of the British Mediterranean fleet. German anger over the surrender of their allies became evident when the flagship of the fleet, the *Roma*, was sunk by a radio-controlled German bomb, killing the commanding admiral and a great number of officers and men. By the end of the month, 76 ships of the Italian navy had surrendered in Malta, including five battleships, six cruisers, six destroyers, and 23 submarines. Admiral Sir Andrew Cunningham sent a message to the British admiralty that read, "Be pleased to inform their Lordships that the Italian Battle Fleet now lies at anchor under the guns of the Fortress of Malta." For Malta, World War II had effectively ended. *See also* AXIS BLOCKADE; DOBBIE, LT. GENERAL SIR WILLIAM GEORGE; E-BOAT ATTACK; GEORGE CROSS; GLOSTER GLADIATOR; GORT, LORD; HMS *ILLUSTRIOUS*;

OPERATION HERKULES; OPERATION PEDESTAL; POST-WAR RECONSTRUCTION.

– X –

XERRI, DUN MIKIEL. During the blockade of the French garrison holding **Valletta** in 1798–99, there were many attempts by the Maltese to overcome the soldiers. A plan was made for a joint effort by those trapped inside the walls with those outside. On 12 January 1799, there were to be simultaneous attacks on a number of major buildings inside the city and on various entrances through the walls. It was hoped that the general confusion of such widespread attacks would bring success. Instead, the plan was discovered in advance, and 45 persons were shot to death in the Palace Square. In the group was one of the leaders of the plan, Dun Mikiel Xerri, a priest. His execution only served to harden the Maltese opposition to the French. *See also* FRENCH INVASION; FRENCH OCCUPATION.

XIMENES DE TEXADA, GRAND MASTER FRANCIS. *See* UPRISING OF THE PRIESTS.

XUEREB, PAUL (1923–1994). Born on 21 July 1923, Xuereb was educated at St. Aloysius College in Birkirkara and Flores College in **Valletta**. During **World War II**, he interrupted his studies to serve as an antiaircraft gunner with the Malta Artillery, earning several medals for bravery. From 1944 to 1946, he worked as a clerk at the **dockyards**. He immigrated to London in 1946 and worked as an accountant while continuing his studies. Xuereb returned to Malta in 1950, first managing a trading firm before becoming a teacher at the Lyceum.

In 1959, he gave up teaching to become the literary editor and assistant editor of the **Malta Labour Party (MLP)** news publication the *Voice of Malta*. He successfully ran in the **elections** of 1962 as a member of the MLP and was reelected in 1966, 1971, 1976, and 1981. In August 1971, he was appointed parliamentary secretary in the **Prime Minister's** office and later served as minister of **trade**, industry, **agriculture**, and **tourism**. Xuereb resigned his parliamentary seat on 27 April 1983 to make way for the leader designate of the MLP, **Dr. Karmenu Mifsud Bonnici**. Never actually sworn in, Xuereb was appointed as acting **president** of Malta from 16 February 1987 to 4 April 1989. Not only did Xuereb serve on numerous company boards, including as chairman of the Mid Med Bank and the Malta Development Corporation, but also he was an accomplished author of historical guidebooks and novels. He died on 6 September 1994.

– Y –

YACHT MARINAS. Located in the center of the Mediterranean Sea, it is no surprise that Malta has become a yachting center. However, it was not always so. As a military base of Great Britain, there was no encouragement given to visits by private yachts. It was only after **independence** that there were significant moves to attract such visits. A marina was developed first in the Ta' Xbiex area, offering attractive rates for slip rental and utilities. As part of economic restructuring, the **dockyards** organization in 2003 developed an entirely new business niche, the overhaul and repair of luxury yachts. This has helped to attract more sailors to the archipelago's deep, natural harbors.

Several new marinas have been opened in Grand, Marsamxett, and Mgarr Harbors, but they still cannot satisfy a burgeoning demand for berthing space. The newest of these, Grand Harbour Marina in Vittoriosa, has added 230 berths, raising the total capacity of Malta's yacht marinas to nearly 1,500 for a current demand estimated at 3,500.

Located on the very site where the **Knights of St. John** first anchored their ships, the newest facility was dedicated on 27 November 2005 by Her Majesty Queen Elizabeth II, who was in Malta for the **Commonwealth** Heads of Government meeting. Grand Harbour Marina is managed and 80 percent owned by a private company, an initial step in government's plan, announced in 2006, to make yacht marinas more competitive through **privatization**. In April 2008, the government announced a call for proposals to add 21 new marinas, offering a total of 4,800 berths and, in June 2009, called for bids on 25-year concessions for private operators to manage the Ta' Xbiex, Msida, and Mgarr marinas.

– Z –

ZAHRA, JOSEPH F. (1955–). Born in 1955, Zahra graduated in 1976 with a first class honours degree in economics from the **University of Malta** and a master's degree in economics in 1979. He cofounded Misco (Market Intelligence Services Co., Ltd.), Misco International, Ltd., and Impetus Europe Consulting, Ltd. He has served as chairman of the Bank of **Valletta** (1998–2004), Maltacom (2003), and their subsidiaries, as a board director of the Central Bank of Malta (1992–96) and the Malta Development Corporation (1995–96). He is today a board member on a number of public and private, local and international companies based in Malta and overseas.

Zahra has a strong personal interest in the arts and culture. He held the chairmanship of the first Malta Council for Culture and the Arts (2002–3) and was a member of the Committee for the Guarantee of Maltese Heritage and Arts (2002–05). In his capacity of chairman of the National Euro Changeover Committee, Zahra was responsible for the changeover in Malta from the local currency to the **euro** on 1 January 2008.

Since 2006, he has served as the chairman of the National Commission for Higher **Education**, responsible for changes and oversight of the higher and tertiary education sector in Malta. For over 10 years, he held the position of visiting lecturer in economics at the University of Malta. Since 2000, he has been a lecturer in managerial economics at the University of Messina.

A published poet and playwright, Zahra was awarded the Gold Medal of the Malta Society for Arts, Manufactures and Commerce from the **president** of Malta. He is married to Lucienne (née Naudi), and they have two children, David and Maria.

ZAMMIT, SIR THEMISTOCLES (1864–1935). A true Renaissance scholar, Sir "Temi" Zammit was successful in many fields, whether as medical practitioner, researcher, historian, professor, or **archeologist**. Zammit was born in **Valletta** on 30 September 1864. Graduating from the Royal **University of Malta** as an MD in 1889, he began his distinguished career focused on medicine. He was a member of the joint **British**-Maltese commission charged with finding the cause of undulate fever, more commonly known as **Malta fever**. It was he who, in 1905, discovered that the microbe was transferred from goats (running wild in the streets of Valletta at the time) to humans, and the test for the disease bears his name: Zammit's Test. In 1920, he left the medical profession to become the rector at the University of Malta, a position he resigned in 1926 to focus on historical and archeological research. The University's emblem and motto were created by him. He authored a number of books covering a variety of subjects related to Malta's history.

As an archaeologist, for over three decades Zammit headed the excavations of the Hypogeum, the Temples of Hal Tarxien, Hagar Qim, and Mnjadra, the **cart tracks**, and the **Roman** baths, among other sites. He wrote books about his discoveries, gaining an international reputation. Zammit founded what later became the National **Museum** of Archaeology and completed his long and productive career as its director, a position later held by his son, Captain C. G. Zammit. His influence over that extensive collection remains to this day. Sir Zammit died on 2 November 1935. *See also* MEGALITHIC TEMPLES.

ZAMMIT DIMECH, DR. FRANCIS (1954–). Born on 23 October 1954, Zammit Dimech studied at St. Aloysius College and the **University of Malta** where he served as president of the Students' Representative Council and earned a doctorate in law in 1979 and an MA in financial services in 1999. After running, unsuccessfully, as a candidate of the **Nationalist Party** in 1981, he was active in the party's youth movement for which he served as president. He was first elected to **Parliament** in 1987 and appointed parliamentary secretary for transport and communications in 1990. Reelected in 1992, he was appointed minister of transport and communications and from March 1994, minister for the **environment** with responsibility for the environment, capital construction, water services, **energy**, waste, and the Planning Authority.

After the Nationalists returned to power in 1998, Dr. Zammit Dimech was reappointed as minister for the environment, serving until 2002, when he was appointed minister of resources and infrastructure. Since his reelection in 2003, he has been in the public eye even more frequently, as minister of **tourism** (reconfigured as tourism and culture under the **Lawrence Gonzi** government), a sector that has grown in importance to the **economy** of Malta and has struggled in recent years.

Bibliography

CONTENTS

INTRODUCTION

Although it is a very small nation, Malta has a rich history and a thriving cultural environment in literature and the arts. In recent years, the volume and quality of works on the history, economy, and culture of the Maltese islands has increased dramatically. There are, thus, more titles included in this new bibliography than the previous one.

The Maltese language is used by a very small community of speakers (slightly over 500,000), and English is an official language of Malta; therefore, this bibliography only includes works in English with an emphasis on those published since 1995, when the first edition of this *Historical Dictionary of Malta* appeared.

The Melitensia Sections of the Library at the University of Malta and the National Library have the most extensive collections of items about Malta existing anywhere. In the United States, there are two collections at collegiate libraries, which emphasize publications about the islands. St. John's University in Collegeville, Minnesota, has the Malta Study Center of the Monastic Manuscript Microfilm Library. The center houses an extensive collection of microfilm copies of medieval manuscripts and archival documents from Maltese, including A. Zammit Gabarretta and J. A. Mizzi's *Catalogue of the Records of the Order of St. John of Jerusalem in the Royal Malta Library*, in addition to a wide range of published works on the island's history, literature, and culture. A similar Malta Study Center exists at Luther College in Decorah, Iowa, featuring a collection of library materials on all aspects of Malta's history and culture, from prehistory to the contemporary.

The European Documentation and Research Center at the University of Malta's main campus in Msida houses documents concerning Malta and the European Union (EU). It has recently published numerous works on Malta's economy and EU membership.

For the casual reader seeking a general overview of Malta's history, the accepted standard continues to be Brian Blouet's *The Story of Malta* (revised edition, 2004).

A more detailed comprehensive history is provided by Stefan Goodwin's *Malta, Mediterranean Bridge* (2002).

In his preface, Goodwin describes Malta as a "missing link for understanding regional interrelationships that remain hidden or poorly understood." His work provides a very readable yet detailed history of the political, economic, social, and cultural developments on the Maltese islands from prehistory to the 21st century.

For even more detailed histories and descriptions of sites and artifacts of Malta's prehistory and early history, readers should consult the "Malta's Living Heritage" series published by Midsea Books in collaboration with Heritage Malta, specifically: *Malta: Prehistory and Temples* by David H. Trump, *Malta: Phoenician, Punic, and Roman* by Anthony Bonnano, and *Malta: The Medieval Millennium* by Charles Dalli, each of which are over 300 pages in length and richly illustrated with hundreds of photographs by Daniel Cilia.

A Chronicle of Twentieth Century Malta by Joseph Bonnici and Michael Cassar offers a 500-page, year-by-year collection of major news stories with photographs and illustrations covering the years 1900 through 1999.

Numerous works have been written about various eras and aspects of the Knights of St. John. Among those, H. J. A. Sire's *The Knights of Malta* is most comprehensive. Meanwhile, Ernle Bradford's *The Great Siege* is still highly recommended as the most readable and gripping account of an event that remains important to the Maltese psyche.

Concerning the modern political and cultural history of Malta, the well-known Maltese historian Henry Frendo has written several important books. His *Malta's Quest for Independence: Reflections on the Course of Maltese History* offers a very detailed and, at times, personal account of Malta in the latter half of the 20th century and as it struggled to become an independent nation-state. Also still very valuable are his earlier *Malta: Culture and Identity* (coauthored with Oliver Friggieri, 1994) and *Party Politics in a Fortress Colony: The Maltese Experience* (1979).

In *Ambivalent Europeans: Ritual, Memory, and the Public Sphere in Malta*, the British ethnographer and social anthropologist, Jon Mitchell, presents interesting insights concerning the impact of globalization and the prospect of EU membership on Maltese attitudes, culture, and traditions, especially through the lens of church festivals (*festi*), band clubs, political party affiliation, and gender.

On Malta's economy, Edward Spiteri's *Malta: From Colonial Dependency to Economic Viability, Maltese Economic History, 1800–2000* (2002) offers the general reader a comprehensive, not overly technical, discussion of how Malta's economy has changed in the last two centuries.

General information on Malta and the EU can be found in *European Integration: The Maltese Experience* (2004) by Christopher Pollacco and *Malta in the European Union: Five Years On and Looking to the Future* edited by Peter Xuereb (2009).

Internet sites about Malta have increased considerably in number and quality. Reliable sources of general information about Malta can be found at the Malta government gateway site (www.gov.mt), the Department of Information site (www.doi.gov.mt), the official tourist website (www.visitmalta.com) as well as commercial sites (such as www.aboutmalta.com). Statistics about Malta can be found on the National Statistics Office website (www.nso.gov.mt), which includes digitized copies of *Malta Blue Books*, covering demographic and economic statistics compiled for the British government and dating from 1821.

I. HISTORY

1. General

Atauz, Ayse Devrim. *Eight Thousand Years of Maltese Maritime History: Trade, Piracy, and Naval Warfare in the Central Mediterranean.* Gainesville: University Press of Florida, 2008.

Attard, Edward. *A History of the Malta Police, 1800–1964*. Malta: Colour Image, 2003.

Attard, Joseph. *Malta: A History of Two Millennia*. Valletta, Malta: Progress Press, 2002.

Blouet, Brian W. *The Story of Malta*. rev. ed. Valletta, Malta: Progress, 2004.

Boisgelin de Kerdu, Pierre Marie Louis de. *Ancient and Modern Malta: Containing a Description of the Ports and Cities of the Islands of Malta and Goza*. . . . 3 vols. London: G. J. Robinson, 1804. Facsimile of the 1st ed. Valletta, Malta: Midsea Books, 1988.

Bonello, Giovanni. *Histories of Malta*. 7 vols. Valletta, Malta: Fondazzjoni Patrimonju Malti, 2000.

Bonnici, Joseph, and Michael Cassar. *A Chronicle of Twentieth Century Malta*. San Gwann, Malta: Book Distributors, 2004.

Bradford, Ernle Dusgate Selby. *Mediterranean: Portrait of a Sea*. London: Hodder and Stoughton, 1971.

Cassar, Carmel. *A Concise History of Malta*. Msida, Malta: Mireva, 2000.

Cassar, Paul. *Early Relations between Malta and the United States of America*. Valletta, Malta: Midsea Books, 1976.

———. *Medical History of Malta*. Vol. 6. London: Wellcome Historical Medical Library, 1965.

Castillo, Dennis A. *The Maltese Cross: A Strategic History of Malta*. Westport, CT: Praeger Security International, 2006.

De Lucca, Dennis. *Giovanni Battista Vertova: Diplomacy, Warfare and Military Engineering Practice in Early Seventeenth Century Malta*. Valletta, Malta: Midsea Books, 2001.

Elliott, Peter. *The Cross and the Ensign: A Naval History of Malta, 1798–1979*. Annapolis, MD: Naval Institute Press, 1980.

Fiorini, Stanley, ed. *Documentary Sources of Maltese History*. Vol.1. Msida, Malta: University of Malta, 1996.

Gambin, Kenneth, ed. *Malta, Roots of a Nation: The Development of Malta from an Island People to an Island Nation*. Valletta, Malta: Heritage Malta, 2004.

Ganado, Albert, and Joseph C. Sammut. *Malta in British and French Caricature, 1798–1815: With Historical Notes*. Valletta, Malta: Said, 1989.

Gauci, Charles A. *The Genealogy and Heraldry of the Noble Families of Malta*. 2 vols. Valletta, Malta: Gulf, 1981–92.

Gerada-Azzopardi, Eric. *Malta Revisited: An Appointment with History*. rev. ed. Valletta, Malta: Progress Press, 1984.

Goodwin, Stefan. *Malta, Mediterranean Bridge*. Westport, CT: Bergin & Garvey, 2002.

Kearney, J. Michael. *Malta Concerto*. Bellevue, WA: Elfin Cove, 2000.

The Malta Stamp Collection, 1964–2004. Marsa, Malta: Maltapost, 2004.

Malta Study Circle. "Malta, the Postal History and Postage Stamps, 1576–1960." Supplement to *Malta, the Stamps, and Postal History, 1576–1960,* edited by R. E. Martin. Malta: Malta Study Circle, 1985.

Rizzo Naudi, John. *Brucellosis: The Malta Experience, A Celebration, 1905–2005.* San Gwann, Malta: Publishers Enterprises Group, 2005.

Savona-Ventura, Charles. *Ancient and Medieval Medicine in Malta: Before 1600 AD.* San Gwann, Malta: Publishers Enterprises Group, 2004.

Testa, Carmel. *The French in Malta, 1798–1800.* Valletta, Malta: Midsea Books, 1997.

Wettinger, Godfrey. *Slavery in the Islands of Malta and Gozo ca. 1000–1812.* San Gwann, Malta: Publishers Enterprises Group, 2002.

Wismayer, J. M. *A Miscellanea of Historical Records.* Sliema, Malta: J. M. Wismayer, 2003.

Zolina, Elizaveta., comp. and ed. *Malta and Russia: Journey through the Centuries, Historical Discoveries in Russo-Maltese Relations.* Valletta, Malta: E. Zolina, 2002.

2. Ancient History

Attenborough, David. *The First Eden: The Mediterranean World and Man.* London: Collins, 1987.

Bonanno, Anthony. *Malta: Phoenician, Punic, and Roman.* Sta Venera, Malta: Midsea Books, 2005.

Casson, Lionel. *The Ancient Mariners: Seafarers and Sea Fighters of the Mediterranean in Ancient Times.* 2nd ed. Princeton, NJ: Princeton University Press, 1991.

Galea, Michael, and John Ciarlo, eds. *St. Paul in Malta: A Compendium of Pauline Studies.* Malta: Conventual Franciscans, 1992.

Galea, Michelle, and Francesca Balzan. *Palazzo Falson: Historic House Museum.* Sliema, Malta: Miranda, 2007.

Grant, Michael. *The Ancient Mediterranean.* New York: Scribner, 1969.

Harden, Donald B. *The Phoenicians.* London: Thames & Hudson, 1963. Reprinted with revisions and extended bibliography. Harmondsworth, Middlesex, UK: Penguin Books, 1980.

Sammut, Felix. *Saint Paul in Malta.* 6th ed. Rabat, Malta: Religjon u Hajja, 2002.

3. Medieval History

Buhagiar, Mario. *The Christianisation of Malta: Catacombs, Cult Centres, and Churches in Malta to 1530.* Oxford: Archaeopress, 2007.

Dalli, Charles. *Malta: The Medieval Millennium.* Sta Venera, Malta: Midsea Books, 2006.

Luttrell, Anthony, ed. *Medieval Malta: Studies on Malta before the Knights.* London: The British School at Rome, 1975.

Pe´rez de Alesio, Mateo. *The True Depiction of the Investment and Attack Suffered by the Island of Malta at the Hands of the Turks in the Year of Our Lord 1565.* Translated with notes by Denis J. Calnan and Giovanni Ercole Testaferrata Abela. 3rd ed. Valletta, Malta: Progress Press, 1965.

Pickles, Tim. *Malta 1565: Last Battle of the Crusades.* London: Osprey Publishing, 1988.

4. Knights of Malta

Abela, A. E. *The Order of St. Michael and St. George in Malta, and Maltese Knights of the British Realm.* Valletta, Malta: Progress Press, 1988.

Balbi, Francesco. *The Siege of Malta, 1565.* Translated from the Spanish edition of 1568 by Ernle Bradford. London: Folio Society, 1965.

Bedford, W. K. Riland. *Malta and the Knights Hospitallers.* London: Seeley, 1894.

Bradford, Ernle Dusgate Selby. *The Great Siege.* London: Hodder & Stoughton, 1961.

———. *The Shield and the Sword: The Knights of St John.* London: Hodder & Stoughton, 1972.

———. *The Sundered Cross; The Story of the Fourth Crusade.* Englewood Cliffs, NJ: Prentice-Hall, 1967.

Breithaupt, Johann Friedrich. *Malta, Island of Christian Heroes: Life in Malta in the Early 17th Century.* Translated by Alfred Scalpello. Valletta, Malta: Fondazzjoni Patrimonju Malti, 2001.

Cassar, Paul. *The Holy Infirmary of the Knights of St. John: "La Sacra Infermeria."* Valletta, Malta: Mediterranean Conference Centre, 2005.

Cavaliero, Roderick. *The Last of the Crusaders: The Knights of St. John and Malta in the Eighteenth Century.* London: Cape, 1960. Reprinted with new afterword by the author. Valletta, Malta: Progress Press, 2001.

Dauber, Robert L., and Michael Galea. *Austrian Knights of Malta: Relations Malta-Austria 1530–1798.* San Gwann, Malta: Publishers Enterprises Group, 2006.

De Ransijat, Bosredon. *The Seven Year Balance Sheet of the Sovereign Military and Hospitaller Order of St. John. . . .* Introduction and glossary by J. M. Wismayer. Naxxar, Malta: Universal Intelligence Data Bank of America (Europe), 1984.

Dijkhof, Hans J. Hoegen. *The Legitimacy of Orders of St John: A Historical and Legal Analysis and Case Study of a Para-Religious Phenomenon.* Amsterdam: Hoegen Dijkhof Advocaten, 2006.

Earle, Peter. *Corsairs of Malta and Barbary.* London: Sidgwick & Jackson, 1970.

Engel, Claire Éliane. *Knights of Malta; A Gallery of Portraits.* London: Allen & Unwin, 1963.

Freller, Thomas. *The Anglo-Bavarian Langue of the Order of Malta.* Malta: Pubblikazzjonijiet Indipendenza, 2001.

——. *The Last Corsairs of Malta: An Incredible True Story.* Sta Venera, Malta: Midsea Books, 2007.

——. *Spies and Renegades in Hospitaller Malta.* Pietà, Malta: Pubblikazzjonijiet Indipendenza, 2004.

Galea, Michael. *German Knights of Malta: A Gallery of Portraits.* Valletta, Malta: Burgelli Publications, 1986.

Grandmaster Aloph De Wignacourt, 1601–1622: A Monograph. San Gwann, Malta: Publishers Enterprises Group, 2002.

King, E. J. *The Knights of St. John in the British Realm: Being the Official History of the Most Venerable Order of the Hospital of St. John of Jerusalem.* 3rd ed. Revised and continued by Sir. Harry Luke. London: Most Venerable Order of the Hospital of St. John of Jerusalem, 1967.

Lo Celso, Luciano, and Adrian Busietta. *The Triangle of Mediterranean: The Knights of Malta between the Kingdom of Naples and Arabs-Barbary states of Maghreb.* . . . Malta: Castello Entertainment, 2001.

Mula, Charles. *The Princes of Malta: The Grand Masters of the Order of St. John in Malta, 1530–1798.* San Gwann, Malta: Publishers Enterprises Group, 2000.

Muscat, Joseph, and Andrew Cuschieri. *Naval Activities of the Knights of St John: 1530–1798.* Sta Venera, Malta: Midsea, 2002.

Nicholson, Helen J. *The Knights Hospitaller.* Woodbridge, Suffolk, UK: Boydell, 2001.

Nicolle, David. *Knights of Jerusalem: The Crusading Order of Hospitallers, 1100–1565.* Oxford: Osprey Publishing, 2008.

O'Malley, Gregory. *The Knights Hospitaller of the English Langue, 1460–1565.* Oxford: Oxford University Press, 2004.

Phillips, Simon. *The Prior of the Knights Hospitaller in Late Medieval England.* Woodbridge, UK: Boydell Press, 2009.

Quintano, Anton. *The Maltese-Hospitaller Sailing Ship Squadron: 1701–1798.* San Gwann, Malta: Publishers Enterprises Group, 2003.

Riley-Smith, Jonathan Simon Christopher. *Hospitallers: The History of the Order of St. John.* London: Hambledon, 1999.

Savona-Ventura, Charles. *Knight Hospitaller Medicine in Malta: 1530–1798.* San Gwann, Malta: Publishers Enterprises Group, 2004.

Setton, Kenneth Meyer, ed. *A History of the Crusades.* 6 vols. Philadelphia: University of Pennsylvania Press, 1955–89.

Sire, H. J. A. *The Knights of Malta.* New Haven, CT: Yale University Press, 1994.

Spiteri, Stephen. *Armoury of the Knights: A Study of the Palace Armoury, Its Collection, and the Military Storehouses of the Hospitaller Knights of the Order of St. John.* Valletta, Malta: Midsea Books in association with Fondazzjoni Wirt Artna, 2003.

———. *Fortresses of the Knights.* rev. ed. Hamrun, Malta: Book Distributors, 2001.

———. *The Great Siege: Knights Vs. Turks, MDLXV: Anatomy of a Hospitaller Victory.* Tarxien, Malta: Gutenberg Press, 2005.

Testa, Carmel. *Romegas.* Sta Venera, Malta: Midsea Books, 2002.

Vella, Andrew P. *Malta and the Czars: Diplomatic Relations between the Order of St. John and Russia, 1697–1802.* Valletta, Malta: Royal University of Malta, 1965.

5. Great Britain and Malta

Abela, A. E. *Governors of Malta.* Valletta, Malta: Progress Press, 1991.

Austin, Douglas. *Churchill and Malta: A Special Relationship.* Stroud, UK: Spellmount, 2006.

———. *Malta and British Strategic Policy, 1925–43.* Cass Series 13. London: Cass, 2004.

Bonham-Carter, Charles. *The Bonham-Carter Diaries, 1936–1940: What the British Governor Thought of Malta and the Maltese.* Edited with an introduction by John Manduca. San Gwann, Malta: Publishers Enterprises Group, 2004.

Chesney, A. G., comp. *Historical Records of the Maltese Corps of the British Army.* London: W. Clowes & Sons, 1897. Facsimile. Valletta, Malta: Midsea Books, 1986.

Cremona, J. J. *An Outline of the Constitutional Development of Malta under British Rule.* Msida, Malta: University Press, 1963.

Crowley, Roger. *Empires of the Sea: The Siege of Malta, the Battle of Lepanto, and the Contest for the Center of the World.* New York: Random House, 2008.

Frendo, Henry. *The Origins of Maltese Statehood: A Case Study of Decolonization in the Mediterranean.* 2nd ed. Malta: H. Frendo, 2000.

Grech, Jesmond. *British Heritage in Malta*. Miller Guides. Luqa, Malta: Centro Stampa Editoriale Perseus, Plurigraf, 2002.

Gregory, Desmond. *Malta, Britain, and the European Powers, 1793–1815*. Madison, NJ: Fairleigh Dickinson University Press, 1996.

Harding, Hugh W. *Maltese Legal History under British Rule, (1801–1836)*. Msida, Malta: University Press, 1980.

Lloyd, T. O. *The British Empire, 1558–1995*. 2nd ed. The Short Oxford History of the Modern World. Oxford: Oxford University Press, 1996.

Louis, William Roger, Alaine M. Low, Nicholas P. Canny, and P. J. Marshall, eds. *The Oxford History of the British Empire*. 5 vols. Oxford: Oxford University Press, 1998–99.

Mallia-Milanes, Victor, ed. *The British Colonial Experience, 1800–1964: The Impact on Maltese Society*. Msida, Malta: Mireva, 1988.

Smith, Simon C. *Malta*. British Documents on the End of Empire 11. London: The Stationery Office, 2006.

Wismayer, J. M. *The History of the King's Own Malta Regiment and the Armed Forces of the Order of St. John*. Valletta, Malta: Said International, 1989.

6. World War I

Brittain, Vera. *Chronicle of Youth: Great War Diary, 1913–1917*. Edited by Alan Bishop and Terry Smart. London: Gollancz, 1981.

Mizzi, John A. *Gallipoli: The Malta Connection*. Luqa, Malta: Tecnografica Publications, 1991.

Zarb-Dimech, Anthony. *Malta during the First World War, 1914–1918*. Malta: A. Zarb-Dimech, 2004.

7 World War II

Abela, A. E. *Malta's George Cross and War Gallantry Awards*. Valetta, Malta: Progress Press, 1989.

Ansel, Walter. *Hitler and the Middle Sea*. Durham, NC: Duke University Press, 1972.

Attard, Joseph. *The Battle of Malta*. London: Kimber, 1980.

Barnham, Denis. *One Man's Window; An Illustrated Account of Ten Weeks of War, Malta, April 13th, to June 21st, 1942*. London: W. Kimber, 1956.

Bennett, G. H., and R. Bennett. *Survivors: British Merchant Seamen in the Second World War*. London: Hambledon, 1999.

Bennett, Ralph Francis. *Ultra and Mediterranean Strategy*. New York: Morrow, 1989.

Beurling, George F., and Leslie Roberts. *Malta Spitfire: The Diary of a Fighter Pilot*. London: Greenhill, 2002. First published 1943 by Oxford University Press.

Bradford, Ernle Dusgate Selby. *Siege: Malta, 1940–1943*. London: Hamilton, 1985.

Clayton, Tim and Phil Craig. *The End of the Beginning: From the Siege of Malta to the Allied Victory at El Alamein*. New York: Free Press, 2002.

Cull, Brian, and Frederick Galea. *Hurricanes over Malta: June 1940–April 1942*. London: Grub Street, 2001.

———. *Spitfires over Malta: The Epic Air Battles of 1942*. London: Grub Street, 2005.

Cull, Brian, Nicola Malizia, and Frederick Galea. *Spitfires over Sicily: The Crucial Role of the Malta Spitfires in the Battle of Sicily, January–August 1943*. London: Grub Street, 2000.

The Epic of Malta: A Pictorial Survey of Malta during the Second World War. London: Oldhams, 1943. Facsimile of the 1st edition with an introduction by Henry Frendo. Malta: Melitensia Editions, Valletta Pub., 1990.

Forty, George. *Battle for Malta*. Hersham, Surrey, UK: I. Allan, 2003.

Foss, Denis, and Basil Entwistle. *Shoot a Line: A Merchant Mariner's War*. Linden Hall: Grosvenor Square Associates, 1992.

Franks, Norman L. R. *Buck McNair: Canadian Spitfire Ace: The Story of Group Captain R. W. McNair, DSO, DFC & 2 Bars, Ld'H, CdG, RCAF*. London: Grub Street, 2001.

Galea, Frederick R. *Call-Out: A Wartime Diary of Air/Sea Rescue Operations at Malta*. St. Julians, Malta: BIEB BIEB, 2002.

Holland, James. *Fortress Malta: An Island under Siege, 1940–1943*. London: Orion, 2003.

Jackson, Robert. *The Royal Navy in World War II*. Annapolis, MD: Naval Institute Press, 1997.

Jellison, Charles A. *Besieged: The World War II Ordeal of Malta, 1940–1942*. Hanover, NH: Published for the University of New Hampshire by University Press of New England, 1984.

Johnston, Tim, and Chaz Bowyer. *Tattered Battlements: A Fighter Pilot's Malta Diary, D-Day and After*. London: Kimber, 1985.

Kurowski, Franz. *Luftwaffe Aces: German Combat Pilots of World War II*. Translated by David Johnston. Winnipeg, Manitoba: J. J. Fedorowicz, 1996.

Leighton, Frank. *Frayed Lifelines: A Siege Survivor's Story*. Victoria, British Columbia, Canada: Trafford, 2003.

Lucas, Laddie. *Malta, the Thorn in Rommel's Side: Six Months that Turned the War.* London: St. Paul, 1992.

Massimello, Giovanni, and Giorgio Apostolo. *Italian Aces of World War 2.* Osprey Aircraft of the Aces 34. Oxford: Osprey, 2000.

McCaffery, Dan. *Hell Island: Canadian Pilots and the 1942 Air Battle for Malta.* Toronto, Canada: James Lorimer, 1998.

Mitcham, Samuel W., Jr., and Friedrich von Stauffenberg. *The Battle of Sicily: How the Allies Lost their Chance for Total Victory.* New York: Orion, 1991.

Mizzi, Laurence. *When War Broke Out.* Translated by Joseph M. Falzon. Valletta, Malta: Progress Press, 2000.

Nichols, Steve. *Malta Spitfire Aces.* Osprey Aircraft of the Aces. Oxford: Osprey, 2008.

Page, Christopher L. W. *The Royal Navy and the Malta and Russian Convoys, 1941–1942.* Naval Staff Histories. London: Cass, 2003.

Ralph, Wayne. *Aces, Warriors & Wingmen: Firsthand Accounts of Canada's Fighter Pilots in the Second World War.* Mississauga, Ontario, Canada: John Wiley, 2005.

Ratcliffe, Christina. *Women of Malta: True Wartime Stories of Christina Ratcliffe and Tamara Marks.* Edited by Frederick R. Galea. Rabat, Malta: Wise Owl Publications, 2006.

Roba, Jean-Louis, and Martin Pegg. *Jagdwaffe: The Mediterranean, 1942–1943.* Luftwaffe Colours vol. 4, sec. 4. Burgess Hill, UK: Classic Publications, 2003.

Rogers, Anthony, ed. *185: The Malta Squadron.* Staplehurst, UK: Spellmount, 2005.

———. *Battle over Malta: Aircraft Losses & Crash Sites, 1940–42.* Stroud, Gloucestershire, UK: Sutton, 2000.

Shores, Christopher, Brian Cull, and Nicola Malizia. *Malta: the Spitfire Year 1942.* London: Grub Street, 1991.

Spooner, Tony. *In Full Flight.* Canterbury, UK: Wingham, 1991.

———. *Night Fighter Ace.* Stroud, UK: Sutton, 2003.

———. *Warburton's War: The Life of Maverick Ace Adrian Warburton, DSO, DFC, DFC(USA).* Bristol, UK: Crécy Books, 1994.

Thake Vassallo, Clare, and Ivan Callus, eds. *Malta at War in Cultural Memory: Representations of "The Madonna's Chosen People."* Valletta, Malta: University Publishers, 2005.

Thomas, David A. *Malta Convoys 1940–42: The Struggle at Sea.* London: L. Cooper, 1999.

Tomblin, Barbara. *With Utmost Spirit: Allied Naval Operations in the Mediterranean, 1942–1945.* Lexington: University Press of Kentucky, 2004.

Twiss, Peter. *Navy Flyer: Reminiscences of a Fleet Air Arm and Test Pilot.* London: Grub Street, 2005.

Vella, Philip. *Malta: Blitzed but Not Beaten.* Valletta, Malta: Published by Progress Press for the National War Museum Association, 1997.

Wade, Frank. *A Midshipman's War: A Young Man in the Mediterranean Naval War, 1941–1943.* Victoria, British Columbia, Canada.: Trafford, 2005.

Warlow, Ben, comp. *The Royal Navy at Malta: A Collection of Old Photographs Taken by the Ellis Family at Malta.* Liskeard, Cornwall, UK: Maritime Books, 1989.

Whelan, John Allison. *Malta Airmen.* New Zealand in the Second World War; Official History 17. Wellington, New Zealand: War History Branch, Dept. of Internal Affairs, 1951.

Williams, Paul R. *Malta: Island under Siege.* Barnsley, UK: Pen & Sword Military, 2009.

Wingate, John. *The Fighting Tenth: The Tenth Submarine Flotilla and the Siege of Malta.* London: L. Cooper, 1991.

Woodman, Richard. *Malta Convoys, 1940–1943.* London: John Murray, 2000.

Wragg, David W. *Malta, the Last Great Siege: The George Cross Island's Battle for Survival, 1940–43.* Barnsley, UK: L. Cooper, 2003.

Zarb-Dimech, Anthony. *Mobilisation in Action: A History of Civil Defence, Malta, 1940–1943.* Malta: A. Zarb-Dimech, 2003.

II. GENERAL DESCRIPTIONS: TRAVEL GUIDES, PHOTO ESSAYS, MAPS

1. Travel

Bianchi, Petra, and Peter Serracino Inglott, eds. *Encounters with Malta.* Malta: Encounter Books, 2000.

Boffa, Charles J. *The Islets of Comino, Filfla, Hagret il-General and the Volcanic One (Graham) that Was.* Valletta, Malta: Progress Press, 2003.

Breithaupt, Johann Friedrich. *Malta, Island of Christian Heroes: Life in Malta in the Early 17th Century.* Translated by Alfred Scalpello. Valletta, Malta: Fondazzjoni Patrimonju Malti, 2001.

Byrd, Melvin Richard. *Malta from Melita and Ogygia: Observations of the Maltese Archipelago.* n.p.: M.R. Byrd, 2003.

Freller, Thomas. *The Cavaliers Tour and Malta in 1663: One Journey and Two Accounts.* Pietà, Malta: Pubblikazzjonijiet Indipendenza, 1998.

———. *Gozo, the Island of Joy: Gozo and Its Visitors: Adventurers, Scientists, Noblemen, and Writers.* Mgarr, Malta: Colour Image, 1997.

Guillaumier, Alfie. *Malta's Towns and Villages.* Translated by Terry Asphar. Mount Vernon, NY: T. Asphar, 2003.

Manduca, John. *City of Mdina and Rabat.* 3rd ed. San Gwann, Malta: Publishers Enterprises Group, 2003.

Quintin, Jean. *The Earliest Description of Malta (Lyons 1536).* Translated by Horatio C. R. Vella. Sliema, Malta: DeBono Enterprises, 1980.

Stephenson, Charles. *The Fortifications of Malta, 1530–1945.* Fortress 16. Oxford: Osprey, 2004.

2. Guidebooks

Azzopardi, Aldo E. *Malta and Its Islands.* Luqa, Malta: Miller Distributors, 1999.

Azzopardi, John. *Mdina: The Silent City, Rabat, Mosta.* Luqa, Malta: Miller Distributors, 1999.

Baedeker's Malta. 2nd ed. Baedeker's Travel Guides. Basingstoke, UK: AA, 2000.

Bain, Carolyn. *Malta and Gozo.* 3rd ed. Oakland, CA: Lonely Planet, 2007.

Borg, Joseph. *The Public Gardens and Groves of the Maltese Islands: A Visitor's Guidebook.* Mgarr, Malta: Colour Image, 2005.

Boulton, Susie. *Malta & Gozo.* 4th ed. Travellers. Peterborough, UK: Thomas Cook, 2009.

Camilleri, Alex, Annalise Falzon, and Alan Deidun. *Malta, Gozo & Comino: Off the Beaten Track: The Ecological Walk Guide.* Malta: Nature Trust, 2003.

Dillon, Paddy. *Walking in Malta: 33 Routes on Malta, Gozo and Comino.* A Cicerone Guide. Milnthorpe, UK: Cicerone, 2004.

Lemon, Peter G. *A Guide to Shore Diving the Maltese Islands.* Lavenham, UK: Lavenham Press, 2000.

Lockhart, Douglas. *Landscapes of Malta, Gozo and Comino.* 5th ed. Sunflower Landscapes. London: Sunflower, 2007.

Magro Conti, Emmanuel. *The Malta Maritime Museum, Vittoriosa.* Insight Heritage Guides 11. Malta: Heritage Books in association with Heritage Malta, 2006.

Manduca, John Borg. *Gozo: Sun, Sea and History.* 8th ed. Welcome Travel Guide. San Gwann, Malta: Publishers Enterprises Group, 2003.

Middleton, Ned. *Maltese Island Diving Guide.* Miller Guides. Malta: Miller Distributors, 1997.

Richards, Brian. *The Best of Malta.* 2nd ed. Globetrotter. London: New Holland, 2008.

Rose, Lesley Anne. *Frommer's Malta & Gozo Day by Day: 22 Smart Ways to See the Region*. Hoboken, NJ: Frommer's, 2009.

3. Photo Essays

Arrigo, Kurt. *Malta: A Coastal Journey*. Malta: 2005.

Beacom, Johnathan and Geoffrey Aquilina Ross. *The Maltese Islands from the Air*. 2nd ed. Balzan, Malta: Proud, 1995.

Boccazzi-Varotto, Attilio, Daniel Cilia, Joseph Bezzina, and Nicola Paris. *Gozo & Comino 360°*. Sliema, Malta: Miranda, 1992.

Bonello, Giovanni. *Nostalgias of Malta: Images by Geo Furst from the 1930s*. Valletta, Malta: Fondazzjoni Patrimonju Malti, 2006.

Bonello, Giovanni, and Graham Smeed. *Malta Picture Postcards, 1898–1906*. Malta: privately printed, 1986.

Bonnici, Joseph, and Michael Cassar. *Malta and Gozo: Then and Now*. Malta: Book Distributors, 1998.

———. *The Malta Grand Harbour and Its Dockyard*. Malta: privately printed, 1994.

Formica, Enrico, Daniel Cilia, and Attilio Boccazzi-Varotto. *Malta 360°*. rev. ed. Sliema, Malta: Miranda, 2002.

Grima, Reuben, and Enrico Formica. *The Museums of Malta 360°*. Sliema, Malta: Miranda, 2006.

4. Maps

Great Britain. *Malta and Gozo*. 4th and 5th eds. London: Geographical Section, General Staff, 1958.

National Geographic Society (U.S.), Cartographic Division, John B. Garver, Jr., John F. Dorr, Laura Robinson Pritchard, and Juan J. Valde´s. *The Historic Mediterranean 800 B.C. to A.D. 1500*. Washington, DC: National Geographic Society, 1982.

United States, Geographic Names Division. *Malta; Official Standard Names Approved by the United States Board on Geographic Names*. Washington, DC: 1971.

III. SELECT TOPICS

1. Archaeology

Blom, Adrian van der, and Veronica Veen. *The First Maltese: Origins, Character and Symbolism of the Ghar Dalam Culture*. Haarlem, Netherlands: FIA Publications, 1992.

Bonanno, Anthony. *An Illustrated Guide to Prehistoric Gozo*. Gozo, Malta: Gaulitana, 1986.

Bonanno, Anthony, Joseph Bartolo, and Mario Mintoff. *Malta, an Archaeological Paradise*. rev. ed. Valletta, Malta: M. J. Publications, 1997.

Buhagiar, Mario. *Late Roman and Byzantine Catacombs and Related Burial Places in the Maltese Islands*. B.A.R International Series 302. Oxford: B.A.R., 1986.

Cilia, Daniel, ed. *Malta before History: The World's Oldest Free-Standing Stone Architecture*. Sliema, Malta: Miranda, 2004.

Ellul, Joseph. *Malta's Prediluvian Culture at the Stone Age Temples with Special Reference to Hagar Qim, Ghar Dalam, Cart Ruts, Il-Misqa, Il-Maqluba & Creation*. Malta: privately printed, 1988.

Ellul, Michael. *History on Marble: A Corpus of Inscriptions in the Presidential Palaces in Valletta, San Anton and Verdala, Malta*. San Gwann, Malta: Publishers Enterprises Group, 1998.

Gregory, Isabelle Vella. *The Human Form in Neolithic Malta*. Sta Venera, Malta: Midsea Books, 2005.

International Conference on Archaeology of the Ancient Mediterranean. *Archaeology and Fertility Cult in the Ancient Mediterranean: Papers Presented at the First International Conference on Archaeology of the Ancient Mediterranean, the University of Malta, 2–5 September 1985*. Edited by Anthony Bonanno. Amsterdam: B. R. Grüner, 1986.

Joussaume, Roger. *Dolmens for the Dead: Megalith-Building throughout the World*. Translated by Anne and Christopher Chippindale. Ithaca, NY: Cornell University Press, 1988.

Maempel, George Zammit. *Ghar Dalam: Cave and Deposits*. Malta: privately printed, 1989.

Micallef, Paul I. *Mnajdra Prehistoric Temple: A Calendar in Stone*. Malta: privately printed, 1992.

Mohen, Jean-Pierre. *The World of Megaliths*. Translated by Helen McPhail. New York: Facts on File, 1990.

Morana, M. *The Hypogeum: A Jewel of Ancient Malta*. Malta: M. J. Publications, n.d.

Pace, Anthony. *The Hal-Saflieni Hypogeum, 4000 BC–2000 AD*. Malta: National Museum of Archaeology, Museums Department, 2000.

Parker, Rowland, and Michael Rubinstein. *The Cart-Ruts on Malta and Gozo*. Gozo, Malta: Gozo Press, 1984.

Sagona, Claudia. *The Archaeology of Punic Malta*. Ancient Near Eastern Studies 9. Leuven, Belgium: Peeters, 2002.

Sagona, Claudia. *Punic Antiquities of Malta and Other Ancient Artifacts Held in Ecclesiastic and Private Collections*. 2 vols. Dudley, MA: Peeters, 2003–6.

Sultana, Sharon. *The National Museum of Archaeology, Valletta: The Neolithic Period.* Insight Heritage Guides 13. Sta. Venera, Malta: Heritage Books in association with Heritage Malta, 2006.

Trump, David H. *Malta: An Archaeological Guide.* 2nd ed. Valletta, Malta: Progress Press, 2000.

———. *Malta: Prehistory and Temples.* 2nd ed. Malta's Living Heritage. Malta: Misdea Books, 2004.

Veen, Veronica. *The Goddess of Malta: The Lady of the Waters and the Earth.* Haarlem, Netherlands: Inanna-Fia Publications, 1992.

Vella, Nicholas C. *The Prehistoric Temples at Kordin III: Kordin.* Insight Heritage Guides 5. Sta Venera, Malta: Heritage Books, 2004.

2. Architecture

Abel, Chris, and Richard England. *Transformations: Richard England, 25 Years of Architecture.* Valletta, Malta: Mid-Med Bank, 1987.

Azzopardi, John, ed. *The Church of St. John in Valletta, 1578–1978: An Exhibition Commemorating the Fourth Centenary of Its Consecration, St. John's Museum, Valletta, 3 June–3 July 1978.* Valletta, Malta: Progress Press, 1978.

Bonnici, Joseph, and Michael Cassar. *The Royal Opera House, Malta.* Malta: privately printed, 1990.

Borg, Malcolm. *British Colonial Architecture: Malta, 1800–1900.* San Gwann, Malta: Publishers Enterprises Group, 2001.

Buhagiar, Vincent, John Ebejer, and Alberto Miceli Farrugia. *Impressions, Aesthetics, Design.* Sta Venera, Malta: Midsea Books, 2006.

De Giorgio, Roger. *A City by an Order.* 3rd ed. Valletta, Malta: Progress Press, 1998.

De Piro, Nicholas. *The Sovereign Palaces of Malta.* Sliema, Malta: Miranda, 2001.

———. *The Temple of the Knights of Malta.* Sliema, Malta: Miranda, 1999.

England, Richard. *Richard England: Architect as Artist.* Edited by Dennis Sharp. London: BookART, 2007.

Fsadni, Michael. *The Girna: The Maltese Corbelled Stone Hut.* Translated by Louis J. Scerri. Malta: Dominican Publication, 1992.

Galea, Michael. *Malta: The Palace of the Grandmasters and the Armoury.* Valletta, Malta: M. J. Publications, 1988.

Ganado, Albert, ed. *Palace of the Grand Masters in Valletta.* Valletta, Malta: Fondazzjoni Patrimonju Malti, 2001.

Heathcote, Edwin, and Richard England. *Richard England.* Chichester, West Sussex, UK: Wiley-Academy, 2002.

Hoppen, Alison. *The Fortification of Malta by the Order of St. John, 1530–1798*. Edinburgh, UK: Scottish Academic Press, 1979.

Hughes, Quentin. *The Building of Malta During the Period of the Knights of St. John of Jerusalem, 1530–1795*. rev. ed. London: A. Tiranti, 1967.

———. *Fortress: Architecture and Military History in Malta*. London: Lund Humphries, 1969.

Hughes, Quentin, Conrad Thake, and Daniel Cilia. *Malta, the Baroque Island*. Sta Venera, Malta: Midsea Books, 2003.

Jaccarini, Carol J. *Ir-Razzett: The Maltese Farmhouse*. Malta: C. J. Jaccarini, 2002.

Johnston, Shirley, and Anthony Cassar de Sain. *Splendor of Malta*. New York: Rizzoli, 2001.

Knevitt, Charles, and Richard England. *Connections: The Architecture of Richard England, 1964–84*. London: Lund Humphries, 1984.

Luttrell, Anthony, ed. *Medieval Malta: Studies on Malta before the Knights*. London: The British School at Rome, 1975.

Mangion, Giovanni, ed. *Maltese Baroque: Proceedings of a Seminar on "The Baroque Route in Malta" Held at the Ministry of Education, Beltissebh, Malta, on 3rd June, 1989*. Malta: Ministry of Education and Council of Europe, 1989.

Munro, Dane, and Maurizio Urso. *Memento Mori: A Companion to the Most Beautiful Floor in the World*. Valletta, Malta: M. J. Publications, 2005.

Sammut, Joseph. *Malta and Gozo: Views and Hues: A Colourful Diversion*. San Gwann, Malta: Publishers Enterprises Group, 2005.

Thake, Conrad, and Quentin Hughes. *Malta, War & Peace: An Architectural Chronicle 1800–2000*. Sta Venera, Malta: Midsea Books, 2005.

3. Arts

a. Art

Biennale of Christian Art. *Contemporary Christian Art: Malta 2002: The Fourth Biennale of Christian Art*. Edited by Vincent Borg. Mdina, Malta: Cathedral Museum Publications, 2002.

Buhagiar, Mario. *The Iconography of the Maltese Islands, 1400–1900: Painting*. Valletta, Malta: Progress Press, 1987.

———. *The Late Medieval Art and Architecture of the Maltese Islands*. Valletta, Malta: Fondazzjoni Patrimonju Malti, 2005.

De Giorgio, Cynthia, and Keith Sciberras, eds. *Caravaggio and Paintings of Realism in Malta*. Valletta, Malta: Midsea Books for the St. John's Co-Cathedral Foundation, 2007.

De Piro, Nicholas. *The International Dictionary of Artists Who Painted Malta.* 2nd ed. Malta: Audio Visual Centre, 2002.

———. *The Quality of Malta: Fashion and Taste in Private Collections.* Malta: AVC Publishers, 2003.

Farrugia, Jimmy. *Antique Maltese Ecclesiastical Silver.* 2 vols. Valletta, Malta: Progress Press, 2002.

Galea, Catherine Sinclair, ed. *Caravaggio, Diaries: Extracts from Fr. Marius Zerafa's Diaries.* Malta: Grimand, 2004.

Giorgio, Cynthia de. *The Image of Triumph and the Knights of Malta.* Malta: Printed by Printex, 2003.

Grima, Reuben, Charles Frederick de Brocktorff, and Daniel Cilia. *The Archaeological Drawings of Charles Frederick De Brocktorff.* Malta: Midsea Books, 2004.

Harker, Margaret. *Photographers of Malta, 1840–1990.* Malta: Fondazzjoni Patrimonju Malti, 2000.

Hibbard, Howard. *Caravaggio.* New York: Harper & Row, 1983.

Inglott, Peter Serracino. *Sacred Art in Malta, 1890–1960.* Edited by Gino Gauci. Valletta, Malta: Said International, 1990.

Manduca, John, ed. *Antique Furniture in Malta.* Valletta, Malta: Fondazzjoni Patrimonju Malti, 2002.

National Museum (Malta), and Antonio Espinosa Rodriguez. *Paintings at the National Museum of Fine Arts in Malta.* Valletta, Malta: Said International, 1990.

Prins, A. H. J., and Joseph Muscat. *In Peril on the Sea: Marine Votive Paintings in the Maltese Islands.* Valletta, Malta: Said International, 1989.

Sammut, Edward. *Notes for a History of Art in Malta.* Valletta, Malta: Progress Press, 1955.

Sciberras, Keith, ed. *Melchiorre Cafa: Maltese Genius of the Roman Baroque.* Valletta, Malta: Midsea Books, for the History of Art Programme, University of Malta, 2006.

———. *Roman Baroque Sculpture for the Knights of Malta.* Valletta, Malta: Fondazzjoni Patrimonju Malti, 2004.

Sciortino, Antonio. *Antonio Sciortino: Monuments and Public Sculpture: Catalogue of the Exhibition Inaugurated at the National Museum of Fine Arts on the 19th December 2000 by H. E. Prof. Guido De Marco, President of Malta.* Malta: National Museum of Fine Arts, 2000.

Terribile, Tony. *Tez ori fil-knejjes Maltin = Treasures in Maltese Churches.* Pietà, Malta: Pubblikazzjonijiet Indipendenza, 2002.

Wain, Kenneth. *Luciano Micallef: A Study.* Msida: Malta University Services, 1993.

b. Literature

Abela, Joseph S. *The Loggia of Malta: A Historical Novel Set in 16th Century Malta*. San Gwann, Malta: Publishers Enterprises Group, 1992.

Andersen, H. C. *A Visit to Germany, Italy, and Malta, 1840–1841: A Poet's Bazaar I–II*. Translated by Grace Thornton. London: P. Owen, 1985.

Arberry, A. J. *A Maltese Anthology*. Oxford: Clarendon Press, 1960.

Attard, Dunstan. *Island I Call Home: Poems from a Mediterranean Island*. Coral Springs, FL: Llumina Press, 2004.

Bartolo, Hella Jean. *The Malta Connection*. Valletta, Malta: Progress Press, 1976.

Briffa, Charles. *Rhythmic Patterns in Maltese Literature*. Valletta, Malta: Midsea Books, 2001.

Butler, Gwendoline. *Coffin in Malta*. New York: Walker, 1965.

Buttigieg, George Gregory. *Of Craft and Honor and a Templar's Chronicles*. Luqa, Malta: Miller Distributors, 2006.

Cassola, Arnold. *The Literature of Malta: An Example of Unity in Diversity*. Sliema, Malta: Minima, 2000.

Davies, Sheila. *The Young Marchesa, A Story of Malta*. New York: Dodd, Mead & Co., 1951.

Dun Karm. *Dun Karm, Poet of Malta*. Translated by A. J. Arberry. University of Cambridge Oriental Publications 6. Cambridge: University Press, 1961.

Ebejer, Francis. *Come Again in Spring: A Novel Set in America*. Malta: Union Press, 1973.

——. *English Plays*. 3 vols. Valletta, Malta: A. C. Aquilina, 1980.

——. *Evil of the King Cockroach*. London: MacGibbon & Kee, 1960.

——. *In the Eye of the Sun: A Novel Set in Malta*. London: MacDonald, 1969.

——. *Leap of Malta Dolphins: A Novel*. New York: Vantage Press, 1982.

——. *Requiem for a Malta Fascist (or The Interrogation): A Novel*. Valletta, Malta: A. C. Aquilina, 1980.

——. *A Wreath for the Innocents: A Novel*. London: MacGibbon & Kee, 1958.

Fairfax, Saxon. *The Switchback*. Valetta, Malta: Progress Press, 1900.

Hamilton, Lyn. *The Maltese Goddess: An Archaeological Mystery*. New York: Berkley Prime Crime, 1998.

Le Fort, Gertrud. *The Song at the Scaffold*. Translated by Olga Marx. New York: Sheed & Ward, 1933.

Marlowe, Christopher. *The Jew of Malta*. Edited by N. W. Bawcutt. The Revels Plays. Manchester, UK: Manchester University Press, 1978.

Monsarrat, Nicholas. *The Kappillan of Malta*. New York: Morrow, 1974.

Pynchon, Thomas. *V.: A Novel*. Philadelphia: Lippincott, 1963.

Sultana, Donald. *The Journey of Sir Walter Scott to Malta*. New York: St. Martin's Press, 1986.

——. *Journey of William Frere to Malta in 1832: Preceded by a Sketch of His Life and of the Frere Family, with Particular Reference to John Hookham Frere: A Monograph in Two Parts*. Valletta, Malta: Progress Press, 1988.

——. *Samuel Taylor Coleridge in Malta and Italy*. Oxford: Blackwell, 1969.

——. *The Siege of Malta Rediscovered: An Account of Sir Walter Scott's Mediterranean Journey and His Last Novel*. Edinburgh, UK: Scottish Academic Press, 1977.

Short, Agnes. *The Crescent and the Cross: A Story of the Great Siege of Malta, 1565*. London: Constable, 1980.

c. Music

Camilleri, Charles, and Peter Serracino Inglott. *Mediterranean Music*. Malta: Foundation for International Studies at the University of Malta, 1988.

Sapienza, Edwige, and Joe Attard, eds. *Charles Camilleri: Portrait of a Composer*. Valletta, Malta: Said International, 1988.

University of Malta, and Paul Xuereb. *The Maltese Opera Libretto: A Catalogue of the Librettos in the University of Malta Library: With an Introductory Essay*. Msida, Malta: Malta University Press, 2004.

4. Economy

a. General

Baldacchino, Godfrey. *Worker Cooperatives with Particular Reference to Malta: An Educationist's Theory and Practice*. The Hague, Netherlands: Institute of Social Studies, 1990.

Baldacchino, Godfrey, Saviour Rizzo, and E. L. Zammit. *Evolving Industrial Relations in Malta*. Luqa, Malta: Agenda in collaboration with Workers' Participation Development Centre, 2003.

Bonanno, Nicolas S. *Capital, Accumulation, and Economic Growth: In Theory and as They Relate in the Maltese Paradigm*. Documents Economiques 44. Fribourg, Switzerland: Editions Universitaires Fribourg, 1989.

Bonnici, Joseph, and Michael Cassar. *The Malta Railway*. rev. ed. Malta: privately printed, 1992.

——. *Malta Tramway and the Barracca Lift*. Malta: privately printed, 1991.

Briguglio, Lino. *Island Economies—Plans, Strategies, and Performance, Malta*. Canberra, Australia: Research School of Pacific Studies, 1992.

Briguglio, Lino, and Gordon Cordina, eds. *Competitiveness Strategies for Small States*. Malta: Islands and Small States Institute of the Foundation for International Studies, 2004.

Briguglio, Lino, Gordon Cordina, and Eliawony J. Kisanga, eds. *Building the Economic Resilience of Small States*. Malta: Formatek for The Islands and Small States Institute of the University of Malta and the Commonwealth Secretariat, London, 2006.

Camilleri, Perit Denis. *Housing Affordability in Malta: A Conference Organized by the Chamber of Architects & Civil Engineers—Malta in Conjunction with the Building Industry Consultative Council*. Malta: The Building Industry Consultative Council, 2000.

Caruana, Carmen M. *Education's Role in the Socioeconomic Development of Malta*. Westport, CT: Praeger, 1992.

Coldman, Alfred. *Malta: An Aviation History*. San Gwann, Malta: Publishers Enterprises Group, 2001.

Debono, John. *Trade and Port Activity in Malta: 1750–1800*. Malta: J. Debono, 2000.

Delia, E. P. *Papers on Malta's Political Economy*. 2nd ed. Malta: Midsea Books, 2006.

Johnson, Tom. *Malta and Gozo Buses*. Telford, UK: British Bus Publishing, 2003.

Lerin, Franc¸ois, Leonard Mizzi, and Salvino Busuttil. *Malta: Food, Agriculture, Fisheries, and the Environment*. Options Me´diterrane´ennes 7. Paris: CIHEAM, 1993.

Pollacco, Christopher. *An Outline of the Socio-Economic Development in Post-War Malta*. Msida, Malta: Mireva, 2003.

Rigby, Bernard. *The Malta Railway*. 2nd ed. Usk, UK: Oakwood, 2004.

Senior, John A. *Malta Bus Album: A Pictorial Record of Buses in Malta & Gozo Spanning Fifty Years*. Glossop, UK: Venture, 2004.

Spiteri, Edward J. *Malta: From Colonial Dependency to Economic Viability, Maltese Economic History, 1800–2000*. Sliema, Malta: Edward J. Spiteri, 2002.

Staines, David Spiteri, ed. *Airliners in Malta: A Historical and Pictorial Review: Eighty Years of Civil Aviation in Malta*. Malta: Malta Aviation Museum Foundation, 2000.

Vella, Catherine C., ed. *The Maltese Islands on the Move: A Mosaic of Contributions Marking Malta's Entry into the 21st Century*. Lascaris, Valletta, Malta: Central Office of Statistics, 2000.

Zammit, E. L. *A Colonial Inheritance: Maltese Perceptions of Work, Power, and Class Structure with Reference to the Labour Movement*. Msida, Malta: Malta University Press, 1984.

b. Banking and Finance

Consiglio, John A. *A History of Banking in Malta: 1506–2005*. Valletta, Malta: Progress Press, 2006.

Pirotta, Godfrey A., and Edward Warrington. *Guardian of the Public Purse: A History of State Audit in Malta, 1800–2000*. Malta: National Audit Office, 2001.

Sammut, Joseph C. *Currency in Malta*. Valletta, Malta: Central Bank of Malta, 2001.

———. *From Scudo to Sterling: Money in Malta, 1798–1887*. Valletta, Malta: Said, 1992.

c. Tourism

Briguglio, Lino. *Sustainable Tourism in Islands and Small States*. 2 vols. London: Pinter, 1996.

Pollacco, John. *In the National Interest: Towards a Sustainable Tourism Industry in Malta*. Malta: Fondazzjoni Tumas Fenech ghall-Edukazzjoni fil-G'urnaliz'mu, 2003.

5. European Union

Berger, Helge, and Thomas Moutos, eds. *Managing European Union Enlargement*. CESifo Seminar Series. Cambridge, MA: MIT Press, 2004.

Cassola, Arnold. *A Maltese in the European Parliament: 1999–2003*. Brussels, Belgium: European Federation of Green Parties, 2004.

European Documentation and Research Centre. *The Constitution for Europe: An Evaluation: EDRC Conference 2005*. Edited by Peter G. Xuereb. Msida, Malta: European Documentation and Research Centre, University of Malta, 2005.

Pace, Roderick. *The European Union's Mediterranean Enlargement: Cyprus and Malta*. London: Routledge, 2005.

———. *Microstate Security in the Global System: EU-Malta Relations*. Valletta, Malta: Midsea Books, 2001.

Pierros, Filippos, Jacob Meunier, and Stanley Abrams. *Bridges and Barriers: The European Union's Mediterranean Policy, 1961–1998*. Aldershot, UK: Ashgate, 1999.

Pollacco, Christopher. *European Integration: The Maltese Experience*. Luqa, Malta: Agenda, 2004.

———. *The Mediterranean: The European Union's "Near Abroad."* Luqa, Malta: Agenda, 2006.

Sajdik, Martin, and Michael Schwarzinger. *European Union Enlargement: Background, Developments, Facts.* Central and Eastern European Policy Studies 2. New Brunswick, NJ: Transaction Publishers, 2008.

Xuereb, Peter G., ed. *The Future of the European Union: Unity in Diversity.* Msida, Malta: European Documentation and Research Centre, University of Malta, 2002.

——, ed. *Malta in the European Union: Five Years On and Looking to the Future.* Msida, Malta: European Documentation and Research Center, University of Malta. 2009.

6. Geography, Geology and Nature

Azzopardi, Anton. *A New Geography of the Maltese Islands.* 2nd ed. Malta: St. Aloysius' College Publication, 2002.

Boffa, Charles J. *The Islets of Comino, Filfla, Hagret il-General and the Volcanic One (Graham) that Was.* Valletta, Malta: Progress Press, 2003.

Bonett, Guido, and Joe Attard. *The Maltese Countryside.* 2 vols. San Gwann, Malta: Publishers Enterprises Group, 2005.

Borgese, Elisabeth Mann, and David Krieger, eds. *The Tides of Change: Peace, Pollution, and Potential of the Oceans.* New York: Mason/Charter, 1975.

Briguglio, Lino. *Malta National Report: Submitted by the Government of Malta to the World Summit on Sustainable Development, Johannesburg, 2002.* Malta: 2002.

Cachia, Charles, Constantine Mifsud, and Paul M. Sammut. *Mollusca of the Maltese Islands.* Vol.1. Marsa, Malta: Grima, 1991–.

Casha, Alex. *Where to Watch Birds and Other Wildlife in Malta.* Ta' Xbiex, Malta: BirdLife Malta, 2004.

Cassar, Louis F., and Darrin T. Stevens. *Coastal Sand Dunes Under Siege: A Guide to Conservation for Environmental Managers.* Malta: International Environment Institute, Foundation for International Studies, 2002.

Fenech, Katrin. *Human-Induced Changes in the Environment and Landscape of the Maltese Islands From the Neolithic to the 15th Century AD: As Inferred From a Scientific Study of Sediments from Marsa, Malta.* BAR International Series 1682. Oxford: Archaeopress, 2007.

Haslam, S. M., J. Borg, and J. M. Psaila. *River Kbir: The Hidden Wonder: A Field Study Guide.* Malta: 2002.

Maempel, George Zammit. *Illustrators and Their Illustrations of Maltese Fossils and Geology: A Historical and Biographical Account.* Contributions to a History of Maltese Geology and Paleontology. San Gwann, Malta: Publishers Enterprise Group, 2007.

Mifsud, Mark. *Maltese Nature in Focus*. Msida, Malta: Mireva, 2003.

Pedley, Martyn, and Michael Hughes Clarke. *Geological Itineraries in Malta & Gozo*. San Gwann, Malta: Publishers Enterprises Group, 2003.

Pedley, Martyn, Michael Hughes Clarke, and Pauline Galea. *Limestone Isles in a Crystal Sea: The Geology of the Maltese Islands*. San Gwann, Malta: Publishers Enterprises Group, 2002.

Sultana, Joe, and Charles A. Gauci. *A New Guide to the Birds of Malta*. Valletta, Malta: Malta Ornithological Society, 1982.

Sultana, Joe, and Victor Falzon, eds. *Wildlife of the Maltese Islands*. Floriana, Malta: Environment Protection Dept., 1996.

Valletta, Anthony. *The Butterflies of the Maltese Islands*. Malta: G. Muscat, 1972.

———. *The Moths of the Maltese Islands*. Valletta, Malta: Progress Press, 1973.

Weber, Hans Christian. *Ornamental Plants of Malta*. Weikersheim, Germany: Margraf, 2008.

———. *Wild Plants of Malta*. San Gwann, Malta: Publishers Enterprises Group, 2004.

Weber, Hans Christian and Bernd Kendzior. *Flora of the Maltese Islands: A Field Guide*. Weikersheim, Germany: Margraf, 2006.

Wood, Lawson. *Sea Fishes and Invertebrates of the Maltese Islands and the Mediterranean Sea*. Valletta, Malta: Progress Press, 2002.

7. Politics

a. General

Baker, Randall, ed. *Public Administration in Small and Island States*. Kumarian Press Library of Management for Development. West Hartford, CT: Kumarian Press, 1991.

Bezzina, Joseph. *Gozo's Government: The Autonomy of an Island through History*. Rabat, Gozo, Malta: Gaulitana, 2005.

Cachia, Francis. *Global Diplomacy Reflected in Malta: A Decade of Decisive Developments in International Affairs: 1993–2003*. San Gwann, Malta: Publishers Enterprises Group, 2004.

Clemmer, Edward J. *Alfred Sant Explained: In-Novella Ta' Malta Fil-Mediterran*. Malta, 2000.

De Marco, Guido. *Momentum*. Valletta, Malta: Office of the President, 2002.

———. *Momentum II*. Valletta, Malta: Office of the President, 2004.

Dobie, Edith. *Malt's Road to Independence*. Norman, OK: University of Oklahoma Press, 1967.

Fenech, Dominic. *Responsibility and Power in Inter-War Malta.* San Gwann, Malta: Publishers Enterprises Group, 2005.

Frendo, Henry. *Malta's Quest for Independence: Reflections on the Course of Maltese History.* Valletta, Malta: Valletta Publishing & Promotion, 1989.

——, ed. *Maltese Political Development 1798–1964: Selected Readings.* Malta: Interprint, 1993.

——. *The Origins of Maltese Statehood: A Case Study of Decolonization in the Mediterranean.* San Gwann, Malta: Publishers Enterprises Group, 1999.

Koster, Adrianus. *Prelates and Politicians in Malta: Changing Power-Balances between Church and State in a Mediterranean Island Fortress, 1800–1976.* Studies of Developing Countries 29. Assen, Netherlands: Van Gorcum, 1984.

Mintoff, Dom, ed. *Malta: Church, State, Labour: Documents Recording Negotiations between the Vatican Authorities and the Labour Party, 1964–1965.* Malta: Malta Labour Party, 1966.

Nalizpelra [Maurice Tanti Burlo]. *Blame It on Dom!* Valletta, Malta: Progress Press, 2003.

O'Donoghue, Sarah. *Industrial Relations and Political Change in Malta.* Msida, Malta: Mireva, 2003.

Office of the Permanent Secretary, Office of the Prime Minister, Malta. *A Profile of the Public Service of Malta: Current Good Practices and New Developments in Public Service Management.* Edited by Charles Polidano. 2nd ed. Country Profiles Series. London: Commonwealth Secretariat, 2002.

Pirotta, Godfrey A. *Malta's Parliament: An Official History.* Malta: Office of the Speaker of the House of Representatives, Malta, and the Department of Information, 2006.

Rossi, Enzo. *Malta on the Brink: From Western Democracy to Libyan Satellite.* European Security Studies no. 5. London: Alliance Publishers for the Institute for European Defence & Strategic Studies, 1986.

Saliba, Evarist. *No, Honourable Minister: Memoirs of a Maltese Senior Diplomat.* San Gwann, Malta: Book Distributors, 2007.

b. Constitutions

Cremona, J. J. *The Maltese Constitution and Constitutional History since 1813.* 2nd ed. San Gwann, Malta: Publishers Enterprises Group, 1997.

Malta Constitutional Conference. *Malta Demands Independence: Official Documents of the Talks Held in London between the Delegation of the Malta Labour Party and the Delegation of the United Kingdom Government in November–December, 1958.* Malta: Malta Labour Party, 1959.

Progressive Constitutional Party, Malta. *Maltese Constitutional and Economic Issues,* 1955–1959. Valletta, Malta: Progress Press, 1959.

c. Elections

Bowler, Shaun, and Bernard Grofman, eds. *Elections in Australia, Ireland, and Malta under the Single Transferable Vote: Reflections on an Embedded Institution.* Ann Arbor: University of Michigan Press, 2000.

Felice-Pace, Joe, and Richard Felice-Pace. *Who's Who in the House, 1921– 2006: Results of Maltese General and Casual Elections.* Valletta, Malta: Midsea Books, 2006.

Giglo, Albert. *Malta: Analysis and Consequences of Elections 1921–2003.* Valletta, Malta: Studia Editions, 2007.

d. Foreign Affairs

Coleiro, Christine. *A Propitious Partner.* San Gwann, Malta: Publishers Enterprises Group, 1997.

Gauci, Victor J. *The Genesis of Malta's Foreign Policy: A Personal Account.* Malta: Agenda, 2005.

e. Political Parties

Frendo, Henry. *Party Politics in a Fortress Colony: The Maltese Experience.* Valletta, Malta: Midsea Books, 1979.

Koster, Adrianus. *Prelates and Politicians in Malta: Changing Power-Balances between Church and State in a Mediterranean Island Fortress, 1800–1976.* Studies of Developing Countries 29. Assen, Netherlands: Van Gorcum, 1984.

Mintoff, Dom, ed. *Malta: Church, State, Labour: Documents Recording Negotiations between the Vatican Authorities and the Labour Party, 1964–1965.* Malta: Malta Labour Party, 1966.

8. Society

a. General

Abela, A. E. *Grace and Glory: Malta: People, Places & Events: Historical Sketches.* Valletta, Malta: Progress Press,1997.

Abela, Anthony M. *Secularised Sexuality: Youth Values in a City-Island.* Valletta, Malta: Social Values Studies, 1998.

———. *Transmitting Values in European Malta: A Study in the Contemporary Values of Modern Society.* Valletta, Malta: Jesuit Publications, 1991.

———. *Values of Women and Men in the Maltese Islands: A Comparative European Perspective.* Valletta, Malta: Commission for the Advancement of Women, Ministry for Social Policy, 2000.

Attard, Lawrence E. *Early Maltese Emigration, 1900–1914.* Valletta, Malta: Gulf, 1983.

———. *The Great Exodus: 1918–1939.* Marsa, Malta: Publishers Enterprises Group, 1989.

———. *Profiles in Maltese Migration: A Series of Nineteen Biographies Covering the Period from 1792 to 2000.* San Gwann, Malta: Publishers Enterprises Group, 2003.

Baldacchino, Godfrey, Antoinette Caruana, and Mario Grixti, eds. *Managing People in Malta: Case Studies in Local Human Resource Management Practice.* Luqa, Malta: Published in collaboration with the Foundation for Human Resources Development, Agenda, 2003.

Boffa, Charles J. *Malta's Grand Harbour and Its Environs in War and Peace: Historical Scenario, World War One and Two, Social Dimensions, People in Wartime, Medical and Health Objectives.* Malta: Progress Press, 2000.

Camilleri-Cassar, Frances. *Gender Equality in Maltese Social Policy?: Graduate Women and the Male Breadwinner Model.* Luqa, Malta: Agenda, 2005.

Carville, Alan, and Mark Avellino. *Malta 24/7.* Valletta, Malta: Progress Press, 2005.

Cassar, Carmel. *Society, Culture and Identity in Early Modern Malta.* Msida, Malta: Mireva, 2000.

Cassar, George, and JosAnn Cutajar, eds. *Sociological Aspects of the Maltese Islands.* Msida, Malta: Indigo Books, 2004.

Catania, Paul, and Louis J. Scerri, eds. *Naxxar: A Village and Its People.* Malta: P. Catania, 2000.

Census of Population and Housing Malta, 2005. Valletta, Malta: National Statistics Office, 2007.

Ciorbaru, Adriana. *Youth Policy in Malta: Report by an International Panel of Experts Appointed by the Council of Europe.* Strasbourg, France: Council of Europe Publications, 2005.

De Piro, Nicholas. *Lost Letters: An Ostensibly Historical Divertimento.* London: Pedigree, 1986.

Gatt, Rose Ann, Christopher Mallia, and Gabrielle Mifsud. *Government and Sport: A Historical Review (1962–2002).* Edited by Michael Aquilina.

Msida, Malta: Institute for Physical Education and Sport, University of Malta, 2004.

Goodwin, Stefan. *Malta, Mediterranean Bridge.* Westport, CT: Bergin & Garvey, 2002.

Leopardi, Edward Romeo. *Malta's Heritage: Selections from the Writings of E. R. Leopardi.* Valletta, Malta: Progress Press, 1969.

Mitchell, Jon P. *Ambivalent Europeans: Ritual, Memory, and the Public Sphere in Malta.* London: Routledge, 2002.

Mizzi, J. A. *Scouting in Malta: An Illustrated History.* Valletta, Malta: privately printed, 1989.

Montalto, John. *The Nobles of Malta, 1530–1800.* Maltese Social Studies 4. Valletta, Malta: Midsea Books, 1980.

Savona-Ventura, Charles. *Contemporary Medicine in Malta, 1798–1979.* San Gwann, Malta: Publishers Enterprises Group, 2005.

Sciriha, Lydia. *Keeping in Touch: The Sociolinguistics of Mobile Telephony in Malta.* Luqa, Malta: Agenda, 2004.

Sultana, Ronald G., and Godfrey Baldacchino, eds. *Maltese Society: A Sociological Inquiry.* Msida, Malta: Mireva, 1994.

Tabone, Carmel. *Maltese Families in Transition: A Sociological Investigation.* Sta Venera, Malta: Ministry for Social Development, 1995.

Xerri, Raymond C. *Gozitan Crossings: The Impact of Migration and Return Migration on an Island Community.* Gozo and the Gozitans 1. Qala, Malta: A&M Printing, 2005.

b. Biographies

Bencini, Alfred J. *Nothing but the Truth: An Illustrated Autobiography.* N.p.: Penprint 1981.

Catania, Charles. *Andrea De Bono: Maltese Explorer on the White Nile (1848–65).* London: Minerva, 2001.

De Marco, Guido. *The Politics of Persuasion: An Autobiography.* Valletta, Malta: Allied Publications, 2007.

Freller, Thomas. *The Life and Adventures of Michael Heberer Von Bretten: The German Robinson Crusoe in Malta.* Valletta, Malta: Valletta Publications, 1997.

Frendo, Henry. *Censu Tabone: The Man and His Century.* 2nd ed. Malta: Maltese Studies, 2001.

Goulston, Jill. *Gozo Glimpses: The Heart of a House.* London: Blackie, 2003.

Mangion, Tony S. *The Maltese: A Collection of Portraits and Biographies.* Malta: privately printed, 2002.

Sammut, Austin. *The Court Martial of Enrico Mizzi, 1917.* Maltese Social Studies. Malta: Midsea Books, 2006.

Sant, Alfred. *Confessions of a European Maltese.* Malta: SKS, 2002.

Smith, Harrison. *Lord Strickland: Servant of the Crown.* Edited by Adrianus Koster. 2 vols. Valletta, Malta: Progress Press, 1984–86.

Zarb-Dimech, Anthony. *Moments in Time: An Album of an Old Maltese Family.* Malta: A. Zarb-Dimech, 2003.

c. Education

Caruana, Carmen M. *Education's Role in the Socioeconomic Development of Malta.* Westport, CT: Praeger, 1992.

Zammit Mangion, Joseph. *Education in Malta.* Valletta, Malta: Studia Editions, 1992.

d. Folklore and Folk Culture

Attard, Robert. *Malta: A Collection of Tales and Narratives.* Zebbug, Malta: Edward De Bono Foundation, 2001.

———. *Malta: A Second Collection of Tales and Narratives.* Zebbug, Malta: Edward De Bono Foundation, 2001.

———. *Malta: A Third Collection of Tales and Narratives.* Zebbug, Malta: Edward De Bono Foundation, 2003.

Camilleri, George, trans. *Realms of Fantasy: Folk Tales from Gozo.* Victoria, Gozo, Malta: privately published, 1992.

Cassar-Pullicino, Joseph. *Folktales of Malta and Gozo: A Selection in English Translation.* Valletta, Malta: University Publishers, 2000.

———. *Studies in Maltese Folklore.* rev. ed. Msida, Malta: Malta University Press, 1992.

e. Food

Borg, Miriam. *Healthy Mediterranean Recipes from Malta: With Calorie Counts and Step-by-Step Photos.* Olive Garland Series. Malta: Karl Borg, 2005.

Calleja, Edward. *Success Bil-Helu 2: Ricetti U Informazzjoni.* Malta: E. Calleja, 2004.

Caruana, Claudia M. *Taste of Malta.* New York: Hippocrene Books, 2009.

Caruana Galizia, Anne, and Helen Caruana Galizia. rev. ed. *The Food and Cookery of Malta.* Totnes, Malta: Prospect Books, 1997. First published 1972 as *Recipes from Malta.* Valleta, Malta: Prospect Books.

Cremona, Matty, and Kurt Arrigo. *A Year in the Country: Life and Food in Rural Malta.* 2nd ed. Malta: Proximus, 2004.

Mattei, Pippa, and Kurt Arrigo. *25 Years in a Maltese Kitchen.* Sliema, Malta: Miranda, 2003.

Mitze, Rainer. *Malta's Mediterranean Cuisine.* Neustadt an der Weinstrasse, Germany: Umschau, 2004.

Parkinson-Large, Pamela. *A Taste of History: The Food of the Knights of Malta.* Lija, Malta: MAG Publications, 1995.

Wirth, Caroline. *The Best of Maltese Cooking.* Narni, Italy: Plurigraf, 1991.

f. Language

Aquilina, Joseph. *Maltese: A Complete Course for Beginners.* 2nd ed. Teach Yourself Books. London: Hodder Headline, 1994.

———. *Papers in Maltese Linguistics.* Valletta, Malta: Royal University of Malta, 1961. Reprinted with corrections. Valletta, Malta: Malta University Press, 1970.

Braunmu'ller, Kurt, and Gisella Ferraresi, eds. *Aspects of Multilingualism in European Language History.* Hamburg Studies on Multilingualism 2. Amsterdam: J. Benjamins, 2003.

Bugeja, Paul. *Maltese: How to Read and Speak It.* 3rd ed. Valletta, Malta: A. C. Aquilina, 1979.

Caruana Dingli, Noel. *The French Language in Malta and the Napoleonic Period.* Valletta, Malta: Progress Press, 2002.

Hull, Geoffrey. *The Malta Language Question: A Case History in Cultural Imperialism.* Valletta, Malta: Said International, 1993.

Sutcliffe, Edmund F. *A Grammar of the Maltese Language, with Chrestomathy and Vocabulary.* Valetta, Malta: Progress Press, 1960.

g. Media

Frendo, Henry. *The Press and the Media in Malta.* Bochum, Germany: Projekt Verlag, 2004.

Sammut, Carmen. *Media and Maltese Society.* Lanham, MD: Lexington Books, 2007.

h. Religion

Azzopardi, John, ed. *Portable Altars in Malta.* Malta: Patrimonju, 2000.

Boissevain, Jeremy. *Saints and Fireworks: Religion and Politics in Rural Malta.* 3rd ed. Valletta, Malta: Progress, 2000.

Ciappara, Frans. *Society and the Inquisition in Early Modern Malta.* San Gwann, Malta: Publishers Enterprises Group, 2000.

Cornuke, Robert. *The Lost Shipwreck of Paul*. Bend, OR: Global Publishing Services, 2003.

Gambin, Kenneth. *Two Death Sentences by the Inquisition Tribunal of Malta, 1639*. Sta Venera, Malta: Midsea Books, 2006.

Jaccarini, Carol, and Mauro Inguanez. *Dom Mauro Inguanez, 1887–1955: Benedictine of Montecassino*. Translated by Victor Buhagiar. Mdina, Malta: Cathedral Museum, 1987.

Kilin. *A Hundred Wayside Chapels of Malta & Gozo*. Valletta, Malta: Heritage Books, 2000.

Luttrell, Anthony. *The Making of Christian Malta: From the Early Middle Ages to 1530*. Aldershot, UK: Ashgate, 2002.

O'Shea, Stephen. *Sea of Faith: The Shared Story of Christianity and Islam in the Medieval Mediterranean World*. New York: Walker, 2006.

Rountree, Kathryn. *Crafting Contemporary Pagan Identities in a Catholic Society*. Farnham, Surrey, UK: Ashgate, 2009.

Tabone, Charles. *Religious Beliefs and Attitudes of Maltese University Students*. Msida, Malta: University Chaplaincy, University of Malta, 20003.

Vassallo, Mario. *From Lordship to Stewardship: Religion and Social Change in Malta*. The Hague, Netherlands: Mouton, 1979.

Vella, Andrew P. *The Tribunal of the Inquisition in Malta*. Royal University of Malta Historical Studies 1. Valletta, Malta: Royal University of Malta, 1964.

Wettinger, Godfrey. *The Jews of Malta in the Late Middle Ages*. Maltese Social Studies 6. Valletta, Malta: Midsea Books, 1985.

Yaffe, Martin D. *Shylock and the Jewish Question*. Johns Hopkins Jewish Studies. Baltimore, MD: Johns Hopkins University Press, 1997.

i. Women

Abela, Anthony M. *Women's Welfare in Society*. Valletta, Malta: Commission for the Advancement of Women, 2002.

Camilleri, Frances. *Women in the Labour Market: A Maltese Perspective*. Msida, Malta: Mireva, 1997.

Deguara, Angele. *Life on the Line: A Sociological Investigation of Women Working in a Clothing Factory in Malta*. Malta: Malta University Press, 2002.

IV. REFERENCE SOURCES

1. General

Malta: Country Study Guide. International Business Publishers, 2005–, published annually.

Malta Year Book. Vol. 1. Sliema, Malta: De La Salle Brothers, 1988–, published annually.
Manduca, John. *Malta Who's Who.* Valletta, Malta: Progress Press, 1987.
Schiavone, Michael J., and Louis J. Scerri. *Maltese Biographies of the Twentieth Century.* Pietà, Malta: Pubblikazzjonijiet Indipendenza, 1997.
Wettinger, Godfrey. *Place-Names of the Maltese Islands: ca. 1300–1800.* San Gwann Malta: Publishers Enterprises Group, 2000

2. Bibliographies

Camilleri, Ninette, and Romaine Petrocochino. *Supplement to A Checklist of Maltese Periodicals and Newspapers: Covering the Years 1974–1989.* Valletta, Malta: Malta University Publications, 1990.
National Library of Malta. *A Checklist of Maltese Periodicals and Newspapers in the National Library of Malta (Formerly Royal Malta Library) and the University of Malta Library.* Compiled by Anthony F. Sapienza. Valletta, Malta: Malta University Press, 1977.
Portelli, Sergio. *A Bibliography of Nineteenth-Century Periodicals in the National Library of Malta Collection.* Valletta, Malta: National Library of Malta, 2000.
Thackrah, John Richard, comp. *Malta.* rev. ed. World Bibliographical Series 64. Oxford: Clio Press, 1998.
Xuereb, Paul. *Melitensia; A Catalogue of Printed Books and Articles in the Royal University of Malta Library Referring to Malta.* Msida, Malta: Malta University Press, 1974.

3. Dictionaries

Aquilina, Joseph, comp. *A Comparative Dictionary of Maltese Proverbs.* Valletta, Malta: Royal University of Malta, 1972.
——. *Concise Maltese-English, English-Maltese Dictionary.* Sta Venera, Malta: Midsea Books, 2006.
Busuttil, E. D. *Kalepin: Dizzjunarju Ingliz-Malti = English-Maltese Dictionary.* 3rd ed. Valletta, Malta: Muscat, 1976.
Cassar, Mario. *The Surnames of the Maltese Islands: An Etymological Dictionary.* Malta: Book Distributors, 2003.
Farrugia, Carlo. *Dictionary for Financial Services: English-Maltese—Maltese-English.* Valletta, Malta: Midsea Books, 2006.

4. Websites

a. General

http://www.aboutmalta.com
https://www.cia.gov/library/publications/the-world-factbook/geos/mt.html
http://www.malta.com
http://my-malta.com

b. European Union

European Union (Malta English-language portal)
    http://europa.eu/abc/european_countries/eu_members/malta/index_en.htm
European Union Commission Representation in Malta (English portal)
    http://ec.europa.eu/malta/welcome_en.htm
Legal Malta (legal information about Malta and the EU)
    http://www.legal-malta.com/european

c. Government of Malta

Department of Information, Malta
    http://www.doi.gov.mt
Government of Malta official website (English-language version)
    http://gov.mt/index.asp?l=2
Heritage Malta, National Agency for Museums, Conservation Practice and
    Cultural Heritage
    http://www.heritagemalta.org/home.html
National Statistics Office, Malta
    http://www.nso.gov.mt

d. Libraries

Melitensia Library at the University of Malta
    http://www.um.edu.mt/library/departments/melitensia
National Library of Malta
    http://www.libraries-archives.gov.mt/nlm/index.htm
St. John's University Malta Study Center
    http://www.hmml.org/centers/malta
University of Malta Library
    http://www.lib.um.edu.mt
WorldCat—World's largest network of library content and services
    http://www.worldcat.org

e. Maps

Interactive map of Malta (Visit Malta website of Malta Tourism Authority)
http://www.visitmalta.com/includes/map/popup1.html
Political map of Malta
http://www.lib.utexas.edu/maps/europe/malta_pol84.jpg
Relief map of Malta
http://www.lib.utexas.edu/maps/europe/malta.gif

f. Media

Di-ve (online news site)
http://www.di-ve.com
Independent (daily newspaper)
http://www.independent.com.mt
MaltaMedia (online news service)
http://www.maltamediaonline.com
Malta Star (online daily)
http://www.maltastar.com/pages/ms09cont.asp
Malta Today (weekly newspaper)
http://www.maltatoday.com.mt
Radio Stations of Malta
http://www.radio-locator.com/cgi-bin/nation?ccode=mt&x=12&y=8
Times of Malta (daily newspaper)
http://www.timesofmalta.com

g. Nongovernmental Organizations

Competitive Malta (organization to improve Malta's economic competitiveness)
http://www.competitivemalta.com/competitivemalta/home.aspx
Din L'Art Helwa (National Malta Trust, heritage preservation organization)
http://www.dinlarthelwa.org
Flimkien ghal Ambjent Ahjar (environmental action organization)
http://www.ambjentahjar.org
Fondazzjoni Patrimonju Malti (Malta heritage preservation organization)
http://www.patrimonju.org/patrimonju/home.aspx
Fondazzjoni Wirt Artna (Malta heritage preservation organization)
http://www.wirtartna.org/main_menu/AboutUs/tabid/1198/Default.aspx
General Workers' Union
http://www.gwu.org.mt

Malta Chamber of Commerce and Enterprise
http://www.chamber.org.mt
Union Haddiema Maghqudin (Malta Workers' Union)
http://www.uhm.org.mt

h. Politics and Law

Alternattiva Demokratika (The Green Party)
http://www.alternattiva.org.mt/page.asp
Legal information about Malta
http://www.legal-malta.com
Partita Nazzjonali (The Nationalist Party)
http://www.pn.org.mt
Partit Laburista (Malta Labour Party)
http://www.mlp.org.mt
Website about Malta's political parties, elections, and the single transferable voting system
http://www.maltadata.com/index.htm

i. Tourist Information

Lonely Planet guide
http://www.lonelyplanet.com/malta
Malta Tourist Board website
http://www.visitmalta.com/main

About the Authors

WARREN G. BERG (AB, Luther College; MA and PhD, State University of Iowa) is professor emeritus of economics, accounting, and management at Luther College in Decorah, Iowa. A native of Chicago, Illinois, he graduated from Taft High School there in June 1942. Shortly afterward, he enlisted in the U.S. Navy, eventually receiving a commission as ensign and serving aboard the USS *LST-896* in the Pacific Theater. He joined the faculty of Luther College in 1948 and, at retirement in 1988, was professor and head of the department. For 25 years during the summer sessions, he and his wife, Jan, were associated with the Institute in American Studies for Scandinavian Educators (teachers from the five Nordic nations of Europe) at Luther College, and for 19 of those years, they were codirectors. In recognition, each was awarded the St. Olav Medal by His Majesty, King Olav V of Norway. In 1990, one of his former students established the Warren G. Berg Endowed Chair in Accounting and Finance.

The Malta connection between Luther College and the island nation started when he was selected as the first senior Fulbright lecturer for the Royal University of Malta during the 1966–67 academic year. That experience led to a steady flow of students from Malta to Luther College, a semester abroad program for Luther students to study in Malta, a variety of faculty exchanges, and the establishment of the Malta Studies Center in the college's library. He was selected for a second Fulbright award to the University of Malta in 1988–89 upon his retirement. The unusual relationship between a small nation and a small college continues to this day.

UWE JENS RUDOLF (BA, MA, University of Cincinnati; MBA, University of Southern California) is professor of accounting and management at Luther College, where he has taught since 1971. Originally hired to teach German, he had completed the coursework and examinations for the PhD in German literature when the college decided to cut his position, but armed with grant money for the purpose, a colleague, Warren Berg (see above), convinced him to abandon his half-written dissertation to retrain as an accountant. After passing the CPA examination, he joined the Department of Accounting and Management headed by Berg, who also introduced Rudolf to Malta, a country he had visited numerous times since 1990, including several extended stays on sabbatical and in research for this book.

Rudolf has extensive teaching and business consulting experience in Europe, Asia, and Africa. He has taught courses in accounting, international business, and global issues. On occasional leave from Luther College, he has worked in France, Germany, China, and Japan and led 16 January-term, study abroad courses for Luther College students in visits to Germany, France, Malta, Italy, Switzerland, Japan, China, Australia, and Iceland. He has also served as director of international studies and study abroad programs at Luther College.

Following closely in the footsteps of Berg, his senior colleague and mentor, Professor Rudolf agreed to take over the updating of this second edition of the *Historical Dictionary of Malta*. Like Berg before him, he was appointed codirector (along with spouse Ruth Caldwell, professor of French at Luther College) of the Institute in American Studies for Scandinavian Educators, serving in that role since 2008.

Breinigsville, PA USA
14 April 2010
236130BV00002B/2/P